CROSSING BETWEEN TRADITION AND MODERNITY:

ESSAYS IN COMMEMORATION OF MILENA DOLEŽELOVÁ-VELINGEROVÁ (1932–2012)

EDITED BY KIRK A. DENTON

KAROLINUM PRESS
PRAGUE 2016

KAROLINUM PRESS
Karolinum Press is a publishing department of Charles University
Ovocný trh 560/5, 116 36 Prague 1, Czech Republic
www.karolinum.cz

Layout by Jan Šerých
Set and printed in the Czech Republic by Karolinum Press
First English edition

A catalogue record for this book is available from the National Library
of the Czech Republic.

The publication of this book has been supported by the grant provided
by Chiang Ching-kuo Foundation for International Scholarly Exchange in Taipei,
Taiwan, Project No. SP001-U-15.

ISBN 978-80-246-3513-2
ISBN 978-80-246-3539-2 (pdf)

The original manuscript was reviewed by Professor Raoul David Findeisen
(Institute of East Asian Studies, Comenius University, Bratislava)
and Professor Olga Lomová (Department of East Asian Studies,
Charles University, Prague).

TABLE OF CONTENTS

LIST OF CHARTS AND FIGURES

ACKNOWLEDGEMENTS

This volume would not have been possible without the generous support of the Chiang Ching-kuo Foundation. Thanks in particular to Maggie Lin of the CCK Foundation for her assistance and good cheer during the proposal submission process. Olga Lomová of Charles University was most generous with her time in organizing the conference in Prague at which many of these essays were first presented and serving as a go-between with Karolinum Press, and its director, Petr Valo, during the review and production process of this book. We are also grateful to Alena Jirsová for all her hard work and care in the preparation of the manuscript.

Milena Doleželová-Velingerová (1932–2012), in the Lu Hsun Library, Oriental Institute, Prague, 1955. Courtesy of Milena Dolezel.

REMEMBERING MILENA: A PREFACE[1]

CHEN PINGYUAN
TRANSLATED BY GRAHAM SANDERS

It was the evening of October 4th when I received a letter from Milena's daughter telling me that her mother had been taken to the emergency room, and asking her friends to write to her without delay. Xia Xiaohong and I immediately sent the following message:

> Milena, we have just learned the news that you are in the hospital, and we are both very worried about you. You have always been so optimistic that we believe this time you will surely overcome your ailment and quickly return to health. We still plan to go to your cottage again as your guests; our previous visit there left us with such beautiful memories. Last month we were still proofreading the manuscript sent by Prof. Wagner of the English translation of *Modern Encyclopedic Dictionaries*. It is all due to your scholarly sensitivity that we even had this opportunity to collaborate. And, as it is a topic that we can continue working on, we await your further guidance. So please get well soon!

Although I spoke this way, I feared in my heart that her situation was fraught with danger. Just as I expected, I learned over the course of two days from various sources that Prof. Milena had indeed passed away in Prague on October 20th. According to the announcement made by her daughter they were planning to hold two memorial services, one in Toronto, where she had worked for such a long time, and one in Prague. We had no way to attend them, as they are so far away, so I felt it best to compose this short piece to convey our thoughts of mourning.

In 2007, Peking University Press published *Modern Chinese Encyclopedic Dictionaries*, edited by Milena and me. The brief author's biographies included this passage:

> Milena Doleželová-Velingerová, born 1932 in Prague, Czech Republic. Employed successively at the Oriental Institute of the Academy of Sciences of the Czech Republic, the University of Toronto in Canada, and Charles University in Prague. She is currently a Research Associate at Heidelberg University in Germany. Her major publications in-

---

1   Originally published in Chinese in *Wenhui bao* (Nov. 14, 2012).

clude: *The Chinese Novel at the Turn of the Century, The Appropriation of Cultural Capital: China's May Fourth Project*, and articles such as "Lu Xun's 'Medicine,'" and "Narrative Modes of Late Qing Novels," among others.

I recall at the time that Milena herself provided a biography that was much longer than this, but I was forced to abridge it to keep it consistent with the rest of the work.

During my studies at Peking University in the 1980s, when writing my doctoral dissertation, "The Transformation of Narrative Modes in Chinese Fiction," I benefitted greatly from *The Chinese Novel at the Turn of the Century*, edited by Milena. But the first time I was able to meet her in person was not until ten years later in Prague, the capital of the Czech Republic.

In August of 1998, after having just taken part in the magnificent 100th anniversary of the founding of Peking University, I came to Prague to attend a scholarly event that was part of a series in celebration of the 650th anniversary of the establishment of Charles University, the oldest university in Central Europe. I was deeply moved that Milena was hosting this small but significant Sinology workshop with such high hopes. We arrived in Prague the day before the workshop, which happened to be the 30th anniversary of the invasion of the Czech Republic by Soviet forces. Strolling along the wide avenues of Prague, everywhere one could see advertisements for a photography exhibition called "1968." Milena had fled to distant lands after the Soviet invasion and had only returned two years ago to take up a position as a Visiting Professor at Charles University. She chose this particular time to hold the meeting not only to show her own strong feelings toward these events and transformations, but also in the hopes that we too would sense the lasting magic of the "Prague Spring."

Two years later, I, along with Professors David Der-wei Wang and Shang Wei of Columbia University, held an international symposium at Peking University called "The Late Ming and the Late Qing: Historical Continuation and Cultural Innovation." Milena in the end came and presented a paper titled "Creating a New World of Fiction: Chinese Short Stories, 1906–1916." Summer in Beijing that year was sweltering and, to make matters worse, the conditions of the meeting venue and the hotel were not very good. Many of the overseas Chinese scholars complained about it for days. But Prof. Milena, who was nearly 70 years old at the time, continued to talk and joke cheerfully both inside and outside the venue; everywhere one could see her tiny but vigorous figure. The reason I describe her this way is because in the middle of the meeting she came running up to "lodge a complaint": the students at Peking University tasked with running the symposium, seeing that she was the most senior scholar there, kept wanting to help her as she went up the stairs. She said she was not that old, that she could handle anything herself, and that there was no need for others to help her. When she noticed that I was a little embarrassed by this, Milena added, "Next time you come to Prague, I will take you out in my car for some fun."

After this, whenever we were at an international conference on late Qing literature, culture, scholarship, or thought, we would see each other again many times. And she really did take us out in her car for some fun just as she had promised, in October of 2006. After that conference, Milena drove her little red car to take Xia Xiaohong and me to her cottage in the countryside, an hour and half outside of Prague. The weather was quite cold, and I remember once we were inside the door, she set about lighting a blazing fire in the fireplace. Then she prepared a meal and we drank wine and chatted together. When we got up the next day, we toured nearby villages, and I watched as she and Xia Xiaohong wrangled playfully over choosing souvenirs. In the sunshine Milena's lined visage appeared particularly charming, and I truly believed that she was not old in the least.

The "English manuscript of *Modern Encyclopedic Dictionaries*" I mentioned in my letter asking after Milena's health was a major collaborative project she undertook with Prof. Rudolph Wagner of Heidelberg University, which was in press at that time [subsequently published in 2014 by Springer as *Chinese Encyclopaedias of New Global Knowledge (1870–1930)*]. Actually, this book began its life in 2007 when Peking University Press released *Modern Chinese Encyclopedic Dictionaries* (Jindai Zhongguo de baike cishu). In the introductory article I contributed as a preface, "Encyclopedias as 'Cultural Projects' and 'Enlightenment Business'," I mentioned: "This book is a collection of articles drawn from a workshop entitled 'Early Modern Chinese Encyclopaedias: Changing Ways of Thought in Late Qing China' held at Heidelberg University, March 26–28, 2006, for which I extend my sincere gratitude to the host, Prof. Milena, and the venue, Heidelberg University."

That year, in late September and early October, I carried the newly published book, still smelling of fresh ink, as we attended a workshop on Modern Chinese Encyclopedic Dictionaries organized by Academia Sinica in Taipei. The whole journey—from settling on topics, organizing research groups, repeatedly discussing our trains of thought on writing, to our mutual deliberation and encouragement over completed drafts, translation into English, and final revisions—was completely strenuous. To tell you the truth, I came to have more than a little admiration in my eyes for Western scholars with such dedication and rigor.

On the very day the workshop officially began there was a big typhoon, which meant the local scholars had no way to attend; so the scholars who had already arrived from abroad, led by Profs. Milena and Wagner, made use of a meeting room beside the hotel to proceed with the workshop. Coming out of the meeting room we ran into violent winds and torrential rains, and Milena was blown along by her umbrella until she fell down onto the ground. But she just gave a laugh, pulled herself up again, and continued on her way. That year, she was already getting close to 75 years old.

Early in the summer of 2009, I went to Budapest, Hungary to attend a workshop called "The International Symposium on the History and Present Condition of Cultural Exchange between China and Central and Eastern Europe," jointly hosted by Beijing Foreign Studies University and Hungary's Eötvös Loránd University. After the meeting, many delegates from China made a detour to Prague, and I was upset that I was unable to go with them and thus lost the perfect opportunity to get together with Milena to have a good chat—it really was a pity. Nevertheless, at the meeting itself I gave a talk titled "Between 'Knowledge' and 'Friendship'—The Meaning of Průšek," in which I raised the contributions of the European Sinologist Průšek, and Průšek's students such as Milena, along with the challenges, revisions, and transformations faced by the next generation of scholars.

Scholars who participate in "international dialogues" are swayed by grand intellectual tides as well as being concerned with their personal contacts in everyday life. Near the end of last year, I published an article called "International Views and Local Feelings: How to Engage in Dialogue with Sinologists." I once delivered the third section of the essay, "There Ought to Be Feelings Behind Research," as a lecture in a classroom at Peking University, and the students were all extremely moved when they heard it. In it, I pointed out:

> Two or three decades ago, exchanges between Chinese and foreign scholars were rare and it was difficult to meet face-to-face. Whenever we did have a chance, we were thirsty for a better understanding of one another. Because of this, we took great pains to make ourselves understood clearly, to listen to one another intently, to seek out common bases for research, to throw ourselves sincerely and deeply into a series of conversations where we might benefit from one another, and became lifelong friends in the process. Nowadays, international academic gatherings are as numerous as the hairs on an ox, and although it is very easy to meet other scholars face-to-face, it is rare to be able to put your heart and soul into a conversation with someone. It is not all about the articles and papers, it is about making toasts to friendship; but we tend not to care so much about the other person's life beyond their scholarly work. If we are reduced to only caring about such things as the other person's status and title, their symbolic capital, we are actually descending to a lower level.

In my article I mentioned a good many direct contacts with foreign scholars, including ones with scholars now deceased such as Ito Toramaru, Maruyama Noboru, Nakajima Midori, and others. They have all given me great amounts of sincere and selfless help.

And now, one more sinologist I admire, Prof. Milena, has passed away—dwelling on it makes me sigh with sadness. The scholarly environment today is so different from thirty or fifty years ago. It is very difficult for the younger generation to fully understand our generation and the ones that came before, why we so cherish the aid we received from each other during tough times, and the lifelong friendships that we built because of it.

That year in Prague, Milena gave me a slim, exquisite volume in English entitled *Wu Xiaoling Remembered* (Prague, 1998). She compiled it together with Prof. Patrick Hanan of Harvard University, and there were a dozen European and North American scholars involved in writing it. In an article entitled "A Chinese Scholar in the Eyes of Sinologists" (published in Qunyan, Dec. 1998), I said of the slim 117-page book "although it is not lengthy, it does warrant the phrase 'profound in feeling and meaning.'" One should note that it is an exceedingly rare occurrence in European and American universities to have a collection published to commemorate a Chinese scholar. Milena came to China for her studies in 1958–1959 and received warm-hearted assistance from Wu Xiaoling, the famed rare book collector and research fellow of the Chinese Academy of Social Sciences. After that time Wu Xiaoling's daughter, Wu Hua (Laura), also became a doctoral student under Milena's guidance when she was at the University of Toronto. These sorts of charming anecdotes are all tiny ripples that should not be overlooked when telling the story of the great tides of international cultural exchange.

October 31, 2012
While at The Chinese University of Hong Kong

INTRODUCTION

KIRK A. DENTON

Prof. Milena Doleželová-Velingerová (hereafter Doleželová) was an important member of the Prague School of Sinology founded by her teacher, Jaroslav Průšek, in the 1950s. Like Průšek, Doleželová was that rare scholar who crossed fluidly over the May Fourth divide—that is, she worked with equal skill on both modern and premodern literature. She published on Song dynasty popular ballads (*zhugongdiao*), the late imperial autobiography *Six Records of a Life Adrift* (Fusheng liuji), late imperial drama and fiction commentary, novels of the late Qing, the modern writer Lu Xun, the Cultural Revolution novel *The Bright Red Star* (Shanshan de hongxing), and, in her later years, late Qing encyclopedia—a scholarly range of which few Chinese literature scholars can boast. In crossing over the premodern and modern divide, her scholarship embodies a healthy skepticism toward what can be called the May Fourth paradigm, which reduces May Fourth cultural modernity to a radical break from the imperial and Confucian past.

Well before "alternative modernities" scholars made it popular, Doleželová promoted the notion that late Qing fiction was modern and that the late Qing period (1894–1911) was an integral part of the early formation of modern Chinese literature. That the late Qing belonged to "tradition" was a notion propagated by May Fourth intellectuals themselves, part of a larger polemical rejection of the past and a form of imperious self-affirmation. With her edited book *The Chinese Novel at the Turn of the Century* (1980), Doleželová questioned both the May Fourth's own rhetorical strategies and prevailing scholarly views, as well as implicitly drawing attention to the fact that scholarship itself is driven by ideological motivations. She tackled the May Fourth legacy more forthrightly in her co-edited (with Oldřich Král) *The Appropriation of Cultural Capital: China's May Fourth Project*.

Doleželová not only crossed the borders of scholarly disciplines and fields, she lived a peripatetic life that involved crossing national, political, and cultural borders: from Nazi occupation to Soviet domination; from Communist Czechoslovakia to Maoist People's Republic of China in the 1950s; from Europe to the United States in 1967; from the U.S. to Canada the following year; and finally back to a now-postsocialist Czech Republic in 1996. Reflecting this multicultural background, Doleželová published in many languages, including French, German, Czech, English, Italian, and Chinese.

As Chinese literary studies entered, belatedly, the poststructuralist era, Doleželová's approach to literature was sometimes dismissed as outdated. It is true that she was influenced by the structuralism and semiotics of the Prague school, in particular the work of Jan Mukařovský, but she was rarely dogmatic or mechanical in applying them to the analysis of texts. Theory was for her a methodological tool more than an explanatory system. What structuralism and semiotics offered her was a view of literature as dynamic, constantly changing in response to both internal (literary) and external (social and political) factors—a far cry from the pure formalism with which structuralism is sometimes associated. They also instilled in her an abiding concern with language as the very fabric of literature. It should be said, furthermore, that Doleželová was at the forefront of introducing literary theory, and theoretical rigor, into Sinology, a field long characterized by its philological orientation.

A collection of essays by her students, most of whom gathered in June 2012 for a small conference to celebrate their teacher's eightieth birthday, the present volume honors Doleželová's career as a Sinologist and her contributions to Chinese literary studies. It also commemorates and carries on the legacy of the Prague School. More important, the collection exemplifies the scholarly values Doleželová herself stood for, in particular her broad range of intellectual interests, her crossing over of the artificial boundary between traditional and modern literature, and her abiding attention to issues of language, narrative structure, genre, and representation.

Doleželová's students, who teach in universities in Hong Kong, the Czech Republic, Canada, and the U.S., are specialists in both late imperial literature and modern Chinese literature. Very few teachers in our field can be said to have produced students who excel in these two fields. The diversity of Doleželová's own scholarship is therefore reflected in the work of her students generally and that included in this volume in particular. The essays range in temporal focus from the Tang dynasty to the present; they deal with mainland China, Taiwan, Hong Kong, and the Chinese diaspora; they focus on genres and artistic forms as diverse as the novel, short story, memoir, autobiography, landscape essay, film, theater, oral performance, and museums. They treat "texts" such as: *Romance of the Three Kingdoms*; the Tang prose master Liu Zongyuan's *Eight Records on Yongzhou*; *zidishu* (Manchu Bannerman tales) adaptations of *Dream of the Red Chamber*; Wang Wenxing's experimental novel *Family Catastrophe*; the permanent exhibit at the National Museum of Taiwan History; Shi Tuo's short-story cycle *Records from Orchard Town*; fiction by Chinese-Canadian writers; and Zhang Yimou's films. Attention to the text—language, tropes, narrative structure, style, etc.—is common to all these essays.

After a "preface" in the form of a short memorial by the renowned Peking University literature professor Chen Pingyuan, the volume opens, appropriately, with Leonard Chan's essay on the Hsia-Průšek debate. This debate, which was instrumental in the early formation of the field of modern Chinese literature in the West, was also key to Doleželová's development as a sinologist in the 1960s. Although his views on the relationship between the literary text and history were not always consistent, Průšek guided his students to analyze texts both in their historical context and as part of a literary system. At the same time, Doleželová's careful close readings and literary interpretations—demonstrated, for example, in her essay on Lu Xun's "Medicine" (Yao)—show characteristics of Hsia's New Critical "close reading" approach to texts. Doleželová's attention to both the historical/literary context and the text is embodied in the essays in this volume.

After Chan's essay, which sets the historical scholarly context, the volume is organized into two parts. The essays in Part I, "Language, Narrative Structure, and Genre," reflect concerns that were at the heart of Doleželová's methodology and of the Prague School more generally. Although Doleželová was no formalist, she demonstrated in her teaching and her writing a detailed attention to the language and narrative structure of literary texts, as well as to the larger literary system with which they interact. Genre, a critical aspect of structuralist narratology, was also a key focus of her research, for example in her work on *zhugongdiao*, autobiography, and the narrative innovations of late Qing fiction.

Anthony Pak and Shu-ning Sciban demonstrate in their respective essays a strong concern for language and narrative structure that was central to Doleželová's scholarship. Pak presents a close reading of Liu Zongyuan's *Eight Records on Yongzhou*, with an eye toward delineating its key structural features as a sub-genre of prose writing—the landscape essay. In a gesture that reminds one of Doleželová's analysis of late imperial drama and fiction commentary, Pak draws from the discourse of Chinese landscape painting to dissect the structural workings of Liu's essays. Sciban's approach is linguistic, with a focus on the use of neologism as a key element of Wang Wenxing's modernist project in the novel *Family Catastrophe*. By looking at his neologisms in light of earlier examples of neologism, moreover, Sciban suggests that the modern—even the modernist—should never be seen as radically disconnected from tradition, an idea that Doleželová emphasized in much of her work and in her teaching. Doleželová insisted on seeing modern works of literature as part of a long-standing tradition, not simply as products of radical modernity or a modern impulse. Ihor Pidhainy's essay analyzes chapters 36 to 38 of *Romance of the Three Kingdoms* in which Liu Bei woos the strategist Zhuge Liang to his cause. This is a pivotal turning point in the larger structure of the novel, Pidhainy argues, in terms of marking a shift from the masculine militarism of the early chapters to a more feminine Daoist strategism in the later ones.

Alison Bailey's essay investigates the eruption of the personal in an unlikely text: *A Bodkin to Unravel the Code*, a seventeeth century legal and forensic text by Wang Mingde. Contrary to the generic norms of the forensic text, Wang weaves personal stories in and around the scientific description of "wounds, scars, and death." A malleable conception of genre is also at play in Dušan Andrš' essay on Shi Tuo's *Records from Orchard Town*. Through detailed analysis of the narrative structure and thematic patterns in the collection, Andrš describes the blending of fiction and prose into a literary work that is fresh and original in its structure and its lyricism. Literary texts, Bailey and Andrš show us, are not simply mechanical iterations of patterns determined by generic norms; they can, and often do, engage creatively with those norms to forge something new. Doleželová affirmed this kind of dynamic, organistic view of genre and the literary system.

Li Zeng's and Ying Wang's essays are concerned with crossing over the borders between genres through adaptation. Zeng looks at the adaptation of fictional texts in two of Zhang Yimou's films and engages in an intertextual, "cross-cultural" reading by suggesting some interesting links between these adaptations and texts such as O'Neill's *Desire under the Elms* and Stephen Foster's song "Old Black Joe." And Ying Wang analyzes in detail the *zidishu* (a form of folk ballad popular among the Manchus in the Qing) adaptations of *Dream of the Red Chamber* and their role in cementing the novel into popular consciousness. This crossing over from genre to genre was an abiding concern in Doleželová's own work, particularly her writing on the mutual interaction of elite and popular literature in *zhugongdiao* and of Western and indigenous Chinese literary traditions in late Qing fiction.

The topics and approaches of the essays in Part II, "Identities and Self-Representations," reflect to some degree new orientations that Doleželová herself was taking in her later work. In this sense, they mark the development of the Prague School into the era of cultural studies scholarship. At first glance, the "national" identities in post-martial law Taiwan addressed in Kirk Denton's chapter would appear to be centered on issues that were not major concerns in Doleželová's work. But the museum, which is Denton's focus, is a knowledge construct and a form of institutional historical memory that functions in ways not unlike the encyclopedia, which was a focus of Doleželová's work in her later years. In their essays, Hua Wu and Xueqing Xu analyze the complex issue of diasporic identities as expressed in fiction by a range of Chinese-Canadian writers. Although she herself lived a "postcolonial" and "diasporic" life, these topics were not central to Doleželová's work. But the imprint of Doleželová's influence can be found in the careful attention Wu and Xu pay to issues of language and narrative structure, even as they draw from poststructuralist, postcolonial theorists, such as Stuart Hall on the fluid and performative nature of identity and Andrea O'Reilly on the construction of motherhood in literary texts. Gilbert Fung and Shelby Chan also cite Stuart Hall in their informative overview of the constantly shifting and hybrid identities of post-retrocession Hong Kong. They also, briefly, bring in Hong Kong translated theatre—often in the form of translations from English to Cantonese, but also from Mandarin to Cantonese—as an example of this hybridity. Although these postcolonial, post-structuralist notions of identity might seem to be far removed from Doleželová's methodology, we should keep in mind that structuralism first recognized the unstable relationship between sign and meaning and the constructed nature of all linguistic representations.

The volume ends with Graham Sanders' essay on *Six Records of a Life Adrift*, a text about which Doleželová herself wrote an influential essay published in 1972. Sanders brings this important autobiography into the digital age by discussing the relevance of its apparently disjointed style and paradoxical elements to our postmodern fragmented selves and loss of faith in notions of personal authenticity. Making a late imperial text speak to the postmodern present is a perfect way to end a volume about the crossing between tradition and modernity.

Individually, the essays constitute new and original scholarship on a wide range of important topics in imperial and modern Chinese literary and cultural studies. As a whole, the volume is a fitting commemoration of the life and work of Milena Doleželová-Velingerová, who will be missed greatly by her students and the larger Sinological community. Below, find a list of her publications as a tribute to her scholarly contributions to the field.

MILENA DOLEŽELOVÁ-VELINGEROVÁ: PUBLICATIONS

Books

Editor/Translator [with James I. Crump]. *Ballad of the Hidden Dragon*. London: Oxford University Press, 1971.

Editor. *The Chinese Novel at the Turn of the Century*. Toronto: University of Toronto Press, 1980.

Editor. *A Selective Guide to Chinese Literature 1900–1949*. Vol. 1. *The Novel*. Leiden: Brill, 1988.

Editor. *Wu Xiaoling Remembered*. Prague: Dharma Gaia, 1998.

Editor [with Oldřich Král]. *The Appropriation of Cultural Capital: China's May Fourth Project*. Cambridge, MA: Harvard University Asia Center, 2001.

Editor/Translator [with M. Henri Day and Augustin Palát]. *Jaroslav Průšek 1906–2006 ve vzpomínkách přátel/remembered by friends*. Prague: Dharma Gaia, 2006.

Editor [with Rudolf Wagner]. *Chinese Encyclopaedias of New Global Knowledge (1870–1920): Chinese Ways of Thought*. Heidelberg: Springer, 2014.

Articles

"Kuo Mo-jo's Übersetzungen von Goethes Werken." *Archiv orientální* 26 (1958): 427–97.

"The Editions of the *Liu Chih-yuan chu-kung-tiao*." *Archiv orientální* 28 (1960): 282–289.

"Kuo Mo-jo's Autobiographical Works." In Jaroslav Průšek, ed., *Studies in Modern Chinese Literature*. Berlin: Akademie-Verlag, 1964, 45–75.

"Vers la théorie de la litérature des narrateurs chinois." *Cina* 8 (1964): 23–27.

"An Early Chinese Confessional Prose: Shen Fu's *Six Chapters of a Floating Life*." *T'oung Pao* 58 (1972): 137–160. [With L. Doležel].

"The Origins of Modern Chinese Literature." In Merle Goldman, ed., *Modern Chinese Literature in the May Fourth Era*. Cambridge, MA: Harvard University Press, 1977, 17–35.

"Lu Xun's 'Medicine.'" In Merle Goldman, ed., *Modern Chinese Literature in the May Fourth Era*. Cambridge, MA: Harvard University Press, 1977, 221–231.

"Typology of Plot Structures in Late Qing Novels." In Doleželová, ed., *The Chinese Novel at the Turn of the Century*. Toronto: University of Toronto Press, 1980, 38–56.

"Narrative Modes in Late Qing Novels.' In Doleželová, ed., *The Chinese Novel at the Turn of the Century*. Toronto: University of Toronto Press, 1980, 57–75.

"Li Xintian's Novel *The Bright Red Star*: The Making of a Revolutionary Hero." In Wolfgang Kubin and Rudolf Wagner, eds., *Essays in Modern Chinese Literature and Literary Criticism*. Bochum: Brockmeyer, 1982, 150–167.

"Chinese Literary Modernity: Cultural Constraints upon Its Understanding." In Jonathan Hall and Abbas Ackbar, eds., *Literature and Anthropology*. Hong Kong: Hong Kong University Press, 1986, 96–115

"Liu Chih-yuan chu-kung-tiao." In William H. Nienhauser, ed., *The Indiana Companion to Traditional Chinese Literature*. Bloomington: Indiana University Press, 1986, 578–580.

"Understanding Chinese Fiction 1900–1949." In Doleželová, ed., *A Selective Guide to Chinese Literature 1900–1949*. Vol. 1. *The Novel*. Leiden: Brill, 1988, 3–45.

"Traditional Chinese Theories of Drama and the Novel." *Archiv Orientálni* 59, no. 2 (1991).

"Pre-modern Chinese Theories of Drama and the Novel." In Michael Groden and Martin Kreiswirth, eds., *The Johns Hopkins Guide to Literary Theory and Criticism*. Baltimore: Johns Hopkins University Press, 1994, 149–155.

"European Studies of Modern Chinese Literature." In *Europe Studies China: Papers from an International Conference on the History of European Sinology*. London: Han-shan Tang Books, 1995, 1134–1151.

[with David Der-wei Wang] "Introduction." In Milena Doleželová-Velingerová and Oldřich Král, eds., *The Appropriation of Cultural Capital: China's May Fourth Cultural Project*. Cambridge, MA: Harvard University Asia Center, 2001, 1–27.

"Literary Historiography in Early Twentieth-Century China (1904–1928): Constructions of Cultural Memory." In Milena Doleželová-Velingerová and Oldřich Král, eds., *The Appropriation of Cultural Capital: China's May Fourth Cultural Project*. Cambridge, MA: Harvard University Asia Center, 2001, 123–166.

"Fiction from the End of the Empire to the Beginning of the Republic (1897–1916)." In Victor H. Mair, ed., *The Columbia History of Chinese Literature*. New York: Columbia University Press, 2001, 697–731.

"La Cina e l'Occidente: incontri e trasvalutazioni." In Franco Moretti, ed., *Il romanzo*. Vol. terzo. Storia e geografia. Torino: Giulio Einaudi editore, 2001, 479–504.

[with M. Henri Day] "Huang Moxi 黃摩西 (1866–1913): His Discovery of British Aesthetics and his Concept of Chinese Fiction as an Aesthetic System." In Ling-Yeong Chiu, with Donatella Guida, eds., *A Passion for China: Essays in Honour of Paolo Santangelo for his 60th Birthday*. Leiden: Brill, 2006.

[with Rudolf Wagner]. "Chinese Encyclopedias of New Global Knowledge (1870–1930): Changing Ways of Thought." In Milena Doleželová-Velingerová and Rudolf Wagner, eds., *Chinese Encyclopaedias of New Global Knowledge (1870–1920): Chinese Ways of Thought*. Heidelberg: Springer, 2014, 229–328.

"Modern Chinese Encyclopaedic Dictionaries: Novel Concepts and New Terminology (1903–1911)." In Milena Doleželová-Velingerová and Rudolf Wagner, eds., *Chinese Encyclopaedias of New Global Knowledge (1870–1920): Chinese Ways of Thought*. Heidelberg: Springer, 2014, 229–328.

Books and Articles in Chinese (under the name Miliena 米列娜)

世紀轉折時期的中國長篇小説 (The Chinese novel at the turn of the century). Changsha: Huazhong shifan daxue, 1990.

從傳統到現代: 19至20世紀轉折時期的中國小説 (From tradition to modernity: Chinese fiction in the transitional period from the late nineteenth century to the twentieth century). Beijing: Beijing daxue, 1991. Reprint 1998.

Edited [with 陳平原]. 近代中國的百科詞書 (Early modern Chinese encyclopedias). Beijing: Beijing daxue, 2007.

"留下了一片赤誠的心: 回憶鄭振鐸教授在捷克斯洛伐克的日子" (Leaving behind a sincere heart: remembering Professor Zheng Zhenduo's days in Czechoslovakia). 光明日報 (Guangming ribao) 19, no. 10 (1959): 3.

"魯迅的《藥》." In 樂黛雲 (Yue Daiyun), ed. 國外魯迅研究論集 1960–1981 (A collection of essays from overseas Lu Xun studies). Beijing: Beijing daxue, 1981, 497–507.

"晚清小説的敍述模式" (Narrative techniques in late Qing fiction). 中外文學 (Zhongwai wenxue) 11, no. 2 (1982): 26–45.

1 "LITERARY SCIENCE" AND "LITERARY CRITICISM": THE PRŮŠEK-HSIA DEBATE

LEONARD K. K. CHAN

> *An honest endeavor to grasp this whole complex process*
> *and to present it in an objective and unbiased way.*
> (Jaroslav Průšek)

> *The literary historian's first task is always the discovery*
> *and appraisal of excellence.*
> (C. T. Hsia)

THE PRŮŠEK-HSIA DEBATE

In a brief summary of his academic career given in the preface of his 2004 publication, *C.T. Hsia on Chinese Literature*, C. T. Hsia (1921–2013) recalls a literary debate of more than four decades earlier. He elucidates his "position as critic of Chinese literature" by citing his own words, which had appeared at the end of an essay: "a refusal to rest content with untested assumptions and conventional judgments and a willingness to conduct an open-minded inquiry, without fear of consequence and without political prepossessions" (Hsia 2004: xi–xii). The essay first appeared in 1963. It was an article written in response to a long review of Hsia's *A History of Modern Chinese Fiction* (1962) written by the renowned Czech scholar, Jaroslav Průšek (1906–1980). Hsia was greatly concerned with the debate; he repeatedly referred to it in his subsequent writings.[2] An important event in the history of modern Chinese literature, the Průšek-Hsia debate is worth re-examining because it illustrates a clash between two trains of thought in literary research.[3]

Hsia and Průšek were both pioneering researchers in the field of modern Chinese literature, and their works had a great impact on Western academia.[4] The two scholars are also immensely well known in the Chinese academy.

---

2   Aside from the foreword in *C. T. Hsia on Chinese Literature* (2004), Hsia mentioned it in Hsia 2002: 135 and 1987: 26.
3   This point is made by Lee 1980: xi–xii; and Wang 2005: 51–56.
4   For a discussion of this impact, see Lee 1980: xi–xii; Wang 2005: 51–56; and Gálik 1990: 151–161.

Many of their works have been translated into Chinese and are frequently quoted. Before a discussion of the significance of the Průšek-Hsia debate, I briefly sketch the cultural and academic backgrounds of the two scholars at the center of the debate.

In late 1940s, before leaving for the US to pursue his Ph.D. in English literature at Yale University, C. T. Hsia was a tutor in the Foreign Literature department at Peking University (Hsia 2002b: 94–115). Not long after he had moved to the US, China experienced a massive change: the ruling Kuomintang was overthrown by the Communists in a bloody civil war. Many intellectuals of different political stances—including Hsia's elder brother, Xia Ji'an, who had worked with Hsia at Peking University—left the mainland and went to Hong Kong, Taiwan, or overseas.[5] After the communist revolution, Hsia gave up on his hope of returning to his home country. In the final years of his Ph.D. study, Hsia was recruited to work on a project of China study sponsored by the US government: he was assigned to write several chapters, among which one was on Chinese literature, for the handbook *China: An Area Manual*.[6] He subsequently decided to develop out of this chapter a project of his own—an entire book on modern Chinese literature. The major part of the book was completed in 1955 and then published with several enlargements and revisions in 1961. A second edition of the book appeared in 1971, and a third in 1999.[7] With the publication of this pioneering work, along with his other important book *The Classic Chinese Novel* (Hsia 1968), Hsia acquired a prominent place in the field of Chinese literature. He would go on to become Professor Emeritus of Chinese at Columbia University and a fellow of the Academia Sinica. He passed away in 2013. *C. T. Hsia on Chinese Literature*, which came out in 2004, is a collection of sixteen substantial essays that Hsia had written during his years at Columbia University.[8]

---

5   After leaving Bejing, Xia Ji'an stayed in Hong Kong for a short period of time, and then went to Taiwan to teach at the National Taiwan University. He launched an important periodical, *Wenxue zazhi* (1956–1960), which later became a camp for liberal intellectuals who advocated democracy and the autonomy of literature. C. T. Hsia gave his support by contributing articles from abroad (Mei 2006: 1–33).

6   The project was led by David Nelson Rowe (1905–1985), an "anti-communist" who was a professor of political science at Yale University. According to Hsia, the handbook had never been formally published; the chapter on "literature" had a clear focus on modern literature, but classical literature was also covered (Hsia 1979a: 3–5). The following book record can be found in the Library of Congress: Chih-tsing Hsia [and others], *China: An Area Manual* (Chevy Chase, MD.: Operations Research Office, Johns Hopkins University, 1954-), edited by David Nelson Rowe and Willmoore Kendall.

7   Liu Shaoming and his co-workers' Chinese translation of the book is based on the second edition. The book was published by Union Press in Hong Kong and Zhuanji wenxue in Taipei in the same year of 1979, and re-published by the Chinese University Press in Hong Kong in 2001. An abridged simplified characters version, by Fudan University Press in Shanghai, came out in 2005.

8   For details of Hsia's publications, see "Chih-Tsing Hsia (C. T. Hsia) Publications" 1985; and Lianhe wenxue 2002.

Jaroslav Průšek first studied European history at Charles University, Prague. Later, while studying abroad in Sweden (and then Germany), he switched to sinology. He went to China in 1932 on a scholarship and studied Chinese socio-economic history. During his stay in China, he made acquaintance with Chinese literary men and artists such as Hu Shi, Bing Xin, Zheng Zhenduo, and Qi Baishi. He also exchanged letters with Lu Xun. After two years in China, he visited Japan, and then went back to Prague via the US in 1937. The journey to China deepened his understanding of Chinese literature, as well as Chinese language, folk culture, and arts. Soon after his return, he published a Czech translation of Lu Xun's *Call to Arms* (Nahan), which had a foreword contributed by Lu Xun. He later published the journal of his China trip under the title *My Sister China* (*Sestra moje Čína*, 1940).[9] In 1945, Průšek started teaching at Charles University. His interests cover a broad range of areas: Chinese thought, history, literature, and arts. Yet he became a well-known sinologist in Europe mainly from his achievements in two areas: "Middle Age folk literature," *huaben* fiction in particular, and "new literature" (*xin wenxue*). In 1953, he became the founding Director of the Oriental Institute of the Czechoslovak Academy of Sciences and devoted himself to promoting international exchange in the field of sinology. After the Prague Spring in 1968, he was expelled from the Communist Party and from the Oriental Institute and prohibited from publishing. He died in 1980. Průšek left behind a large collection of works.[10] His major publications in English are: *Chinese History and Literature* (1970), and *The Lyrical and the Epic: Studies of Modern Chinese Literature* (1980).

From the above brief description, it is not difficult to discern the great disparity between Hsia and Průšek. A Chinese student trained at Yale University—a bastion for the American "New Criticism" school of literary criticism—Hsia uses the benchmark of European literature in his review of Chinese literature. His thinking tends towards Anglo-American liberalism, and he strongly resists Communism and Communist regimes. Průšek was primarily trained in the European theoretical tradition. That the curiosity and imagination he had for China grew into fond attachment and sympathy is not difficult to understand if we take into consideration his political thinking: he was first attracted by national liberalization, and later found his ideal in socialism. In the 1960s, Průšek lost confidence in Communism. After the Prague Spring in 1968, he was put under severe political suppression and eventually died in grief. The Průšek-Hsia debate had taken place before Průšek changed his political thinking. At that time, the Western camp, head-

---

9   An English (Průšek 2002) and a Chinese (Průšek 2005) were subsequently published in the early 2000s.

10 For overviews of his work, see Merhaut 1956: 347–355; Merhaut 1966: 575–586; Šíma 1994.

ed by the US, was in direct confrontation with the Russian-led Communist Eastern block. It was the beginning of the Cold War period. It should be recalled that the book Hsia was recruited to write and that initiated his career as a specialist in Chinese literature—*China: An Area Manual*—was a reference work for the US army, a product of the West's strategy of containment of the Communist camp.

In March 1961, Yale University Press published Hsia's *A History of Modern Chinese Fiction*, the first literary history of its kind in English. Previously, the major focus of western studies of Chinese literature was on traditional/classical literature; modern literature was seldom studied, and it was often treated as a branch of area studies and complementary to socio-political analyses (Link 1993: 4–6). Hsia's pioneering and voluminous book of 600 pages attracted much attention among scholars of sinology and received a very positive response. David Roy claims it to be "the best book" in the field (Hsia 1979a: 11). However, in the following year, in a very prestigious journal of sinology *T'oung Pao*, the book was the subject of a long [48 pages] and harsh review by Průšek (1962) called "Basic Problems of the History of Modern Chinese Literature and C. T. Hsia, *A History of Modern Chinese Fiction*."[11] Hsia, who had just started working in the Department of Chinese and Japanese (forerunner of the current East Asian Languages and Cultures) at Columbia University, found this review article potentially damaging to his budding career,[12] so he decided to write a rebuttal in the same journal titled "On the 'Scientific' Study of Modern Chinese Literature: A Reply to Professor Průšek."[13] As a sequel, Průšek's student Zbigniew Słupski (1964) also wrote a review article "Some Remarks on the First History of Modern Chinese Fiction" in the journal *Archiv Orientální*. This article seems to have gone without any notice from Hsia. However, I will refer to it because it is helpful for us to understand Průšek's basic thinking, and the differences between Průšek and Hsia.

In terms of the exchange of essays that constitute this debate, it is clear that ideology and personal grievances marred both Hsia and Průšek in their

---

11   This article is also collected in Průšek 1980: 195–230. A Chinese translation can be found in Průšek 1987: 211–253.

12   Hsia says in retrospect: "When *A History of Modern Chinese Fiction* was published in March, 1961, I was little known in western academia, while Průšek had long been a spokesman for communist literature in Europe. He had written the long and harsh review on the sinology periodical *T'oung Pao* with an intention to strike me, to throw me to the ground and make sure that I won't be able to stand up again" (Hsia 2002a: 138). Also refer to Hsia 2004: xi.

13   Hsia 1963: 428–474. See also Průšek 1980: 231–266. But since the book is not edited in the highest standard and contains some mistakes, it is not used as main reference here. Hsia's article was later collected in *C. T. Hsia on Chinese Literature* (2004: 50–83). For a Chinese version, see Hsia 1979a. Quotations in this paper are based on the original passage in *T'oung Pao*, although the Chinese translation has also been consulted.

writing.[14] For instance, Průšek condemns Hsia for giving "a completely distorted picture" of the "ideological problems in the Liberated Areas during the War and of Mao Tse-tung's views, especially his 'Talks at the Yenan Literary Conference,'" and that "the criteria according to which C. T. Hsia evaluates and classifies authors are first and foremost of a political nature and not based on artistic considerations." Had the author moderated his "political animosities" and concentrated on the grasping of "the great literary process which is [was] going on in China today," he suggests, the considerable information that the author has brought together in his work would have become more useful. Průšek's conclusion is: "Thus the value of his book is greatly depreciated, for practically none of it can be used without critical examination and reassessment. In many places, too, the book sinks to the level of malicious propaganda" (Průšek 1962: 370, 358, 402-403). Průšek's student Słupski later did a detailed examination of the two chapters on Lao She in Hsia's book. Citing Hsia's final statement of his book: "A literary history, to be meaningful, has to be an essay in discrimination and not a biased survey to satisfy extrinsic political or religious standards," Słupski protests that Hsia "never misses the opportunities of besmirching a leftist writer." He concludes by saying "[Hsia] substitutes for literary scientific standards his subjective political sympathies and antipathies," and the book is "a book of practically very little value" (Słupski 1984: 142, 151-152).

Hsia of course denies Průšek's accusation of "dogmatic intolerance," stating that "I am afraid it is Průšek himself who may be guilty of 'dogmatic intolerance' insofar as he appears incapable of even theoretically entertaining any other view of modern Chinese literature than the official Communist one." If there is any "intolerance" in his own work, he says, it would be intolerance for bad writing, which is a consequence of his commitment to "literary standards," not "political prejudices" (Hsia 1963: 431, 434).

Both parties accuse the other of political bias, and each declares himself defender of the artistic value of literature. Literature and politics thus intertwine in a most suffocating way in the debate. While the two debaters' ingenious and serious thoughts on "literature" and "politics" are indeed admirable, it is important to bear in mind that Cold War politics does play a significant role in the debate. In this essay, however, I do not delve into this issue in further detail. Instead, I focus on the disparate attitudes and stances Průšek and Hsia take regarding "literary research," and the insight we can gain from the disparity.

---

14   Průšek says in the very beginning of his article that Hsia's work is saturated with "dogmatic intolerance," "disregard for human dignity." Hsia replies that it Průšek is advocating a "dogmatic scientific approach" (Průšek 1962: 357; Hsia 1963: 429; and Gálik 1990: 154-155).

"LITERARY SCIENCE" AND "LITERARY PROCESS"

At the very beginning of his rejoinder, "On the 'Scientific' Study of Modern Chinese Literature," Hsia questions the validity of the "scientific" approach accentuated by Průšek:

> I remain completely skeptical whether, beyond the recording of simple incontrovertible facts, the study of literature could assume the rigor and precision of "science" and whether, in the study of any literary period, an inflexible methodology could be formulated once for all. (Hsia 1963: 428–429)

He slights Průšek's search for "objectivity" as working in the confinement of "presuppositions" and "political prepossessions" (Hsia 1963: 459, 474), implying that Průšek's vaunted notions of "scientific method" or "objectivity" are a fantasy. Whether or not literary research should or can follow scientific standards of research is a topic that can be explored through different perspectives and approaches—I do not delve into the topic here. To understand Průšek's conception, we have now to examine the source of his literary theories.

Průšek returned to his home country from China in the autumn of 1937. He started teaching at Charles University in 1945. Before obtaining "habilitation," he had already joined the world renowned "Prague Linguistic Circle," which was based at Charles University, and had presented in the Circle's lecture series.[15] He shared the same theoretical conception with other key members of the Prague School, for example Jan Mukařovský (1891–1975) and Felix Vodička (1909–1974).[16] For literary theorists of the Prague School tradition, the words "science" and "scientific method" were standard fare and referred simply to an attempt to demystify the "literariness" of language. If we go over the "List of Lectures Given in the Prague Linguistic Circle (1926–1948)," we can find titles such as "Literary History and Literary Science," "The Science of Verbal Art and Its Relation to Adjacent Sciences," and "Method of Detailed Observation in Literary Science."[17] In the original titles, the Czech word for "science" is "věda,"[18]

---

15   Průšek presented twice in the lecture series of the Circle: "On the Semantic Structure of a Chinese Narrative" (1939.6); "On the Aspect of the Chinese Verb" (1948.12). See Kochis 1978: 607–622; Galan 1985: 207–214.

16   Regarding literary theories of the Prague School, see Chan Kwok Kou, "Literature / Structure / Literature of Acceptance—Felix Vodička's Theory of Literary Historiography" and "Literary Structure and the Process of Literary Evolution" in Chan Kwok Kou 2004: 326–361, 362–387. For Průšek's connection with the Prague Linguistic Circle, refer to Doležel 1994: 592–595.

17   J. V. Sedlák, "Literary History and Literary Science" (1929), F. Wollman, "The Science of Verbal Art and its Relation to Adjacent Sciences" (1935), and A. Bém, "Method of Detailed Observation in Literary Science" (1936). See Kochis 1978: 607–622.

18   Refer to "A List of Lectures on Poetics, Aesthetics and Semiotics Given in the Prague Linguistic Circle, 1926–1948" in Galan 1985: 207–214. Topics listed include both the original Czech version which is equivalent to the German term "Wissenschaft." The meaning of "Wissenschaft" is not limited to natural sciences; instead, it embraces a wider perspective and points to different systems of knowledge that are obtainable through hard empirical work.[19] The Prague School considers lifting the mysterious veil enshrouding literature to be the objective of "literary science," in particular the "literariness" of language. For instance, in the words of Roman Jakobson, leader of the Russian Formalist school and later a key member of the Prague Linguistic Circle, "The object of study in literary science is not literature but 'literariness,' that is, what makes a given work a literary work."[20] In the European tradition, literature is commonly accepted as a discipline of study or knowledge.[21]

A positive sense of the "scientific" research of literature is easily discernible in Průšek's review. Right from the beginning of the essay, Průšek says: "it is only natural that the attitude and approach of every scholar or scientist is determined in part by subjective factors ... all scientific endeavor would be vain, should the investigator not aim at discovering objective truth." Near the end of the review, he again proclaims: "The preliminary requirement for the author of such a work [i.e. a history of modern Chinese literature] would have to be, at the very least, an honest endeavor to grasp this whole complex process and to present it in an objective and unbiased way" (Průšek 1962: 357, 404).

From these assertions, we can recognize that for Průšek:

(1) literary study is an earnest quest for knowledge; a scholar in this discipline is not really different from a scientist; and the aim of this quest is to uncover the truth of an objective nature;

(2) the object of literary study is not a simple and easily discernible entity, but a very complex process that requires in-depth investigation.

The first point raises the issue of whether there is objective truth in literary study—a notion that Hsia dismisses. To Průšek, the history of modern

---

and English translation. In Galan's English translation, the term "science" is avoided and "study" is used instead.

19   Wellek (1960: 1–19) mentions that "Literaturwissenschaft" refers to systematic knowledge; he disagrees that it should be translated as "science of literature," since "science" in English connotes natural sciences. See also in Wellek 1963: 1–20. Quotations hereafter are based on the latter.

20   Roman Jakobson, "On Realism in Art" (1921). This is quoted from Bradford 1994: 127. See also Warner 1982: 69–81; and Striedter 1989: 20–21.

21   In his translation of the preface in Werner Mahrholz's *Literaturgeshichte und literaturwissenschaft* (1933), Li Changzhi (2006: 9–135) says that "Literature is also a 'study,' a specialized study, a science." This helps to prove that "literary science" is a common concept in the European tradition. See also Wellek's "The Revolt Against Positivism in Recent European Literary Scholarship" (Wellek 1963: 256–281)..

Chinese literature "exists" out there. It is the literary historian's responsibility to collect and investigate all the clues he can gather in order to uncover "objectively" the "real" process of literary development. That process is a complicated one, and an unbiased and honest attitude, suggested by the qualifier "scientific," is required to undertake such research. For Průšek, the scientific method is thus a legitimate strategy of research into literature, as it is for all academic disciplines.

The notion of "whole complex process" necessitates a thorough discussion. Imagining the entity of literature [and also of literary history] as a supraindividual complex is a conception derived directly from the Prague School aesthetics. The term "literature" refers not to a collection of literary works, but an abstract concept of "supraindividual relationship" and "system" or "structure" that can be defined in terms of a "part-whole" relationship. As Mukařovský put it, structure is a "whole whose nature is determined by its parts and their reciprocal relationships, and which in turn determines the nature and relationships of the parts" (in Galan 1985: 35). The Prague School's theory of "structure" comprises two central notions. First, it stresses the social character of literature and arts. "Literary structure" takes on meaning only when it enters into the social structure. Second, "structure" is dynamic, not static; "literary structure" is in constant flux, because it is locked in a dynamic, mutually-influencing relationship with different social and historical forces.[22] Průšek's "whole complex process" can be taken as a historical presentation of this pluralistic dynamic structure; it explains how Průšek arrived at his conviction about the social character of literature and the dynamic process of literary development.

With this theoretical background, we can better understand why Průšek criticizes C. T. Hsia for not being able "to give a systematic analysis of an author's work"; and he "facilitates his argumentation by laying stress on certain things and suppressing or remaining silent on others, or by attributing a significance to them which they do not possess" (Průšek 1962: 377-378). To Průšek, Hsia fails to grasp the concept of "whole." For instance, in order to study literary writers, Průšek suggests that:

> We do not limit ourselves to accidentals, but submit his oeuvre to systemic analysis, seeing in its individual traits not isolated and chance singularities, but the components of a unified artistic whole, welded by the author's artistic personality. The order of importance of these individual elements is determined by the artist's intention, just as is the way in which he binds and makes use of all these elements for the realization of his creative conception. This intention—and also the artistic procedures employed for the realization of his conception—reflects the author's philosophical outlook, that

---

22   See Galan 1985: 33-36; Steiner 1978: 356-359; Chan Kwok Kou, 2004: 362-369.

is, his attitude toward the world, toward life and toward the society in which he lives, and then too, his relation with established artistic traditions, and so on. The special nature of all these attitudes is then determined by the author's ideological and artistic individuality; we see him as a member of a given human society and, at the same time, as an artist of specific qualities. (377)

Průšek's strategy is without doubt a demonstration of the Prague structuralist methodology. The logic of the theory can be better understood by consulting works of Mukařovský, for instance "The Individual and Literary Development" (1977a: 161–179), "Personality in Art" (1977b: 150–168), "Intentionality and Unintentionality in Art" (1977b: 89–128), and "The Concept of the Whole in the Theory of Art" (1977b: 70–81). Actually, setting aside the politico-ideological factor, Průšek's criticism of Hsia's work is based primarily on ideas advocated by the Prague School. The same theoretical fount shaped his "discoveries" (or "inventions") of characteristics of modern Chinese literature, as can be seen in these statements: "[There can be no question that] subjectivism and individualism, joined with pessimism and a feeling for the tragedy of life, along with an inclination to revolt and even the tendency to self-destruction, are the most characteristic qualities of Chinese literature from the May Fourth Movement of 1919 to the outbreak of war with Japan" ("Subjectivism and Individualism in Modern Chinese Literature," 1957, in Průšek 1980: 3); "the roots of the exquisite modern Chinese short story, such as the short stories of Lu Hsün [Lu Xun], in so far as they have roots in old Chinese literature at all, are not to be found in old Chinese prose but in poetry" ("Introduction to Studies in Modern Chinese Literature," 1964, in Průšek 1980: 56); and "The main literary stream in Old China was that of lyric poetry, and this predilection runs through the new literary production as well, so that subjective feeling dominates and often breaks up the epic forms" ("A Confrontation of Traditional Oriental Literature with Modern European Literature in the Context of the Chinese Literary Revolution" 1964, Průšek 1980: 84).

These observations, deep and insightful, rose far above the level of the theoretical discussions of literary history undertaken by contemporary mainland Chinese critics, whom Průšek held as orthodox. His findings also threw new light on the study of Chinese literary history: for example, he regarded the "link" between "old" and "new" literature as highly important, and therefore chose the late Qing period as one of the focal points of his research. The recent wealth of scholarship in late Qing literature is very much indebted to Průšek and his students' earlier work.[23] His achievements show that the

---

23   It goes without saying that his debate opponent, C. T. Hsia, was also one of the trailblazers of late Qing literary research.

method of "scientific" research can be rewarding and inspiring. Nevertheless, when we say "inspiring," we ought to consider at the same time how much "imagination" is involved in the research—to fill in the missing "links," to correlate "tendencies" and so on—of uncovering the "whole complex process." Therefore, we need to problematize the concept of objectivity in Průšek's claimed "objective truth."

"LITERARY HISTORY" AND "LITERARY CRITICISM"

Let us turn to Hsia's defense. Hsia is annoyed by Průšek's accusation that he conducted his literary study in a "non-scientific," "subjective" way. He refutes the criticism by adapting Průšek's own measuring scale. He said "'Objectivity,' ... appears to mean uncritical compliance with the reigning opinion; to depart from it is to incur the risk of 'subjectivity.' Not only that, it is to betray one's sheer arrogance and 'dogmatic intolerance'" (Hsia 1963: 431). He also asserts that "it is his [Průšek's] dependence on a 'scientific' theory of modern Chinese history and literature and his unvarying habit of judging every work by its supposed ideological intent that have frequently misled him into simplifying a text or misinterpreting its import" (474). He goes on to say that "with all my 'subjectivity,' I have at least tried to do justice to every author and every work without having first to accommodate my honest reactions to a predetermined theory of modern Chinese fiction" (474). Hsia considers Průšek's "objectivity" not truly objective, and although accused of being "subjective," he regards himself as fair and unbiased. In other words, Hsia does not refute Průšek's argument by denying the importance of "objectivity" altogether; instead, he stresses the importance of "independent judgment":

> Thus, whatever historians and reporters may say of China since 1949, if one finds the literature produced since that date to be infinitely dreary, then this cultural fact should be taken into careful account in one's objective evaluation of the period. This inductive method seems to me far more scientific than the contrary method, the deductive method adopted by Průšek of first broadly defining the historical image of a period and then finding literature to fit that image. (Hsia 1963: 439)

Hence, Hsia also strives for "objective evaluation" and is concerned about being "more scientific." The question is: how can "objectivity" be achieved?

In the 1950s, when C. T. Hsia launched his study of modern Chinese literary history, the critical norm in mainland China was a politically-motivated form of literary criticism. Significant works of literary history, such as those by Cai Yi, Wang Yao, Zhang Bilai, Liu Shousong and Ding Yi, while they varied in quality, all served a Communist propaganda function.[24] Hsia disapproved of this political direction in the study of literature. He says the following in the preface to *A History of Modern Chinese Fiction*:

> I have tried mainly to elicit order and pattern from the chaotic mass of modern Chinese fiction—the most fruitful and important branch of modern Chinese literature—and to test this pattern against the Communist idea of the modern Chinese literary tradition. (Hsia 1999: xlvi)

He also says the following in his rejoinder to Průšek's review of his book:

> In dealing with the modern period in China, because so many of the native critics, aside from the question of their dubious training in their craft, were too much involved in the making of this modern literature to be unpartisan, the need to start from scratch appeared especially imperative. (Hsia 1963: 430)[25]

Hence Hsia's "objectivity" can be interpreted as a method that is free from manipulation by the mainstream and by staying true to one's own reading experience and judgment.[26] In other words, "objectivity" in Hsia's conception points to a respect for the literary texts and materials that are the "objects" of his research; it also implies "sincerity" on the part of the scholar, who is not bound by preconceived ideas.

We can thus understand why Hsia has the following definition for "the tasks of the literary historian": "A critical examination of the major and the representative writers of the period along with a succinct survey of that period designed to make their achievement and failure historically comprehensible" (Hsia 1963: 429). He further states that:

> [F]or a pioneer survey of modern Chinese fiction, the primary task is, I repeat, discrimination and evaluation: until we have elicited some order and patterns from the immense body of work available for examination, until we have distinguished the possibly great from the good writers, and the good from the poor, we cannot begin the study of influence and technique, however temptingly scientific the latter kinds of study may be. (429)

---

24   The works include: Cai Yi 1952; Wang Yao 1951–53; Zhang Bilai 1955; Liu Shousong 1956; and Ding Yi 1957.

25   Hsia later said: "I had read all criticisms on modern Chinese novels written by Chinese and Western critics that were available, but they weren't of much use to me" (Hsia 1979a: 6). This shows his determination to work on his own.

26   In Hsia's own words: "should go about the task empirically" and "form his own opinion about the vitality and culture of an age." See Hsia 1963: 439.

Hsia considers the primary tasks of the literary historian to be "critical examination" and "discrimination and evaluation." He therefore strategically dismisses tasks that are important to Průšek—for example "systematically study the relations between modern experiments in fiction and the native literary tradition," "systematic study of the impact of western literature upon modern Chinese fiction," "a broad comparative study of the narrative techniques employed by Chinese writers of fictions" (Hsia 1963: 429). This interpretation helps us understand Hsia's conviction that "the literary historian's first task is always the discovery and appraisal of excellence" (Hsia 1999: xlvi). Here we find the definitive divergence between Průšek's and Hsia's conceptions of literary history: in Průšek's conception, literary history should aim for a "systematic," "objective" study of the "whole complex process," whereas Hsia believes that a literary historian should first strive for "objective evaluation" on individual authors and works; for Hsia, the principle job of a literary historian is that of a critic. Průšek thus complains in his review: "Instead of employing a truly literary scientific method, C. T. Hsia is content to adopt the procedures of a literary critic—and of a very subjective critic at that" (Průšek 1962: 367).[27] Hsia does not distinguish between the work area of a literary historian and that of a critic; he quotes René Wellek (1903–1995) to justify his position: "[The literary researcher] must ... be a critic in order to be a historian" (Hsia 1963: 435). Wellek (1960: 14–15) believes that as a form of art literature is itself a "structure of values," and hence there is "the necessity of critical judgment" and the need for "aesthetic standards."

Wellek was teaching at Yale when Hsia was a graduate student there. Wellek's thinking was akin to that of the school of "New Criticism." Similar to Cleanth Brooks (1906–1994), who was Hsia's teacher and a prominent New Critic, Wellek disapproved of the positivist method of literary historiography. Brooks had written an essay entitled "Literary History vs. Criticism," in which he criticizes the "scientific" appearance of literary history at that time, which he claims was little more than an accumulation of verified historical data that had not been filtered by critical review. He concludes: "If the profession lacks an interest in literature as literature, they may become blind alleys" (Brooks 1940: 412).

Hsia's disapproval of Průšek's views can be understood against the background of the struggle between New Criticism and the positivist methods of literary research that had dominated American academia since the nineteenth century and that prioritized science. Yet, Průšek's "literary science" is

---

27   Průšek's student, Słupski makes a similar comment in a harsher tone: "The main characteristic feature of C. T. Hsia's work process is the absolute lack of systematic literary scientific viewpoints and the isolation of the studied subject from its historical connections. As a result, the conclusions he arrives at are distorted and superficial and are valid, at the very most, as subjective impressions of a reader" (Słupski 1964: 152).

different from the scientific theory being criticized by New Critics; the two theories in fact stand in diametrical opposition. In his "The Revolt Against Positivism in Recent European Literary Scholarship," Wellek (1963: 279–280) cites the Prague School as a prominent case of anti-positivism. But despite the differences, there is a commonality between Hsia and Průšek, or between New Criticism and the Prague School: the "literariness of literature" forms the core of their thinking. The two differ only in the fact that the former focuses more on the texts, whereas the later stresses literary process; this difference forms the different rationales behind their arguments. In an early essay "The Theory of Literary History," Wellek elucidates the issue:

> While there is … no substantial difference between the literary historian and the critic in the question of evaluation, there is a real difference between them in one substantial point: the literary critic is preoccupied with an individual work of art or an individual author, the literary historian tries to trace the development of literary art. (Wellek 1936: 191)[28]

BUILDING OF "THE GREAT TRADITION"

Hsia considers literary criticism a responsibility of literary historians. For modern Chinese literature in particular, because the existing works of literary history were often driven by political ideology, he sees a great need to "re-evaluate" important works and writers through an impartial critical eye. In the process, Hsia gradually sketches out the shape of the "tradition of 'new literature'" or "the 'genuine tradition' of Chinese culture" (Hsia 1979a: 16–17; 1979b: 1–3). Hsia's line of thinking, which has started from the text-focused theory of the New Criticism, eventually leads to Leavis's conception of "The Great Tradition," a conception filled with moral intensity (Samson 1992: 151–152).

In the preface to the Chinese version of *A History of Modern Chinese Fiction*, Hsia mentions "the great British critic Leavis's work that is dedicated entirely to the discussion of British novels—*The Great Tradition* (1948)" (Hsia 1979a: 6). He says he has benefited greatly by the work.[29] In his early days in Shanghai, he read Leavis's *Revaluation: Tradition and Development* (1936) and *New Bearings in English Poetry* (1932), works that inspired him in writing his doctoral thesis (Hsia 2002b: 111–112). From *A History of Modern Chinese Fiction*

---

28 Wellek was a graduate of the Charles University in Prague, and a member of the Prague School. His work "The Theory of Literary History" is an important article of the Prague School. Refer to Chan Kwok Kou 2004: 367–369.

29 In "Yelu sannian ban" (Three and a Half Years in Yale), Hsia (2002b) further elaborates on Leavis's influence.

to his renowned "Obsession with China," Hsia shows a deep concern with humanity, and Leavis's influence is clear. In this regard, the Průšek counterpart is the Prague School concept of "social function" of art, plus a version of humanist Marxism. It is worth comparing Hsia and Průšek's social and humanistic concerns and the roots of their thinking. Here I focus only on the "formalistic" aspect of Hsia's concept of tradition.

In his *A History of Modern Criticism*, Wellek describes Leavis as "the most influential English critic of this century after Eliot." Capturing the essence of his work as "culture against civilization, of a value-charged understanding against scientific explanation," he commends the British critic for having "valiantly fought for the central concern of criticism" (Wellek 1986: 241, 264). I mention Wellek here because half a century before his book was published, he was involved in a polemical discussion with Leavis,[30] a discussion that bears some resemblance to the Hsia-Průšek debate.

In 1937, Wellek sent an essay to *Scrutiny*, a review journal edited by Leavis. Commenting on Leavis's *Revaluation: Tradition and Development*, he praises the work as "the first consistent attempt to rewrite the history of English poetry from the twentieth century point of view." But he says that Leavis should "more explicitly" and "systematically" explain the review criteria adopted in the book, and "defend this position more abstractly." (Wellek 1937: 375–376) In a "reply" to Wellek, Leavis expresses his disagreement. He considers abstract and generalized explanations to be within the domain of "philosophy"; literary criticism, he says, is a different kind of academic discipline, one that focuses on the actual experience of reading: "The ideal critic is the ideal reader ... Philosophy ... is 'abstract' ... , and poetry 'concrete.' ... The business of the literary critic is to attain a peculiar completeness of response and to observe a peculiarly strict relevance in developing his response into commentary" (Leavis 1937: 60–61). The argument between Wellek and Leavis centers on the different expectations the two scholars have for literary discussions. Whereas Wellek holds that literary history (he considers Leavis to be "rewriting the history of English poems") should be on the level of generalized, abstract thinking and should present "systematic" reasons for judgments made, Leavis, as a "literary critic," thinks that concrete works are the focus of his study, and his writing is nothing more than his reading experience presented in a concrete form. He considers Wellek's demands for generalization relevant only within the context of philosophy.[31]

---

30   In a book review collected in a book on Leavis published after his death, Wellek talks about the argument of fifty years earlier: "This polemic has pursued me all my life," René Wellek 1988: 707–709.

31   For a discussion of the theoretical meaning of the two's polemic, refer to Samson 2009: 26–31.

Leavis's conception that a critic's responsibility is to make concrete judgment and present analyses is probably homologous to Hsia's idea that the primary task involved in his *A History of Modern Chinese Fiction* is to present analyses of authors and works. Leavis never made explicit the importance of writing literary history; instead, he propagated the value of literary criticism in modern culture and devoted himself to promoting literary education through literary criticism.[32] But throughout his writing—from *Revaluation: Tradition and Development* and *New Bearings in English Poetry* to *The Great Tradition*, and in many of his essays—he re-mapped British (and later American as well) literary history. A unique view of literary history is presented in these works. One of the striking features of *The Great Tradition*—a work that greatly influenced Hsia—is that only very few novelists are admitted to this "Great Tradition."[33] The work defines itself to a large extent by "exclusions,"[34] and consequently names of many famous novelists (such as Laurence Sterne, Henry Fielding, Charlotte Brontë, William Thackeray, and Thomas Hardy) are omitted. Hsia once said that:

> Britain in the Victorian Age had no entertainment such as movies and television. Many people liked to read novels, and there were a vast number of novelists in those days. But nowadays, no more than ten of those novelists are still being read, and only two of them are considered must-read writers by learned English readers: Dickens and Eliot. Even Thackeray and Hardy are secondary. A book of literary history that is rigorously written is not only for people of the contemporary age; it provides the strictest judgment for readers of later generations. (Hsia 1979b: 11)

Hsia's claim echoes the judgment made in *The Great Tradition*. Leavis's "strictest judgment" screens out many famous names, and only a handful of writers are admitted to the list. This is of course a process of "canon-making," a re-mapping of literary history through the establishment of a concretely recognizable literary tradition. It is also remarkable that this literary tradition is not structured on a novelist's literary lineage or heritage; it is based on Leavis's own "observation." The "tradition" is built up by bring-

---

32   One scholar comments that "Leavis was supremely a publicist for criticism and the idea of criticism ... Leavis placed literary criticism ... at the heart of English studies; historical scholarship became marginalized, a matter for specialists only. In the recent past criticism had been part of the profession of letters; after Leavis it seemed to be firmly rooted in the academy" (Bergonzi 1990: 56). See also Atherton 2005: 143–150.

33   The great authors cited by Leavis in the beginning of the book are: Jane Austin, George Eliot, Henry James, Joseph Conrad, amongst these authors Eliot is given the highest regard. The last chapter of the book is on Charles Dickens's *Hard Times*, and Leavis later wrote *Dickens the Novelist* (1970). It seems like Leavis's list of "Great Tradition" has to be supplemented.

34   Refer to Horne's comment: "Leavis's enterprise defines itself, to a startling degree, by its exclusions, its resounding negations." Horne 2004: 166.

ing together Leavis's judgments on the greatness of individual writers. Aside from artistic value, the most important criteria held by Leavis are "a vital capacity for experience, a kind of reverent openness before life, and a marked moral intensity" (Leavis 1948: 9).

It seems plausible to suggest that Leavis's conception of the "Great Tradition" forms a prototype for Hsia's study of modern Chinese literature. Hsia says the following in the preface to the Chinese edition of *A History of Modern Chinese Fiction*: "[If] we believe that the Chinese literary tradition should always be in relation to the real world, be concerned with the realities of life, and be rich in Confucius benevolence, then we can say that this tradition has truly made important headway only after the beginning of the twentieth century" (Hsia 1979a: 15). And he says the following in "Joint Review of Four Modern Chinese Literary Histories": "All literary works that stand the test of time are closely related to 'life.' They expose the truths of life, or at least tell the author's own view of life" (Hsia 1979b: 19).

Hsia's criteria stand close to those of Leavis's—we can see the building of a "new tradition," one that counters the canonical norms in mainland Chinese scholarship, taking place in *A History of Modern Chinese Fiction*.[35] There is a close resemblance between Hsia and Leavis even in their methodology. Although over 600 pages, the number of writers covered in *A History of Modern Chinese Fiction* is not so considerable. The selection criteria are rigorous, more so when compared with other works on modern Chinese literature that were available at that time. Hsia included in his inventory names that were largely ignored by literary historians at that time, writers such as Zhang Ailing, Qian Zhongshu, Shen Congwen, Zhang Tianyi, and Shi Tuo. He says the following in his rejoinder to Průšek: "A lonely genius working in supposed defiance of the Zeitgeist may ultimately sum up that age much more meaningfully than a host of minor writers walking fully in step with the times" (Hsia 1963: 439).

Neither "literary criticism" nor "literary history" can exist independent of value judgment. After establishing a reliable standard of judgment, it is possible for both Leavis and Hsia to make use of the standard to "judge hundreds and thousands of cases" (*duan qianbai zhi gong'an*). Hsia's view, though striking at that time, has now become a commonly accepted notion in academia. His idea of not being bound by existing dogma and concepts has been proven correct, especially in light of the "rewriting of literary history" movement in China in the 1980s and its "revisionist" attention to the very writers Hsia had championed decades earlier.

When we say that "tradition" is built up through the application of critical consciousness, the existence of a certain kind of force that works to make links and determine structures is implied. The "greatness" endowed by Lea-

---

35   See Hsia 1979a: 16–17; 1979b: 1–3.

vis in just a handful of key writers suggests a commonality that allows for the creation of a "whole." Similarly, Hsia's *A History of Modern Chinese Fiction* discusses only a limited number of topics and writers; he proclaims in the preface to the work that as a "literary historian," he tries to "elicit order and pattern" from chaos, so as to test the pattern against "the Communist idea of the modern Chinese literary tradition" and "the example and challenge of the Western tradition."[36] In that sense, although *A History of Modern Chinese Fiction* emphasizes the "discovery and appraisal" of elite writers, Hsia's thinking incorporates the idea of a "tradition," and this implies the existence of a "whole." Just as Leavis deems it unnecessary to give a full explanation to Wellek of his criteria for literary evaluation, Hsia does not bother to describe in any tangible detail the nature of his standards.

CONCLUSION

Hsia and Průšek both made significant contributions to the study of modern Chinese literature. Both were pioneers in their field, and the fruits of their research are valuable today. The debate between the two epitomizes a clash between two kinds of research methods. Both parties think that literary study should give objective, verifiable results, yet they offer different approaches to the process by which objective "truth" is uncovered. Průšek's views are based on the following premise: literature is a structure that transcends individual parts, and along with the passage of time, it changes into a structure of process that keeps on evolving. This structure of process is highly complex, and thus a "scientific" method and an "objective" attitude are crucial for uncovering the complete picture of the structure. Also, since the "complete picture" or the "whole" constantly interacts with individual elements, such as writers or works, it is also important to consider the individual elements in order to get at the truth. Hsia suggests that literary study should start from individual works. The essence of "objectivity" lies in the impartiality of the subject who undertakes the study; the hidden tradition can be gradually grasped by engaging in empirical studies in an in-depth manner, and accumulating experience gained from each individual study.

In terms of methodology, Průšek, and the Prague School, favor an approach that is precise, systematic, and comprehensive. But the existence of the "literary structure"—which Průšek claims transcends individual parts—is something that is beyond verification and can only be taken as a possibility. The "literary structure" is further in doubt because of the fact that Průšek accepted, rather uncritically, Chinese left-wing ideology as fact; the bound-

---

36   Hsia 1999: xlvi. A similar view is stated in 1963: 430.

ary between ideal and reality is blurry and the basis of the "objectivity" in his argument dubious. When the logical development of his theory leads away from reality, disparity arises and many of Průšek's historical judgments lose their validity. As for Hsia, whether it is the humanism-centered theory that originated at Yale or Leavis's notion of surrounding life with literature and taking literature as the hub of humanistic spirit, he has done great work in drawing correspondences among individual works; the critic's ability to empirically prove the value of works is taken to be more important than the method being used. But just like Leavis's building of the "Great Tradition" of British literature, in Hsia's *A History of Modern Chinese Fiction* there is a stronger sense of "presentness" than "historicity." The book's greatest achievement lies not in the mapping of history, but in "the discovery and appraisal of excellence."

While they are clearly a factor motivating the two sides, the debate between Hsia and Průšek should not be reduced to Cold War politics. There is an important lineage between Průšek and his Prague School's theoretical thinking, as well as the modern ideological trend of nationalism in Czechoslovakia and other countries in Eastern Europe. Between the two world wars, countries such as Czechoslovakia and Poland experienced a period of revival of nationalism after the breakdown of the Austro-Hungarian Empire. Like socialism, avant-garde literary thinking is another manifestation of the people's political ideal and, at the same time, a symbol of liberation (Tihanov 2004: 61–81). Probing into the "whole complex process" of the Chinese literary history—for example, the heritage of "lyricism" that seems to have a close resemblance to the avant-garde trend—provides support for their imagination of a general structure that transcends the parts; the notion of "scientific" method forms a basis upon which they can turn their imagination into a belief. The starting point in Hsia's thinking is just the reverse. Having witnessed a time when political doctrines were given precedence, when right and wrong were made as obvious as black and white and yet nothing was reliable, Hsia strongly resists the idea of collective consciousness, and he has lost confidence in orders that are externally imposed. He thus counts on himself. Relying on his own critical judgment and the theoretical basis of the New Criticism, he examines individual writers of new literature and their works, individually. Looking at Hsia's *A History of Modern Chinese Fiction* from a different angle, one may say that Hsia's independent endeavor shows his own obsession with China. Through his own efforts, he tries to recalibrate the scales used to weigh the value of modern Chinese literature.

Nearly three decades after the debate took place, Marián Gálik, another of Průšek's students, re-examined the debate: "There was no victory and no defeat in this Průšek-Hsia duel. But it is necessary to say that Průšek was better in his other studies. All the students of modern Chinese are recommended to devote more time to his other works" (Gálik 1990: 155). Gálik's comment seems reasonable. Many of Průšek's other works are indeed of a better quality than his review on Hsia, and his writings have inspired many later scholars. The same can be said for Hsia. Many of his most mature observations, such as "obsession with China" and "the tradition of new literature" (*xinwenxue de chuantong*), were made after the debate. If we "let history be the judge," we can say that in the debate both Hsia and Průšek had victories and defeats. As regards critical evaluation of individual authors, Hsia's unique insight has been affirmed by literary history; it has been proved that effective "literary criticism" has the power to alter the course of the development of "literary history." Průšek, on the other hand, has made contributions not to the field of critical evaluation, but analysis. His observations on the "lyric" and "epic" trend in modern Chinese literature have made a strong impact on the study of late Qing and twentieth-century Chinese literature. It has to be mentioned here that Průšek's grasp of the development of literary history is not based upon logical permutation or scientific measurement; it is a process of induction based on his close observations of literary activities at that time and on his own experience. In other words, his achievement brings out the difference between "literary science" and "natural science." The "science" in "literary science" hints at a return to "Wissenschaft"—the source of the humanistic spirit, which involves extensive study and critical inquiry, prudent reflection and clear discernment. The meaning of the Hsia-Průšek debate lies not in determining a winner; the debate is important because it helps us understand the flexibility and breadth of literary historiography, and how literary explanations and evaluations from different theoretical orientations can best be accommodated.

PART I:
LANGUAGE, NARRATIVE STRUCTURE, AND GENRE

2 HOW TO DO THINGS WITH NEOLOGISMS: A STUDY OF WANG WENXING'S LANGUAGE

SHU-NING SCIBAN

> *I have never created a language;*
> *I am only revealing what a language can do.*
> (Wang Wenxing)
> (Zhou Yizheng 2011: 11)

INTRODUCTION

Wang Wenxing (also known as Wang Wen-hsing) (b. 1939), a prominent Modernist writer from Taiwan, was the winner of the Taiwan National Cultural and Art Award (Taiwan guojia wenyi jiang; literature category) in 2009 and of the Huazong International Chinese Language Literature Award (Huazong shijie huawen wenxue jiang) in 2011. Wang began writing creatively when he was still in high school and his first fictional work, "The Lingering Night" (Shouye), was published in 1958 when he was a freshman in university. Till now, Wang has produced twenty-three short stories, one novella, three novels, and one play; obviously, he is not prolific, considering his writing career has spanned more than fifty years. Nevertheless, his first novel, *Family Catastrophe* (Jia bian; 1973), was selected as one of the best one-hundred Chinese literary works published in the twentieth century (selection organized by *Yazhou zhoukan* magazine in Hong Kong) and one of the thirty best literary works published in the second half of the twentieth century in Taiwan (selection organized by the Council for Cultural Affairs in Taiwan through *Lianhe bao*). Though Wang's stories examine social, economic, and cultural problems of contemporary Taiwan, it is his language that attracts most attention, particularly the innovative language used in his three novels.

Christopher Lupke (2003: 482) describes Wang's novels as follows: "*Family Catastrophe*, Wang Wenxing's first novel, is one of the most uniquely structured novels in any language," and "*Backed against the Sea* [*Bei hai de ren*; Vol. 1 and 2, 1981 and 1999], Wang's subsequent novel, extends the linguistic and structural experimentation of *Family Catastrophe* … The language is a *tour de force* of linguistic play." Wang's innovative language uses numerous typographical designs, including traditional characters, simplified characters,

national phonetic symbols (or *zhuyin fuhao*), alphabetical letters, punctua-
tion, characters with alternative scripts, neologisms, "incorrect" characters,
bold font, created signs, and empty space; in addition, there are words and
phrases altered from standard phrases, and irregular syntaxes (e.g., syntax
with ungrammatical word order, syntax with excessive repetition of words).
These writing strategies present a profound challenge to conventional reading practices.

Considering the reception of Wang's language and style over the past
fifty years, one finds that it has been like a journey beginning with a bumpy
road that has turned smooth in the recent decade. When *Family Catastrophe*
was published, as Sung-sheng Chang (1993: 111) notes, it "created an immediate stir, followed by intermittent, energized discussions"; however, "*Backed
against the Sea* [Vol. 1] has been largely neglected since its publication."[37]
Compared with other canonical writers, the number of studies that have
been done on Wang Wenxing's works is not large and those focusing on his
language and style are even fewer.

Yan Yuanshu (1973) was the first to discuss the realism in Wang's writing and claims that the most important aesthetic virtue of *Family Catastrophe*
is vividness. Ouyang Zi (1973) presents a remarkably detailed discussion on
particles and exclamations used at the ends of sentences, the mixture of classical and vernacular vocabulary, the unconventional use of characters with
acoustic effects, and the ungrammatical repetitions of words. Chang Han-
liang (1973) investigates many aspects of the language in *Family Catastrophe*,
particularly the characters, claiming that Wang has brought into full play the
ideographical nature of Chinese characters, and that they are visually effective and acoustically precise. Scrutinizing the unconventional style in *Family
Catastrophe*, Edward Gunn (1984: 38) writes that "changes in Wang's style may
be taken as symbolically connoting the mood of the story." Zheng Hengxiong
(2013: 347) employs the musical structure of harmony and counterpoint to
find that "Wang's *Backed against the Sea*, with its complex polyphonic musical
texture, is unique and unprecedented in twentieth century Chinese fiction."
In his meticulous analysis of the rhetorical effect of Wang's innovations of
characters, lexicon, and syntax, Zhou Guozheng (1984) believes that *Family
Catastrophe* is an outstanding and sensational novel with a highly irregular
language. Examining the strategies of Wang's literary style (e.g., neologism,
unconventional use of existing characters, alphabets, Mandarin phonetic
signs, typographic designs, newly coined phrases, syntactical deviations and
so on), I have asserted that Wang's innovative language aims at constructing
acoustic, visual, and semantic effects (Sciban 1995). In addition, Sung-sheng

---

37   For different opinions on Wang's language of *Family Catastrophe* in the 1970s and 1980s, see Yang
Xiaojing 1999: 31–54.

Chang's (1993) monumental book, *Modernism and the Nativist Resistance: Contemporary Chinese Fiction from Taiwan*, which delineates the historical, cultural and literary background of the Modernist movement in Taiwan and Wang's aesthetic views, lays a foundation for understanding Wang's art of writing.

This review of the scholarship on Wang's language reveals that a consensus has been reached among academic critics that Wang's innovative use of language is unprecedented and effective. Though Wang's aesthetic of literary language is accepted generally, questions such as exactly how the individual linguistic and stylistic features are constructed and applied remain unanswered. As Wang is considered an "iconoclast" (Shu 1980) and "the greatest anarchist of style since Lu Xun" (Gunn 1991: 161), these questions are worth scrutinizing in hope that they will lead to a more thorough understanding of Wang's language and of the historical development of Chinese writing. As a response to the call for a comprehensive study of Wang's linguistic and stylistic features, in this chapter I investigate the neologisms in *Family Catastrophe*, perhaps the most ambitious and "disturbing" feature of Wang's linguistic experimentation.

Sung-sheng Chang (2001: 10) encapsulates the goals of *Xiandai wenxue* (Modern literature), the magazine Wang Wenxing co-founded,[38] and underlines the most important two: first, experiment with, search for, and create new artistic forms and style; second, draw lessons from Western literary works, art trends, and critical thought. Neologisms clearly reflect the spirit of the first goal. In his *Rewriting Chinese*, Gunn (1991: 99, 102, 153) mentions three writers who have used neologisms in their stories. Besides Wang Wenxing, there are Lu Xun (1881–1936) and Wang Zhenhe (1940–1990). However, unlike Wang Wenxing, Lu Xun and Wang Zhenhe did not develop neologisms into a major feature in their writings. Gunn (1991: 99) registers only one neologism "猹" (pronounced as *zhā*, an animal like a badger) created by Lu Xun and used in his story "Hometown" (Guxiang); Lu Xun is also reported to have created another two neologisms "女人 [one character]" (a female third-person pronoun, likely to be pronounced as *tā*) and "虫遷 [one character]" (as a replacement for the 遷 to be used in the name of the Han historian Sima Qian 司馬遷, pronounced as *qiān*) (Han 2007: 79). As for Wang Zhenhe's neologisms, I have not found any, but Chang Han-liang (1992: 133–156) has discussed the unique use of character font in Wang Zhenhe's two stories, "A Mouse Serves Tea to Guests (Laoshu peng cha qing renke) and "The Time of Your Life (Rensheng gewang). Sung-sheng Chang (1993: 74), in her comparative discussion

---

38   Wang Wenxing co-founded *Modern Literature* with classmates including Bai Xianyong, Ouyang Zi, Chen Ruoxi, Ye Weilian, Li Oufan, Liu Shaoming and so on, in March 1960 when he was in his junior year in university.

of Wang's style, states: "What significantly distinguishes Wang Wen-hs-ing's literary experiment from that of other Modernist writers, such as Wang Chen-ho [Wang Zhenhe], is its rigorous professionalism." Han Shiqi (2007: 79–80) points out a number of other intellectuals in the May Fourth era who created neologisms. In most cases, the creations of these neologisms were for the purpose of translating new or foreign ideas; none of them were meant to become a widely accepted literary feature, as Wang Wenxing intended. In other words, Wang makes neologism an important feature of fictional style.

Instead of evaluating the neologisms Wang creates, I focus on questions that concern the mechanism of the neologisms used in *Family Catastrophe*: What is considered a neologism? How many neologisms are there in *Family Catastrophe*? What are their rhetorical functions? And, what are their forma-tive principles?

WHAT IS CONSIDERED A NEOLOGISM IN THE STUDY OF WANG WENXING?

According to the *Oxford Dictionary of English* (2012), neologism is "a newly coined word or expression." The *Cambridge Encyclopedia of Language*'s (Crys-tal 1997: 73) description is "The invention of new words is perhaps the most obvious way to go beyond the normal resources of a language: completely fresh creations, such as Shakespeare's *incarnadine*; new constructions, such as Hopkins's 'widow-making unchilding unfathering deeps' (*The Wreck of the Deutschland*); and new parts of speech, as in Othello's very lip (=kiss), 'To lip a wanton in a secure couch.'" Obviously, originality and creativity are essential to a neologism. However, the specific linguistic construction of a neologism is flexible; it can be a word or a phrase.

When applying the above mentioned notions of neologism in a Chinese language text, we need to clarify what a word is, because of the confusion that often arises in understanding the relationship of characters to words. In the pre-modern period, most Chinese words were monosyllabic; the language, however, has gradually evolved so that, today, many Chinese words are bi- or multisyllabic. In other words, a Chinese word today can be either one char-acter or more than one character. In Chinese terms, "character" is called *zi*, and "word" is *ci*. Ideally, the study of Chinese neologisms should exam both single-character words and multi-character words.

I first look at characters created by Wang Wenxing, which in Chinese are *zichuangzi* (self-created characters); however, it should be noted that Wang uses other forms of neologisms. Since Wang is a Taiwanese writer, I use the *Zhongwen da cidian* (The encyclopedia dictionary of the Chinese language) (Zhongwen 1962)—the largest dictionary published in Taiwan which lists

49,905 characters—to determine the qualification of single-character neologisms; in other words, in this study, a character must be excluded from the dictionary to be considered a neologism. It should also be noted that, in the entire list of neologisms found in *Family Catastrophe*, the only one that has been excluded from this study is 口+伯 (*bo*, not).[39] Although this character is not found in *The Encyclopedia Dictionary of the Chinese Language*, it appears in the word 口+基 口+路 口+伯 (*jilubo*, cherubim) in Chinese translations of the Bible.[40]

HOW MANY NEOLOGISMS ARE THERE IN *FAMILY CATASTROPHE*?

According to my research, Wang Wenxing creates forty-five neologisms in *Family Catastrophe*. I have consulted all five versions of *Family Catastrophe*, and the script of each of the neologisms in all the versions has been examined. In a conversation I had with Wang in 1995 (Huang Shuning 2013), he described his writing process. After finalizing what to write, he puts to paper a writing plan; i.e., the plot of the story. The next step is the daily composition of a small section of the story, following the plot as close as possible, avoiding any change or alteration. During the process of composing, he often uses dots, lines, or symbols, instead of characters, to record the words that come into his mind. Once he is satisfied with the words or the sentence, he will immediately copy it in character form on a blank piece of paper, before he forgets it. The next day, he will move on to the next section of the plot, not looking back at what he wrote the day before. Because this kind of writing requires strenuous effort, Wang can write only thirty characters a day. What he writes down in characters is the first version of the story. It is referred to as the manuscript of the story. The second version is the clean copy that Wang prepares for his publisher; the paper he uses is standard composition paper with printed squares. The second version is very easy to read, compared with the first version, which has many changes such as deletions, insertions, additions, switches, and so on, as well as some minor changes. The third version, in the case of *Family Catastrophe*, is the formal publication by Huanyu Publishing Company in 1973. The fourth and fifth versions are the editions printed by Hongfan Bookstore in 1978 and 2000, respectively. I examine all versions available because Wang is known for

---

39 In this paper, Wang's single-character neologisms are typed with the Chinese script components, the "+" sign between each component and unbroken underlining under all components of one neologism.

40 The three-character word "口+基 口+路 口+伯" is seen in many places in the Chinese translation of the Bible. One instance is in *Chu Aiji ji* 出埃及記 (Exodus) 25: 18–21.

being extremely careful about the language he uses and constantly revising his writing. In 2000, Wang Wenxing donated the manuscripts and the clean copies of his two novels to the library of his *alma mater*, National Taiwan University. These manuscripts and the clean copies were published along with Wang Wenxing's own reading of the two novels by Xingren wenhua shiyanshi in 2010, entitled *Wang Wenxing shougao ji* (The collection of Wang Wenxing's manuscripts),[41] allowing the public to access the first two versions of Wang's novels for the first time.

WHAT ARE THE RHETORICAL FUNCTIONS OF NEOLOGISMS IN *FAMILY CATASTROPHE*?

Being a figure of speech in the category of tropes, neologisms have a function that turns a general depiction into a specific kind by means of new words or expressions. Referring to his unconventional writing, Wang in an interview with Lin Jingjie (Lin 2011: 28) says: "I have given myself a high degree of freedom in choosing this road [of writing unconventionally] in the past few decades. The freedom has nothing to do with wanting to impress people by being different, but reflects that I feel desperate to write this way, like a cornered beast struggling for survival" (幾十年下來, 我都給自己很大的自由, 走這條路。這很大的自由呢, 不是標新立異, 而是絕地求生, 是一種困獸之鬥).[42] As revealed in Wang's aesthetic of language described by S. Chang, Gunn, and Sciban, Wang aims at achieving a literary language that is effective in its acoustic and visual representation of a character's speech and thinking and of the narrator's narration, a style modeled after the masters of nineteenth-century realism (e.g., Gustave Flaubert, Guy de Maupassant, and so on).[43] However, at the same time, Wang also wishes to produce a realistic description that reflects the psychology of the characters or the narrator in the story, a style that Shan Dexing calls "symbolic realism" (Shan 1987: 185). Knowing this, one can say that Wang has enlarged the space between words

---

41   The publication of Wang's manuscripts and the recording was organized and edited by YI Peng (易鵬) at National Central University.

42   Lin Jingjie is also the director of *Xunzhao Bei Hai de ren* 尋找背海的人 (The man behind the book), the documentary film on Wang Wenxing distributed by Sumu Meiti company or Fistisa Media in 2012. Lin has won several national and international awards for the films he directed at the Asia Pacific Film Festival, Taipei Film Festival, Golden Horse Awards and Golden Harvest Awards. He took the International Critics' Week Award at the Venice Film Festival with his 2007 film *The Most Distant Course* and the gold medal in the category of biography film at the 46th Worldfest-Houston: International Film and Video Festival, April 12–21, 2013 for *The Man behind the Book*.

43   Wangs' Western influences are discussed in details in Shan Dexing's interview with Wang (Shan 1987; rpt. 2013). The short English version of this interview is also seen in Shan Dexing (1984).

(not lines) and condensed the meaning of his language through his unique writing style. The rhetorical functions of the neologisms found in his first novel attest to this idea.

The forty-five neologisms in *Family Catastrophe* are used for the following rhetorical purposes: depicting sounds, shape-color, senses of taste and smell, sense of touch, emotions-feelings, and synaesthesia. Chart 1 below lays out the distribution of the neologisms' rhetorical functions and a description of each function follows.

Chart 1: Rhetorical Functions of Neologisms in *Family Catastrophe*

Figures of Speech	Depicting Sounds	Depicting Shapes/ Colors	Depicting Senses of Taste and Smell	Depicting Senses of Touch	Depicting Emotions and Feelings	Synaesthesia	Single Rhetoric Function
No. of neologisms	41	12	1	3	21	3	6

Note: The total number of neologisms is 45. Due to their multifunctional nature in rhetoric, some neologisms are counted more than once.
Source: Author.

DEPICTING SOUNDS (ONOMATOPOEIA)

Depiction of sounds is the most important function of Wang's neologisms. Out of the 45 neologisms, 41 belong to this category; for instance, 氵+格氵+羅 (*geluo*, sound of gargling):

去拿冷開水氵+格氵+羅一下嘴腔。嘴裏帶有暑氣，氵+格氵+羅以後才不會中暑。

(Go gargle with some cold water and rinse your mouth. You've swallowed a great deal of the sun's heat. Get rid of it so you won't have heatstroke.)
(Sec. 77)[44]

"*Geluo*" represents the gargling sound that is represented by "格羅," the right-hand components of the two characters of the neologism. In the context of the quotation, water is emphasized so the water radical 氵 is placed on the left of each of the characters.

---

[44] The translation is Susan Dolling's (Wang 1995: 92) with the author's modification for the purpose of description of the literal meaning of the quoted text. As the novel is divided into 172 sections (15 under alphabetical indicators from A to O, representing events in the current story time; and 157 under Arabic numbers from 1–157, representing events in the past story time), it is rather easy to find a quotation from the novel, in either the original or the translation, without a specific page number. For this reason, the page numbers of quotations novel will not be given in this paper.

DEPICTING EMOTIONS AND FEELINGS

Depiction of emotions and feelings is the second most frequently used function of Wang's neologisms. Out of forty-five neologisms, twenty-one belong to this category. As Sciban (1995: 27) describes, Wang's interest in psychological fiction began from the very first story he wrote, so the high frequency of the appearance of this rhetorical function is understandable and, to a certain degree, anticipated. For instance, 口+猴 (*hou*, exclamation for showing excitement) in the following sentence:

口+猴! 三仟塊錢可以做好多事!

(Hou! One can do **many things** with three thousand dollars!)
   (Sec. 122)

The neologism *hou* is created with 口 (*kou*, mouth) as its radical indicating its exclamatory function and the character of 猴 (*hou*, monkey) representing its pronunciation. The sentence is quoted from the teenager protagonist Fan Ye's speech when he learns that his father may bring extra income into the family. The character of "monkey" not only describes the sound of the exclamation, the charm of it is that it also reflects the excited mood of the protagonist.

Interestingly, several images of animals, insects and plants are used in Wang's neologisms for symbolic descriptions of a character's personality, mood, or manner of action. In addition to monkeys, these images also include those of geese, ducks, ravens, spinach, and cypress trees.

DEPICTING SHAPES AND COLORS
(OR GRAPHICS AND COLOR SCHEME)

Depiction of shapes and colors is the third most frequently used function of Wang's neologisms. The purpose of this function is to describe the physical appearance of a character or an object. Traditionally, in both Western and Chinese rhetoric, they are treated as two different figures of speech—one is a description of colors, the other of graphic composition. However, because the two figures of speech both deal with the sense of seeing, I combine them. Out of the forty-five neologisms, twelve belong to this category. For instance, 湯+灬 (*tang*, hot) as seen in the sentence below:

范曄湯+灬紅着他的臉

(Fan Ye's cheeks were burning hot.)
   (Sec. 133)

The neologism *tang* or hot is constructed with 湯 (*tang*, soup) on the top and 灬 (*huo*, fire) at the bottom. Obviously, the top component designates the pronunciation, whereas the bottom serves as the radical conveying the meaning of being hot. This neologism is better defined as "to blush," according to the context that details the humiliating behavior of the protagonist's father at his office. Fan Ye blushes or feels embarrassed for his father when hearing about it from his father's colleague. It seems that this neologism could be replaced with the existing character 燙 (*tang*, hot) for the same pronunciation and the same meaning. In fact, 燙 is used in Sec. 86 of the same novel:

她的腦勺後貼著繾纏短短的燙修頭髮，像塊圓型的麵餅一樣。

(The tiny, neatly woven curls of her permed hair made the back of her head look like a round packet of noodles.)
    (Sec. 86)

Comparing the contexts of the two *tang*s, one finds that the neologism 湯 +灬 depicts the color of Fan Ye's face when he blushes, and the regular character of "hot" 燙 describes actual heating, as in the process of perming hair. It is then clear that with 火 (*huo*, fire) used at the bottom of 燙 projecting a vivid image of camp fire, this character is a good choice for describing the meaning of burning hot required in the phrase of perming hairs, whereas 灬, the radical form and a simpler version of 火, conveying the association of warmth from fire but without the threating sense of flame, is a better choice for describing the blushing of a person's face.

YIJUE OR SYNAESTHESIA

In C. Hugh Holman's (1980) *A Handbook of Literature*, synaesthesia, as a figure of speech, is defined as "applied in literature to the description of one kind of sensation in terms of another."[45] Though this figure of speech has been used commonly in Chinese literature, it was not introduced into Chinese rhetoric until 1962 by Qian Zhongshu (1985: 63–78), who calls it *tonggan,* though other scholars refer to it as *yijue.*[46]

Synaesthesia is the fourth most frequently used rhetorical function of Wang's neologisms. Out of the forty-five neologisms, three belong to this category. For instance, 口+辣 (*la*, stinging) in the sentence below:

---

45 Holman's definition is quoted in Li Yazhou and Li Dingkun 2005: 227.

46 Qian Zhongshu's "Synaesthesis" (Tonggan) was first published in *Wenxue pinglun* (Literary criticism) in 1962, issue no. 1. The author did not see this version, but its reprint in his *Qi zhui ji* (Seven supplemental essays) (rev. ed.) (1985: 63–78). Later scholars such as Chen Weijun use *yijue* (1991).

在椅子上坐太久, 膝以下會有輕微瘝<u>口</u>+辣 ...

(If he sat for a long time in his chair, he would feel a tingly, stinging sensation from his knees to his toes...)
　　(Sec. 14)

The neologism *la* depicts the stinging sensation one experiences in one's legs after sitting for a long time. The common description of the feeling could be conveyed by 麻 (*ma*, numb). "瘝<u>口</u>+辣" has probably been transformed from 麻辣 (*mala*, spicy and hot) to give a precise description of the sensation in one's legs after sitting in the same posture for a long time, which is both numb as well as stinging, similar to what one experiences when eating spicy and hot food. In addition, because *mala* is not used for the taste of food in this context, different radicals are assigned to the two characters: 疒 (radical for illness) to 麻 and 口 (mouth, radical for loan words) to 辣. In brief, the neologism 口+辣 is created by means of associating the feeling of eating spicy and hot food with that of sitting for a long time.

DEPICTING SENSES OF TOUCH

Depicting senses of touch is, along with synaesthesia, the fourth most frequently used function of Wang's neologisms. Out of the forty-five neologisms, they belong to this category. An example, as seen in the sentence below, is 扌+久 (*jiǔ*, to twist):

父親然後自己也扌+久絞一把, 蓋蒙他自己臉上。

(After that, Father [rinsed out and] twisted the towel and covered up his own face.)
　　(Sec. 11)

The normal verb for twisting (a towel) is 紏 (*jiū*). With the radical 糸 at the left, 紏 can suggest the image of the twisted towel, not a bad choice for the visual presentation of the actions of the father. However, with 扌 (the hand radical) at the left, foregrounding the hand movement, and with 久 (*jiǔ*, long time) at the right, serving as the indicator of the pronunciation, the neologism adds an element of duration to the twisting movement, as well as giving the character a pronunciation of jiǔ that is more commonly used in daily conversation than that of *jiū* represented by the character 紏.

DEPICTING SENSES OF TASTE AND SMELL

Depicting senses of taste and smell is the least used rhetorical function of Wang's neologisms. There is only one instance of this use of neologism; 口+活 (*huo*, an exclamation)

口+活, 通下空氣。

  (Huo, circulate the air.)
    (sec. 25)

Fan Ye's mother utters this sentence when she closes the window on the day a neighbor holds a funeral. After the ceremony is over, smelling the stuffy air, she opens the window to circulate air in the house. Character construction in Chinese exclamations usually places the 口 (*kou*, mouth) radical to the left. This neologism's construction follows this rule. What is unique about the neologism is its right-side component, 活 (*huo*, to live or alive), which serves as the indicator of the pronunciation of the character and, more important, conveys the mother's fear and dislike of the smell of the stuffy air, somehow associated with death, and her sense of relief.

WHAT ARE THE FORMATIVE PRINCIPLES OF WANG'S NEOLOGISMS?

When filming *The Man behind the Book,* a documentary on Wang Wenxing, Lin Jingjie set up his camera on the balcony of Wang's apartment, a space Wang uses to write his fiction, in order to document the actual process of Wang's writing. Though the audience could see the author's physical movements in producing the very first version of his story, our question on how exactly Wang creates his neologisms remained unanswered, because, after all, the camera can only view a person externally, not internally. Based on the shapes and rhetorical functions of the 45 neologisms, this study attempts to capture the internal perspective by inducing three formative principles of Wang's neologisms.

PICTOPHONETIC

In terms of shape, *xingsheng zi* or "pictophonetic" is the dominant formative structure of the neologisms. Forty-four of the forty-five are constructed as pictophonetic characters; only one neologism (i.e. 足+晢) is constructed as a *huiyi zi* or "associative compound."

The structure of a pictophonetic character possesses two formative components: a semantic symbol and a phonetic symbol. The former is often the character's radical, which gives the general semantic meaning of the character and in most cases appears on the left side. The latter, the phonetic symbol, is often on the right side, and gives an indication of the pronunciation of the character. For instance, 口+矮 (sigh). The 口 (*kou*, mouth) at the left is a radical that can be used to designate a semantic association with some sort of exclamation, while the 矮 (*ai*, short) at the right indicates the pronunciation of the neologism.

ACOUSTIC QUALITIES

In terms of pronunciation, most of the neologisms reflect the acoustic qualities of utterances in authentic speech, or the sounds that occur in the story.

Wang is a writer who is particularly sensitive to the acoustic effect of his language. Many critics have noted this characteristic in his writing. Chang Han-liang (1973: 125), for instance, states: "For the sake of precision (mainly the acoustic precision), he creates many characters." The number of neologisms, forty-one out of forty-five, that function as onomatopoeia also reflects this feature. For instance, 口+辣 (*là*, a particle at the end of a sentence).

快吃! 快點兒! 來不及口+辣!

("Eat faster! Hurry! You will be late!")
    (Sec. 18)

In this example, the particle at the end of the sentence would normally be 了 (*le*) or 啦 (*la*), but Wang uses instead the neologism 口+辣. This neologism, in my opinion, should be pronounced *là*, because its phonetic symbol on the right side is 辣 (*là*, spicy hot). This example is taken from the speech of Fan Ye's mother, who is pushing Fan Ye to eat fast to avoid being late for school. The neologism *là*—sounding longer than *le* and *la*—prolongs the pronunciation of the particle at the end of the sentence and therefore reflects Fan's mother's impatience, thereby depicting her mood and tone in a more vivid manner than could conventional particles 了 and 啦. Since the neologism 口+辣 can be used as a synaesthesia, as I discussed earlier, as well as an exclamation, it is clear that Wang's neologisms must be understood in their specific context. To appreciate Wang's writing, one must engage in "slow reading" so as to catch and savor his innovative linguistic devices and style.

IMAGE AND SOUND

Yixing biaoyi, or "to convey meaning by means of image," and *yisheng tuoyi*, or "to convey meaning by means of sound" are frequently used principles in the creation of Wang's neologisms. The majority of Wang's neologisms are rhetorically multifunctional. Out of the forty-five, only twelve have a single rhetorical function; thirty-three have more than one rhetorical function. The multifunctional nature of the neologisms clearly reflects the author's aesthetics of literary language and the fundamental style of his fiction—symbolic realism. The neologisms 口+猴 and 口+辣 discussed above demonstrate the principles of conveying meaning by image and sound. The neologism口+猴 reveals the excited mood of the protagonist through the image of a monkey, and the neologism 口+辣 depicts Fan Ye's mother's impatience through the pronunciation of "spicy hot."

These principles for creating neologisms are often found in classical Chinese poetic language. According to Huang Lizhen (1999: 143), Du Fu (712–770) has a famous line in "Ballad of the Army Carts" (Bing che xing) that exemplifies the principle of using sound and image to convey meaning. That line is: "the carts squeak and rattle, / The horses neigh and neigh. / Bows and arrows at their waist, / the conscripts file out" (車轔轔, 馬蕭蕭, 行人弓箭各在腰). In Du Fu's time and earlier, 轔轔 (*linlin*) could be written as 鄰鄰 (*linlin*), as seen in "Che lin" (Rattles of carts), a poem from the Qin state in the *Book of Songs* (Shijing). Nevertheless, the image of a cart embedded in the character 轔 is helpful in depicting the rolling movement of the wheels of the carts. At the same time, 轔轔 serves as an onomatopoeia of the rolling sound of the wheels. In "Ode of Mulan" (Mulan ci), one finds the example of the principle of using sound to convey meaning in the lines of "when Little Brother hears Elders Sister [Mulan] is coming [home], he whets the knife, quick quick, for pig and sheep" (小弟聞姊來, 磨刀霍霍向豬羊) (Frankel 1977). The sound 霍霍 (*huohuo*), an onomatopoeia of the cutting knife, reflects the excited mood of Mulan's younger brother as he anticipates his sister's return after so many years away from home (Huang 1999: 145).

CONCLUSION

In his stylistically innovative fiction, Wang maximizes the metaphorical space between characters in his text, filling the space with rich meaning created by means of colors, shapes, sounds, emotions, and feelings; his works are therefore challenging to read. Yet, Wang does want his stories to be understood. He has recently given several public lectures on his two novels. *Six Lectures on Family Catastrophe* (*Jia bian* liu jiang) records the six lectures he gave at National Central University in Zhongli, Taiwan.[47] His frankness in replying to questions from the audiences on how he wrote the novel is apparent. In the preface of *Family Catastrophe*, Wang urges his readers not to read fast, only one thousand characters per hour and for only two hours per day. If one follows his advice, one should be able to understand his writing. While I have not tested this out on actual readers, I hope I have made clear that Wang's neologisms are not that difficult to understand and appreciate.

First of all, Wang has followed the traditional "six formation principles" (*liushu*) of Chinese characters to construct his neologisms in *Family Catastrophe*. He has used "pictophonetic" and "associative compounds" to create all forty-five of them. Second, while the neologisms' multifunctional rhetorical nature is remarkable and rarely seen in modern Chinese literature, it is a development from classical Chinese poetics, where it was a common practice. Perhaps, separately, each of the two characteristics of Wang's neologisms is not difficult to understand, but their combination is. In addition, the frequency of their use can pose a challenge for readers. However, through the use of neologisms, Wang offers a new rhetorical strategy for modern Chinese narrative art, and, at the same time, continues the innovative traditions of Chinese characters and classical Chinese poetics. His unique method not only introduces neologisms as a new figure of speech in Chinese rhetoric, but may also inject a new spirit of creativity in a young generation of writers.

---

47   See Wang 2009. The six lectures were organized by Kang Laixin 康來新 who is also the editor of this book. It is worth noting that Jian Yingying 簡瑛瑛 at National Taiwan Normal University also invited Wang to give lectures on *Backed against the Sea*. The publication of those lectures is forthcoming.

3 TOWARDS AN ANALYTICAL APPROACH TO THE LANDSCAPE ESSAY: TEXTUAL ANALYSIS OF LIU ZONGYUAN'S *EIGHT RECORDS ON YONGZHOU*

ANTHONY PAK WAN-HOI

INTRODUCTION

The landscape essay (*shanshui youji*) is one of the most important genres of classical Chinese prose. And in the field of the landscape essay, *Eight Records on Yongzhou* (Yongzhou baji)[48] by Liu Zongyuan (773–819), is considered the best of the kind. Though Liu Zongyuan's landscape essays have received adequate attention in the academic world, most of the research focuses on how the political turmoil of his time gets reflected in his essays and his intellectual life,[49] and only a few scholars have investigated his essays in terms of their structures and/or from the perspective of genre.[50]

In this chapter, I treat the textual structure of Liu Zongyuan's *Eight Records*, with particular focus on a textual analysis of description—the most crucial element of the landscape essay—so as to decipher the inner structure of its descriptive expression. The close relationship between descriptive and lyrical expressions can then be identified. Traditional Chinese painting theories are introduced as well to help formulate the structural analysis of these

---

48 They are: "Record of an Excursion on Which I First Discovered the West Mountain" (始得西山宴游記), "Record of the Box-iron Pool" (鈷鉧潭記), "Record of the Little Hillock West of the Box-iron Pool" (鈷鉧潭西小丘記), "Record of Reaching the Small Rock Pool West of the Little Hillock" (至小丘西小石潭記), "Record of Yuan Family Slough" (袁家渴記), "Record of the Rocky Trough" (石渠記), "Record of the Rocky Gorge" (石澗記), and "Record of the Mountain of Little Stone City-walls" (小石城山記). See Zhonghua shuju bianjibu 1979: 3: 762–774.

49 The political reform led by Wang Shuwen (753–806) was stopped abruptly when the Emperor Shunzong (761–806), who had supported the reform, was forced to abdicate and died only months after he had ascended the throne. Wang was sentenced to death and supporters including Liu Zongyuan were banished from the court. Liu was exiled to Yongzhou (now Lingling of Hunan province), the far southern side of the empire. Details can be found in Ye Shufa 1998: 40–58. Scholars like Li Chunyu (2012), Tang Chengfeng (2012), and Jo-shui Chen (1992) focus mostly on the sentiment caused by banishment shown in literary works by Liu Zongyuan.

50 Studies by Wang Liqun (2008) and Tosaki Tetsuhiko (1996) are among the best.

expressions. Though literary works and painting are of course different by nature, they share enough factors that an analysis of landscape essays can benefit from an understanding of traditional Chinese painting and the terms that are used to describe it.

CHINESE PROSE: ITS CONTENT AND RELATED EXPRESSIONS

Prose (*sanwen*) is one of the most difficult to define literary genres in Chinese literature.[51] In its broadest sense, prose includes all kinds of writings except poetry and fiction. In order to develop an analytical tool for understanding prose in China, we have to examine its content, which can cover a broad range of things. To contend with this breadth of content, we must employ some generalizing terms. There are at most four kinds of content that can be detected in Chinese prose: event (*shi*); object (*wu*); feelings, affection, or sentiment (*qing*); and reason, principle, theory, logic (*li*).[52]

An analytical tool that is suitable for Chinese prose has to be common and generally recognized. I propose using "mode of expression" for this purpose. Mode of expression is a common device found in any writing, whether poetry, fiction, or prose, including the landscape essay. There are five modes of expression to be considered: expository (*shuoming*), descriptive (*miaoxie*), narrative (*xushi*), argumentative (*yilun*), and lyrical (*shuqing*). These five modes of expression can then present and/or represent the above-mentioned four kinds of content. The following table lists all elements of these kinds of content and their related modes of expression.

In order to work as an effective tool for textual analysis, the above-mentioned five expressions should be all-inclusive, and every single sentence in a text should fall into one of the five categories. Yet it is possible that a sentence can, for instance, be both expository and argumentative—that is, it can have more than a single function. For example, a sensory description of a scene can, on the one hand, be a descriptive expression and, on the other, function as evidence of an argument that the scene being described, for example, is the best the author has ever seen.

---

51   William H. Nienhauser (1986a) has a comprehensive entry on Chinese prose.

52   The former two involve concrete matters, the latter two abstract matters. "Object" includes both living and non-living objects. Human beings, animals and plants, etc. are living objects, whereas non-living objects include natural and human objects. Natural object includes mountain, river, moon, sun, etc. Human object means those made by human beings such as buildings, bridges, gardens, etc. In Chinese, *qing* and *li* have rich philosophical connotations. For more details, see Hansen 2003: 620–622 and Cua 2003: 364–370. Though people (*ren*) and scenery (*jing*) are common content in an essay, people are in fact a kind of living object, whereas scenery is a combination of objects. Thus, they should be put under the category of object, instead of being classified separately.

Content			Mode of Expression
Type	**Aspect**	**Details**	
Event 事	Character	Background	Exposition
		Action	Narration
		Image	Description
		Speech	Narration
	Event	Background	Exposition
		Course	Narration
		Commentary	Argumentation, lyrical expression
Object 物	Living	Image	Description
		Action	Narration
		Speech	Narration
		Commentary	Argumentation, lyrical expression
	Non-living	Image	Description
		Information like characteristics, type, function, etc.	Exposition
		Experience with author	Argumentation, lyrical expression
Feelings 情		Reaction, response, emotions	Lyrical expression
Reason 理		Thought, logic, principle, theory, law	Argumentation

I first identify the basic features and forms of each of these modes in order to be able to then use them to identify which mode a given sentence belongs to.

EXPOSITORY EXPRESSION

Exposition is a plain expression that provides information, especially background information. Its basic form is the declarative sentence. Examples of exposition in the landscape essay often occur at the beginning of the essay, when the author states the time the journey took place and provides readers background information on the location and nearby areas.

NARRATIVE EXPRESSION

Narration is common in the essay and functions like a storyteller telling stories. Its basic form is characters with actions (i.e., someone + verbs). In the landscape essay, narration always involves telling readers the course of the sightseeing trip: who are the ones travelling and what they do during their journey. Narration always forms the frame of the text in which descriptive and lyrical expressions can be embedded.

DESCRIPTIVE EXPRESSION

Description is not a necessity in an essay. Yet for the landscape essay, since natural scenery is usually the focus, description is a crucial element that enhances readers' impressions of and feelings about the described objects. Its basic linguistic forms are adjectives and adverbs or any other figure of speech that describes the object.

ARGUMENTATIVE EXPRESSION

Argumentation is a common element in the essay. Its function is to convince readers, with evidence developed in the text, to share the author's viewpoint. Its basic form is therefore argument and supporting evidence. In the landscape essay, argumentation may not be as common as in other prose genres, but in Liu Zongyuan's landscape essays arguments are presented through the author's experience during the journey.

LYRICAL EXPRESSION

Lyrical expression is the core element in the essay. It serves to show the author's personal feelings. Its basic form is an emotive adjective followed by the subject "I." In the landscape essay, lyrical expressions are often represented in description. After the sensory description, the reaction of the author to the scene always follows—both what I call "personal feeling" (*ganshou*) and "deep feeling" (*gankai*).

The following table shows the basic forms of the five modes of expressions:

Expressions	Aims	Basic Form
Expositive	To provide information	Declarative sentence
Narrative	To tell events	Characters + Actions
Descriptive	To depict figuratively	Objects + adjectives/adverbs
Argumentative	To convince	Argument + evidence
Lyrical	To express one's feeling	Subject + emotions

FEATURES OF THE LANDSCAPE ESSAY

In his *A Study of the Landscape Essay in Ancient China*, Wang Liqun (2008) discusses the landscape essay as a literary genre and tries to place the genre on the map of classical Chinese literature. Wang first investigates the development of the "consciousness of landscape" (*shanshui yishi*) in Chinese history, and starts his discussion with topography (*diji/yudizhi*), a genre related to the landscape essay, in the Wei-Jin period (220–420), and then travelogue (*xingji/youzongji*) in the following Northern and Southern Dynasties period (420–589). Wang argues that these two genres gradually developed into the more mature forms of the landscape essay. The genre reached its maturity in the Tang dynasty, especially through the creative works of Liu Zongyuan. According to Wang, by their very nature, the kinds of landscape essays Liu wrote should be distinguished from the earlier genres like topography and travelogue, the former which reports details of the features of a geographical area and the latter focuses more on the journey itself. According to Wang, the landscape essay has four main features. From the content point of view, the most important feature is the author's "expression of personal feelings" (*shufa ganshou*), whereas the crucial feature is its sensory "description of landscape" (*miaoxie jingguan/shanshui zhi xie*). Though "narration of the journey" (*youzong jishu*) is a necessity in landscape essay, it is not the focus. From the linguistic point of view, the landscape essay is written in classical Chinese prose, which thus differentiates it from other genres written with rhyme, such as the landscape poem (*shanshui shi*) and landscape rhapsody (*shanshui fu*) (Wang 2008: 2–30).

In his well-written study on Liu Zongyuan's *Eight Records*, Tosaki Tetsuhiko (1996) provides prodigious information about *Eight Records*, ranging from lexical meaning of classical Chinese, emendations, detailed description of Tang objects, etc. Tosaki even made a fieldtrip in 1991 to the Lingling (present-day Yongzhou) area of Hunan. Tosaki dedicates a chapter to "record" (*ji*), a term whose history he traces back to the Han dynasty; he emphasizes that "record" bears many functions, including exposition, narration, and argumentation. To Tosaki, Liu Zongyuan was one of the most important writers in the genre of "records." Liu injected his personal feelings into the record, thus enriching and enlarging the scope and depth of the genre. The essay reached its historical apogee in Liu's hands, Tosaki argues, and later writers followed and developed his style (Tosaki 1996: 824–854).

In the West scholarship, though Hargett (2001: 555–559) does not discuss in depth the features of the landscape essay, he does mention that Liu Zongyuan's well-known landscape essays are "significant," because they are "China's first landscape essays of literary note in which travel narrative, scenic description and expression of personal sentiment played key roles."

Wang Liqun accurately identifies the basic features of the landscape essay: descriptive and lyrical expressions are the crucial elements, whereas information (i.e., in my terminology "exposition"), and narration are a necessity. Yet Liu Zongyuan's landscape essays transcend this narrow scope, as Tosaki correctly shows, and Liu develop a more personal style in which argumentation is his main concern. Liu's form of argument is not objective, as the term might suggest, but lyrical in nature; Liu's argumentation is in fact a mixture of the argumentative and lyrical modes of expressions.

ANALYTICAL TOOLS OF DESCRIPTIVE EXPRESSION

As a crucial element of the landscape essay, descriptive expression and its details have to be investigated in depth. I propose five elements that can be employed for analysis:

Descriptive Subject: Unlike its counterpart in western languages, the subject in Chinese appears only occasionally. Thus, the subject of description, the sole source of sensations of description, may generally be understood as the author of the essay.

Temporal and Spatial Positions of the Descriptive Subject: These two positions are important especially for scenic description because the timing and angle of his position in the scene have crucial impact on the sensations felt by the subject. Yet, this kind of information is not always offered in a text.

Descriptive Object: The object is crucial because its feature and characteristics are the focus of the description. The object can be depicted as a whole and in parts, so any analysis of the object should work out the details of the object and its various parts.

Temporal and Spatial Positions of the Descriptive Object: Theoretically, for landscape description, the time should be identical whether we consider things from the perspective of the viewing subject or the object viewed. The spatial position from which the subject views the object and the position of the object itself are almost always different.

Descriptive Core: This refers to the lines of description directly related to the Descriptive Object. The scene can be depicted as a whole, from a wide perspective, or its parts can be described one by one, from a closer perspective. We can employ detailed analysis of description here by using the tools for sensory description listed in Appendix II.

Take the first essay of *Eight Record*, "Record of an Excursion on Which I First Discovered West Mountain," as an example. The journey begins with Liu discovering the distinctiveness of West Mountain:

This year, on the twenty-eighth day of the ninth lunar month [November 9, 809], while sitting in the West Pavilion of the Temple of the Dharma Lotus, I gazed at West Mountain and, for the first time, really noticed its extraordinary appearance. So I ordered my servants to accompany me across the Hsiang River, following along Tinting Stream. We cut a path through the forest growth and burned the dry brush that stood in our way until we reached the highest point on the mountain. We ascended by pulling ourselves up and then stretched out our legs to enjoy the scene. The land of several prefectures spread out below our mats. The towering and low-lying formations of spacious mountains and deep lakes resembled anthills and caves. A thousand li appeared as but a few inches. Things appeared crowded together or piled up—nothing below escaped our view. White clouds wound about in the clear blue atmosphere, and the sky extended to the far beyond so that the view was the same in every direction. (Strassberg 1994: 141–142)

今年九月二十八日, 因坐法華西亭, 望西山, 始指異之。遂命僕人過湘江, 緣染溪, 斫榛莽。焚茅茷, 窮山之高而止。攀援而登, 箕踞而遨, 則凡數州之土壤, 皆衽席之下。其高下之勢, 岈然洼然, 若垤若穴, 尺寸千里, 攢蹙累積, 莫得遯隱。縈青繚白, 外與天際, 四望如一。(Zhonghua shuju bianjibu 1979: 3: 762)

The elements of this descriptive expression are as follows:

Elements	Particulars	Original Text
Descriptive Subject	Liu Zongyuan (understood)	/
Descriptive Object	surrounding prefectures from the West Mountain	數州之土壤
Temporal Position of the Subject	the 28th of Ninth lunar month of AD 809 (no particular time mentioned)	今年九月二十八日
Spatial Position of the Subject	on the West Mountain where Liu was sitting on the mat (understood)	攀援而登, 箕踞而遨
Temporal Position of the Object	the 28th of Ninth lunar month of AD 809 (no particular time mentioned)	今年九月二十八日
Spatial Position of the Object	down from the West Mountain and the scene that are under his mat	衽席之下

Since the descriptive core is the center of the landscape essay, it needs to be analyzed in close detail. Doing so then sets the foundation for explaining the relationship between descriptive and lyrical expressions. In terms of the descriptive core of the above descriptive expression, the Descriptive Object is the pronoun "its" (*qi*), which refers to "the surrounding prefectures from the West Mountain" (數州之土壤) in the previous sentence. Yet of this expansive area, the focus of its core is the area's terrain (*shi*). The followings is a dissection of the sensory description of the terrain:

Descriptive Object	Senses	Attributes	Aspects	Original Text	Type of Wording
Terrain (勢)	visual	shape	high and low	高下	adjective
		shape	protrusive	岈然	adverb
		shape	recessed	洼然	adverb
		size	enormous, spacious, wide	尺寸千里	noun, exaggeration
		direction	horizontal	攢蹙	verb
		direction	vertical	累積	verb
		shape	hillock	垤	noun, vehicle
		shape	hollow	穴	noun, vehicle

In order to differentiate the descriptive element from that of the lyrical, detailed analysis has to be conducted. Any description of the Descriptive Object can be separated into two kinds, pure description and description with personal feeling. Pure description denotes objective sensory description without the explicit feelings of the Descriptive Subject. Take the phrase "this is a red and lovely apple like a baby's face blushing scarlet" as an example. The adjective "red" is objective and therefore pure "sensory description" (*ganjue*) and "lovely" involves the Descriptive Subject's reaction to the apple's appearance; the latter is description with personal "feeling" (*ganshou*). If the Descriptive Subject further expresses his feelings about the apple, we would call this "deep feeling" (*gankai*). And for sensory description, figurative language is always employed like the metaphor in the example here. Since an apple is not necessarily associated with a baby's face, this figure of speech is purely the Descriptive Subject's choice; it is therefore a subjective and lyrical expression.

To conclude, in a Descriptive Core, only sensory description is descriptive expression, whereas "feeling," "deep feeling," and any figurative language should be considered lyrical expressions. The combination of descriptive and lyrical expressions in the Descriptive Core can be explicated in the following lines from "Record of the Small Rock Pool":

I sat down above the pond and was completely surrounded by bamboo and trees on all four sides. I felt solitary without anyone else there. The scene chilled my spirit and froze my bones. I became hushed, melancholy, and remote. The scene was far too quiet to linger long. (Strassberg 1994: 141)

坐潭上，四面竹樹環合，寂寥無人，淒神寒骨，悄愴幽邃。以其境過清，不可久居。(Zhonghua shuju bianjibu 1979: 3: 767)

The passage begins with a scenic description, which is then followed by the Description Subject's reaction, and the Subject's deep feeling brings it to a close. Bamboo trees and the soundless environment are objective, but the reaction to this scene—solitude and coldness—is certainly Liu's own feeling, and so is his conclusion that the place is too silent to linger too long. The above analysis can be summarized in the following chart:

Expression	Kind	Original Text
Descriptive	sensory description	四面竹樹環合, 寂寥無人
Lyrical	feeling / subject's reaction	淒神寒骨, 悄愴幽邃
Lyrical	deep feeling	以其境過清, 不可久居

STRUCTURAL ANALYSIS OF DESCRIPTIVE EXPRESSIONS: INSIGHTS FROM TRADITIONAL CHINESE PAINTING

The notion that poetry shares the same origins with painting (*shihua tongyuan*) may be applied to Chinese prose as well. In this section, I develop some analytical tools from Chinese painting that are suitable for understanding Chinese prose in general and the landscape essay in particular.[53]

Liu Zongyuan clearly had insights similar to those of Zong Bing (375–443), an influential Chinese painting theorist, about the artistic representation of landscape. In his famous article on painting "Introduction to Painting Landscape" (Hua shanshui xu), Zong demonstrates how a painting could capture a real landscape:

> However, the Kun-lun mountains are immense and the eyes' pupils small. If the former come within inches of the viewer, their total form will not be seen. If they are at a distance of several miles, then they can be encompassed by inch-small pupils. Truly, the further off they are, the smaller they will appear. Now, if one spreads thin silk to capture the distant scene, the form of Kun-lun's Lang peak can be encompassed in a square inch. A vertical stroke of three inches will equal a height of thousands of feet, and a horizontal stretch of several feet will form a distance of a hundred miles. (Bush/Shih 1985: 37)

> 且夫崑崙山之大, 瞳子之小, 迫目以寸, 則其形莫覩, 迴以數里, 則可圍於寸眸。誠由去之稍闊, 則其見彌小。今張綃素以遠暎之, 則崑閬之形, 可圍於方寸之內。豎劃三寸, 當千仞之高; 橫墨數尺, 體百里之迴。(Yu 2000: 583)

---

53   For a discussion of the cross-disciplinary issue on literature and painting, see Murck/Fong 1991.

Similar to the idea that our eyes can capture images from a distance and condense a thousand miles of landscape into a square inch, in his essay "Record of an Excursion on Which I First Discovered the West Mountain" Liu expresses the notion that he captured the scene surrounding West Mountain with his eyes. He writes: "a thousand *li* (unit of measures) appeared as but a few inches" (*chi cun qian li*). This shared discourse of visuality suggests that insights from traditional Chinese painting can benefit an analysis of descriptive expression in Liu Zhongyuan's *Eight Records*.

Unlike Western painting, in which one single perspective dominates the whole work, a Chinese painting be divided into three parts, each of which can have its own perspective. This kind of perspective, referred to as "scatter perspective" (*sandian toushi*), is considered the distinguishing artistic feature of traditional Chinese painting. It allows for varying scenes with changing viewpoints; in other words, images from different perspectives can be included in a single painting (Wang/Tong 1981: 14-20). Therefore, the spectator has to adjust his perspective when his eyesight moves from one part of the painting to another. This changing visual perspective is similar to the literary device called "foot-step movement" (*buyifa*) used to describe changing scenes from the perspective of a moving Descriptive Subject. Since the landscape essay and landscape painting share the same Descriptive Object—the landscape itself—the "scatter perspective" and the "foot-step movement" suggest a particular form of descriptive expression useful to investigating the inner structure of Liu Zongyuan's essays.

In addition to "scatter perspective," the discourse of traditional painting has a concept called "three distances" (*san yuan*) developed by another well-known painting theorist Guo Xi (ca. 1020-ca. 1090). In his essay "The Lofty Message of Forest and Streams" (Linchuan gaozhi), Guo clearly explains the "three distances" as follows:

Mountains have three types of distance. Looking up to the mountain's peak from its foot is called the high distance. From in front of the mountain looking past it to beyond is called deep distance. Looking from a nearby mountain at those more distant is called the level distance. High distance appears clear and bright; deep distance becomes steadily more obscure; level distance combines both qualities. The appearance of high distance is of lofty grandness. The idea of deep distance is of repeated layering. The idea of level distance is of spreading forth to merge into mistiness and indistinctness. (Bush/Shih 1985: 168-169)

山有三遠, 自山下而仰山巔謂之高遠, 自山前而窺山後謂之深遠, 自近山而望遠山謂之平遠。高遠之色清明, 深遠之色重晦, 平遠之色有明有暗。高遠之勢突兀, 深遠之意重疊, 平遠之意沖融而縹縹緲緲。(Yu 2000: 639)

"High distance" represents the viewpoint from low to high, "level distance" from near to far, and "deep distance" from front to past and beyond; the three distances represent, respectively, the low, middle, and high levels of view-point and follow the typical traveler who starts his sightseeing at the bottom of the mountain and ends it at the top. This is also a common perspective in the landscape essay, where scenic description comes from the perspective of the moving Descriptive Subject. Obviously, "level distance" can describe scenery that is at the same level as the Subject—for instance when he describes a scene walking along a stream. Applying the "three distances" theory can benefit our understanding of Liu Zongyuan's landscape essays and help reveal their visual effects and compositional design.

Chinese terms for patterns in painting often come in pairs of characters that are not so much contrasting as they are poles suggesting a larger whole. For example, open (*kai*) and close (*he*) in Chinese painting are not contrastive in their literal senses; rather, together they emphasize the unity of two directions and form a whole in the landscape painting. Individual items scattered in a painting attract the viewer's attention and help him explore and expand the space (opening), whereas some sort of unifying force, such as mist or fog, can then mingle through the whole scene (closing). The same understanding can be applied to other patterns, such as "guest-host" (*binzhu*) and "abstract-concrete" (*xushi*) (Zhang/Tan 2001: 8–11, 14–19). As in a banquet, the guest-host pattern enables the pair to interact with each other in a prescribed manner and produces a harmonized atmosphere. As for abstract-concrete pattern, both items complement each other and provide spectator a balanced space to enjoy. The structure of the descriptive expression in Liu's landscape essays can be interpreted with the above-mentioned patterns and the underlying principle of these expressions can therefore be disclosed.

TEXTUAL ANALYSIS OF DESCRIPTIVE EXPRESSION IN *EIGHT RECORDS*

"RECORD OF AN EXCURSION ON WHICH I FIRST DISCOVERED WEST MOUNTAIN"

This text starts with narration informing readers that Liu is on an excursion in Yongzhou, the county to which he had been banished by the imperial government. After narrating how he and his friends climbed West Mountain and reached its pinnacle, the text depicts the surroundings from that perspective.

As shown in the previous section, Liu depicts the panoramic view from West Mountain, not the mountain itself. He draws attention to just one feature of West Mountain—the fact that the mountain is the highest point in the area—and for this reason he can take in the entirety of the surroundings. Descriptive elements in this text serve two purposes: to support the narration of Liu's travel around Yongzhou and to serve as evidence to prove Liu's statement that, until this trip, he had never really travelled before.

For this purpose, as I have indicated, description is limited to the scenery around the mountain, not the mountain itself. But this description serves to indirectly suggest the height and grandeur of the mountain from which the scenery is observed. It is the height of West Mountain that allows Liu to take in the entirety of the vista. Liu employs the adverbs 岈 (*xia*, spaciousness and wideness of mountains) and 洼 (*wa*, means hollow or cavity) and the more metaphoric expressions 垤 (*die*, hillock) and 穴 (*xue*, hollow) to describe the contrasts between high and low in the landscape around West Mountain.

Though the scenery viewed from West Mountain appears small in area to the eye, it actually covers thousands of miles; the visual perception concentrates the size of the surrounding area, in particular its depth and width. Four adjectives in particular enhance the impressions of visual relief perceived by the spectator: 攢 (*zuan*, to gather, to assemble), 蹙 (*cu*, to contract), 累 (*lei*, to accumulate), 積 (*ji*, to pile up) all are used here to describe different shapes of the terrain. Seemingly every detail, including the assembling, contracting, accumulating, and piling up, cannot escape Liu's vision from the top of West Mountain. These details indirectly emphasize that West Mountain is the highest point in the area, thus justifying Liu's later comment that West Mountain is unlike any mountain around.

Liu's description ends with a kind of blurring effect in which, for instance, the land and sky seem to merge. Two colors—青 (*qing*, cyan) and 白 (*bai*, white)—represent the blending color of trees, land, water, and sky, while two verbs—縈 (*ying*, literary means to wreath with vine) and 繚 (*liao*, literary means to wind, to encircle)—enhance the merging effect of the above two colors. No details of a particular scenic spot are described; instead, Liu provides us with a general impression that the terrain around West Mountain, whether hillocks or hollows, can be grasped in its entirety from the top of the mountain.

Of the "three distances" developed by Guo Xi, these particular lines of description fall into the category of "deep distance": Liu Zongyuan (the Descriptive Subject) covers all areas in his vision, beginning with the terrain in front of him, moving to the nearby prefectural area, and ending with the land and sky merging in the horizon. As for the aesthetic pattern of this description, when the surrounding area is described, it expands the space and opens a grand vista; with the blurred color and imagery wrapping up the scene, a sense of closure is conveyed. As a whole, then, the aesthetic pattern is one of "opening and closing." In addition, when the focus is brought back from the external scene to Liu himself (the focalizer), his personal feelings naturally emerge to conclude the description with a strong idiosyncratic flavour.

Liu's description serves perfectly as evidence to show the characteristics of West Mountain that Liu mentions in the following sentences, which are widely believed to be his claim that though he was exiled, he was still special and outstanding like West Mountain, and those in power, like the inferior hills around West Mountain, could not equal him.

> My mind numbed, my body shed, I became one with the myriad transformations. Only then did I understand that I had not yet begun to make excursions and that this occasion was the first time. (Nienhauser 1973: 74)

> 心凝形釋, 與萬化冥合。然後知吾嚮之未始游, 游於是乎始。(Zhonghua shuju bianjibu 1979: 3: 762)

Liu expresses his personal feeling of this mountain; his mind and body merge with it and even with the Universe (*wanhua*) in a kind of adaptation of the philosophical idea of "Uniformity of Things" (Qiwu) from Zhuangzi (BCE 369–286). Though Liu is generally considered a typical Confucian intellectual, when he was exiled to a wasteland like Yongzhou, his thinking inevitably shifted from Confucianism to Taoism and Buddhism (Chen 1992: 81–98). The outstanding feature of West Mountain certainly touched Liu to the bottom of his heart, and therefore serves as an evidence of his argument that he had not really travelled in any real sense until this moment.

"RECORD OF THE BOX-IRON POOL"

The second essay of *Eight Records* is about Box-iron Pool. Its descriptive expression in this text is brief, only fifty-seven characters in total (see Appendix I):

> So it increases in ferocity as it flows. It gnaws at its banks along the way, so it is wide along its sides and deep in the middle, finally coming to a halt where it encounters rocks. The water's froth then forms swirling wheels and slowly moves on. The calm and clear surface of the pond extends for about one and a half acres. Surrounding it are trees, and there is a spring high above it. (Strassberg 1994: 152)

> 其顛委勢峻, 蕩擊益暴, 齧其涯, 故旁廣而中深, 畢至石乃止; 流沫成輪, 然後徐行。其清而平者, 且十畝。有樹環焉, 有泉懸焉。(Zhonghua shuju bianjibu 1979: 3: 764)

Different from the first essay analyzed in the previous section, here we have a kind of microscopic scene, with all the focus on the stream itself, especially the flow of water along a stretch of the stream. As a result, the description is full of motion. The water at first falls fast from on high and hits the rocks in the pool below, where it swirls, slows down, and forms the Box-iron Pool. Liu concludes the scenic description with a "long shot" by introducing shrubs and springs around the pool.

As concerns the Descriptive Object, the water and its flow are the focus, whereas the trees and springs around are peripheral; as a whole, then, the two form a kind of balanced "guest-host" pattern. The description is a typical example of "level distance," in which Liu first depicts scenery close to him and then widens his focus to include a broader scope of description. Before the description begins, we are given information to suggest that Liu, the Descriptive Subject, is travelling from the upper end of the stream and following it downward. Liu then employs a "scatter perspective": he follows the stream downward and along the way eyes scenes from a variety of perspectives.

"RECORD OF THE LITTLE HILLOCK WEST OF THE BOX-IRON POOL"

Though the descriptive expression in this text is not terribly long, the metaphors Liu uses for rocks are highly imaginative:

> The rocks on the hillock were pointed pinnacles that rose bearing soil on their backs; they were so numerous that you could barely count them, vying with one another in strangeness of shape. Some of them piled up steeply and bowed down, like horses and cattle drinking from the creek. Others formed pairs that darted heavenwards, like black bears and brown bears climbing up a hill. The hillock was small, not quite one *mu* (0.0667 hectare), and so could be acquired in its entirety. (Wong 2007: 500)

> 其石之突怒偃蹇, 負土而出, 爭為奇狀者, 殆不可數。其嶔然相累而下者, 若牛馬之飲於溪; 其衝然角列而上者, 若熊羆之登於山。丘之小不能一畝, 可以籠而有之。(Zhonghua shuju bianjibu 1979: 3: 765)

This small piece of description again is a concentrated one in which rocks are the principal object. Strange-shaped and grotesque rocks cover the hill. Two kinds of rocks are the focus, one that stretches upward and the other downward. In order to enhance the feeling of dynamics and energy, Liu introduces metaphors of fierce and powerful animals, such as horses, bulls, black bears, and brown bears. The adverbs 嶔 (*qin*, high and steep) and 衝 (*chong*, protrusive) set the tone of the description and emphasize the sturdiness and solidity of the hillock. The two metaphoric expressions then introduce to the scene further motion and power and make the rocks come alive. The bear metaphor is employed to depict those rocks that seem to ascend (like bears climbing upward), whereas the livestock drinking water is used for those rocks that appear to be descending. Following the metaphors, the text narrates the process through which Liu and his friends purchased the hill and cleaned up its surroundings. Another short description of the scene from the hillock depicts the mountains, clouds, brooks, birds, and animals with a joyful quality:

Gazing out from amidst this, the loftiness of the mountains, the floating of the clouds, the coursing of the stream, the frolicking of the birds and animals—all these joyfully displayed their talents by performing in homage to this hill. (Strassberg 1994: 143–144)

由其中以望, 則山之高, 雲之浮, 溪之流, 鳥獸之遨遊, 舉熙熙然迴巧獻技, 以效茲丘之下。(Zhonghua shuju bianjibu 1979: 3: 765)

Compared with the detailed description involving almost every aspect of sensation discussed above, here minor elements, such as mountains, clouds, streams, birds, and beasts, are made to serve as background for the rocks; together they form a picture in the "abstract-concrete" pattern. In the end, we are presented with the "feeling" (i.e., response to the scene) and the "deep feeling" that Liu develops step by step from the scenic description:

one's eyes are comforted by the clear, quiet images [of the water], one's ears are lulled by the murmuring sounds, one's spirt soothed by a far-reaching void, one's heart eased by an abyssal serenity. (Nienhauser 1973: 73)

則清泠之狀與目謀, 瀯瀯之聲與耳謀, 悠然而虛者與神謀, 淵然而靜者與心謀。(Zhonghua shuju bianjibu 1979: 3: 765)

Two different expressions join together to form a sentence pattern in which all the elements correlate with one another. The first two sentences involve sensory description (i.e., the coolness and the murmuring sound that the eyes, skin, and ears could grasp), whereas the next two sentences involve Liu's deep feeling (i.e., the silence and calmness that his heart feels). If the sensory description mentioned here is objective, then the "deep feeling" is Liu Zongyuan's subjective response. The subjective "deep feeling" comes from the scene itself. Therefore, it is quite common to say that descriptive and lyrical expressions are intertwined factors for scenic description.

"RECORD OF REACHING THE SMALL ROCK POOL WEST OF THE LITTLE HILLOCK"

This is the most detailed and intensive description among the essays in *Eight Records*, and the Descriptive Object is the Small Rock Pool:

Its bottom was entirely of rock. Along its edges, the rock bottom curved and protruded forming rises, islets, archipelagoes, and crags. Emerald vines on viridian trees grew thickly entwined or hanging down. Uneven in length, they waved back and forth in the wind.

There are a hundred or so fish in the pond who seem to be swimming in the air without any support. Sun rays penetrate down through the water, and their shadows spread out on the rock bottom as they contentedly remain immobile. Suddenly, they swim off, swiftly darting back and forth, seeming as happy as this traveler.

I gazed at the southwest corner of the pond, which was bent like the Dipper and wound about like a snake, the water flickering light and dark. Its edges were serrated like a dog's teeth, and I could not discover the source of the water. I sat down above the pond and was completely surrounded by bamboo and trees on all four sides. I felt solitary without anyone else there. The scene chilled my spirit and froze my bones. I became hushed, melancholy, and remote. The scene was far too quiet to linger long, so I wrote this down and departed. (Strassberg 1994: 141)

全石以為底, 近岸, 卷石底以出。為坻, 為嶼, 為嵁, 為岩。青樹翠蔓, 蒙絡搖綴, 參差披拂。潭中魚可百許頭, 皆若空遊無所依。日光下澈, 影布石上, 佁然不動; 俶爾遠逝; 往來翕忽, 似與游者相樂。潭西南而望, 斗折蛇行, 明滅可見。其岸勢犬牙差互, 不可知其源。坐潭上, 四面竹樹環合, 寂寥無人, 淒神寒骨, 悄愴幽邃。(Zhonghua shuju bianjibu 1979: 3: 767)

The text is occupied mostly by description and has the highest percentage of description among the eight essays. There is little exposition in the beginning and at the end, and only a bit of lyrical expression can be identified near the end—the rest is description. The Descriptive Object is obviously the pool, in which the water and the rock are the two main components. The rock provides not only the base for the pool, but defines the space above water level with different kinds of formations: 坻 (*di*, small islands), 嶼 (*yu*, hilly islands), 嵁 (*kan*, hillock with uneven shapes), and 岩 (*yan*, steep hill). Since islands and hills in a pool cannot match in size real islands and hills, the landscape described here should be regarded as an exaggeration, and the focus is on their variety of shapes and forms. Unlike the abstract-concrete pattern in "Box-Iron Pool," Liu here demonstrates the pattern in a different way. Juxtaposed to the hardness implied by the rock islands in the pond, the text brings in the softness of the water, trees, and plants to complete the scene, give it a peaceful quality, and form a harmonious unity.

The focus of the essay then shifts to the pond itself and the fish swimming in it. With the light and shadow introduced by the sunlight, the pond water appears clear all the way to the bottom and the fish take on interesting visual effects as a result, sometimes appearing two-dimensional, sometimes three-dimensional. Hundreds of fish are there, like dummies (伲 *yi* dummy-like), seemingly immobile in the pool. The shadows of the fish project onto the background of the pool's rocky bottom, making it appear as if the fish are hanging in air. The focalization of the description moves to the shape of the pool and in particular to one corner of it. Liu then describes the surrounding bamboo trees and how they produce a lovely but chilly effect on him, so much so that he decides he must leave. In the end, the place is too desolate, and the coolness and soundlessness of the landscape chill his body; he loses heart and is overcome by sadness and loneliness.

This is another perfect example of a descriptive expression combining both lyrical and descriptive modes to depict a landscape with a strong personal color. The sunlight shining through the water, the fish swimming here and there—these all could be seen by anyone at the site and are therefore objective, "scenic description." But metaphors such as "like dummies" to describe the lack of movement of the fish and their position at the bottom of the pool, and then comments that those fishes seemed to be playing joyfully with Liu—these are certainly Liu's subjective "feelings."

The essay forms a steady development from "sensory description," to personal "feeling," and finally to "deep feeling." The latter emerges when Liu is reluctant to stay any longer at the site, where deadly silence and chilly air dominate. The solemnness and loneliness of the scene would seem to reflect Liu's feelings of isolation living in political exile in Yongzhou. In following him as he walks along the pond and then sits alone amid the bamboo trees, the reader feels empathy for Liu and his feelings of isolation.

"RECORD OF THE YUAN FAMILY SLOUGH"

Description is the dominant part of this text and accounts for fifty percent of the whole essay. The Descriptive Object of the following lines is the slough:

In between are islands, and tiny brooks, deep pools, shallow banks all intertwined around and about. Lying deep and murky through level land, down slopes it fumes and foams. The skiff floats as if it were reaching the end, but then suddenly another view, and it again seems endless. Hillocks rise out of the water, hills of beautiful stone sprouting green groves on top, winter or summer always luxuriant. In their slopes are many grottoes, at their bases numerous white pebbles. Their trees are primarily maples, rhododendrons, medlars, oaks, gums and citrons. The grasses epidendrum and iris. There is also a strange plant, similar to the bean, which has crept helter-skelter over the rocks in the water. Each time the wind blows down from the four mountains around, it shakes the large trees, conceals in luxuriance all the grasses, waves riotous reds and startled greens. In a flourish of fragrance, it surges billows and swirls rapids, backs them up into gorges, and wildly tosses and overhanging plants. With each season the scene changes, yet it is generally as I have written, although there is no way to completely describe it. (Nienhauser 1973: 76–77)

其中重洲、小溪、澄潭、淺渚，間廁曲折。平者深黑，峻者沸白。舟行若窮，忽又無際。有小山出水中。山皆美石，上生青叢，冬夏常蔚然。其旁多岩洞。其下多白礫; 其樹多楓、栴、石楠、梗、櫧、樟、柚; 草則蘭、芷，又有異卉，類合歡而蔓生，轇轕水石。每風自四山而下，振動大木，掩苒眾草，紛紅駭綠，蓊葧香氣; 沖濤旋瀨，退貯溪谷; 搖颺葳蕤，與時推移。(Zhonghua shuju bianjibu 1979: 3: 768)

At first, the essay details general information about the slough, its size, depth, the number of islands there, colors, and shape. Then the focus shifts to the various parts of the slough, and the essay here is full of names of trees, plants, grasses, and floral vegetation; though Liu identifies them by name, he does not include adjectives to provide readers with attributes. Hills, stones, shrubs, and caves are also mentioned in a desultory manner. Audio and olfactory images make the waters come alive and the flowers smell lovely, giving the scene substance and liveliness. The above paragraph introduces the whole slough through descriptive detail that captures the experience one might have in enjoying such a natural scene. By adding images like the wind that suggest movement, a static mode is given a dynamic quality, and then enhanced with audio and olfactory effects.

Here the Descriptive Subject lingers and his eyes dart around one object of beauty to another, and the landscape is thus presented in an almost cinematic fashion. The general flow of the narrative is from a description of the upper side of the slough to the lower side. The reader is presented with a comprehensive and detailed description using a "level distance" visual effect. Though these kinds of expressions have a quality of generalization, the richness and concreteness of the objects is what readers feel most poignantly.

"RECORD OF THE ROCKY TROUGH"

Scenery description accounts for more than half of this essay. After a very brief expository introduction, we are presented with a lengthy description of Rocky Trough:

There a languid spring whose sound suddenly grows loud, then, just as suddenly, grows faint. The width of the brook is only about a foot or perhaps two, while its length is some ten or so paces. When the flow of water encounters a large rock, it meekly submits and emerges from beneath it. Continuing on beyond the rock, I found a rock pool covered by sweet rush and surrounded by green moss and lichen. Then I turned west, and the flow sank beneath the rocks of a cliff to the side and northward dropped down into a little pond. The area of the pond is not quite one hundred feet. It is clear and deep, with many mullets. I meandered northward, zigzagging and glancing at the unlimited view alongside. Finally it flowed into Yuan Creek. Along the banks there are bizarre rocks, extraordinary trees, rare plants, and fine arrow bamboo: one can sit down and rest amidst them. When the wind shakes their tops, a poetry echoes through the valley. I observed the scene as all became quiet and then began to hear sounds from far away. (Strassberg 1994: 145–146)

有泉幽幽然, 其鳴乍大乍細。渠之廣或咫尺, 或倍尺, 其長可十許步。其流抵大石, 伏出其下。逾石而往, 有石泓, 昌蒲被之, 青鮮環周。又折西行, 旁陷岩石下, 北墮小潭。潭幅員減百尺, 清深多鯈魚。又北曲行紆餘, 睨若無窮, 然卒入於渴。其側皆詭石、怪木、奇卉、美箭, 可列坐而麻焉。風搖其巔, 韻動崖谷。視之既靜, 其聽始遠。(Zhonghua shuju bianjibu 1979: 3: 770)

Our Descriptive Subject walks along a brook while enjoying the wonderful scenery. The description is neat and layered. By employing "scatter perspective," the description follows the Descriptive Subject's steps to describe the flow of the brook, its direction, its depth, etc. Though the Description Object is consistently the Rocky Trough, the essay also introduces other objects, such as springs, stones, flowers, and bamboo, and then rocks, small ponds, and fish. Yet, amid these objects, the water and its movement are the focus—the former the "guest" and the latter the "host."

The description follows the movement of Liu (the focalizer), and scenes are disclosed gradually to expand the reader's field of vision. And when Liu stops walking and sits down, he becomes the center, with all the natural objects surrounding him (see figure below):

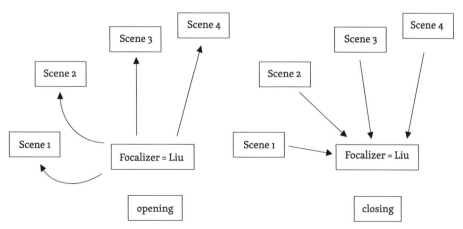

Figure 1: Open Close Pattern.
Source: Author.

And when Liu spots the trough's far end, it becomes the focus of attention. This type of description produces a "level distance" visual effect. In the end, more objects are introduced into the text, and motion caused by the wind evokes the wideness and spaciousness of Rocky Trough. The last two lines adopt "deep distance" to describe the scene, reminding readers that our sight will follow the music of the wind to pass through the top of the hillock and to the far distance behind.

"RECORD OF THE ROCKY GORGE"

In this essay, description does not dominate; there are only eighty-two characters of description, i.e., only thirty-five percent of the essay. Instead, it serves mainly as an explanation for and evidence of Liu's argument that no one in the past could match the happiness he feels in enjoying the scenery there:

The water here exceeds Stony Brook by threefold. Broad rocks form the bottom and extend to the banks, resembling a bed, a foundation, an open mat, or a threshold to an inner chamber. The water covers it evenly, its flow like embroidery, sounding like a strummed Ch'in zither. I lifted up my garment and waded in barefoot. I broke off some bamboo to sweep away the dead leaves and removed the decaying trees, from which we were able to construct eighteen or nineteen folding chairs. I sat down on one and found a flowing tapestry and crashing sounds below my seat. Trees the color of kingfisher feathers and rocks with patterns like dragon scales shaded me from above. (Strassberg 1994: 146–147).

其水之大, 倍石渠三之一, 全石為底, 達於兩涯。若床若堂, 若陳筵席, 若限閫奧。水平布其上, 流若織文, 響若操琴。(Zhonghua shuju bianjibu 1979: 3: 771)

The Descriptive Object of this piece is Rocky Gorge. To represent the broadness of said gorge, the text employs four metaphors to produce a sense among readers of the enormity of the space: the rocks are like a "bed" (床) and a "hall" (堂), like "setting up a banquet in a dining hall" (陳筵席), or like the huge area from a threshold to the "deep end of a quarter" (限閫奧). Then the lines shift the focus from the gorge to its water. Two metaphors are employed here to describe the water: "embroidery" (織文, knitting pattern) to capture its motion and "Ch'in zither" (操琴, playing qin) its murmuring sound.

The softness of running water is accompanied by the hardness of plants and rocks to fill out a pretty standard landscape description. Obviously, the gorge itself is the focus and the host, and its description is supported by guest images such as its flow, its sound, plants, and rocks:

The interwoven flow, the strumming roar, both beneath these seats; kingfisher-plumed trees, dragon-scaled rocks, both sheltered from above. (Nienhauser 1973: 74).

交絡之流, 觸激之音, 皆在床下; 翠羽之木, 龍鱗之石, 均蔭其上。(Zhonghua shuju bian-jibu 1979: 3: 772)

Again, we find a "guest-host" pattern. The host and its various guests create a balanced atmosphere that Liu clearly favored.

"RECORD OF THE MOUNTAIN OF LITTLE STONE CITY-WALLS"

Similar to the essay above, description in this essay does not constitute a major component of the essay, only 66 characters, or about a quarter of the essay. The description again serves as evidence of Liu's argument that the scene was probably made by an "inspired designer."

On top of the rocks were shapes resembling battlements and roof beams, beside which there were fortresses that looked like doors. We peered in and it was pitch dark inside. We cast a pebble in and heard it fall with a plop into the water; the crystal resonance last for a long while before it ceased. As we walked round the fortresses we could look into the great distance. There was no soil on this rocky pile but on it beautiful trees and bamboo stalks grew healthily, exotically, some in clusters, others wide apart, as if they had been carefully arranged by an inspired designer. (Wong 2007: 502)

其上為睥睨梁欐之形; 其旁出堡塢, 有若門焉, 窺之正黑, 投以小石, 洞然有水聲, 其響之激越, 良久乃已, 環之可上, 望甚遠。無封土壤而生嘉樹美箭, 益奇而堅, 其疏數偃仰, 類智者所施設也。(Zhonghua shuju bianjibu 1979: 3: 773)

The description is brief, and its focus is confined to the hill itself. Though the perspective is not as defined as those mentioned in Guo Xi's taxonomy, descriptions here are obviously narrated from a low angle. A "deep distance" perspective is then suggested when the text goes on to describe the vista afforded after climbing up to the top of the fortress.

CONCLUSION

To overview the general structure of each of the essays in *Eight Records*, we can find that Liu Zongyuan generally puts information at the beginning, though sometimes at the end as well. Whereas event and scene form the main part, feeling and/or thinking usually come next and become the center of the text.[54]

To conclude, though the descriptive expressions do not necessarily dominate Liu's eight essays, as one might expect, they play an important role in injecting lyrical expression and/or argument into the text. Description is obviously the most crucial element in Liu's *Eight Records*. As shown in the preceding analysis, the description in Liu's landscape essay is basically in the form of binary patterns, though instead of contrasting, the two parts of the binary join together to form a perfect, higher-level harmony. Aesthetic patterns like "abstract-concrete," "guest-host," and "open-close" can be interpreted as representing a kind "yin-yang" concept in Liu Zongyuan's mind.

Lyrical expression was always the main reason that Liu wrote the essays. He uses two channels for expressing his feeling. The first starts with sensory description, then proceeds to his response (feeling), and ends with deep feeling. The second also begins with sensory description, then proceeds to an established argument and his comments, which closely relate to Liu's personal experience, especially his political exile.

Argumentation in Liu's essay is not necessarily logical, objective, or based solely in reason, but is heavily colored by his personal feelings. With Liu, emotions and thoughts are not contradictory. In fact, they are intertwined with the background of the political turmoil of his time. The beauty of a scene moves him and then provokes in him thoughts about his own life, leading him to think deeply about his personal suffering. Thus, Liu's "arguments" are closely related to his own personal history and can easily be considered part of his feelings and thought, though reasoning is also involved. We may capture this duality with the term "emotional thought."

---

54   The following are the patterns of the eight essays: (1) West Mountain: feeling, event, thinking, event, scene, feeling/thinking, event, feeling, thinking, information; (2) Box-iron Pool: information, scene, event, feeling; (3) Hillock: information, scene, event, scene, event, scene/feeling, thinking, feeling, information; (4) Rock Pool: information, scene, scene/feeling, feeling, information; (5) Slough: information, thinking, information, scene, feeling, information; (6) Trough: information, scene, information, event, information, feeling; (7) Gorge: event, scene, event, scene, thinking, information; (8) Rocky City: information, scene, scene/thinking, thinking.

APPENDIX I: DESCRIPTION AND TOTAL CHARACTERS IN EIGHT RECORDS

Essay	Description *#	Total Characters #	%
Record of Excursion on Which I First Discovered the West Mountain and Peace	59	372	15.86
Record of the Box-iron Pool	57	208	27.40
Record of the Little Hillock West of the Box-iron Pool	128	408	31.37
Record of Reaching the Small Rock Pool West of the Little Hillock	145	239	60.67
Record of Yuan Family Slough	162	324	50.00
Record of the Rocky Trough	149	271	54.98
Record of the Rocky Gorge	82	234	35.04
Record of the Mountain of Little Stone City-walls	66	263	25.10

* excluding other descriptive elements serve as parts of exposition, argumentation, narration, and lyrical expressions
# in Chinese character

APPENDIX II: TABLE OF SENSORY DESCRIPTION

Sensory Description	Attributes	Aspects		Examples (in Chinese)
Visual Sensation	Colour	Types	Cool	藍, 紫
			Warm	紅, 黃
		Degree	Dark to light	深, 淺
			Thin to thick	稠, 稀; 濃, 郁; 淡, 薄
		Directness	Direct	紅
			Indirect	紅蘋果
	Brightness	Degree	Strong to Weak	強, 弱; 明, 暗
		Changes		閃爍不定 忽明忽暗
	Shape	Types		圓, 橢圓, 半圓, 扁, 正方, 長方, 菱, 梯, 塔, 管, 三角, 多角, 卷, 曲, 串, 蛇狀
		Length	Long to Short	長, 短
		Height	High to Low, Tall to Short	高, 矮; 高, 低
		Regular to Irregular		不規則、整齊不平
		Density		疏, 密
	Direction/Position			東南西北、遠近、前後、左右、內外、上下
	Size/Volume			大, 小
	Line			直、橫、彎、折
	Motion/Motionless	Degree		動, 靜
	Number			多少, 具體數目
Auditory Sensation	Volume	Low to High		無聲到大聲
		Degree		強, 弱
		Style		雄壯, 柔和
	Range	Degree		寬, 窄
	Tone	Degree		高, 低, 轉, 平
	Speed	Degree		快, 慢, 停
Tactile Sensation	Heaviness/Lightness	Degree		輕重、飄沉
	Thickness/Thinness	Degree		厚, 薄
	Dryness/Wetness	Degree		乾, 濕, 黏, 糊
	Hardness/Softness	Degree		柔軟、堅硬、脆爽
	Coldness/Hotness	Degree		冷, 凍, 涼, 溫, 暖, 熱
	Roughness/Fineness	Degree		粗糙、光滑、癢痛、滑溜、凹凸不平

Olfactory Sensation	Smell	Type	香, 臭
		Degree	濃, 淡
Gustatory Sensation	Taste	Type	甜, 酸, 苦, 辣, 鹹
		Degree	濃, 淡

4 NEGOTIATING A MORTGAGE AND WOOING A MINISTER: GENDER, STRUCTURE, AND MEANING IN CHAPTERS 36–38 OF THE *ROMANCE OF THE THREE KINGDOMS*[55]

IHOR PIDHAINY

In teaching *Romance of the Three Kingdoms* (Sanguo zhi yanyi; hereafter *Three Kingdoms*), Milena Doleželová enjoyed teasing her class with the description of this book as the first of the great novels to examine a "ménage à trois"—that of the kingdoms of Shu, Wei, and Wu and their respective rulers.[56] The importance of this theme in later domestic novels, particularly *Golden Lotus* (Jin Ping Mei) and *Dream of the Red Chamber* (Honglou meng), showed insight into power relations that existed at both the familial-social and imperial-political levels. In this chapter, I use the famous section from *Three Kingdoms* in which Liu Bei woos Zhuge Liang to become his minister (chapters 36–38) in order to demonstrate a shift in the novel from a Confucian and "military" (*wu*) culture to that of a Daoist and "civil" (*wen*) culture—that is, Liu Bei swings his focus from his military brothers, Guan Yu and Zhang Fei, to the Daoist military strategist Zhuge Liang. This is a movement from brute strength, which up to this point has dominated the novel (in addition to the two "brothers," witness also Dong Zhuo, Lü Bu, and Cao Cao, among others), to the cunning and wiles of various strategists, including Zhuge Liang. Concurrently, there is a transformation of gender values: these strategists are effete and feminine, whereas the two female characters who appear in this section, both surnamed

55 This essay was dually inspired by my advisor Richard John Lynn, whose course on the Chinese novel I took in my first year as a graduate student and when I served as Professor Doleželová's TA several years later. A much earlier version of this paper was presented at the MCAA annual meeting in 2007 in St. Louis. I would like to thank Rania Huntington for her comments at that panel and also Robert Hegel for his remarks.

56 Milena Doleželová made these remarks during a session that she taught on the Chinese novel in the summer of 2003. The literature on *Three Kingdoms* is extensive. Important studies in English include Hsia 1968: 34–74; Plaks 1987: 361–496, and Besio 1997, and Besio/ Tung 2007. For introductory bibliographies to the novel, see Nienhauser, 1986: 670–671; 1998: 396–398. For translated citations from the text, I use Roberts 1991, unless otherwise stated.

Xu, are trumpeted as the greatest of heroes (surpassing the men of the story). Finally, the central motif of Liu Bei's courtship of Zhuge Liang also speaks of a changing relationship among the men than was present earlier in the novel.

The origins of the novel go back to actual events from the latter third of the second century up to the latter third of the third century. Early accounts were preserved in historical records, the most important being the *Chronicle of the Three Kingdoms* (Sanguo zhi), which though written at the end of the third century, did not gain its current form until the fifth century, when a massive commentary was added that dwarfed the original text.[57] The stories of the period though continued to appear in a variety of formats (drama, poetry, prose narrative) over the next millennium, with the novel not appearing before the fourteenth century (and our earliest confirmable date for the novel going back only to 1522). Authorship is ascribed to Luo Guanzhong, who is dated to the fourteenth century. As was the norm with other novels, *Three Kingdoms* was published by a variety of printing houses with a stream of versions created by editors over the centuries. As time passed and the narrative-editorial tradition developed various interests, *Three Kingdoms*, like other early novels, was shaped into a fairly different type of work: that of a literati novel. The most important of the editor-authors was that of the father and son team of Mao Lun and Mao Zonggang in the mid seventeenth century, who greatly reshaped the narrative through incisions, excisions, commentary and other editorial paraphernalia that defined the late imperial novel.[58] *Three Kingdoms* has provoked a flood of responses, the basic thrust of which centers on the question of how/why the righteous (Liu Bei and Zhuge Liang) lost out to the less righteous (Cao Cao). The Mao edition also brought into play the question of structure and organization of narrative, a topic of more recent scholarly interest.[59]

The overlay of the military-political with the romantic has its roots in the *Songs of Chu* (Chuci), where the poet and political official Qu Yuan purportedly writes of his own troubles as an official whose advice and assistance has been rejected by his ruler. Qu Yuan read his relationship to the emperor through the metaphor of a court woman to her ruler/husband and this has been a common trope in Chinese writing up to the present day. My reading of Liu Bei's courting Zhuge Liang is done within this context and framework.[60]

---

57 See Hayden, "The Beginning of the End: The Fall of the Han and the Opening of Three Kingdoms," in Besio/Tung 2007: 43–51; and Hoyt Tilman, "Selected Historical Sources for *Three Kingdoms*: Reflections from Sima Guang's and Chen Liang's Reconstructions of Kongming's Story" in *ibid.*, 53–69.

58 One notes that the novel begins with the verse of Yang Shen (1488–1567), who wrote them more than a century after Luo was putting brush to paper.

59 See Roy, "*How to Read* The Romance of the Three Kingdoms," in Rolston 1990: 145–195.

60 Louie (2002: 22–41) calls into question the unequivocally heterosexual reading of the relationships among the male heroes of this story. Song Geng (2004: 157–172) writes of the desexualized nature of the hero in these novels. The *haohan* hero is in contrast to the *caizi* hero: the *caizi* hero is after sex; the haohan is after loyalty.

The novel begins with a remarkable flourish—with the political and military fathers of the narrative set out before the reader. In the first chapter, the history of the realm is presented, from the Warring State period through the Qin into the Western Han up to Wang Mang's usurpation, then through the Eastern Han up until the troubles of emperors Huan (Han Huandi) and Ling (Han Lingdi) and, finally, Xian (Han Xiandi). The various players—wives, lovers, mothers, in-laws, favorites, eunuchs, and hangers-on—appear in quick order, before and after the great preliminary event, the Rebellion of the Yellow Turbans (Huang mao; "Scarves" in Roberts' translation). The rebellion introduces the reader to the ever-present triangulation that occurs repeatedly throughout the book.

The rebellion is lead by Zhang Jue, a Daoist of sorts, whose encounter with the Daoist sage, Zhuangzi, incites his attempt to overthrow the Han.[61] Together with his two brothers, they form a triumvirate that challenges imperial power and is only defeated through the general call to arms of the people. The Yellow Turbans are summarily displaced, their leaders killed and their corpses dismembered and indeed metaphorically buried under the continued rebellion of various related bandit warriors. The imperial victory lies in the hands of two other budding triumvirates: Liu Bei, Guan Yu, and Zhang Fei, on the one hand, and Liu Bei, Sun Jian, and Cao Cao, on the other. This second group consists of the fathers of the three kingdoms— Shu, Wei, and Wu— that will arise after the abdication of Emperor Xian (Han Xiandi) and the demise of the Han. The author of the work has carefully managed to insert all three men into the first chapter, though all three are still minor players at this point. Indeed, only Cao Cao takes a clear role at court, and that is as a young hothead arguing (perhaps correctly) for an immediate purge of the enemies of the emperor. Liu Bei, who is perhaps the clearest protagonist in a novel that has hundreds of characters, is followed on his series of minor posts in the provinces. Sun Jian disappears altogether for a while. Nevertheless, the three houses are introduced at the start of the work.

Liu Bei's status is highlighted by his being part of two triangular relations. His first, with Zhang Fei and Guan Yu, differs from that with Cao and Sun in that a harmonious balance is achieved almost immediately in the former, whereas in the latter competition and rivalry win out in the end.[62] The first triangular relationship is symbolically captured in the peach-swearing scene, one of the most famous in the novel—and one that is used to denote the special nature of the relationship between Liu Bei and his two leading generals.

---

61   Zhuangzi is identified through his toponym, *Nanhua laoxian*, the ancient immortal of Nanhua.
62   The rivalry between Zhuge Liang and the two brothers is examined through various understandings of *yi* in Jiyuan Yu, "The Notion of Appropriateness (Yi) in *Three Kingdoms*" in Besio/Tung 2007: 27–40.

As this scene stands in stark contrast to that of Liu's courting of Zhuge Liang later, it warrants our attention.

Each of the three men belongs to a lower status than most of the heroes encountered in the volume. Zhang is a common farmer and butcher; Guan, though perhaps of somewhat higher status, is an outlaw with blood on his hand; and Liu claims—rather dubiously—royal blood, several generations removed. The oath taken at Zhang's farm is indicative of their rather democratic relationship:

> We three, though of separate ancestry, join in brotherhood here, combining strength and purpose, to relieve the present crisis .... We dare not hope to be together always but hereby vow to die the selfsame day. (Roberts 1991: 12)

There is already a discordant element in the relationship: Liu Bei swears brotherhood and yet must be the leader and ruler. The fraternal and hierarchical is bound to clash, and will indeed be acerbated with Zhuge Liang's entry into Liu's service. The ritual was performed with the sacrifice of a black bull and a white horse, likely a borrowing of a Mongol tradition.[63] This bloody sacrifice is indicative of the military qualities associated with the opening chapters of the novel and stands in contrast to Liu's performance in convincing Zhuge to serve as his advisor.

Violence is at the forefront of the novel, and it is exuberantly portrayed in the opening chapters. Masculinity, it seems, can only be achieved through the handling of weapons and letting of copious amounts of blood. A paramount but low-key example is that of Zhang Fei's whipping of a bullying official, a certain unnamed district inspector who arrives at Anxi County where Liu Bei has been given a minor post as reward for his assistance to the throne. The arrival of the official signals the gradual diminution of the status of the militia supporters of imperial power. The inspector immediately shows his disdain for Liu and goes about highhandedly "ruling" as he sees fit. Zhang Fei, having bristled at the poor treatment of Liu, encounters the inspector hounding locals into swearing false complaints against his elder brother, and thereupon proceeds to beat the inspector until he is a pink pulp. It is only the sudden arrival of Liu at the scene of the pummeling that spares the inspector a certain death. Not only is the scene bloody, it reads as a celebration of Zhang Fei's breaking rules and laws and going against administrative protocol in pursuit of a higher justice. Although Liu and his brothers need to disappear

---

63   Roberts (1991: 3: 1560fn25) notes Xiongnu had sacrificed white horses in pre-imperial times. For examples of Mongol sacrifice of white horses and black ox, see Curtin 1908: 84 and Bawden 2009: 4. Note also that the American modernist poet, Ezra Pound, picks up on the exact use of sacrificial animals in his own poetry. See Canto 58 of his Odes (Pound 1972: 319).

for a while, they find a protector willing to hide them and it is not long after that they are once again called forth to participate in governing the realm.

Masculinity is thus defined in the early chapters as brute force wielded through prized swords—often atop prized stallions. Many of the heroes of the novel have a personalized weapon that is specially named and ride a specific horse that too is known by a personalized name. Perhaps the ultimate paragon of masculinity in the early part of the book is Lü Bu, an extraordinarily powerful general who is first encountered after the Commander Dong Zhuo has been invited to the capital with his army. Dong, who stumbled upon the boy Emperor and his cousin in flight from troublesome eunuchs, quickly gains hold of the court and threatens to depose the Emperor and replace him with his cousin as the first move in his quest for rule of the realm. However, Ding Yuan, a counselor, stands up to Dong Zhuo, and with the backing of his adopted son, Lü Bu, cows the would-be tyrant in his tracks.

Dong Zhuo quickly realizes that Lü Bu is the signal element that he needs to win the empire. His pursuit (or courtship) of Lü Bu is the first important courting of a valuable lieutenant by a leader in the novel. It begins with the battle scene between Ding Yuan's forces and Dong Zhuo's, where Lü is introduced as a magnificent warrior: "Lü Bu, his topknot bound in a golden crown, wearing a millefleurs battle robe, girded with armor and a belt bearing a motif of lions and reptiles" (Roberts 1991: 41–42). This is followed by a description of Lü's crown, clothing, armor, horse, and halberd and then by his defeat and pursuit of Dong Zhuo. Dong opines: "Lü Bu is extraordinary ... if only I could win him to our side, the realm would be ours with little trouble" (Roberts 1991: 42). Lü Bu thus is the essential embodiment of masculine values in the early part of the novel—a living, breathing Chinese Heracles. He is, however, neither virtuous nor very intelligent.

Li Su, a townsman of Lü Bu, offers to buy his talents on behalf of Dong Zhuo. This is done through flattery and bribery—here Lü Bu receives the renowned horse, Red Mare (Chitu ma), as a sort of signing prize. In return, Lü speedily beheads his adopted father Ding Yuan and presents this prize to his newly adopted father Dong Zhuo. Dong then holds a drinking session with him during which he offers Lü Bu gifts of armor and battle gown, dressing him as his prized matador. However, unlike Liu Bei, who spends day and night with his confidantes, Lü and Dong part without much ado. This difference underlines Dong's and Lü's surrender to the passions of female flesh—and thus suggests that they are not pure enough to be ultimate representatives of "military" (*wu*) masculinity.

The fealty of Lü allows Dong Zhuo to gradually gain control of the Han court, whose officials are to a man cowed. Dong replaces the teenage emperor with his much younger cousin and begins the process of becoming an emperor. However, this situation soon comes undone. Dong's control of the court is based solely on intimidation and violence. He attempts to shock with sudden and summary executions of several courtiers. And yet, this does not stop opposition to him: the powerful courtier Yuan Shao leaves court, Wang Yun and others plot his demise, and Cao Cao even attempts to assassinate him.

Cao Cao serves as yet another example of a potentially loyal minister. The traditional characterization of Cao is that he is a perverse hero (奸雄), which is not an unfair depiction of the fictional character, but a rather contentious proposition when it comes to the historical figure. Cao falls short of Liu Bei, but at first Cao differs little from his later antagonist. Both are of dubious background (Cao's father was adopted by a eunuch), both battle against the Yellow Turbans, and both are loyal to the emperor. Cao goes so far as to offer and then attempt to assassinate Dong Zhuo. He fails to do so, and so flees and becomes an outlaw. For a brief moment—when he is captured by government troops and put under the watch of a local official, Chen Gong—Cao serves as a model in the novel. Chen responds to him in Damascine wonder and releases him and leaves his post to join him as his first obtained lieutenant. The moment passes as Chen encounters the reality of joining a rebellion—the slaughter of innocents for one's own self-preservation. In this particular scene, Cao mistakenly kills the family of a close friend of his father and then kills the close friend to ensure his silence. When Chen abandons Cao and goes off into the obscurity of the night, Cao recognizes the cause and effect involved, but feels not in the least troubled.[64]

Cao's killing of his father's blood brother contrasts with the earlier Peach Tree Oath that Liu, Zhang and Guan swore together. But Cao's more practical approach to political (and military) attachments will ultimately win out. Indeed, it will be cunning that topples Dong Zhuo through his most powerful, but weak link: the warrior Lü Bu.

Cao manages to manipulate the situation so that he can raise an army and incite a battle against them. However, Dong Zhuo's reliance on Lü Bu and the warrior Hua Xiong proves successful in checking the rebellion. It is only at that point that Liu Bei and his lieutenants come to the fore of the battle, killing Hua and forcing Lü to flee. But it is a pyrrhic victory, because the rebels are not cohesive and fall out amongst themselves, with neither Cao's cunning nor Liu's powerful lieutenants succeeding in replacing Dong.

Dong Zhuo's final downfall is achieved only through the machinations of yet another court official, Wang Yun, who ensnares Dong and Lü in a triangular relationship with his slave girl, Diaochan. In a scene that has captured the imagination of readers for centuries, the slave girl comes to Wang Yun in the depth of his garden to offer her services to her benefactor in his time

---

64   Hsia (1968: 49–50) notes that Chen Gong ends up following Lü Bu after abandoning Cao, while displaying the best of 'a man of ability' in his allegiance to this new, rather weak leader.

of need. Wang kneels before his "adopted daughter" and hatches the scheme by which she will be given to both men and thus cause an enmity to arise between them. The scheme works—Dong Zhuo throws away his opportunity to rule and is killed, while Lü Bu strikes out on his own, taking Diaochan as his prized beauty. And yet the ultimate goal of re-establishing the emperor's authority fails: after Dong has been killed, some of his lieutenants seek to avenge his death and Wang serves as the required victim. The emperor is no more secure then before, and soon falls into the hands of Cao Cao.

Wang Yun's stratagem underlines a struggle between *wen* and *wu* in the novel. Employing one of the few female protagonists in the novel, the scene represents a standard trope: the scheme of using a beauty to overturn the power of male political order.[65] That Diaochan is an active participant does not hide Wang's ultimate power in his machinations in using a slave girl as bait between the two men.[66] Wang's use of *wen* to overcome the might of his opponents shows that violence can be checked, and opens the possibility of the overcoming of the military forces that are marshaled by men such as Dong, Lü, Yuan Shao, and Cao Cao. Diaochan's successful playing of the two men also foreshadows Zhuge Liang's equally successful scheme of sidling up with Sun Ce to defeat Cao's armies at the Battle of Red Cliff.[67]

Let us now turn to the end of Chapter 34 and beginning of chapter 35, where Liu Bei, fleeing from the henchmen of a royal relative, miraculously jumps the River Tan, which could only have been accomplished through "Heaven's will" (Roberts 1991: 269), as Liu Bei acknowledges. The commentary likewise notes this improbable incident: "It is not only the reader who cannot believe it, but [Liu] Xuande himself cannot believe it."[68] Heaven's will is now leading Liu Bei on the path to meet his future admired one—Zhuge Liang. Liu Bei's search begins by chance with his being found by a Daoist sage's novice, who immediately recognizes Liu Bei from the descriptions given him by his master Stillwater (Shui Jing). This man is the first of a series of Daoist figures

---

65 The phrase emperor toppling beauty (*qingcheng*) is traced back to Ban Gu's *History of the Han* (Hanshu), in a description of the future Consort Li of Emperor Wu (Hanshu 57). The tradition though was far older, as can be seen in Liu Xiang's (77–6 BCE) *Liennü zhuan*, whose seventh chapter on depraved women lists a series of ancient empire toppling beauties.

66 However Louie (2002: 28–30) observes Diaochan is merely a foil to a masculine power. Lü Bu's death should signal her being prized by Guan Yu. Instead, he slaughters her. Louie's comments follow those of Hsia on the "subconscious hatred" of the *haohan* toward women.

67 Scholars and readers alike have noted Guan Yu and Cao Cao's on-again off-again relationship. Indeed, there is a special sense to Cao's gallant treatment of the true warrior, Guan, over his rather callous relationship with scholars and advisors. Cao's pursuit of Guan is parallel to that of Liu's of Zhuge. Although Cao is not successful in his pursuit, nevertheless, Guan spares his life in a moment of feeling deep loyalty for him following Cao's flight along the Huarong Trail after the disastrous Battle of Red Cliffs.

68 Jiang 1988: 271. All translations from the commentary, unless otherwise indicated, are my own. Future references will be indicated.

that Liu Bei is to encounter before his final discovery and courtship of Zhuge Liang. The Maos rightly note that these figures all foreshadow Zhuge Liang (Jiang 1998: 283).

Chapter 35 functions as a preface to chapters 36, 37, 38, because in this chapter, Liu Bei's search for the perfect (Daoist) minister begins.[69] Stillwater, whom Liu Bei at first is unable to recognize, is the first occurrence of the effete Daoist in the novel. Liu is earnestly entreated to join his forces (in essence to be the true Minister).[70] Stillwater also spurs Liu on by refusing him. Nevertheless, he does let Liu Bei know of a certain "sleeping dragon," which is one of Zhuge Liang's names, and is visited during the night by Shan Fu (Yuanzhi). Soon after leaving his refuge, Liu Bei also encounters Shan Fu and takes him on as his minister.

Chapters 36 to 38 on the whole feature the following: a clear delineation of the competition among the three competitors: Liu Bei, Cao Cao, Sun Quan; the search for the true minister (one who takes this role because it is the will of Heaven); a series of competitive engagements among the various characters, whether friend or foe; and the triumph of the feminine over the masculine.

The triangular competition is mostly engaged through proxies. Cao Cao and Liu Bei do not directly meet in these chapters. Instead, Cao Cao has Cao Ren (along with Li Dian) go to battle Liu Bei (with Shan Fu). The defeat of Cao Ren does not immediately draw Cao Cao, rather he moves behind the scenes to detach Shan Fu from Liu Bei. Liu's side is likewise upheld by Madame Xu (Xu shi), Shan Fu's mother. Similarly, Sun Quan and Liu Bei do not directly engage in battle; rather, it is Liu Bei's relative Liu Biao who stands in for him in this competition. Indeed, only Sun Quan and Cao Cao directly battle (i.e., when Cao demands Sun's son as hostage and Sun turns him down). This will ostensibly be the cause that leads to Cao Cao's defeat and a shift in the fortunes among the three powers.

Every relationship in these chapters is one of competition.[71] This is obviously the case when opponents meet on the battlefield, such as Cao Ren and Liu Bei, but it is also fairly clear when non-aligned, but not neutral in view parties meet—for example, when Cao Cao engages with Madame Xu (Xu shi). However, it is also the case in other relationships such as Liu Bei's and Shan Fu's negotiation over his leaving his employment or Liu Bei's and Zhuge Liang's later negotiation for Shan Fu's replacement.

---

69 Mao (Jiang 1998: 266) states unequivocally that chapter 35 begins the section on Liu Bei's search for Zhuge Liang. Here I am focusing on ch. 36-38 as a single unit, as there are structural features tightly linking the chapters, which are not present in ch. 35.

70 Liu Bei: "I have been anxious to find a worthy man who has absented himself from the world of men. But, alas, I have yet to encounter him." (Jiang 1998: 270)

71 See Plaks (1987: 399-476) reading of irony in the novel.

Let us consider the sequence of events leading up to Shan Fu's release. Cao Cao has contrived to use Madame Xu to entice her son Shan Fu (his assumed name) to work for him. Madame Xu refuses and turns the tables by enraging him so that he will order her execution. However, before she can claim victory (her son would have good reason to work for Liu Bei), an advisor calms Cao Cao down and Madame Xu is comfortably housed in the palace. Cao Cao then gains the upper hand through an intermediary who manages to forge Madame Xu's calligraphy in a letter calling for Shan Fu to come home. This does the trick, and Cao Cao is temporarily victorious. However, Madame Xu ups the ante: when her son arrives, she scolds him as unmanly and unfilial and then commits suicide, which fixes her son as permanently disabled (impotent) and unable to assist Cao in any manner (indeed he is passively hostile afterwards). Madame Xu's victory is also a triumph for Liu Bei (though neither author nor editor sees his hand in any of this).

Before this scene, Shan Fu needed to cautiously work his way out of Liu Bei's employment. Shan Fu was fully informed (and had directed) Liu Bei's army and his loss would not only have meant that Liu needed to find a replacement, but also that Cao would have within his grasp a man who was fully aware of every aspect of Liu Bei's situation and strategy. Shan Fu's claim of filial devotion swayed Liu Bei, but other advisors dropped hints that the best policy was to restrain Shan Fu until Cao killed his mother. Liu Bei found that aspect repugnant and was intent on honouring filial devotion and releasing Shan Fu. Shan, however, was ever cautious in his "negotiations" with Liu, and it was only after their parting that he returned to recompense Liu with the name of a possible successor—Zhuge Liang. His awkwardly expressed "my emotions were so conflicted, I forgot to mention ..." (279) was denuded of its true strength by Liu Bei's almost pathetic belief that his advisor was returning to him. It goes unsaid that the reason for not revealing this information was fear that Liu Bei was going to have him ambushed. Indeed, the caution both men employ and the tears they manage to shed does not hide their careful negotiation over Shan Fu's release.[72]

The author then has a quick follow-up scene between Shan Fu (Xu Shu) and Zhuge Liang: Zhuge Liang on hearing that Shan Fu has recommended him for a post, turns his back on his "friend" with disdain—no doubt to start his own preparations for encountering Liu Bei. This sets up the next encounter: the long negotiation between Zhuge Liang and Liu Bei. This is the famous Three Visits to the Thatched Cottage. The author is at pains to portray Liu

---

72   Roberts (1991L 1036fn10) suggests that Liu Bei and Shan Fu are testing each other here. On the other hand, Louie (2002: 34) reads the tears that the men shed at their parting as excessive and not particularly Confucian, and perhaps indicative of a passionate sexual relationship. I tend to see them engaged in stereotypical roles of friends parting while they plot on how best to deal with the situation at hand.

Bei's sincere desire to have the smartest and best to be his chief advisor and to allow for enough time to pass before Zhuge Liang accepts Liu Bei's hasty proposal. However, there is a sneaking suspicion that Liu Bei's ardent desire to attract Zhuge Liang is in part because of Shan Fu's earlier rejection of him—it is Zhuge Liang who enforces the slow, drawn-out courtship. It is only when Liu Bei has proved his single devotion to Zhuge Liang by coming, absurdly, three times to look for him[73] that Zhuge Liang finally gives in to his master with nary a snag. Indeed, Zhuge Liang has long been preparing for their eventual union and has already worked out their dream home—that is, the mortgaged property I refer to in the title of my paper.

In the competition between them, both Zhuge Liang and Liu Bei are aware that they are negotiating a union. Liu Bei raises the ante each time he goes in search of Zhuge Liang; Zhuge Liang treats his suitor with a studied indifference (managing to be away twice and only on the third time being home). Indeed, during the final visit Zhuge Liang is lost in sleep while Liu Bei humbles himself for a good amount of time by his bedside. Zhuge Liang's swift recovery from sleep is ingenuous and face-saving for Liu Bei, but nonetheless does not fool either of the two brothers who have noted Liu Bei's foolish pursuit of this man. Zhang Fei notes to Guan Yu,

> The insolence! Our brother standing in attendance, while he pretends to sleep peacefully on! Let me go out and torch the rear. We'll see whether that gets him up or not. (Roberts 1991: 290–291)

After the relation has been consummated, so to speak, there are a series of competitions that help to unwind the narrative from this climax. First there is Cao Cao and Sun Quan and the negotiation over sending a hostage to court. Sun Quan's parries are not successful and the two go to battle. Then there is the competition between Lady Xu (Xu shi) and two villains (Gui Lan and Dai Yuan). (Lady Xu—the wife of Sun Quan's younger, incompetent, alcoholic brother— is a minor figure, but I discuss her heroism later in the chapter.) Finally there is the concluding battle between Sun Quan and Liu Biao, who serves as proxy for Liu Bei. It is interesting that Liu Bei's relation to both men is quite complicated: he is both allied and in conflict with both at different times.

These competitions are always set within the greater framework of the search for a true minister: this is a Confucian ideal, but here the position is to be filled by Daoists only. The search for a true minister is connected to a number of related points. First, there is the question of genuine versus false. This question comes up throughout the novel, but is most forcefully dealt with in the scene between Cao Cao and Madame Xu: Cao has argued that her son (Shan

---

73   Zhang Fei's chides Liu Bei: "I think you overrate this village bumpkin" (Roberts 1991: 290).

Fu) serves a false minister; she turns this argument on its head and states un-equivocally that Cao is the false one and Liu the true one. Her baiting almost succeeds, but Cao is restrained from killing her by his own wily ministers.

Liu Bei, though indicated as the true leader, is in search of a true minister. In his search, however, he is hampered by his own inability to see true worth. A case in point is his initial lack of clarity on Stillwater's status. Stillwater actually sent his young novice out to lead Liu Bei over to his farm. Liu Bei then propositions Stillwater, but is turned down. Liu Bei's next man is Shan Fu, who makes a scene to catch the attention of Liu Bei. Shan Fu is a competent enough advisor, and yet is not the promised one, which becomes painfully obvious in the fact that Shan Fu is actually an assumed name for Xu Shu, who had killed a local bully and had to flee his home. Shan Fu's playing of Liu Bei and himself being fooled by Cao Cao both indicate his own lack of discernment. Indeed, it is his mother who pointedly admonishes him for his failures in this regard.

Liu Bei's knowledge of Zhuge Liang's name is the only clue he has to his existence. His search for him is marred by a comedy of errors. Liu Bei literally misidentifies six people for Zhuge Liang—one or two might seem plausible, but Liu Bei is so worked up about finding his true minister, that he sees him everywhere—whether it is in the face of Zhuge Liang's younger brother or his much older father-in-law. There is more in this than simple narrative exuberance on the part of the author: Liu Bei is literally blind when it comes to true talent, and we should read this as a character flaw. His blindness is not unique nor is it of the same quality as that of Guan Yu and Zhang Fei, who also are blind when it comes to Zhuge Liang. Indeed, their blindness is not one of misidentification, but in not recognizing his talent upon his arrival. This blindness, of course, will be remedied by Zhuge Liang over time, when he manipulates them in the name of Liu Bei's state. Their final recognition of his worth will confirm this.

The lack of recognition might have to do with the cultural prerequisites involved. Whereas Zhang Fei and Guan Yu represent the hyper masculine as-pects of war and the military, Zhuge Liang stands for the feminized element of culture in the tradition. This is of course a very simplistic reading—in making this point baldly, I want to draw attention to a broad shift in values in the novel from that of the masculine to that of the feminine or, in more Confucian terms, from the military (wu) and to the civil (wen). This latter reading is possible, but it should be noted that Zhuge Liang has no disdain for military campaigns, though it is also true that he never relies on brute force, being rather more attracted to the seduction of his opponent through trickery.[74]

---

74   See Louie (2002) for a discussion of wen/wu. For a discussion of Guan Yu as the ultimate wu man, see Louie 2002: 22–41; for idealized wen men from before Three Kingdoms, see 59–68. Note also Xueping Zhong's (2000: 9–12) question of this paradigm.

One aspect of this shift is the move from Cao Cao to Liu Bei/Sun Quan. Cao Cao is the military leader par excellence. Co-incidentally his interest in women is always one of conquest (of course, Zhuge Liang's wily suggestion that the southern campaign is only about the capture of two women is quite interesting and perceptive). Liu Bei is in many ways similar to Cao Cao— he too is a military man, though not of the same grade and quality. His interest in women though present (witness his various marriages and his strong filial devotion to his mother) never manages to match his love of potent generals and advisors (thus the anger he exhibits when hearing that Zhao Yun almost lost his life rescuing his son and attempting to save his wife). It is only in Sun Quan that we have a ruler who is fully controlled by his women (his mother and aunt). Although, the men of the south make war, women are ever present.

In the chapters under consideration, women also play a role. I am referring here to the two Xus. That they share surname is not merely coincidence; it also reinforces their common position as paragons of virtue. Here the virtue is that of a loyal minister. But let us take a step back to Liu Bei's miraculous flight across the River Tan discussed earlier. This flight was to escape soldiers nominally under the control of his relation Liu Biao, but who were acting on behest of Lady Cai (Cai shi, Liu Biao's second wife), who hated and feared Liu Bei because of her own selfish machinations at her husband's court. She is a typically bad woman (noticeably, there are not many women in this novel!). It is in Chapter 36 that we encounter Madame Xu whose virtuous suicide leads the narrator to commend her for standing up to Cao Cao and checking him in his desire of obtaining a proper minister:

> Mother Xu's integrity
> Will savor for eternity.
> She kept her honor free of stain,
> A credit to her family name...
> In life, her proper designation;
> In death, her proper destination.
> Mother Xu's integrity
> Will savor for eternity. (Roberts 1991: 281–282)

Mao's praise for Madame Xu is even stronger. In his prefatory remarks to chapter 36, specifically referring to her, he writes

> Amazing women who surpass amazing men—not only to be rarely seen in *Liennü zhuan* but also rare to be seen among accounts of heroic men. (Jiang 1998: 276)

騎婦人勝似騎男子, 不獨烈女傳中罕見之, 即豪士中罕見之.

And in his introductory comments to chapter 37, he notes that Madame Xu is a wise/sagely woman (*xian mu*). Following this discussion, Mao turns to discuss Zhuge Liang. This pairing is not accidental, and he explicitly equates the wisdom of Madame Xu to that of Zhuge Liang.

The second Xu is Lady Xu, the wife of Sun Quan's younger brother. The circumstances of her own heroic actions are much more threatening to her personally. Instead of a tyrant and a weak son, she loses a husband and faces two disloyal officers, Gui Lan and Dai Yuan, who murdered her husband. Moreover, Gui Lan takes a passionate liking to Lady Xu and offers her the option of himself or death. Lady Xu is able to outwit these two and through a false pretense entices them into an ambush. With their heads firmly planted at the altar, she is able to worship at the altar of her dead husband secure in having obtained proper vengeance. The narrative voice conveys its message through a poem:

> So able and so chaste – in this world all too rare! –
> The widow lured two villains into her cunning snare.
> Vassals base chose treachery, vassals loyal chose death;
> To this Southland heroine does any man compare? (296)

Mao simply notes, "that by the time Sun Quan had arrived with his troops, this woman had already killed the bandits. In consulting the *Book of Changes* (Yijing) she is a diviner, and in wielding troops she is a military leader. Such a marvelous woman, I'm afraid, would not even yield to Wolong of Nanyang [Zhuge Liang]" (Jiang 1998: 299).

比及孫權兵到, 女將早已殺賊矣。其卜易則知是女先生, 其用兵則是女將帥。如此奇婦人, 恐不讓南陽臥龍也。

Mao here establishes the second female Xu as Zhuge Liang's equal, claiming for her the same heavenly gift that he has (in the role of consulting the *Book of Changes*).

The two Xus are presented as heroines who surpass even the male heroes in valor. That their descriptions are clothed in both military and Confucian values speaks about the texts re-ordering of gender values. Although they are exceptional, it must be noted that there are a number of other women, such as Diaochan, who are equally acclaimed in the novel in their heroic abilities.

In examining the central motif of this section, gender issues arise. Liu Bei's pursuit of Zhuge Liang, which resembles a male suitor for female lover, is the most obvious example. This construction of meaning should however be understood within the context of the tradition: the relation of Ruler to Minister was analogous to that of Husband to Wife. Liu Bei's pursuit of Zhuge

Liang, I believe, is structured ingeniously to present a reverse situation in which the ruler is the one yearning, and not the minister. The much older Liu Bei (whose equally aged companions Guan Yu and Zhang Fei are chagrinned by their brother's susceptibility to these younger Daoists) makes the effort necessary to attract the brilliant and heavenly-blessed Zhuge Liang. Zhuge's play-acting about not being interested gives way to an acceptance that he has a happy future based in a beautiful home in the west—the region of Shu (Sichuan). This reading suggests that the state (with its ruler and ministers) works much like a family (and is the inverse of later domestic works such as *Golden Lotus* or *Dream of the Red Chmaber*, in which relations between men and women are analogous to political relations.

In this chapter, I have suggested that there is a shift of values in regard to rulers of state. The world in the early part of the *Three Kingdoms* is Confucian, military, and male. With chapters 36–38, we see shift toward a Daoist, cultural, and female world, at least for contending parties from the south. Gender relations are fairly complex in the novel. For example, male gender roles include those that we conventionally consider both male and female. These roles are in part determined by the hierarchical structure of society and particularly by the relation between ruler and minister. However, traditional attributes of male roles are taken on by the women and are praised by author and commentator. The ease with which male and female characters inhabit both male and female realms speaks of the Daoist flexibility deemed necessary in a world neither wholly Confucian nor fully masculine.

5 INTERSTITIAL MEMORIES: THE FORENSIC LIFE OF WANG MINGDE[75]

C. D. ALISON BAILEY

"There are more things in Heaven and Earth, Horatio,
than are dreamt of in your philosophy."
Hamlet Act One, Scene 5.

"The recollected past is not a consecutive temporal chain
but a set of discontinuous moments lifted out of the stream of time."
Lowenthal 1985: 208

INTRODUCTION

According to Wu Pei-yi (1990: 197), the golden age of Chinese autobiography was in the seventeenth century when writers forsook the historiographical model to craft a more fluid genre influenced by vernacular literature. While some self-narratives in this era are couched as nostalgic journeys towards enlightenment, others are more fragmented, surreptitiously slipped into other texts as interlinear commentary, travel literature, or informal jottings. One, albeit unusual, example is Wang Mingde's (fl. 1674) *Dulü peixi* (A bodkin to unravel the code). Wang, a prominent jurist working in the Board of Punishments, inserted into the final part of this highly theoretical text his *Supplement to The Washing Away of Wrongs*, a forensic manual that becomes a space where the personal erupts in interesting ways. It is here that we learn something of Wang's childhood and where the figure of Wang as meticulous jurist is transformed into a story-teller and memoirist, interspersing his recommendations for cures and advice on how to read forensic signs with tales of ghosts and

---

75   This essay is greatly indebted to the warm creative energies and inspiration of Milena Doleželová-Velingerová. It was she who initiated my interest in the seventeenth century and helped train me to read between the lines. The shared project with Milena and my dear *tongxue* Hua Laura Wu on the great fiction commentators Jin Shengtan, Mao Lun, Mao Zonggang, and Zhang Zhupo was deeply exciting and engaging. Milena shared her hospitality and knowledge with us, and created unforgettable memories. When I last saw her at the Atlanta AAS in 2008 we talked about my work on Wang Mingde, and I know she would have appreciated the complexities and hybridities of his fascinating text.

foxes and memories of his own and family servants' injuries and illnesses. Wang's anecdotes combine natural observation, experimentation, practice, hearsay, and memory. Much is elided: there is no journey toward self-knowledge, no introspection, nor do the momentous events of the Qing conquest impinge. Instead Wang's experiences and values are linked specifically and associatively to the forensic problems he outlines in a format that is simultaneously liberating and confining. In this chapter, I interrogate the generic boundaries of autobiography through an examination of Wang's forensic life.

SUPPLEMENT TO DEATH BY BURNING

In the long quote below, taken from "Supplement to Death By Burning" in Juan 8 of the *Dulü Peixi*, Wang Mingde combines a detailed description of a complex forensic procedure with a reference to his father Wang Yongji (1600–1659) whose technical expertise amazed onlookers and provided evidence to convict a murderer. This narrative brings together many of the tropes shaping Wang Mingde's "forensic life": memory, specialist knowledge, a mystery solved, and signs of trauma or violence. In this chapter, these tropes re-appear in discussions of case histories, the supernatural, and childhood memories.

There is a type of extremely wicked person who, after killing someone, will use fire to destroy [the body], so that there is no corpse or bones for examination. What method can then be used to determine the crime [and punishment]? The time when someone was killed must be carefully investigated. At what place was the destruction by fire undertaken? Unfortunately, unless the place where the corpse was destroyed by fire is established, the evidence clarified, and the body's wounds examined on the spot, there will be no way to establish the facts. Whenever such a doubtful case is encountered, if the place where the burning was done has in fact been established, set up a site to examine the corpse and bring the perpetrator there to bear witness by personally indicating the place. Have the grass scythed and completely cleared away, burn a lot of firewood at a very high heat and scatter several pecks of sesame seeds over the fire and then sweep up with a broom. If this is truly the place where the burning [of the corpse] took place, then the oil within the sesame seeds will penetrate the earth and form the outline of a human body and the sesame seeds will collect in the places where there are injuries, so that their shape, whether large or small, round or square, long or short, slanted or straight, will appear. Nothing will coagulate in the places where there are no injuries. However, even if the shape of the injury is visible but there is no way to see the scars, this is still not sufficient to fully have cognizance of the perpetrator's heart. Therefore, remove the collected sesame seeds and, in the place where the outline of the body is, burn a fire fiercely and then throw water over it; then with another fierce fire steam and decoct vinegar and swiftly cover the spot with a brightly lacquered gold table,[76] wait a moment and then take it up for examination. On the surface of the table will be seen the complete outline of a human figure and all details of the injuries and scars will be visible … . When my honored father was serving in Hangzhou, a villain killed someone in the city and burned the body in front of the Examination Grounds. My father got the perpetrator and personally investigated the site of the burning to establish [his guilt]. Everyone described this as a miracle then, but I did not ask my honored father at that point how he had achieved it. So now I have carefully written a supplement in order to provide aid when there is no corpse available for examination.[77]

The early Qing jurist Wang Mingde's influential *A Bodkin to Unravel the Code* is an original, meticulous readers' handbook for legal practitioners to master and implement the new Qing code. Organized into eight *juan*, Wang's lengthy treatise provides a detailed guide to central legal issues that departs from the standard commentarial line-by-line explication of the statutes. Instead the text offers users a clear distillation of knowledge of Ming and early Qing legal codes and their antecedents, introducing key concepts, memorization tools, cross-referencing devices, technical apparatuses, and charts for procedural regulations. Unusual in structure and scope, Wang's text is invaluable for its meticulous guidance on legal minutiae but it is also a profound meditation on the ideals of the imperial legal system. His voluminous array of prefatory materials includes a history of legal philosophy and theory that celebrates the centrality of (Confucianized) law in ordering the state. He deals with precise definitions of terms and their importance in adjudication, but he also does not forget the importance of stories—to provide a human-centred focus to remind the practitioner that at the basis of law are the people affected by that law. With his emphasis on the moral necessity to get it right—to follow due process—he is underlining the duty of legal practitioners to be careful. Careless, ignorant, or biased application of the law has severe consequences and causes miscarriages of justice. Wang Mingde stresses again and again that the law deals in matters of life and death; he therefore insists on accountability, informed and meticulous investigation, and, most vitally, impartiality. The legal practitioner must, above all, set aside bias and self-interest and serve the vulnerable by ensuring that victims, alive or dead, see justice done. To this end, his final chapter, *juan* 8, uses the Song dynasty forensic text *Xiyuan lu* (The Washing Away of Wrongs)[78] as a means to stress the vital importance of forensics in solving crimes but also to underpin his own strongly held belief in righting wrongs.

---

76   This refers to Jinzhou lacquer. See Will 2007: 87; Huang 1984: 375.
77   See Wang Mingde 2001: 314; Sung Tz'u 1981: 39.
78   For a translation into English, see Sung Tz'u 1981.

The preface to Wang Mingde's *Dulü peixi* is dated 1674 and a postface by Wang is dated 1676.[79] There is no official biography of Wang in the *Qing Shi Gao* (Draft history of the Qing), nor is there evidence of other writings by him. [80] However, it is possible to glean quite a lot of detail about his life from the prefaces and text of his book, as well as from local gazetteers, and, indirectly, from the life of his father, Wang Yongji (jinshi 1625; d. 1659), who went over to the Qing in 1644, when Wang Mingde would have been in his twenties. Wang senior became a high-ranking official under the Shunzhi emperor (r. 1644–1661). A native of Gaoyou (Jiangsu), Wang Yongji served during the Ming as a magistrate in Datian, Fujian, and in Hangzhou, where he is still remembered for his role in building a sea wall and providing granaries for famine relief. His career under the Qing was meteoric, reaching the heights of Grand Secretary twice, vice-president and president of the Board of War, as well as holding high-ranking positions in the Board of Revenue in charge of Yellow River and Grand Canal projects, in the Board of Works and the Censorate, while suffering periodic demotions for accusations of involvement in cliques and examination scandals. After his death, he was posthumously given the titles of Junior Guardian and Grand Guardian of the Heir Apparent and President of the Board of Works (Hummel 1943: 845–846; Wakeman 1985: 2: 909 *passim*). Wang Yongji has a biography in the *Erchen zhuan* (Ministers who served two dynasties) and is described by Wakeman as one of the most able of the "turncoat" officials. His son, Wang Mingde, certainly endorses that opinion—his accounts of his childhood memories of Wang Yongji's actions as a magistrate combine deep admiration and wonder at his abilities.[81]

Wang Mingde makes several references to his father, mother, and grandparents in *juan 8*, in his *Supplement to The Washing Away of Wrongs*, which, in addition to providing a vehicle for his ethical concern for justice, becomes a space where personal memory, somatic associations, and the supernatural intertwine in fascinating ways. Wang Mingde's childhood memories of his father's official exploits and experiences in far-flung posts jostle with anecdotes of Gaoyou neighbors' troubles and tales of the strange. He records the remedies and first aid he and his family dispense and reveals his specialist knowledge of both medicine and forensics. In this chapter, I present the prominent legal scholar as a storyteller and anecdotist whose narratives of

---

79 See Wang Mingde 2001.
80 Wilt Idema notes that it is the literary collection that was the "preferred format" for elite men and women to leave behind "an account of themselves" (Idema 2011: 231). Wang's literary preferences seem to be for fiction rather than poetry and his reminiscences are anecdotal sketches rather than lyrical expressions of the self.
81 Wang's account of his father is admiring but is not designed as a standard posthumous biographical record by a filial son intent on enshrining and enhancing the family's reputation through extolling his parent's illustrious official career. Instead it is Wang Yongji as district magistrate whom his son recalls and emulates.

bodily harm are linked associatively to the forensic text to which they are bound. I suggest that the reader of Wang's unusual hybrid text will discover within its lines an assertion of selfhood, a form of non-linear autobiography that does not fit any standard generic shapes or unified textual registers and that displays elements of memoir, fiction, *biji*, case history, anecdotes of the strange, and legal-medical-scientific observation.

While Pei-Yi Wu's 1990 study of Chinese autobiography continues to be an essential source, studies of Chinese life writing—autobiographical and biographical—have grown enormously over the past twenty-five years, particularly in regard to women's lives. Joan Judge and Ying Hu (2011: 287–289) provide an annotated appendix of traditional auto/biographical genres that encompass many variations of formats in which aspects of the self are depicted or voiced. A broad range of texts and variants from official biography, annalistic biography, hagiography, epitaph, necrology, letters, inscriptions, colophons, *biji*, commentary, diaries, records of merits and demerits, prefaces, and, vitally, poetry all offer entrance points to narrations of selfhood, both public and private.[82] The late Ming and particularly the early to mid-seventeenth-century were, as Wu suggests, periods of unprecedented self-writing fueled by intellectual trends encouraging individual expression and, more tragically, by a widespread compulsion to record the traumas of the Qing conquest and loss of the Ming.[83] Wu (1990: 235), and Martin Huang after him, point to the retreat from individualist expression as Qing orthodoxy became entrenched and it was both dangerous and ideologically unsound to continue valorizing late Ming sensibilities.[84] Wang Mingde was a man of the Qing: his father changed sides and rose high in service to the conquerors; Mingde himself worked in the capital on the new Qing code, and he was praised for his loyal and righteous death at the hands of anti-Qing rebels. His account of life in the late Ming elides all mention of the deep malaise and grief of the times[85] and of the conquest itself: an expression of his generation's coming to terms with *realpolitik* most certainly, but nonetheless a notable absence.

Wang Mingde's *zi* was Liangshi and his *hao*, Jinqiao, and like his father he came from Gaoyou, Jiangsu province. Pu Zhiqiang (2004: 217*ff*), the civil rights lawyer now disbarred in the PRC, in his masters' thesis on Wang estimates he was born in the final years of the Tianqi era (around 1621–1627) and died circa

---

82   See Drysburgh/Dauncey 2013 for an overview of Chinese life writing, especially 21–56.

83   See Lynn Struve's (2004, 2009) many magisterial studies of this period and its concomitant outpourings of grief and heroic resistance. For a particular case study that examines one man's deployment of different autobiographical genres to give expression to his loss, see Grace S. Fong 2009.

84   Martin Huang 1995: 1–2, 8. Huang sees a move toward a fictional representation of self.

85   Lynn Struve (2004) discusses an extraordinary example of the horrors endured by one victim of the conquest of similar background to Wang Mingde.

1681. Pu suggests that because his education was disrupted by the rebellions and wars leading to the Qing conquest, Wang did not pass the requisite exams to become an official but instead, through his father's status as an important Qing official, became a *yinsheng*, or student by inheritance (Pu 2004: 220). He served in the Board of Punishments as a Department Director (*langzhong*) for several years (probably 1668–1672) (Pu 2004: 222) before being dispatched to take up a post in water control in Shaanxi (1673 onwards) (Pu 2004: 223). His book was probably written during his years in the capital, apparently a time of comparative peace and productivity for him in between the turmoil shaping his early and final years (Pu 2004; He Qinhua 2000).

Wang went to serve as prefect in Huguang (Hanyangfu) when Provincial Military Commander Tan Hong rebelled for the second time in 1680–1681.[86] Wang Mingde was in charge of transporting grain during this crisis and fled to Sichuan when he was pressured to join the rebels, swearing to kill himself rather than serve them. He was saved from an unsuccessful drowning attempt and later shaved his hair and temporarily became a monk. Qing troops defeated and wiped out Tan Hong and his followers in 1681 (Pu 2004). In the aftermath, Wang Mingde fled homeward, traveling in great hardship through Sichuan over wild mountains and through steep valleys by night, so badly damaging his hands and feet that his servant had to carry him for miles.[87] Wang died en route, and his biography in his hometown gazetteer comes under the section for the Loyal and Heroic (*zhonglie zhuan*) because he died in service to the Qing. It is interesting to note that Wang's servant, Liu Zhenyu, is mentioned by name in this account, a telling detail that suggests both the high esteem in which Liu's loyalty to his master was regarded, and also that the writers of the local gazetteer were familiar with Wang's story in greater detail that the bare outline provided here. The biography describes Wang in standard terms as upright and straightforward. We also know that Wang Mingde's second son, Wang Xinzhan, collated and corrected the manuscript of his father's text, suggesting that he too had some legal expertise (He 2000: 2: 443; Wang 2001 *passim*).

In a postface to the (undated) edition held by Zhou Houyu of Jiangsu, Wang Mingde's text is described (and praised) briefly in terms of its legal contributions and scope before the author goes on to comment on the fictional aspects or fictional turn (*xiaoshuo jiayan*) he finds intruding into Wang's *Supplement to The Washing Away of Wrongs*.[88] Wang's inclusion of the famous medical forensics text in his final chapter, *juan* 8, was significant for future legal knowledge, introducing it to a new audience. After Wang Ming-

---

86 Pu Zhiqiang (2004: 224) estimates Wang first went to serve there in 1678.
87 Wang Mingde 2001: 1–2. See also He Qinhua 2000: 2: 443.
88 See Wang Mingde 2001: 389. See also Sung Tz'u 1981.

de, it became standard practice to attach the edited forensic manual to the Qing Code, using mainly Wang Mingde's version in addition to some others.[89] Wang (2001: 308–309) notes in his introduction to *juan* 8 after his inclusion of the "original text" (*yuanwen*) that he had heard of *The Washing Away of Wrongs* early in life but only came upon an incomplete copy in Wang Kentang's commentary of the Ming Code many years later.[90]

SUPPLEMENT TO THE WASHING AWAY OF WRONGS

Wang's *juan* 8 is a lengthy text divided into two sections. He provides "the original text" of *The Washing Away of Wrongs* that is similar to but much briefer than the version translated by Brian McKnight from chapter 3 to halfway through chapter 5. He added his own lengthy philosophical preface and afterword and in between repeats sections of the original text followed by a commentary in small characters and a supplement in large characters pertaining to that section. His commentaries and supplements (over twenty in number) vary in length from a few lines to several pages. He states that he is emulating the methodology of the great statecraft writer Qiu Jun (1420–1495), author of the massive statecraft tome *Daxue yanyi bu* (Supplement to the extended meaning of *The Great Learning*) (Wang 2001: 311). However, while Qiu Jun cites directly from particular classics based on specific topics related to ruling the state, follows with quotes from later commentators, and then adumbrates on those topics and commentaries with his own opinions, he does not, as does Wang Mingde, use this forum to insert his own memories, descriptions of his father's and his own exploits in the fields of detection and medicine, nor make excursions into the realms of the supernatural.

Wang's *Supplement* is an uneasy but endlessly fascinating mixture of the practically useful and the idiosyncratic. While his re-introduction of the forensics text into legal discourse is lauded and his knowledge of the impact of violence on the human body acknowledged to be as specialist and authorita-

---

89 See Pierre-Etienne Will, cited in http://lsc.chineselegalculture.org/Documents/E-Library?ID=394

90 Wang says "over 40 years later," which would have made him very young on first hearing of it. Wang Kentang's text was used by Wang Mingde as a basis for his own study of the Code while deviating from the commentarial structure of the earlier book. See Wang Kentang (*jinshi* 1589), *Wang Yibu xiansheng Lüli jianshi* (Mr. Wang Yibu's [Kentang] Commentaries to [The Great Ming Code]). See He Qinhua (2006: 2: 231–254) for details of extant editions and biographical data on this highly influential late Ming jurist. Wang Kentang's father, Wang Qiao (*jinshi* 1547), played a role in the composition of Wang Kentang's volume. Wang Mingde refers repeatedly to Wang Kentang's work throughout his text, often to elaborate on or to differ from his predecessor's opinions in the context of precedents and variations in law from Ming to Qing. Also see, *The Great Ming Code: Da Ming Lü* 2005: 296–297; and Qiu 2008.

tive in nature as the foregoing legal chapters of his book, contemporaries and later scholars have had difficulty knowing how to come to terms with the fictional, supernatural, and personal asides that increasingly dominate the last chapter. What begins as a fairly chaste description and expansion of aspects he feels are missing from the brief entries in the original *The Washing Away of Wrongs* increasingly veers towards the non-canonical.

His supplemental sections vary in length, but certain parts inspire longer interlinked anecdotes and descriptions than others. In particular, his discussions connected to the sections on suicide by hanging, drowning, death by fire, scalding wounds, injuries from falling, being crushed or kicked, poisoning, acupuncture, and lightning take on lives of their own, reminiscent of Jin Shengtan's (1610?–1661) famous list of things that cause him delight slipped into his 1656 commentary to the *Xi xiang ji* (Story of the western wing). In contrast to Jin, however, the anecdotes, reminiscences, and strange tales Wang provides in his supplements have a certain internal logic, spinning off associatively from the main topic, sometimes hewing closely to it and sometimes in a more attenuated fashion. Almost invariably the links between his narratives are based on the physical effects, supernatural outcomes, and remedies for the categories of harm outlined in the forensics text. And while the original text deals overwhelmingly with the dead body and signs of injury causing death, Wang Mingde provides numerous examples of first aid, cures, medical interventions, and lives saved, in addition to his insistence on ensuring that correct diagnoses for cause of death are found to avoid miscarriages of justice and further deaths. If someone dies mysteriously and his family cries out for justice and revenge, Wang will invariably prove that death to be accidental—thus reiterating his constant stress on the need to be careful and impartial when investigating a crime.

Embedded within Wang's two sets of commentaries—the small character extrapolations of the original text and the extended supplements (and indeed across the *Dulü peixi* as a whole)—are a variety of different overlapping registers or genres that provide hints of the individual emerging between the lines. James Olney likens memory to Ariadne's thread, forever hidden but revealing the shape of the process of a person's *bios*, or lifetime: "The thread necessarily remains hidden, unconscious, unknown to the individual until the time when it rises to consciousness *after the fact* to present itself to him as recollections that he can then trace back ... to discover the shape that was all the time gradually and unconsciously forming itself" (Olney 1980: 240–241). While Wang Mingde's self-representations work towards no particular *telos* or goal nor is the reader given a chronological account of a life from birth toward old age, the layered strands of narrative circle, repeat, trace backward and forward, and link disparate moments into something like an eclectic whole. Anecdotes, fragments, traces, associations—all linked within the exigencies of this forensic text—combine to give shape to someone who was a legal and medical expert, a believer in the worlds of spirits and ghosts, a storyteller, and an strongly ethical individual who insisted on averting wrongful judgments. As Wang (2001: 310–311) makes clear, bodies speak, bones tell stories, and those words give up their meanings to the discerning reader.

CASE HISTORIES

As befitting a commentary to a forensics manual, Wang Mingde's supplementary material combines medical-legal details that begin by confirming the earlier text's conclusions and add extra examples Wang seems to have derived from either his father's or his own experience dealing with cases. His additions or recommendations vary from insisting on the use of a new Hangzhou oiled yellow umbrella to shade the site of the investigation of a body as his father was wont to employ (Wang 2001: 317) to adumbrating on different kinds of fatal poisons omitted in the earlier text (346–355). His examples are frequently couched as anecdotes, or what might be described as "cases" in the way Charlotte Furth (2007: 129) defines the earliest examples of medical narratives: "any instance bracketed off from surrounding text and presented as a set of particulars." Furth sees a development in types of case history over time from the earliest "invitations to wonder" (129) to more complex classificatory arguments that work through analogical reasoning based on taxonomies, exemplars, and precedent (17). Wang uses hypothetical cases in some of his earlier *juan* to provide models or grids for calculating precise levels of punishment and allocation of degrees of guilt between offenders. These examples rarely seem to be drawn from real life cases he might have encountered; rather, they tend to present more theoretical situations couched in an "if … then …" formula (*juan* 5 and 7). Wang stresses that his study of the Code is collaborative work, acknowledging earlier scholars and thirty-eight colleagues in the Board of Punishments with whom he discussed many aspects of his work. With certain important and striking exceptions,[91] the main body of the *Dulü peixi* is a careful, meticulous, and objective study of how to master the Code. This objectivity, however, breaks down in the final chapter.

---

91   Wang introduces into *juan* 3 (which deals with serious crimes) a discussion of sorcerous, voodoo like practices utilizing mud images, *gu* poison, and fetuses, to be found in Fujian, Guangdong, Sichuan and Henan, and mentions that his father was active in squashing the use of *gu* poison for revenge in Fujian when serving as an official (Wang 2001: 60–61). Further on he inserts a Newgate Calendar style narrative of a thief who blames his mother for his downfall (298–299). In addition, his prefatorial emphases on key concepts as mnemonic devices and sections on how to read the Code are reminiscent of the seventeenth century fiction commentaries by Jin Shengtan and others.

In the last chapter, Wang turns from the hypothetical to the personal, drawing from both legal and medical examples to supplement the forensic text's lacunae but also providing "invitations to wonder." He insists that his examples are true: based on personal or family experience, learned from a neighbor or colleague, or local history backed up by confirmation. These are all things I have heard or seen, he argues. This repeated formula and brisk, no-nonsense style of the narratives, providing protagonists' names, place, and often year of the event, resemble the *zhiguai* (records of the strange) as a form of reportage or "unofficial history" (Zeitlin 2007: 171).

Judith Zeitlin, in her essay on the case histories of the late Ming doctor Sun Yikui, notes the strong resemblances between the reportage style of the *zhiguai* genre and the medical case history: "These are brief, anecdotal accounts of events, purportedly witnessed or heard about by the author, which are written in simple prose, mainly unadorned by literary figures such as allusion or metaphor. The narrative moves at a fast clip; dialogue is often included, and evaluative or interpretative comments are occasionally tacked on at the end" (Zeitlin 2007: 171–172). The difference lies in the role of the author-narrator who is "presented as the main actor in the story," the "chief protagonist" whose credibility and specialist knowledge is the key issue at stake (171–172). Wang Mingde is often the chief protagonist of his anecdotes, particularly those involving medical knowledge. The more supernatural or strange accounts are usually about someone else—a neighbor, an acquaintance, or an official his father knew—and are recounted mainly in the third-person objective historian narratorial style common to the *zhiguai* genre. In both types of narrative Wang is drawing on literary or specialist models to give expression to his experience and interests. Zeitlin points to the various affinities between late Ming detective fiction and drama and the medical case, particularly in terms of providing evidence and proving earlier, mistaken suppositions to be wrong (173). "From a narratological point of view," she writes, "the entrance of the narrator-doctor-hero onto a case after it has already been bungled by a previous incompetent doctor is one of the most common plot types in the Ming medical case" (181).

Wang stresses that he is not a medical specialist and often introduces into his accounts the figure of an old experienced doctor who either confirms his diagnosis or who offers useful advice or cures. Nonetheless, it is often Wang who saves the day, giving first aid to injured servants or drowning people, or advising on safe herbal treatments for childbirth problems when physicians are stumped (Wang 2001: 352–355). Zeitlin (2007: 177) argues that Sun Yikui's case histories "can be read … as something of an autobiographical project" in their cumulative effect, a form of "self-promotion as self-fashioning" (176) similar to a gentleman's *bieji* (178). Wang's self-fashioning project is rather different—scattered associatively across one chapter, offering hints or suggestions of the author as hero-doctor-detective, but also providing stories of his father's exploits as an official (rather than in a more personal vein) that by extension add to the consequence of his proud son.

Wang Yongji's complex and apparently miraculous procedure to reveal the wounds on a body destroyed by fire and therefore catch a criminal quoted at the beginning of this essay is the longest of such accounts. Wang follows this with his own observations of how grass and other plants grow more luxuriantly where bodies have been burned and take on the outline of those bodies (Wang 2001: 335). He tells of returning several years later to the site where his father in Shunzhi 8 or 9 oversaw the mass killing by soldiers of a heterodox sect that had taken over an abandoned temple in the deep mountains and duped foolish members of the local populace. Wang notes that among the wild grass could be seen the outlines of bodies, providing proof of the killings. He adds that if the burning takes place on mountainsides or rocks, then the cracks and splits in the rock can also serve as visual evidence (335). Wang's *Supplement to Death by Burning* is one of the longest in the chapter (333-339) and offers the full gamut of descriptions of fire's destructive power and strange effects, alternating between natural observation and detection, records of acquaintances' house fires, and speculations on fiery punishments for immorality (337).

If fire captures Wang's imagination so, too, does poison (346-355). The author's childhood experience in the semi-tropical wilds of Fujian and Guangdong when his father served there seems to have been a catalyst for his interest in dangerous plants (347 and elsewhere). However, the focus in his supplement on poison is not on deliberate poisoning as a crime but accidental poisoning that can be mistakenly believed to be deliberate. In one section, when discussing the historical example of the wife of a Han general poisoning an empress (355), he is skeptical, arguing that it is much more difficult for a woman to undertake poisoning than a man because she would inevitably have to use accomplices to buy and administer the poison (355). He warns against the habits of drinking tea that has stood for a few days in warm seasons, tea that comes from a pot with too much lead in its composition, or water from a vase that has held flowers (348). This last bit of information allows Wang, with the help of a doctor's confirmation, to solve the case of mysterious death of one of his friends whose family was considering a lawsuit (348-349).

Two friends of Wang spent a pleasant evening together at one of their homes, drinking until dawn. The guest slept over in an elegantly appointed room but was found dead in the morning. The dead man's relatives felt things were amiss and were on the verge of making an official accusation, but decided it was a case of bad luck. They raised it with Wang who denied categorically that it was a question of ill fortune. He carefully investigated the circumstances surrounding the death. Apparently the body had been found half in bed and half leaning off it. A flower vase was on the couch beside the bed and several stems of the flowers were scattered around. On enquiring what plant it was, Wang was told that it was Winter Sweet (*lamei*) (Chimonanthus, Yellow Plum, Calycanthus fragrans or praecox).[92] "I said, 'I have heard that Winter Sweet is exceptionally poisonous and its seeds are like those of the croton plant. He must have been exceptionally thirsty after drinking so much and therefore drank the water from the vase.' I enquired if the vase was still there. 'Yes, it is still there.' I quickly dragged the respected friend of the deceased with me to investigate and found that there were only a few drops left in the vase." An elderly doctor present confirmed the dangers of drinking Winter Sweet water from a vase and directed that the mouth of the deceased should be examined to see if it was slightly open, because all fragrant and colored flowering plants have an unpalatable bitter taste. This was the case, and thus the suspicions of the assembled company were dispelled and the lawsuit halted (349).

Further on in the supplement on poisoning, Wang narrates the mysterious case of the death of a local dignitary hosted by a gentleman named Tian in the final year of the Wanli era (1620) in the Ming in Fujian. Mr. Tian had arranged a banquet in a newly acquired garden pavilion and all was going well—it was summer, and the lotuses were in full bloom. However, less than halfway through the banquet, the guest was stricken dumb. Believing he had drunk too much, his host had him carried home, but he died soon afterward. Because the county was notorious for *gu* poisoning, the host was widely accused of poisoning the guest for an unspecified revenge motive. The accused was tried, but they failed to get a verdict without evidence of his guilt; the case was classified as "doubtful" and remained unsolved for years.

It was not until over ten years later that a new official, finding the circumstances suspicious, re-opened the case. After thoroughly questioning those present at the banquet and investigating the circumstances, plants, and garden pavilion where it was held, he learned that the accused had no ill intentions toward the deceased and thus had no desire to wreak vengeance by poisoning him. He went to the long deserted garden with the magistrate and local people to undertake a public investigation. He proved *in situ* that the garden pavilion was the habitat of a poisonous snake that had dropped down from the rafters and bitten the victim. And since this was such a public and careful investigation, all suspicions were cleared and long-standing wrongs washed away. Wang heard this story as a child when his father was serving

---

92   http://www.efloras.org/florataxon.aspx?flora_id=3&taxon_id=200008496: the plant is used medicinally but some sites suggest its seeds can be toxic. Also: http://www.efloras.org/florataxon.aspx?flora_id=610&taxon_id=200008496.

in Datian. He comments that only a true gentleman would have investigated so carefully so long after the event (351). In both cases of suspicious poisoning Wang, as protagonist and as the narrator of an old anecdote, uses the motif of the hero-detective to prove that neither case was deliberate, thus washing away the wrongs of false accusations.

SIGNS AND WONDERS

Wang Mingde makes no secret of his belief in ghosts, heavenly requital, demons, and animal spirits. In his supplement on suicide by hanging, which he begins by giving first aid suggestions for saving the life of someone found in time (320), he soon devolves into a discussion of the tradition of hanged ghosts (*yigui*) who hope to induce other victims to take their place. He acknowledges that this is the stuff of vulgar or deluded folklore that a gentleman would find merely amusing. However, he then cites the famous dictum that Confucius did not speak of the strange (*zi buyu guai*) and argues that the Master may not have *spoken* of it, but the strange was already a common part of the world and Confucius certainly was not saying that it did not exist (321).

He follows this statement with the semi-slapstick tale of a certain Mr. Zhang from Wang's hometown of Gaoyou who fell asleep while his wife remained awake. A thief peered in the bedroom window, awaiting the chance to climb inside, and saw a female ghost by the bedside, crying and pleading with the wife, who sighed loudly and started weeping. As the thief watched intently, the wife prepared to hang herself as the ghost expressed her gratitude. The thief cried out, but the husband was snoring soundly and did not hear, so the thief had no choice but to find a bamboo stick from the eaves and poke it through the window to strike at the ghost. The husband awoke, and the thief shouted at him to open the door so he could help rescue the wife. The wife had no idea why she was trying to kill herself, the husband did not know who was shouting outside the house, and the thief had forgotten that he had come there to steal. Later, they found the spectral trace of a rope on a beam near the bed (321). Wang quotes a saying that the world is large enough that anything is possible and who can tell what might or might not be real?

Many other examples of the supernatural in the *Supplement* point to Wang's acceptance of a world that encompasses the strange. In his lengthy disquisition on avoiding poisonous miasmas and mold found in clothing, neglected courtyards, long-locked rooms, and closed spaces (349–351), he describes the eerie discovery of the perfectly preserved skeletons of three large fox cubs in a sealed chest inside a storage room that had been locked for over 100 years. The chest had no obvious entry or exit point and had originally stored material, none of which remained. No explanation or moral is given—Wang frames the story simply as another example of the reality of strange phenomena that cannot be explained. As with many of Wang's anecdotes of the strange, this dates back to the late Ming and was verified by a family neighbor.

Another such anecdote with similar dating and verification describes the tragically ironic example of a fire in the imperial stables for which the attendant in charge was punished with immediate execution. The attendant had taken over his duty the very day of the fire and by rights the blame lay with the former attendant. However, due to the intervention of a certain Mr. Chen Baiyu from Gaoyou, who followed the doctrine of building up ledgers of merit (despised by Wang),[93] the former attendant was let off and the new one executed. On the day of the execution, the former attendant fell ill and his body was covered with purple stripes and red-hot marks. Relentless pain caused him to cry out day and night without cease, but there was no blood or swelling, only crimson markings resembling those made by execution by a thousand cuts (*lingchi*). Mr. Chen visited the former attendant, who said that he would die within three days and that Mr. Chen would also not escape the same fate. And this came about exactly as predicted. Wang writes: "I know for certain that this happened." He regrets that Mr. Chen—a true gentleman—had been taken in by the false doctrine of ledgers of merit and likens his decision to save the life of the former attendant at the expense of the new one to Mencius' parable of the king who spares a sacrificial ox but allows a sheep to be slaughtered in its stead. The king feels compassion for the ox, but cannot extend that compassion to others, in particular to his own people (Mencius 1970: 55; Wang 2001: 336-337).

Wang's lengthiest ghost story, found in the afterword to the *Supplement to The Washing Away of Wrongs* (382-383), bears a resemblance to a tale by his younger contemporary Pu Songling (Bailey 2009). Written in a more elegant style than most of his rather workman-like stories of the strange and with no reference to the standard formulae of verifiable details, this tale of a ghost seeking revenge on her murderer once again takes up the theme of washing away of wrongs studded throughout Wang's text. The murderer, a handsome young scholar, was on the point of being released by a sympathetic official who could not believe so refined and elegant a gentleman could be guilty of such a crime. The ghost appears to the official and accuses him of covering up a wrong that must be righted. It is only after the official is driven mad that the

---

93   Lynn Struve (2009) points to the important role played by the habit of keeping ledgers of merit and demerit to the practice and development of self-writing in the late Ming. It is possible that Wang Mingde's dislike of this genre was linked to the common sentiment of the time that late Ming forms of individualistic expression and pre-occupation with the self were significant factors in that dynasty's decline and fall.

case is re-opened and the young scholar's guilt established. Wang uses this story to comment on the absolute necessity for impartiality in judgments and for the rights of victims to be heard. Here Wang's sentiments closely resemble those found in contemporary fiction and drama where justice must be seen to be done and Heavenly *bao*, or requital, restores balance.

WRITTEN ON THE BODY: CHILDHOOD SCARS, CHILDHOOD MEMORIES

When I was around 4 or 5 years old I accompanied my honored father when he went to take up a position in Fujian. We were near Wulin [Hangzhou]. On the boat was a copper-lined stove with a mud base, used for making tea. It was the height of summer and everyone was very lightly clad. The stove was alight all day long to supply everyone with tea. It was red hot and the water kept a-boil. I was playing and lost my footing, and fell with my back against the side of the stove. The boiling water spilled out and although I was quickly rescued, my back was already scalded [cooked.] My honored Mother, Madame Zou, was very strict and decisive by nature and was still angrily blaming me, but my Father stopped her [?], wanting to find a doctor. However, the boat was traveling through a remote area, and there was no doctor to be found. Therefore my honored Mother ordered that [the afore-mentioned] remedy be used: [a mixture of ice pellets and two or three parts of musk combined together into a fine consistency and spooned into the open shell of freshwater pearl mussels. The flesh of the mussels is then made into a paste, placed in the shell, and the musk and ice mixture added to it once again. A chicken feather is used to smear the paste onto the scalds.] It was very easy to get mussels from the river ... and in a few days the pain subsided and in a couple of months everything returned to normal. To this day, I still have traces on the skin of my back which show up whiter than other parts. My father was amazed at the cure and asked my mother how it was derived. (Wang 2001: 340–341)

Wang Mingde's childhood memories are, within the context of the text in which he chose to enshrine them, inextricably linked to forms of trauma and violence. His memories are written on the body—scars and somatic associations that remind him of the past, but perhaps also serve as Freudian "screen memories" to shield deeper memories.[94] Wang's choice of a forensic text to accommodate representations of his self is telling—but within the welter of injuries, deaths, harm, and dangerous beings, much remains unsaid, unexpressed. Patrick J. Hutton, in his *History as an Art of Memory*,

---

94 "Screen memories are mnemic images that displace deeper, hidden memories. By comparison with the memories that they shield, they are of lesser consequence, arouse fewer emotions, and relate to more recent experience" (Hutton 1993: 67).

links Wordsworth and Freud together in a discussion of the ways in which childhood memories can stand out with "an inexplicable vividness" to offer ways of understanding something vital about the self (1993: 67). Freud's auto-biography, according to Hutton, presents a public persona, the way in which he wished to be "recognized by the world" (62). It is in his case studies that a reader can find scattered "vignettes of his personal experience with doubt and fear" (60).

Similarly, Wordsworth's childhood memories as described in *The Prelude* are what the poet calls "spots of time" that evoke "vivid images of troubling psychological intrusions into otherwise ordinary days: his discovery of the ruins of a gibbet in a hollow in the countryside at age five," seeing a dead man in the distance at eight, waiting fruitlessly at a crossroads for his father to return home and his father dying soon after. "All of these images were me-mentoes of mortality suddenly and magically interjected into the course of his everyday life and, as such, laden with wonder and fear," as Hutton puts it (1993: 52–55).

Wang Mingde spent his childhood observing his father's work as a mag-istrate. He travelled to remote and dangerous regions, absorbing tales of poisonings, ghosts, and fire. He suffered illness and injury and helped others who fell ill or suffered physical harm. He lived through the great, violent, tragic upheavals of the Ming fall and Qing conquest. His father chose to join the winning side and Wang Mingde was, by all accounts, including his own, a good servant of the Qing—not for him the passionate anguish of martyrdom or torn loyalties shown by so many of his peers. There is no introspection, no doubt or fear, no lyrical revelations of the self to be found in his *Supplement to The Washing Away of Wrongs*. His narratives mark physical, somatic "spots of time" rather than emotional expressions. And yet, it is precisely all those bodily associations that beg the question: why choose this form to talk about yourself? Why interweave your stories into a framework of wounds, scars, and death?

Wang Mingde does not give us direct answers to these questions, but it is possible to trace a way through the maze he has left for us by using the con-necting threads of memory and story. As suggested before, Wang's *Supplement* to the famous forensic text provides descriptions of cures, remedies, first aid, and solutions to mysteries that allow wrongs to be righted and order to be re-stored. One brief memory of his childhood is of helping his grandmother chip off bits of silver from an ingot and cutting his finger so badly that the blood flowed copiously. His grandmother quickly puts a salve on the wound and binds it up tightly so that no blood could run out or water enter it. It healed quickly, and the finger was just as before. Although it was just a tiny remedy, he writes, it was very effective, just as the work of a magistrate should be, so that the injustices of life and death can be resolved (332). Wang's parents and grandmother and Wang himself find cures and solutions to save the day. His fascination with the strange, his desire to save lives, and his delight in the role law has played to regulate the world (Wang 2001: 5–7) combine to suggest a man who found a way to deal with the dangers surrounding him.

6 FROM "CINEMATIC NOVEL" TO "LITERARY CINEMA": A CROSS-GENRE, CROSS-CULTURAL READING OF ZHANG YIMOU'S *JUDOU* AND *TO LIVE*

LI ZENG

Among all existing literary genres, as Kamilla Elliott (2003: 113) observes, novels "have been pronounced 'cinematic' whatever decade or style in which they were written." Historically, from pre-cinematic times to the twentieth century, novels written by authors like Charles Dickens, Thomas Hardy, James Joyce, and F. Scott Fitzgerald displayed in one way or another a strong authorial visual sense and possessed certain cinematic devices, "such as the flashback and parallel editing between stories" (Magill 1980: 74). Perhaps mainly because of "the camera-eye" that Leon Edel said novelists since the nineteenth century have cultivated (Elliott 2003: 122), novels have found favor with filmmakers as vehicles for their own artistic creativity. If there exist many filmic adaptations of great novels in the West, it is equally true, especially since the end of the Cultural Revolution, that novels in China have inspired Chinese filmmakers, such as the internationally renowned film director Zhang Yimou, and become an inexhaustible resource for them.

Indeed, almost all of Zhang Yimou's internationally acclaimed feature films, such as *Red Sorghum* (Hong gaoliang), *Judou*, *Raise the Red Lantern* (Dahong denglong gaogao gua), *To Live* (Huozhe), and so forth, are adaptations of popular novels of his contemporaries. In this essay, I discuss some "cinematic" fulfillments in two Zhang Yimou's films, *Judou* (1990) and *To Live* (1994), respectively adapted from Liu Heng's *Fuxi Fuxi* (1988) and Yu Hua's *To Live* (Huozhe; 1992), both of which feature certain "cinematic devices" or styles. As the director of his film-to-be, and often the co-screenwriter of the verbal-to-visual transformation process, Zhang Yimou believes that a good adaptation is "to reduce the complexity of the events [in the original work], and make the story simple and popular." However, as the essay will illustrate, Zhang's "simplification" and "popularization" of each of the original stories under discussion are always full of creativity, and this often results in a highly selected, distorted, yet more dramatically charged representation of the fictional and real worlds.

I choose these two films because they are among Zhang's representative films and because they convey explicit criticism of Chinese society and tradition as well as concerns about the lack of humanity in modern Chinese history. In that sense, they are different from films like *Red Sorghum*, which eulogizes humanity and life (Zhang Huijun 2008: 110–111). Furthermore, that they are perhaps Zhang Yimou's most controversial films—banned as they were in Mainland China for their criticism of entrenched cultural and authoritative political discourses—they are therefore interesting in terms of their politics. Moreover, since in both cases the authors of the original novels were also co-screenwriters for the films, which garnered prestigious international film festival awards and huge critical and public favor abroad, the films need to be set in larger contexts. Through cross-genre and, more interesting, cross-cultural analyses of these films, I demonstrate how, in turning cinematic novels into literary cinema, Zhang Yimou successfully brought to life what is seeded as "cinematic" promise in each of the original novels. Zhang's *Judou* and *To Live* are to be discussed chronologically according to their release dates. But before I set about this, a brief description of the immediate context in which Zhang Yimou's filmic adaptations emerged is necessary.

"CULTURAL REFLECTION" AND CONTEMPORARY "ALLIANCE" BETWEEN FILM AND NOVEL

Like his Fifth-Generation filmmaking colleagues, Zhang Yimou participated in a nationwide intellectual movement in the mid- and late-1980s called "cultural reflection" (*wenhua fansi*), alternatively known as "historical reflection" (*lishi fansi*). At that time, having been recently exposed to Western literary trends and translated works of Western and other foreign literatures, young Chinese writers and artists sensed the relative inferior position of contemporary Chinese literature and art. They then embarked on a broad reassessment of the value of traditional Chinese culture and launched a "searching-for-roots" (*xungen*) movement in literature aimed at criticizing the existing structural character of the nation by returning to traditional cultural experiences and memories that had been attacked by radical ideologies and politics over the course of the twentieth century (Yeh 2001: 230–236). In doing so, however, as noted by Sheldon Hsiao-peng Lu, these young writers and artists established a basic thematic continuity with the legacy of modern Chinese literature:

This critical enterprise is sustained by an ambivalent attitude toward China's past: an iconoclastic attack on tradition in the fashion of the intellectuals of the May 4th Movement (1919) and, at the same time, a return to, or a search for, the deep roots that gave life to Chinese civilization in the first place. (Lu 1997: 8)

At the same time, as Li Tuo, one of the searching-for-roots writers, argued, they realized that the searching-for-roots literature movement "first had to learn from the Western modernists and then try, on that basis, to absorb Chinese traditional culture" (Yeh 2001: 250).

Thus, for searching-for-roots writers like A Cheng and Mo Yan, "[nature], tradition, customs, and marginality then become ... raw materials of a new sociocultural architecture" (Zhang Xudong 1997: 338), as illustrated by such representative works as A Cheng's "King of Chess" (Qi wang; 1984) and Mo Yan's *Red Sorghum* (Hong gaoliang jiazu; 1987). Similarly, the Fifth-Generation filmmakers used "national history, a history understood as a unified cultural picture, as the ontological realm of meaning to be opened up by a chaotic montage of styles and techniques" (Zhang Xudong 1997: 339). Rhetorically, these writers and filmmakers moved away from the iconoclastic thrust of Chinese modernity, including that of the Cultural Revolution, subverted the linear concept of modern Chinese history in the authoritative discourse, and interrogated the causes of historical catastrophe and the reasons for China's lack of humanity. In alignment with such rhetorical strategies, Fifth-Generation filmmakers Chen Kaige, Zhang Junzhao, and Zhang Yimou produced such works of "new cinema" as *One and Eight* (Yige he bage; 1983), *Yellow Earth* (Huang tudi; 1984), and *Red Sorghum* (1988).

To a great extent, post-Mao writers and filmmakers worked together toward a common goal—to invent a new national consciousness of Chinese history through re-presenting Chinese modernity. Writers and filmmakers recognized the "alliance" between their respective art forms. Mo Yan, for instance, remarks: "In my opinion, there's always an affinity between fiction and film. Many famous fictional works have been adapted into films. [In China], since the 1980s, about ninety percent of those successful films are based on an 'original novel.' Fictional works offer a literary foundation for film and television" (Cheng 2010: 23).[95] Zhang Yimou also asserts: "By all means I feel grateful to novels for providing us with fine story frames and great potential for further story development. From this perspective, I still believe that film is very dependent on literature" (Cheng 2010: 211). The alliance or affinity between the two art forms is also seen in the facts that post-Mao "art films" by the Fifth-Generation filmmakers in the mid-1980s-early-90s were often, if not always, evaluated or critiqued by literary critics and scholars against literary standards and that writers like Liu Heng, Mo Yan, Su Tong, Yu Hua, and so on were

---

95   Unless noted otherwise, all English translations of Chinese speeches from Chinese works are mine.

both novelists and screenwriters who, from time to time, even revised or expanded their original novels as they were finishing or after they finished their screenwriting.[96] Working shoulder to shoulder, these artists not only shared similar philosophical and aesthetic concepts regarding inventing a national history and representing Chinese modernity, but also interacted with each other in artistic and cultural forms. As a result, novels increasingly displayed cinematic features and cinematic devices and were therefore ready for filmic adaptation. Of those fictional writers who worked with Zhang in his literary film adaptation processes, Su Tong, whose novella *Wives and Concubines* (Qiqie chengqun; 1990) was adapted into Zhang's film *Raise the Red Lantern* (1991), confessed that he was conscious of "creating distinct visual images which, apart from being suitable in setting the atmosphere, can be seen and touched" (Cheng 2010: 69). And his fictional works contained "strong visual qualities. Some scenes can be transplanted into a film without any editing or revision. This is especially apparent in the novel *Rice*" (Cheng 2010: 250).

As early as the 1940s, Sergei Eisenstein commented on this kind of "inter-art" phenomenon by remarking that "from Dickens, from Victorian novel, stem the first shoots of American film aesthetic" (Elliott 2003: 3). In a similar way, I would say that from contemporary novels written by authors like A Cheng, Mo Yan, Liu Heng, Su Tong, and Yu Hua stem the first shoots of China's Fifth-Generation's film aesthetic, especially that of Zhang Yimou's.

JUDOU: SHIFT IN FOCUS FROM NOVEL TO FILM

Released in 1990, *Judou* is one of Zhang Yimou's most famous early films. Right after its release, *Judou* was officially shown in Hong Kong. In 1992 when a ban was lifted and the film was shown in Mainland China, most Chinese audiences, like earlier Hong Kong viewers, responded either unfavorably or lukewarmly—uneasiness was reportedly caused by the incestuous sexuality depicted in the film (Jenny K. W. Lau 1991: 154; Lin 2005: 120). By contrast, when it was shown abroad, the film was favorably received by Western spectators and critics. Moreover, it earned Zhang Yimou several international film festival awards, among which was the Luis Bunuel Award of the 1990 Cannes Film Festival, and became the first Chinese feature film to be nominated for an Oscar in 1991.

Judou has fascinated not only many audiences abroad but also a large number of film critics and scholars. Some critics and scholars, such as Jenny

---

96 For example, Yu Hua revised and expanded his book *To Live* (originally published in 1992) from about 70,000 words to about 120,000 words as he was working on the screen-script for Zhang's *To Live* in 1994 (Wang Daming 2006: 60–74).

Kwok Wah Lau, think of the film as highly Chinese in its exploration of such ethic issues as *yin* (excessive eroticism) and *xiao* (filial piety)—even though the film is consciously criticizing these notions (1991: 157–162). Others, like Rey Chow (1995: 171), claim to see in it an "Oriental's orientalism"—that is, "in its self-subalternizing, self-exoticizing visual gestures," the film puts on "an exhibitionist self-display" which "turns the remnants of orientalism into elements of a new ethnography." Still others theorize a Chinese Oedipal complex from the character interactions in this film (Lin 2005: 119–123). I join this chorus of diverse interpretations of the film with a cross-genre, cross-cultural analytical reading. My discussion of *Judou* further points out the non-monolithic characteristic of contemporary Chinese cinema and the complexity of cultural relations underlying *Judou*.

Judou is based on Liu Heng's novella *Fuxi Fuxi* (translated into English as *The Obsessed*), which was published in 1988. Together with Liu Heng who was invited to render the screenplay in this verbal-to-visual transformation process, Zhang was the co-screenwriter. Set in a mountain village in China in the 1920s, the film centers on a love triangle among a dye-house master Yang Jinshan, his young wife Judou, and his nephew apprentice Yang Tianqing. The cruel, impotent dye-house master, Yang Jinshan, brings home a young and beautiful bride named Judou, expecting that she will bear him a male heir to continue his family line. Tianqing, the owner's nephew, has eyes for Judou from the first time he sees her and develops strong sympathy and affection for her after witnessing her being abused by her husband. The dye-house master's mistreatment and the discovery of Tianqing's secret passion for her lead Judou to make advances to Tianqing who resists at first but eventually succumbs to her seduction and his own sexual desire. As a result of their transgressions, Judou and Tianqing have a son whom the old Yang Jinshan initially believes to be his own. As time goes on, Yang Jinshan becomes paralyzed by a stroke, and changes from a victimizer to a victim as he watches his wife and nephew carry on their affair in front of him. While the young lovers suffer psychologically and physically from their illicit relationship, their son, Yang Tianbai, in his confusion about who his father is, becomes angry and frustrated. Tianbai accidently drowns his acknowledged father and eventually willfully kills his biological father. In the end, in an act of futile defiance, Judou sets fire to the Yang dye-house and vanishes in the blaze (Zhang Yimou 2005).

At several levels, the film is significantly different from the original novella. In the latter, for example, the story setting is mostly open farmland rather than an enclosed dye-house; and the triangular story takes place over a longer period and during a more recent time, from the mid-1940s to the latter part of the 1960s. Moreover, in the novella the illicit affair between Judou and Tianqing produces not one but two sons who, together with their mother

Judou, survive Tianqing, who commits a suicide, and both grow up and get married with children of their own (Liu Heng 2006: 10–70). But, most important, in his adaptation of the novella, Zhang Yimou shifts the narrative center from the male protagonist Yang Tianqing to Judou.

Published in 1988 when many literary writers and artists were participating in the nationwide searching for roots—from which iconoclastic politics had alienated the Chinese people—*Fuxi Fuxi*, in my reading, is first and foremost a passionate, yet ironical celebration of masculinity in its Chinese style. The title of the novel draws our attention to the Chinese myth of Fuxi and Nuwa, two human-headed and snake-tailed siblings who become spouses and who sacrifice themselves in order to give birth to mankind.[97] The love affair between Judou (as aunt) and Tianqing (as nephew) in the novella is an incestuous one, clearly a taboo after Fuxi and Nuwa brought civilization to mankind. Nevertheless, what Liu Heng is concerned with in the novella is not so much the transgression, but about man's spontaneous, persistent sexual desire—the illicit relationship and its defiance of patrilinear morality mainly provide a context for this representation of androcentrism.[98] In other words, in Liu's art, the phallus is the focus and functions as the source of all human suffering and crises. This focus is indicated first by the fact that *Fuxi fuxi* was originally entitled *Benr Benr*—a slang term for the male genitals; second, it is suggested by Liu's replacing Nuwa by Fuxi in the Fuxi-Nuwa mythical pairing (Chang 2006: i; Huot 1993: 86); and, finally and most importantly, it is manifested in Yang Jinshan's impotence and the humiliation and violence caused by it, in the dramatic depiction of Tianqing's self-displayed, upside-down naked body in the suicide scene and in the fooling-around behavior of Tianqing's heir (his second son in his adulthood).[99] This ironical celebration of masculinity under Liu Heng's pen thematically echoes the contemporaneous cultural revival of masculine images in the visual arts (Gao 2003: 250), and is enhanced through the many monologues by the male protagonist Tianqing.

---

97   As recorded in a Tang dynasty (618–907) text, the mythical story goes like this: "Long ago, when the universe had first come into being, there were no people in the world, only Nu-kua [Nüwa] and her brother on Mount Kun-lun. They considered becoming man and wife but were stricken with shame. And so (Fu-his [Fuxi]) and his sister went up on Kun-lun and (performed a sacrifice), vowing: 'If it is Heaven's wish that my sister and I become man and wife, let this smoke be intertwined. If not, let the smoke scatter,' whereupon the smoke was intertwined, and his sister did cleave unto him" (Plaks 1976: 35–36).

98   Even though it is true that apart from being the title, Fuxi is neither a character in the text nor alluded to overtly, the novella, as Marie-Claire Huot points out, metaphorically portrays man's primitive, myth-like sexual desire. For example, in their love-making Tianqing and Judou are represented as "two big pythons intertwining and becoming one" (Huot 1993: 86).

99   Another example is the talks about Tianqing's legendary penis size by young boys at the end of the novella (un-translated in the English version).

While admitting that Liu Heng's work "is about the realistic mentality of those who are genuinely Chinese" and declaring that his turning the book into a film was to express "the Chinese people's oppression and confinement" (Kuoshu 2002: 153), in the film Zhang Yimou shifts the narrative center from the male protagonist Tianqing to the female Judou. Zhang explains his main reason as follows: "Women express this [oppression or confinement] more clearly on their bodies because they bear a heavier burden than men" (in Kuoshu 2002: 153). The shifted focus and point of view, most obviously illustrated by the title of the film and the strong female lead, allow the director to create a Judou who can symbolize both the burdens of patriarchal tradition and a defiance against that tradition. This adaptation erases the trace of the Chinese male mythical figure Fuxi and thus permits new perspectives and readings centering on the female protagonist. If Zhang was well known since his directorial debut *Red Sorghum* for his fetishizing woman and depictions of sexual transgression, then in *Judou*, along with that fetishism, he becomes fascinated with depicting another sexual taboo—namely, incest. While shifting the narrative focus from the fictional male to the filmic female for thematic reasons, Zhang turns certain of Liu Heng's actions and plots that bear cinematic qualities and can contribute to the new filmic theme, into cinematic point-of-view structures. An example is Yang Tianqing's acts of secretly peeping at Judou's body. In the novel, Tianqing's voyeurism through a hole in the wall of a pigpen used as the family toilet is basically an act to relieve himself from his built-up sexual frustration:

Finally, [Tianqing] worked the stopper-shaped stone loose … . He heard a bunch of kindling drop on the ground. She was moving toward the pigpen now. In a moment he heard the gate open. Finally she was at the place where one stands or squats … . His gaze darted through the hole, passed the ragged edges of the basket, tore through the wisps of morning mist and plunged into a strange new world. He was lost in a welter of strange sensations; of light and shade, colour and texture. What could not be, was. It was destiny. Tianqing had finally opened the last and most secret chapter in the book of life. He was dazed with excitement. He sought swift release, which left him more confused than ever at his turbid body. (Liu Heng 1991: 31–32)

In the film, instead of peeping into a pigpen, Tianqing peeps at Judou's naked body through a peep-hole in the wall separating the barn from the bathing room. Knowing that Tianqing has been peeping at her, Judou then tries to seduce him by performing a slow strip for him as he (and the audience) watches from his hiding place. However, by slowly turning her naked body toward "Tianqing, the camera, and the audience, …seizing and fixing the viewer," Judou reverses the point-of-view "from object being looked at into subject possessing the look" (Cui 1997: 309–310). Thus, besides her body, Judou reveals her bruises and tears as well. This powerful sexual undercurrent forges a bond between the two characters; the scene also functions to highlight for the audience the themes of sexual abuse and cultural oppression.

With this gender- and sexuality-oriented perspective, Zhang makes the film a critique of the decayed, male-dominated Chinese culture. That is, on the one hand, Zhang Yimou symbolically probes a cyclic sexual interplay in which his female protagonist, with acute awareness of her suffering, functions as a central agent whereby the sexually-impotent husband restores his patriarchal power and the socially-emasculated lover fulfills his sexual desire. On the other hand, Zhang invests in Judou a spectacularly defiant spirit, despite the fact that in serving as an object of masculinity, Judou's desires for escape as well as for love are suppressed and eventually punished by either physical or psychic pain.

JUDOU: A POSSIBLE CROSS-CULTURAL RELATIONSHIP

I have been interested in exploring the illicit relationships in *Judou* from a comparative perspective ever since I first saw the film in Toronto in 1991. While watching it, I couldn't help recalling the American playwright Eugene O'Neill's (1888–1953) *Desire under the Elms*, which I had read years before. Although it is a fact that Zhang Yimou's film was adapted from Liu Heng's *Fuxi Fuxi*, I propose here that the incestuous liaison in *Judou* bears similarities to O'Neill's play, first produced in 1924.

The triangle relationship of *Judou*, to a large extent, is the Ephrain-Abbie-Eben plot of *Desire under the Elms*. *Desire under the Elms* is set on a farm in New England in 1850. Like Yang Jinshan in Zhang Yimou's film, the old farmer Ephraim Cabot brings home a young and beautiful bride, Abbie Putnam. Like Judou, Abbie finds herself with passionate feelings for Eben Cabot, her husband's son from a previous marriage, but she initially conceals her passion before finally making advances. Like Tianqing, Eben at first resists his stepmother's advances but eventually succumbs to Abbie's seduction. As in the Judou-Tianqing affair, Abbie and Eben have a son of their transgressions whom the old Ephraim, just like the old Yang Jinshan, initially believes to be his own. And toward the end of the play Abbie smothers her baby son in an effort to prove her love for Eben and testify to the strength of her own passion. Thus, by sacrificing the life of an infant rather then two adults' lives as in *Judou*, the relationship among the mother, two fathers, and the baby son in the play ends with an unresolved questioning of the interplay between human desire and ethical prohibition (O'Neill 1988: 317–378).

My reading of *Judou* in connection with O'Neill's play provoked me to look for a possible cross-cultural influence on Zhang's cinematic structure and vision. In my examination of Western literary influences embedded in the May Fourth literary legacy inherited by post-Mao writers and artists that possibly inspired Zhang Yimou in making *Judou* or in depicting taboo sexuality, I paid a special attention to Cao Yu's spoken drama (*huaju*) play *Thunderstorm* (Leiyu; 1934). As modern Chinese literary historians have noted, among attributions of foreign ancestry for Cao Yu's *Thunderstorm*, were O'Neill's *Desire Under the Elms* and Antony Chekov's *Three Sisters* (Mc-Dougal/lLouie 1997: 173, 178, 180; Wang Weiping 2005: 90).[100] The similarity between *Thunderstorm* and *Desire Under the Elms* is believed to lie not only in plot scenario but also in dramatic theme and vision.[101] Typical is Joseph S. M. Lau, who writes: "by design, Fan-yi is modeled upon Abbie Putnam in her defiance of traditional morals" (1970: 25). Perhaps, via Cao Yu, *Desire Under the Elms*' "desire," a libidinal force that symbolizes the rebellious spirit for his time in the Nietzschean sense, inspired the Chinese film director to create a defiant Judou who struggles against a decayed Chinese culture. In his search for motifs and inspirations for the transgression of his *Judou* outside the overdetermined social realities, I believe, Zhang Yimou either directly inherited or was aesthetically/philosophically akin to this May Fourth literary legacy, which had already absorbed Western thematic and technical elements unknown to the Chinese tradition. In either situation, Cao Yu's *Thunderstorm* could function as a pathway for Zhang's creation of *Judou*. We know that Zhang loved *Thunderstorm* and even adapted it for film with *Curse of the Golden Flower* (Mancheng jindai huangjin jia; 2006). At the Los Angeles Premiere of his new transgression-obsessed film, Zhang spoke clearly of his borrowing from Cao Yu: "The film is actually adapted from a very famous stage play in the 1920s and 1930s called *Thunderstorm*, which is a very powerful story, very dramatic. And I've always loved it, and the interpersonal tensions that are revealed in that story are something I thought we could really tackle with this film" (Zhang Yimou 2007).

During the mid- and late 1980s, when Zhang was exposed to Western cinematic trends, translated works of Western and other foreign literatures,

---

100 Cao Yu's *Thunderstorm* has become the most performed play in the history of modern Chinese drama ever since its first publication in 1934 and successful stage premiere in 1935. There have been quite a few film adaptations of the play made in the 1930s, 1980s, and 1990s respectively (McDougall/Louie 1997: 177), as well as a 2003 reproduction in the popular form of TV series.

101 *Thunderstorm* is a melodrama that blends incest with generational revolt, political drama of class struggle, predestined fate, and bloody revenge. Its major incestuous relationship can be summarized as such: Fanyi, the neurasthenic wife of Zhou Puyuan, a wealthy owner of a coalmine in north China, has a forbidden love relation with her stepson Zhou Ping who abandons her later and courts a house maid Sifeng without knowing she is his half-sister. The play ends with Fanyi's own son and Sifeng dying by accident, Zhou Ping committing suicide, and Fanyi and Shiping, Zhou Puyuan's former mistress and mother to Zhou Ping, incarcerated in an asylum; the male protagonist Zhou Puyuan is left surveying his ruined life—that is, he loses his women and most of his children (McDougall/Louie 1997: 178).

and staged theatrical works including O'Neill's, he clearly absorbed Western modernist characters, narrative structures, and artistic techniques. In this intertextual light, the tall elms in *Desire under the Elms* and the high-hung strips of colorful cloth in *Judou* can, in one way or another, be seen to symbolize man's irresistible desire, longing for libidinal and psychic liberation. In O'Neill's play, the desire that flows through the elms and drips from them is a dynamic "something" present in all things:

[Ephraim] Cabot—(*at the gate, confusedly*) Even the music can't drive it out—somethin'. Ye kin feel it droppin' off the elums, clibmin' up the roof, sneakin' down the chimney, pokin' in the corners! They's no peace in houses, they's no rest livin' with folks. Somethin's always with ye. (O'Neill 1988: 363)

Likewise, in Zhang's film, the colorful strips of cloth are omnipresent and pervade the film's visual aesthetic. Judou's fulfillment of love and the tragic interplay between the characters' sexual desires and social norms all take place under them. It is perhaps the filmic manifestation of the libidinal desire and defiant spirit in Judou tangibly transformed from Western culture that has helped the film, and its director, be so well received by Western audiences.

TO LIVE: A TRANSCENDENTAL SOFT MELANCHOLY?

Produced in 1994, the film *To Live* is a direct adaptation from a novel of the same title first published in 1992. Yu Hua, author of the novel *To Live* and co-screen writer for its filmic adaptation, is a well-known writer of fiction in China. Yu Hua first emerged on the literary scene in the 1980s as a prominent avant-gardist highly regarded for his metafictional narratives, but he has more recently shifted to more commercial, market-oriented fiction. In his exploration of different narrative modes, from "experimental" to "plain realism," Yu has changed from a resentment-fueled young writer to a mature novelist who observes and represents the Chinese world "with sympathetic eyes" (*tongqingde muguang*) (Yu 2004: iii). It was with the latter's maturity and calm that the novel *To Live* was written. Ever since its publication in 1994 (the same year when the film *To Live* was completed and sent to compete at the Cannes Film Festival), the novel has enjoyed rapidly increasing popularity at home and abroad, including being on the bestseller list in China, drawing widespread critical and popular acclaim in Hong Kong and Taiwan, being translated into more than seven languages, and garnering the Bingxin Award for Chinese Literature (Bingxin wenxue jiang) at home (2002) and literature awards from Italy (1998) and Taiwan (1994) (Hong 2004: 111–112).

Yu Hua's *To Live* (2004) is about the trials and adversities of the protagonist, Xu Fugui, from the 1940s to the 1980s, a half century during which China witnessed much upheaval. Through his own stories, an aged Xu Fugui (meaning "fortune," a name his parents hoped would lead to a life of prosperity and happiness) tells a young intellectual outsider about his life. As the novel begins, Fugui, the son of a rich landlord, loses his inheritance as well as mansion to gambling debts, and his father dies of anger. Suddenly poor, Fugui resolves to lead an honest, hardworking peasant life. Nevertheless, his fate thereafter is nothing but tragedy. Through poverty, hardship, and a series of accidents, Fugui loses all his loved ones one by one—his wife, son, daughter, son-in-law, and grandson. When he goes to town to buy some medicine for his ill mother, he is recruited to be a Nationalist soldier to fight in the civil war; in his unexpected absence, his mother dies at home and his daughter becomes mute due to an illness. Returning to his family from the civil war, Fugui witnesses the execution of Long'er, the new landlord of his former family mansion. Having enabled his family to survive for a while, Fugui experiences the loss of his only son during the Great Leap Forward; his son Youqing, an elementary school student, dies in a mishandled blood transfusion for the pregnant school principal. Fugui's wife Jiazhen becomes ill and weak after the death of their son. The next tragic experiences come during the Cultural Revolution when first his daughter Fengxia dies of complications when she goes to the hospital in labor; she is survived by her baby son, Kugen. Then Fugui's wife dies of illness and a broken heart. Having lived for a few years with his grandson and son-in-law through commuting between his village and the city where they live in the late 1970s-early 1980s, Fugui's son-in-law Wan Erxi, a transportation worker, dies in an accident at work and, ironically, his grandson passes away when overeating beans Fugui had given him. Surviving all his family members and friends (one of whom, Chunsheng, Fugui befriended during the civil war and who rose to become a district leader, but who committed suicide during the Cultural Revolution), Fugui lives on with an old cow whom he names "Fugui."

Although a portrayal of the life of a Chinese peasant, Yu Hua was initially all inspired by an American song titled "Old Black Joe." In the "Author's Postscript" of the English edition of the novel, Yu confesses to his readers:

> I once heard an American folk song entitled 'Old Black Joe.' The song was about an elderly black slave who experienced a life's worth of hardships, including the passing of his entire family—yet he still looked upon the world with eyes of kindness, offering not the slightest complaint. After being so deeply moved by this song I decided to write my next novel—that novel was *To Live*. (Yu 2003: 249)

According to Yu's statement, it was the "simplest lyrics" in the song—about an elderly black slave's kind attitude toward the world after "a life's worth of hardships"—that sparked his depiction of Fugui's life—"a life imbued with upheavals and suffering, but also tranquility and happiness" (Yu 2003: 249). Certainly, the American song conveys no complaint or hostility, just "soft melancholy," to use Ken Emerson's words (1997: 259). And it inspired Yu Hua perhaps in the way the song's thematic "soft melancholy" seemed genuine and "transcendent" (chaoran) (Yu 2004: iii), and thus could be typologically applied to anyone, such as his peasant character. What Yu Hua may not know about this "Old Black Joe," however, is that the "folk" song was composed as a parlor song by the white songwriter Stephen Collins Foster (1826–1864) in 1853 and that the "soft melancholy" expressed in it is not the true voice of an elderly black slave or the authentic "folk" expression of black slaves' life experience.

A subgenre in the history of American popular music, "parlor songs," usually composed by white songwriters, emerged along with socioeconomic development of the American middle-class during the nineteenth century. Featuring sentimental themes, such as love songs, poetic meditations, and praise of nature, parlor songs flourished nationwide in the United States in the mid-nineteenth century when "the human condition received an intimate articulation" in literature and art (Tawa 1980: 123), against the backdrop of a bustling and hustling American society torn by rampant industrialization, massive immigration, slavery, and political corruption. As one of the most prolific songwriters of his time, Foster composed a great deal of popular songs that melded "parlor songs" and "minstrel songs," another subgenre in American pop music popularly performed by "black-faced" stage entertainers and loaded with "jokes, biting satires, grotesque dances, and songs with texts in an imitation-Negro dialect" (Tawa 1980: 89). Even with their humanitarian undertones, Foster's minstrel songs (often subtitled "Ethiopian Songs") were often moderated so that they were appropriate as entertainment "in genteel parlors" (Tawa 1980: 90). As Foster himself admitted in an 1852 letter to E. P. Christy, a minstrel-troupe manager: "I find by my efforts I have done a great deal to build up a taste for Ethiopian songs among refined people by making the words suitable for their taste, instead of the trashy and really offensive words which belong to some songs of that order" (Tawa 1980: 99). Like some other parlor song composers, Foster's efforts to moderate his Ethiopian melody songs for their popularity in American polite circles contributed to a tender music environment where "minstrel and parlor works approached each other in musical style and theme, ... minstrel shows increasingly introduced sentimental parlor songs into their formats" (Tawa 1980: 97). By the 1850s, Foster could move back and forth between "parlor song" and "minstrel song" in composition because the gap between these two subgenres became so narrow and the boundaries blurred (Tawa 1980: 95).

From this mid-nineteenth-century American music tradition, with its tenderness and sentiment, the "blackface" parlor song "Old Black Joe" came into being. Its second stanza and chorus read as follows:

Why do I weep when my heart should feel no pain
Why do I sigh that my friends come not again
Grieving for forms now departed long ago?
[I hear their gentle voices calling "Old Black Joe."]
Chorus
I'm coming, I'm coming, for my head is bending low;
I hear those gentle voices calling, "Old Black Joe". (Emerson 1997: 257–258)

Stereotypical to a certain extent, the song "distills the world-weariness" and becomes "the singer of 'Old Folks at Home' and the Uncle Tom figure in 'My Old Kentucky Home'"—two most famous parlor songs by Foster, and "is all too easily exaggerated and caricatured by distorting the chorus's dialogue with the dead into a slave's cringing obedience" (Emerson 1997: 256–258). But, with "its soft melancholy and elusive undertone, rather than any formal musical correspondence," the song "comes closest of Foster's famous songs to the African-American spiritual, and it approaches that tradition with sympathy and respect" (Emerson 1997: 259; 258). With "sympathy and respect," Foster's "Old Black Joe," along with his other sentimental Ethiopian songs, pays heed to the human condition of African Americans and demonstrates a broad awareness of brotherhood. The song, therefore, was not only heard frequently by middle-class Americans but also appreciated by African American activists like W. E. B. Du Bois (1868–1963) who praised Foster's "Old Black Joe" and "Old Folks at Home" as "songs of white America [that] have been distinctively influenced by the slave songs or have incorporated whole phrases of Negro melody" (Emerson 1997: 258).

Misreading the "soft melancholy" of the "Old Black Joe" as authentic African American cultural expression, and touched and inspired by it, Yu Hua starts his novel from a highly subjective perspective—that is, to portray an ordinary Chinese peasant modeled on the "Old Black Joe" with "transcendent" views and "kindness" toward life's sufferings and crises. Perhaps, the distorted yet intimate articulation of "Old Black Joe" not only resonated in Yu Hua's emotional world as a sensitive writer who grew up during the catastrophic Cultural Revolution, but also nurtured his literary imagination: in the early 1990s, when Chinese avant-garde literature was losing readership because it had become increasingly unreadable (i.e., lack of clear plot lines and characters with transparent psychological motivations), Yu was tossing around the idea of abandoning radical experiments and finding a new, realistic mode in which to write an ordinary story. *To Live* was well received, becoming a bestseller and paving the path for Yu to be one of the most popular realist novelists of contemporary China, both at home and abroad. The talented Chinese novelist turned his "misapprehension" of the American song into a best-selling, internationally acclaimed novel. This kind of influence Yu receives from Foster is described by Harold Bloom (1973: 30) in these terms: "Poetic influence—when it involves two strong, authentic poets,—always proceeds by a misreading of the prior poet, an act of creative correction that is actually and necessarily a misinterpretation."

If we approach *To Live* in this intra-textual context, we find Yu not only "creatively corrects" the American song, but also his own earlier fiction and creative vision. Those experimental fictional works, such as "On the Road at Eighteen" (Shiba sui chumen yuanxing) and "The Past and Punishment" (Wangshi yu xingfa), now appear as merely chaotic fragments of thought and limited slices of the world. Under the influence of the American song, Yu seems to recognize in writing *To Live* that his basic concern is not about the relationship between the writer and reality—he more than once considered as his aim the exploration of multiple aspects of reality through words (Li 2011: 150)—but about that between man and his fate. To emphasize man's unchangeable yet reciprocal relationship with fate, in *To Live* Yu only mentions in passing or even depoliticizes all the sociopolitical upheavals and mercilessly sends all Fugui's loved ones to death, but at the same time allows his protagonist to survive all these deaths so as to testify to the strength and perseverance of man's basic will to live on. For Yu, this kind of relationship between man and his fate is more like "a friendship," because in it man and his fate "are grateful to each other," and they are "dependent on each other" even when "they fight against each other" (Wang Daming 2006: 27). The central theme of the novel emerges through the love-and-hate interdependence of Fuigui and his fate—that is, "'to live' [is] the most fundamental, instinctual, 'primitive' desire" (Liu Kang 2002: 115).

Unlike Foster, the "composer" of "Old Black Joe," Yu Hua dissolves into his fictional world, following the natural lead of Fugui's fate, and becoming an honest observer with "the camera-eye:"

> This scoundrel of forty years ago was today sitting bare-chested on the grass, the sunlight filtering through gaps between the tree leaves and into his squinting eyes. His legs were covered with mud, and patches of white hair sprouted from his shaven head. Sweat trickled down over the wrinkles on his chest. At that moment his old ox was in the golden water of the pond, with only its head and back exposed. I saw the water slapping against the ox's long black back, just as water crashes on the shore. (Yu 2003: 43)

In portraying such an ordinary Chinese peasant, Yu adopts a "plain" realistic mode, or a so-called "down-to-earth realism," adorned only with

irony and humor, and with the restraint of "guiding the reader's comprehension of the events" (Liu Kang 2002: 90). Furthermore, he re-enforces
the realist narrative with a dominant "mimetic or figural mode of dialogue,"
and the characters' "reported speech," and with "reporting of their outward
movements: walking, eating, speaking, crying, and laughing" (Liu Kang
2002: 116). Through these and other "cinematic" features, along with the realistic point of view and the depoliticizing of the wrenching Chinese social
changes, Fugui's character becomes at once absolute and real. This ordinary
personage is identifiable to common Chinese people, whose lives have been
shaped by violent past and who face a frightening new world almost devoid
of traditional morality. At the same time, the image of an ordinary man with
"broad tears" (*yanleide kuanguang*), to use Yu's own words (2004: v), is ap-
pealing to an international readership in whom a sensation of familiarity
is awakened.

Critics of Yu Hua have paid special attention to some repeated descriptions in the novel. For example, Hua Li (2011: 150), writes: "the small mortuary
and the concrete slab appear three times in Yu Hua's novel *To Live*. The protagonist Fugui experiences the death of his son, daughter, and son-in-law in the
same hospital, and their bodies are each laid out in turn on the same concrete
slab" (150). Hua Li attributes this style to Yu's life experiences and impressions from his childhood (149–150). But Yu's fondness of music in general and
the specific influence of the lyrics and melodic recurrence in "Old Black Joe,"
I believe, also play an indispensible role here. Like the melodic recurrence of
the chorus in the song, "I'm coming, I'm coming, for my head is bending low;/
I hear those gentle voices calling, 'Old Black Joe,'" which functions as a means
for heightened eloquence, structural unity, and ready comprehension, the
author's critically recognized repetition creates a narrative effect of tension-
and-calm. It is in the rhythm of this structural repetition in the novel that
engenders Yu's "soft melancholy."

TO LIVE: FROM SOFT MELANCHOLY TO HARSH CRITICISM THROUGH MISE-EN-SCÈNE

If Yu Hua's (mis)reading of "Old Black Joe" results in portraying an ordinary
Chinese personage and his fate intertwined with hardships and numerous
deaths of loved ones so to "affirm the strength and perseverance of human
dignity and the will to muddle through and go on living under even great
adversity" (Li 2011: 154), then Zhang Yimou's (mis)interpretation of the novel
revolves around a different spiritual sphere—that is, a critical representation
of modern historical turmoil and sociopolitical upheavals that are realistically enacted through the dramatic changes of an ordinary Chinese family.

Unlike his earlier allegorical films "where a story of the past (say in the 1920s or 1930s) serves as an indirect critique of the present and Chinese history as such" (Lu 1997: 121), in this filmic adaptation of *To Live* Zhang Yimou foregrounds what is depoliticized in the original novel—a long span of modern Chinese history from a pre-Communist time through the early People's Republic and the Cultural Revolution, to the post-Mao era, and situates Fugui and his family in this setting to create a series of mise-en-scène that critically expose the effect of politics and history on ordinary people's lives.

Because of its explicit criticism of totalitarianism and the many failed political campaigns in modern Chinese history, the film was banned in China, even as it was showered with praise abroad, including winning the Grand Jury Prize and Best Actor award (Ge You for the role of Fugui) at the Cannes Film Festival in 1994.[102] For the same reason, the film has drawn a great deal of attention from critics and scholars for whom it becomes an important visual art source in their critique of modern Chinese history and society. Hui Faye Xiao, for example, points out that the film "[strikes] a sharp contrast between intimate familial bonding and the bloodsucking—both literally and metaphorically—party-state. In order to counter political totalitarianism, [the cinematic narrative] established the antagonism of the cold-blooded state toward the heart-warming family" (2014: 20).

Dramatically charged and narrated in a way that is different from the novel, the film *To Live* is a story about Fugui and his wife Jiazhen, who struggle to survive through decades of historical turmoil and political upheaval that victimize the couple and their children. In many ways, the adapted film is significantly different from the original text. First of all, most of the story setting is changed from a rural village to a city, except for the section that takes place in the turbulent late 1940s when the husband Fugui loses his ancestral mansion through gambling and inadvertently takes part in the civil war before returning to his family. So the couple and their children are transformed from peasants (in the novel) to city dwellers (in the film). Enabling his family to make a living mainly by supplying boiled water to families in their neighborhood (in the film), Fugui also performs shadow-puppets—something he is good at and proud of—in order to survive and to fulfill his obligations to propagate state ideology (as during the Great Leap Forward). In the filmic version, the seemingly accidental deaths of the couple's son and daughter are closely tied to political events. Different from the novel, their son Youqing, an elementary school student, is killed during the Great Leap Forward when

---

102 A major reason for the government to ban the film is reportedly that Zhang sent it to the Cannes Film Festival for competition without obtaining prior permission from the Chinese government (Lu 1997: 120–121). Why Zhang did so in the first place, I believe, was because he knew the film wouldn't have had a chance to get such a permission.

the car of the district chief Chunsheng (who happens to be Fugui's old friend from civil war days) hits a wall behind which Youqing is sleeping, exhausted by long hours of participating in his school commune's iron smelting campaign. As in the novel, their daughter Fengxia dies in the Cultural Revolution in a hospital after giving birth to a son; but here her death is caused explicitly by the mishandling of her labor complications by some inexperienced Red Guard nurses and ironically by the inability of the experienced and qualified Doctor Wang who, taken out of prison to help save Fengxia, passes out due to overeating of the steamed buns given him by Fugui. Unlike the novel where every family member dies except Fugui, in the film, the couple, their grandson Mantou ("Little Bun"), and their son-in-law Wan Erxi all survive. Toward the end of the film, the family survivors sit together for dinner at the couple's home (Zhang Yimou 2007).

With fidelity to the original novel, the film retells Fugui's (and Jiazhen's) stories chronologically. By foregrounding almost all the historical and political events elusively set in the background of the original text, however, Zhang Yimou internalizes the temporal narrative in his mise-en-scène so as to interweave the family drama with the half-century long historical and political turmoil. And, to enhance the mise-en-scène and the mirroring of the family's tragedies and the historical and political events, Zhang introduces "shadow play" (*yingxi*) into the film.[103] To a great extent, the story of the fate of the shadow play parallels the ups and downs of the lives of Fugui's family caused by historical and sociopolitical changes. During the civil war, Fugui and Chunsheng are captured by Nationalist soldiers while they tour the provinces with Fugui's shadow play troupe. On the battlefield, Fugui's boxed collection of puppets is almost destroyed by a Nationalist army officer because it is blocking his way, but a fellow soldier comes to the rescue. After the battle, Fugui and Chunsheng are the only survivors among hundreds of dead Nationalist army soldiers; the collection of puppets is once again saved in the chaos, this time by the victorious People's Liberation Army soldiers after they chase the terrified Fugui and Chunsheng. In the Great Leap Forward in the late 1950s, the metal box holding the puppets and the iron parts of the puppets are targeted for smelting, but Fugui and Jiazhen save them one more time by persuading the town leader that the traditional art form can be appropriated positively for socialist construction; consequently, Fugui puts on shadow-play shows day and night to uplift the spirit of his fellow workers as they smelt iron in the commune. Finally, during the Cultural Revolution, Fugui is

---

103 The idea of creating and inserting the shadow play in a film had been on Zhang's mind for a previous film plan failed to carry out. His strategically apt incorporation of it in *To Live* witnesses his creative impulse and readiness for advocacy of Chinese ethnography in his art in the age of globalization.

impelled to destroy the puppets for fear that they would be seen as feudal and reactionary artifacts whose characters are considered "four olds" (*sijiu*). The scene in which the out-of-date puppets are burned suggests not only "a gesture of a complete break with the past" (Lu 1997: 122), but also a more radical replacement of it by the sweeping revolution in which every Chinese must perform on the national "revolutionary stage" (*gemingde dawutai*).

A traditional Chinese folk art, shadow play is by its nature comic and entertaining. Zhang's strategy for incorporating shadow play into the film results in a series of ironies that not only caricature history and the immediate present, but also ridicule the distortion of characters—for example, the paranoia of Fugui during political campaigns. The chain of ironies begins when Fugui borrows a set of shadow play puppets from the now rich Long'er and forms a shadow-play troupe to make a living; this enables him to change his social status from "landlord" to "poor city-dweller" after the revolution; meanwhile, Long'er, the former owner of a shadow play troupe whose "fortune" in gambling with Fugui allowed him to take over Fugui's ancestral mansion prior to the Communist victory, is executed by the Communist government because of his landlord status. And it is through this "exchange of roles" that Fugui transforms from a "good-for-nothing," who loses his inheritance and his ancestral mansion in the late 1940s, to a poor but dedicated performer of shadow play, a hero of the revolution and war veteran, and a useful member of the "new society." Moreover, because of his transformation, his wife Jiazhen comes back to him with their daughter Fengxia and a newborn baby boy Youqing. In another ironic twist, after the battle in which the Nationalist soldiers are all killed, Chunsheng gets into an abandoned army truck and pretends to drive it, expressing to Fugui his dream of becoming a truck driver; but Chunsheng's dream turns into a nightmare: years later, now the district chief in Fugui's town, he accidentally kills Fugui's son by driving into a wall and eventually commits suicide during the Cultural Revolution because he is accused of being a "capitalist roader." In the latter part of the film, the chain of ironic events revolving around the shadow play is given a figurative connection with the "role play" of Chinese people on the national "revolutionary stage" during the turmoil of the Cultural Revolution. Like the shadow-play puppet, "everything, including the family, has become subservient to the rule of central government"; although people "at the wedding party attending the marriage of Fengxia and Erxi sing a 'traditional' Communist song, which praises Mao as being 'dearer than mother and father'" (Cornelius 2002: 33), later in the hospital, Fengxia dies at the hands of Mao's Red Guards.

Just as the shadow play is metaphoric—its rise and fall parallels the cyclic sociopolitical changes in modern Chinese history interwoven with the ups and downs of the physical and psychic life of the characters—so too is the film's music. Like the narrative repetition that produces the tension-and-calm effect in the novel, the theme music, a stream of melancholic melodies produced mainly by the Chinese musical instruments *banhu* and *erhu*, repeats itself again and again during major life incidents throughout the film. Here, consistent with the spirit of the novel, the repeated bitter-sweet melody, while echoing the "soft melancholy" of "Old Black Joe," functions as another metaphoric trope in the film that links ups and downs, as well as sad and happy moments, of Fugui's family with the oppressive political milieu. With these audio-visual effects, the film "brings us back to a historical experience which is much more emotional and dramatic than the written texts" (Chen/ Haque 2007: 177).

In Zhang Yimou's art, soft melancholic attitudes toward hardships and crises are metaphorically and realistically blended into the drastically chang- ing sociopolitical fabric and a tender or even "happy" ending. Seen this way, Zhang's film *To Live* is a harsh critique of modern Chinese sociopolitical up- heavals and at the same time indicates the film director's reconciliation with Chinese history as such. As Sheldon Hsiao-peng Lu points out: "By an ironic reversal [referring to the different ending of the film], Zhang finally salvaged and vindicated temporality. Despite all the horrific personal losses and col- lective sufferings, the Chinese family perpetuates itself, and 'Little Bun' and little chicks will *live*" (1997: 122).

CONCLUSION

In the West, the sibling resemblance between the visual art and literature can be traced back theoretically to Horace's (65–8 BCE) "as is painting so is poetry" phrase that "has become the general epigraph, title, or slogan of many essays on poetry and painting" (Elliott 2003: 9). In China, Su Shi's (1036–1101) complimentary remark on Wang Wei's (701–761) talent in painting and poetry epitomizes the Chinese aesthetical thinking on the relationship between the visual art and literature: "When one savors Mo-chieh's (Wang Wei) poems there are paintings in them, when one looks at Mo-chieh's pictures, there are poems" (in Bush 1971: 25). This kind of aesthetic history, in China or in the West, places the visual and literary arts in a relationship of mutual influence, leading to descendants that feature both qualities. A modernist "inter-art" phenomenon in post-Mao China, as we have seen in the preceding discus- sion, emerged between the novel and film; together, these two genres were at the forefront of debates about contemporary ideological, economic, and social change, and they most successfully depicted the implications of those changes for personal life and for society.

Examining Zhang Yimou's *Judou* and *To Live* against Liu Heng's *Fuxi fuxi* and Yu Hua's *To Live*, the two novels Zhang's films are based on, from a cross-genre perspective and in a large, cross-cultural context leads to a better understanding of Zhang Yimou's filmic works. If in *Desire under the Elms*, by portraying modes of unholy lust and infanticide, Eugene O'Neill conveys a Nietzschean viewpoint that man's desire alone can enable him to transcend himself, and if in Liu Heng's *Fuxi Fuxi*, his metaphorical, ironic celebration of Chinese man's primitive, myth-like sexual desire responds thematically to his contemporary call for a cultural revival of masculinity, then in *Judou*, by audaciously transforming Western or Chinese age-old adultery and incest motifs, Zhang Yimou symbolically probes a cyclic sexual interplay in which his female protagonist functions as a central agent for patriarchal power and sexual fulfillment.

On the other hand, if in the American song "Old Black Joe," Stephen Foster approaches the African American tradition with an outsider's sympathy and respect, singing about an old black slave in sorrow without bitterness, and if Yu Hua, in his *To Live*, creatively appropriates the Old Black Joe's "soft melancholy"—his inspiration from Foster's song—in portraying with "sympathetic eyes" an ordinary Chinese peasant's fundamental desire to live on after loosing all his loved ones, then in Zhang Yimou's *To Live*, by foregrounding what is depoliticized in the original text, the film director creates a series of realistic mise-en-scène to critically reveal Chinese people's collective strife in modern history and contemporary society with a humanitarian focus on Fugui's family.

The examination of Zhang Yimou's *Judou* and *To Live* from cross-genre and cross-cultural perspectives is exciting and meaningful because this kind of study, as we have seen, can not only reveal how certain motifs are recreated in the verbal-to-visual transformation process, but also why writers and artists use certain plots and characters for specific purposes in a particular place and time. Moreover, in intertextualizing Zhang Yimou's *Judou* within a larger cross-genre, cross-cultural context, it becomes apparent that it is precisely the familiar traits of Western culture in the Chinese film that are the basis for its positive reception among Western audiences. With regard to *To Live*, Zhang Yimou establishes an interplay that both connects to and disengages from the original literary source; with such a deliberate temporal/spatial (dis)continuity with the original fiction, as well as its cross-cultural inspiration, the film always echoes a compassionate tone.[104]

---

104 Some critics are more impressed than others by this expressed compassion and the connection the film has with the novel. For example, Wang Yichuan (1998: 234) believes that the film has a sort of "tender toughness" in Fugui's character.

7 REWRITING *HONGLOU MENG* IN THE ORAL PERFORMING ARTS: THE CASE OF *ZIDISHU* (OR THE MANCHU BANNERMEN TALE)

YING WANG

INTRODUCTION

As one of the classics of Chinese vernacular fiction, *Dream of the Red Chamber* (Honglou meng; henceforth *Honglou meng*), also known as *Story of the Stone* (Shitou ji), presents a different case of dissemination and recycling than the Ming masterpieces of vernacular fiction. While its predecessors in the Ming dynasty, such as *Romance of the Three Kingdoms* (Sanguo zhi yanyi), *Water Margin* (Shuihu zhuan), and *Journey to the West* (Xiyou ji), moved from an oral to a written tradition whereby the stories and characters were circulated in oral performing arts or in theater long before they were written into vernacular novels, the opposite was true for *Honglou meng*. After the publication of the Cheng-Gao woodblock edition in 1791, China witnessed a *Honglou meng* craze that produced numerous rewritings in different literary genres, including fiction, opera, and oral performing arts. Through these re-creations, particularly through theater and oral performance, Cao's masterpiece was introduced to a broader audience and its stories and fictional characters became familiar in every household. Among the oral performing arts that played a significant role in popularizing *Honglou meng*, zidishu, or the Manchu Bannermen tales, presents a unique and interesting case for the Manchu ethnicity and elite status of its writers and target audience, as well as for its ability to reach the non-Manchu populace by successfully reshaping the novel's original stories and characters to fit the generic features of oral performing art.[105]

Zidishu was one of the oral performing arts prevalent among Manchu Bannermen in Beijing, Shenyang, and Tianjin in the mid and late Qing dynasty.[106]

---

105 *Zidishu* (prevalent in northern China) is recognized as one of the three major storytelling forms of the nineteenth century that played a significant role in popularizing *Honglou* meng; the two others are *tanci kaipian* and *Yangzhou qingqu* from southern China.

106 For detailed discussions on *zidishu*, please see Guo Xiaoting 2013; Lin Junjia 2012; Cui Yunhua 2005; Yao Ying 2007; Suet Ying Chiu 2007.

Literally, *zidi* means "sons and younger brothers" and *shu* refers to "tales." As the term suggests, *zidishu* is an art form that was created and performed by members of the Eight Banner system,[107] a definition that is consistently confirmed by scholars and bibliographers alike.[108] A *zidishu* text entitled "Ziditu" (A portrayal of Bannermen) describes this art in detail, providing information about its origin, writers, musical instruments, performers, melodic features, and targeted audience:

> I have heard that the two characters "zidi" were rooted in a storytelling genre, which was created by some influential families and great clans.
> In those bygone days, most of our bannermen were wealthy and privileged.
> They often listened to opera singing at home and were familiar with its melodies.
> They criticized *kunqu* and the southern tunes as being too difficult to understand;
> Meanwhile, *yi* melodies and northern songs were too vulgar.
> So, the bannermen created a kind of storytelling text with chapters.
> They intended to gain the elites' attention and popularize it [*zidishu*] among common people.
> Having set the three-string plucked lute with *zidishu's* tunes, following its musical scores as well as meter, performers shared their joy with others.
> Who knows how these clever bannermen learned *zidishu* so well by themselves?
> When there was a family gathering or banquet, they might join in and have some fun.
> Based on their intention, a listener called these "bannermen tales."[109]

曾聽說子弟二字因書起，
創自名門與巨族。
題昔年凡吾們旗人多富貴，
家庭內時時唱戲狠聽熟。
因評論昆曲南音推費解，
弋腔北曲又嫌粗。
故作書詞分段落，
所為的是既能警雅又可通俗。
條子板譜入三弦與人同樂，
又誰知聰明子弟暗習熟。
每遇家庭宴會一湊趣，
借此意聽者稱為子弟書。 [110]

---

107 According to Geng Ying, who wrote a preface to *Honglou meng zidishu*, Manshu zhenjun from the Qing dynasty indicated that *zidishu* was a kind of art form created by members of the Eight Banner system (Hu Wenbin 1983: 1).

108 All modern scholars of *zidishu* agree on this definition (e.g., Guo Xiaoting 2013, Lin Junjia 2012, Geng Ying 1983, Cui Yunhua 2005, Yao Ying 2007, Hu Wenbin 1985, and Suet Ying Chiu 2007).

109 English translations in this chapter are mine unless indicated otherwise.

110 This translation is taken from Suet Ying Chiu 2007: 7–8.

Since all of the information about *zidishu* here came from a *zidishu* practitioner who lived when the art was still prevalent, we accept the description as accurate. A perusal of the miscellaneous writings on *zidishu* further convinces one of the precision of the above account. The modern *Honglou meng* scholar Hu Wenbin (1985: 141) defines *zidishu* thus:

Zidishu (the Manchu Bannermen tales), also called *"qingyin zidishu"* (the Bannermen tales in pure tunes),[111] is a kind of ballad singing/storytelling art by and for the Manchu. According to the research of the ballad singing/storytelling experts, [the art] was prevalent in the area of Beijing and Shenyang of the northeast part of China from the years of the Qianlong Emperor's reign (1735-1795) to the end of the Qing Dynasty (1644-1911) lasting about one and a half centuries. After the decline of its performance, *zidishu*'s melodic texts were adopted in various northern ballad singing/storytelling genres such as Drum Lyrics, Henan Narrative-Singing, and Song and Dance Duets that are still performed on stage today.

子弟書又稱清音子弟書, 是我國滿族民間的曲藝。根據曲藝專家們的考證, 是從乾隆年起至清末為止, 子弟書在北京地區, 東北瀋陽等地方盛行長達一個半世紀左右。子弟書演出衰落以後, 其曲本為北方各種大鼓, 墜子, 二人轉等曲種所採用, 至今還在曲壇上廣為演唱。

Guo Xiaoting (2013) further indicates that *qingyin zidishu*, like *jingyin zidishu* (Bannermen tales of Beijing) and *wei zidishu* (Bannermen tales of Tianjin), is a regional label, indicating that the referred works were published in Shenyang. According to Guo, in Qing historical documents, the Manchu language was often called *qingyu* and books written in Manchu language *qingshu*. So it is logical to refer to those *zidishu* published in Shenyang, the old Qing capital, as *qingyin zidishu* (Bannermen tales of Shenyang).[112]

The generic features of *zidishu* are similar to *guci*, or Drum Lyrics. However, whereas the former contains only singing parts, the latter has both chanting and speaking sections. *Zidishu* can be divided into chapters: they vary in chapter numbers (with a range from one to thirty), but each chapter normally contains eighty to one hundred stanzas. The lyrics of the tales adopt the thirteen rhymes habitually used by northern oral performing arts of China. Mainly heptasyllabic in line length, additional words can be inserted in a line of *zidishu* for balance. Most *zidishu* start with the eight-lined and heptasyllabic-opening poem(s) and end with a closing verse that varies from two to eight stanzas.

---

111 There are several different interpretations of this term. For other interpretations, see Guo Xiaoting's explanation below and the next footnote of this article.

112 Other interpretations of this terminology include: (1) the elegance of the tales; (2) performances without music accompaniment; or (3) the amateur nature of the art. For detailed analysis, see Guo 2013: 22-23.

The earliest existing piece of *zidishu* is believed to be Luo Songchuang's (n.d.) block-printed edition of "Lady Zhuang Burns Incense to Worship" (Zhuangshi jiangxiang), which dates to 1756. Since this piece demonstrates all of the generic and stylistic features of a full-blown *zidishu*, the formation stage of the art can be traced to earlier times, to the early Qianlong period from 1735 to 1756, or even to the Yongzheng period (1722–1735). The art peaked during the reigns of the Jiaqing (1796–1820) and Daoguang (1820–1850) emperors with the production of the best works and the appearance of representative *zidishu* writer-performers such as Shi Yukun (n.d.) and Helü shi (n.d.). In the seventeenth year of Jiaqing (1813), the Qing court sent some members of the royal clan and Bannermen to Shenyang and the art of *zidishu* became popular there in the following years. When *Zidishu* became a trade of blind professional storytellers in Tianjin at the turn of the twentieth century, it ebbed in popularity and gradually disappeared from the stage (Guo 2013: 1–19).

Since most of the *zidishu* writers were anonymous or used a pseudonym, we know very little of their personal lives. However, as a group, they left ninety *zidishu* pieces (over 20% of the extant texts) reflecting the daily concerns and activities, family relationships, and social interactions of the Bannermen society during the mid- and late Qing. These so-called original creations of Bannermen provide a rich socio-cultural and literary context for all of the *zidishu* works and the backgrounds of their authors. Guo Xiaoting's study on *zidishu* and the Qing Bannermen society, in particular, offers a close reading of these contemporary stories/ballads, which piece together a social panorama of their respective writers.

For the present study, the most relevant background information of the *zidishu* writers includes the following. First, the Bannermen were provided with sufficient government allowance, or "money and grain" (*qianliang*), and lived comfortably. After the Manchus occupied Beijing, there were several hundreds of thousands of Bannermen who settled in the inner city of Beijing and a soldier was allocated three to four taels of silver monthly in addition to rationed rice. This amount, at the time, was equivalent to the salary of a county magistrate of the seventh rank. Some Bannermen were much more affluent, because they had either inherited large property of land and/or were given high-ranking official posts due to their blood lineage (*yinsheng*). This relatively comfortable existence allowed Bannermen to devote their time and energy to write *zidishu* (Guo 2013: 30–32). Second, except for one piece written in both Chinese and Manchu, all other extant *zidishu* texts are in Chinese. This fact, combined with the Kangxi (1654–1722) emperor's decision to abolish the special civil examination held for the Bannermen in 1687, indicates the Bannermen's high level of education in Chinese language and culture. Indeed, Bannermen valued education, and within their community, both private and public schools were established for teaching children from eight or ten years old on. In addition, they formed an avid readership of vernacular Chinese fiction and the most enthusiastic audience of the Beijing theater. Good education and being well versed in Chinese literature prepared the Bannermen writers in the new literary genre of *zidishu*. Finally, the lifestyle of Bannermen can be described as leisurely but restricted in profession and activity scope. The Qing court forbade Bannermen from working in any profession other than in the imperial government or its military. They lived in the inner city of Beijing where no theater or other professional entertainments were permitted. If Bannermen wanted to watch plays or oral performing arts, they had to travel to the outer city and return before the curfew. This was partly why Bannermen developed their own oral performing art, *zidishu*, which they performed mainly in their own households or in other small venues as amateurs. Indeed, *zidishu* was an art form by Qing Bannermen for the entertainment of other Bannermen and their families. The form was born and thrived in this particular historical and socio-cultural context.

If the performance of *zidishu* disappeared on stage in the early Republic, many of its lyric texts were well preserved and are still extant to this day. Recent studies indicate that about 80% of the more than 400 extant *zidishu* texts are adaptations of previous historical, fictional, and theatrical works, and the other 20% are reflections of the contemporary lives of the Bannermen (Guo 2013: 179). Among the fictional adaptations, *Honglou meng zidishu* are outstanding in both quantity and quality. They also present an interesting case of comparison with the many other forms of *Honglou meng* rewrites, including fictional sequels, imitative works, oral storytelling, and opera scripts, produced during the same period. In joining these other rewrites, *Honglou meng zidishu* made a significant contribution to the interpretation, dissemination, generic transformation, and popularization of Cao Xueqin's masterpiece. This study intends to examine this group of writings in the following three perspectives: First, what stories or themes did the *zidishu* writers and/or performers select from the original, and what does this tell us about these rewriters and performers in terms of their socio-cultural identity? Second, how were the chosen stories and characters told differently in the *zidishu* texts, in terms of characterization, ideology, and artistic presentation? How did the *zididshu* writers differ from other rewriters in terms of their ways of responding to and critiquing *Honglou meng*? Last, what were the contributions of *zidishu* to popularizing and re-creating Cao's original? More specifically, the particular thematic and artistic strategies of a representative text, entitled "Destiny of Dew and Tears" (Lulei yuan), are probed for their successful generic reformulation from a fictional piece to a ballad-singing/storytelling script.

GENERAL INFORMATION ABOUT *HONGLOU MENG ZIDISHU*

Yisu (1981) records thirty-nine titles of *Honglou meng zidishu* texts, although not all of these titles are extant. In 1983, Hu Wenbin edited a collection of *Honglou meng zidishu* that contains twenty-seven works. A Taiwan scholar, Lin Junjia (2012), published another collection with thirty-two pieces of *Honglou meng* ballad. In addition to those included in Hu (1983), Lin's collection adds two different versions of "Baoyu and Daiyu Exchange Feelings" (Eryu lun xin), "Daiyu Buries Flowers" (Daiyu zang hua), "Baochai Gives Birth to Baoyu's son" (Baochai chan yu), and the two early missing chapters for the "The Jade Is Fragrant and the Flower Talks" (Yu xiang hua yu) piece contained in Hu Wenbin's collection. The two-chaptered "Baoyu Visits the Sick Daiyu" (Tanbing) is taken verbatim from "Lin Daiyu Laments the Autumn" (Beiqiu) and may be used as a separate piece only for performance, so it is not in fact an addition to Hu's edition. I use Hu Wenbin's and Lin Junjia's collections as my primary sources.

Although the texts are not dated, we are informed that *Honglou meng zidishu* were circulated and performed not long after the publication of the Cheng-Gao edition of the original *Honglou meng* in 1791. A piece focusing on Lin Daiyu's story, entitled "Daiyu Laments the Autumn" (Beiqiu) was certainly one of the earliest *zidishu* produced and performed by Manchu Bannermen in Beijing. De Shuoting , in his *Caozhu yichuan* (A string of grass beads) from 1817, describes the performance of "Daiyu Laments the Autumn" in Beijing in a popular song, *zhuzhi ci*, and it reads: "'Daiyu Laments the Autumn' of the Western Melody really pleases one's ears" (西韻《悲秋》書可聽) (Hu 1985: 142; Guo 2013: 16). Beneath this description, De Shouting further explains that "*Zidishu* has two melodies called the Eastern Melody and the Western Melody. The Western Melody is close to *kunqu*. 'Daiyu Laments the Autumn' tells Lin Daiyu's story from *Honglou meng*" (子弟書有東西二韻, 西韻若昆曲。《悲秋》即《紅樓夢》中黛玉故事) (Hu 1985: 142).[113]

Like other *zidishu* writers, the authors of *Honglou meng zidishu* concealed their authorship, electing to use pseudonyms or simply remaining anonymous.[114] This is not surprising, as ballad singing or oral performing arts have historically been performed in the venues of "*goulan wasi*" (entertainment places and amusement parks) and are considered to be low art forms. In addition, the Qing court forbade Bannermen from taking in any performing arts as a profession, and the most severe punishment was to be stripped of

---

113 Whereaas the Western Melody was close to *kunqu*—gentle and lingering, and dealing with romantic stories, the Eastern Melody was similar to the *yiyang* tune—thumping and impassioning, usually relating the stories of war and heroes. See Guo 2013:23.

114 In Hu Wenbin's collection, ten works have pseudonyms and seventeen are anonymous.

one's Bannerman status; thus, open association with ballad singing was not a wise career move. Even for Han Xiaochuang, the most accomplished and prolific *zidishu* writer, one can hardly find any reliable source of information about his personal life. The practice of anonymity might also be related to the Bannermen writers'/performers' motives for writing and performing—that is, for play or self-amusement. In these circles, amateur performers (*piaoyou*) enjoyed a higher status than did the professional ones (*jianghu yiren*) (Chiu 2007: 68–144). Although we are unable to find useful information about the writers' personal lives, they often mention their purposes and circumstances in their respective *zidishu* texts.

To most of the writers, to "divert oneself from boredom" (*jie menfan*) or to "amuse oneself to while away the time" (*xian xiaoqian*) was one of the main reasons behind their creations. They describe writing scenarios when they were inebriated or had leisure time on a long spring afternoon or an idle autumn night. Such descriptions are consistent with their lifestyles as privileged Manchu Bannermen who depended on a government allowance and lived a life of leisure. As the Qing court prohibited them from taking on other professions except for serving the court or the military, the Bannermen who did not have a real post would idle about, trying to find some diversions from their boredom. The opening poem to "Baoyu Thinks of Daiyu and Shows Affection to Fivey" (Siyu xihuan) provides an apt image of the writer amusing himself by writing:

The mild breeze of spring moves and waves in the bright sunny day,
Willows are seductive and flowers glow, and their beauty comes naturally.
Instead of playing a musical instrument and performing the pure melody,
I momentarily take out an ancient inkstone to write about beautiful ladies.
As a change, I write a piece of *zidishu* as a new ballad,
And leave out the old tunes and stereotypical conventions.
I have completed this rustic work that other might laugh at,
[But in so doing,] I lament the deep passion [of Cao Xueqin] and distract myself from
    boredom.

和風動瀲豔陽天，
柳媚花明出自然。
不向絲桐拂正調，
暫從古硯寫紅顏。
換出筆墨新文詠，
除去宮商舊套刪。
演成俚句堪人笑，
閑歡癡情解悶煩。
(Hu 1983: 291)

This poem not only informs us of the purpose and circumstances of the composition of the piece, it also tells us that he was good at playing music and composing ballads. This is obviously a writer who could fulfill the dual duty of writing lyrics and composing tunes for *zidishu*. We could assume that he performed *zidishu* as well, since the word "*yancheng*" may be understood as to "complete the telling of the story." Here, "telling" is ambiguous, for it can mean either narrator telling the story to his readers, or a performer singing the ballads to an audience. The common understanding of the *zidishu* performance also confirms that the Manchu amateur performers were cultured and well versed in literature, and many of them played the *sanxian*, a stringed instrument. One can therefore imagine that they could have readily assumed the triple status of writer, composer, and performer of *zidishu*.

Writing to appreciate and critique their parent novel was a common attribute of the authors of *Honglou meng zidishu*. In rewriting the stories of *Honglou meng*, the *zidishu* writers consistently played a dual role as appreciative reader of Cao's masterpiece and an "inferior" rewriter whose "rustic" writing cannot be compared with the superior skills of the original (ironically, both the original and rewritten texts are often mentioned in the same breath).

In the opening poems, or *shipian*, or the very end of the *zidishu* text, several authors explicitly declare their admiration for *Honglou meng*, praising Cao Xueqin's remarkable imagination and ingenious portrayal of the characters. In "Baochai Helps with the Embroidery" (Baochai daixiu), a *zidishu* based on the episode of Xue Baochai helping Aroma with an embroidery for Jia Baoyu in chapter 36 of *Honglou meng*, Han Xiaochuang states that: "It is so difficult to write the tender emotions and jealous intentions of this chapter; I mock myself as an old awkward writer whose writing cannot be compared to the remarkable writing of *Honglou meng*" (此一回柔情醋意真難寫, 笑老拙怎比紅樓筆墨奇) (Hu 1983: 71). An anonymous writer who wrote "Charmante Scratches a 'Qiang' and Mystifies a Beholder" (Chunling huaqiang), a story taken from chapter 30 of *Honglou meng*, also echoes Han in praising Cao Xueqin by saying: "I admire [the author of] *Honglou meng* and wonder how he came up with such a marvelous depiction, and how he was able to produce more and more fine writing like this" (羨紅樓何處得來生花筆, 似這般花樣他越寫越多) (Hu 1983: 66).

Linda Hutcheon in her book, *A Theory of Adaptation*, identifies the characteristics of an adaptation as follows:

- An acknowledged transposition of a recognizable other work or works
- A creative *and* an interpretive act of appropriation/salvaging
- An extended intertextual engagement with the adapted work

Therefore, an adaptation is a derivation that is not derivative—a work that is second without being secondary. It is its own palimpsestic thing. (Hutcheon 2006: 8–9)

As appreciative and sophisticated readers, as well as adaptors, of *Honglou meng*, the *zidishu* authors certainly played a role that is far beyond entertaining themselves. In fact, they contributed to the interpretation and the "salvaging"/dissemination of Cao Xueqin's novel: they evaluated and critiqued *Honglou meng* from both ideological and artistic perspectives. Even as they declare their genuine veneration for *Honglou meng*, they cannot help but rewrite it in accordance with their own moral, sentimental, and aesthetic values. More important, changes had to be made from the fictional original to fit the story into the genre of the ballad. The writers' self-deprecating gesture seems to be disingenuous, as they not only placed their own writings on par with Cao Xueqin's original, but in the *zidishu* texts in question, one also senses a desire for self-display in some of the most modified and flowery pieces, particularly those of Han Xiaochuang.

IDENTIFYING WITH CAO XUEQIN: *ZIDISHU*'S APPRECIATION AND RE-PRESENTATION OF *HONGLOU MENG*

Generally speaking, the *Honglou meng zidishu* texts are faithful rewrites of Cao Xueqin's original. In contrast to the fictional sequels that were produced in the same period and that focused on altering the tragic ending of Gao E's continuation, the majority of the stories in the *zidishu* series were chosen from Cao Xueqin's first eighty chapters, and only five of thirty-two texts retell stories from Gao E's last forty chapters. The five pieces are: "Baoyu and Adamantina Listen to Daiyu Play the Zither" (Shuangyu tingqin) from chapter 87; "The Story of the Stone" (Shitou ji) and "The Destiny of Dew and Tears" from chapters 96 to 98 and 104, "Baoyu Thinks of Daiyu and Shows Affection to Fivey" from chapter 109, and "Baochai Gives Birth to Baoyu's son" from chapter 120. Among these five pieces, "The Story of the Stone" completely alters Gao E's treatment of Baoyu's wedding and Daiyu's death and may be read as a critical response to Gao and an attempt to return to Cao Xueqin's original design.[115] Han Xiaochuang's "The Destiny of Dew and Tears," by contrast, presents a case of deepening sentimentality and enhanced artistry in the section describing the doomed love between Daiyu and Baoyu, and Daiyu's untimely death.[116] Such a disproportionate selection of material and the more outright challenge to Gao E's writing

---

115 I deal with this piece specifically in the second part of this study.
116 A more detailed analysis is provided in the third part of this study.

clearly demonstrate the *zidishu* writers' preference for the first of the two parts of the novel.

In addition to this obvious preference for Cao Xueqin's part, the *Honglou meng zidishu* writers were also quite selective and focused in their reworking of the characters, themes, and stories. I argue that such choices are not random but reflect the rewriters' understanding and appraisal of the original, their resonance with the values and sentiments of Cao Xueqin, and their tastes as cultural elite and as a unique group of literati. Sharing the lifestyle of the Bannermen and living in a time of dynastic and personal decline, this group of rewriters might have had more in common with Cao Xueqin than other *Honglou meng* readers of that period did. The *Honglou meng zidishu* can be divided into four different subgroups in terms of their subject matter: (1) the stories of Baoyu and Daiyu and their doomed love (ten texts); (2) the episodes related to Skybright (five texts); (3) Grannie Liu's series (ten texts); (4) a group of episodes considered to be "*yunshi*" or tasteful events (seven texts).

The first two subgroups deal with the theme of *qing*, a theme that is most prominent in *Honglou meng* but was severely undermined or even absent in the fictional sequels to it. By the time Cao Xueqin wrote *Honglou meng*, the subject of *qing* had already occupied center stage in Chinese vernacular fiction and drama for more than a century, and almost all the ramifications of *qing* had been treated in different fictional genres. If *Jin Ping Mei*, a milestone in dealing with the subject of desire, demonstrated "various forms of an individual's private desires in their fullest social context" (Huang 2001: 59), different implications of emotions, such as love and feeling (*qing*) versus lust or carnal passion (*yu*) or of *qing* versus reason/principle (*li*), had been continuously explored in the genre of erotic fiction, scholar-beauty fiction, and the novel of manners. The concept of *qing* was used or misused, abused and rescued, represented or misrepresented, and defined and redefined in connection with different ideologies, such as the Confucian sense of moral judgment, Buddhist or Taoist ideas of enlightenment, or the popular belief in karmic retribution. In two Qing literary novels, *A Supplement to the Journey to the West* (Xiyou bu) attributed to Dong Yue (1620–1686), and *The Unofficial History of Confucian Scholars* (Rulin waishi) by Wu Jingzi (1701–1754), the literary discourse on the subject of *qing* was elevated to a higher and more sophisticated level in which the psychology of *qing*, as well as the stereotypical literary representations of it, are scrutinized and mocked by the two Qing novelists. This long-lasting and multifaceted discourse on the subject of *qing* in vernacular fiction and drama finally gave rise to *Honglou meng*, a novel that is considered "a profound novelistic rehearsal as well as rethinking of all of the major motifs of *qing* throughout its history" (Huang 2001: 84).

As a novel that dwells deeply and complexly on *qing*, *Honglou meng* invites its readers to a whole range of representations and interpretations of this subject, which may be summed up in two sets of dichotomies: the dichotomy of "lust of the mind" (*yiyin*) versus the "lust of the flesh" (*pifu lanyin*); and the dichotomy of individual desire and subjectivity versus Confucian rituals and social expectations. Although a heavily loaded word that could mean different things for different fictional characters in various situations in *Honglou meng*, *qing* as a literary concept and image is mainly contrasted with *yu* and *li*—two dichotomous literary and ideological concepts. In contrast with *yu*, or the "lust of the flesh," *qing* is purified, raised to an emotional level and to a spiritual bond, and deemphasizes (although is not completely stripped of) carnal pleasure. *Qing* is best embodied in the love shared by Jia Baoyu and Lin Daiyu, Baoyu's affection for and emotional bond with all the beautiful and talented girls in the Prospect Garden, including his female cousins and maids, as well as in his friendships with several effeminate men. In opposition to *li*, *qing* in *Honglou meng*, particularly in the character of Baoyu, represents a kind of individualistic desire or subjectivity that challenges Neo-Confucian morality and rituals, refusing to be contaminated by worldly gains and social corruption and devaluing Confucian careerism and the utility of learning. If the dichotomy of "lust of the mind" and "lust of the flesh" mainly works within the part that contains the story of the "mirror of the romance" (*fengyue baojian*), an earlier text embedded in the novel,[117] the contrast between individual desire and the social mandate is best revealed in the part about Prospect Garden—a little heaven created by the author to allow the individual desires of Baoyu and his female companions to grow and thrive. In addition, many other issues raised in earlier literature, "such as the narcissistic nature of *qing*, representation versus desire, and the illusionary nature of the autonomous world of *qing*, are further explored in *Honglou meng*, with great subtlety" (Huang 2001: 83).

In dealing with the theme of *qing*, the *zidishu* writers echo *Honglou meng*'s sublimation of *qing* but concentrate on the love shared by Baoyu and two female characters, namely Daiyu and her double, Skybright. In fact, the *zidishu* rewrites make the two female characters into personifications of *qing*.

---

117 Several modern scholars keenly note the amalgamation of the two stylistically and ideologically different texts in the novel—an earlier text entitled *The Precious Mirror of Romance* (*Fengyue baojian*, a namesake for the mirror given to Jia Rui in chapter 12) and a later narrative named *The Story of the Stone* (*Shitou ji*) referring to Cao Xueqin's original text. Consisting of the chapters on Jia Rui, Qin Keqing, Qin Zhong, the You sisters, and Duo Guniang (or Miss Duo), the narrative of *The Precious Mirror of Romance* unfolds at a relatively hurried pace with a melodramatic style that contrasts with the lyric quality of much of the first eighty chapters of the novel. More important, these chapters present an orthodox ideology in dealing with *qing* and *yu*, described by Wai-yee Li (1993: 233) as comprising "a world (*ching-chieh*) of the Precious Mirror where love is carnal and transgressive (i.e., *ch'ing* is often the equivalent of *se*), and where the mythic-fantastic realm is invoked to reimpose order and to dramatize the opposition between obsessive sexual passion and well-defined moral imperatives."

In some ways, the two female characters replace Jia Baoyu to occupy center stage of the retold stories and both ballads of Daiyu and Skybright focus on the heightened emotional points of their lives. While Daiyu's cycle relates her meeting with Baoyu for the first time, her burial of the flowers in the spring, her desolate laments in the autumn, and her emotional and tragic death after hearing the news of Baoyu's marriage to Baochai, Skybright's cycle focuses on mending Baoyu's cloak when she is ill, her dismissal by Lady Wang, her meeting with Baoyu before her death, and finally, Baoyu's writing a long elegy for her. In these *zidishu* texts, Daiyu and Skybright are not only further idealized as the most desirable lovers for Jia Baoyu but are poetized as muses for the poet. The poet's role is played by both Baoyu, the fictional character in the ballad, and the *zidishu* author who sometimes speaks in his own voice but often uses Baoyu as a mouthpiece. Inspired by Daiyu's and Skybright's beauty, talents, moral purity, and, most important, their intensified *qing*, the poet— Baoyu/the author—expresses his deep love for them and his profound loss at their deaths.

"Baoyu and Daiyu Bury Flowers" (Shuangyu maihong), a work written by an anonymous writer, recasts the episode of Baoyu and Daiyu burying flower petals in chapter 23 of *Honglou meng*. Although the title is "*shuangyu*" ("two jades" signify Baoyu and Daiyu, because their names share the same character of "yu" or jade), this is really a piece about Lin Daiyu and her lament at the fading flowers and the passing of spring. The opening poem clearly indicates who actually inspired the author to write this piece:

> The most talented would suffer from the deepest sorrow;
> The person who pitied flowers did not stay for blossoms.
> Now her fragrant tomb is already buried by green grasses;
> In her days the spring breeze coiled about the painted tower.
> The fallen red petals were splendid on the ground;
> A forest of pretty birds sung pleasantly.
> Who is able to understand Daiyu's refined intention?
> She ends up becoming a topic of people's discussions about romance.

> 絕世聰明絕代愁，
> 惜花人不為花留。
> 於今香塚埋芳草。
> 當日春風繞畫樓。
> 滿地落紅飛燦爛，
> 一林姣鳥叫勾輈。
> 顰卿雅意誰能解，
> 只落得千古風流作話頭。
> (Hu 1983: 27)

The poem starts with the poet's comment on Daiyu's deepest sorrow—flowers quickly fading as a metaphor of the untimely passage of youth and beauty—then moves to the poet's sighing over Daiyu's fate—her appreciation of the flowers' beauty and their fleeting existence but her inability to enjoy the flowers anymore. The poet then imagines that Daiyu's fragrant tomb, created especially for the flower petals, now would have grown a lot of green grass since she is no longer there to care for it; this further turns his imagination back to Daiyu's days when the fallen petals inspired her to act as the flower burier and to lament them as a poet. Those days of fading spring were still beautiful with Daiyu there to feel and acknowledge them. The poem finally ends with an expression of profound regret—that people nowadays cannot really understand Daiyu's sorrow and actions, but can only treat them as the result of her disappointment in love. To the author of this poem, Daiyu's "refined intention," or qing, is something that goes beyond personal love. In fact, the poet repeats this claim at the very end of the zidishu text, where the last sentence reads: "I sigh that Daiyu's pity for the flowers is as endless and deep as the sea; my pen fails to depict her ten thousand different sorrows" (歎顰卿無邊芳意深如海, 筆尖難畫佳人萬種愁) (Hu 1983: 30). Although the poet does not explain directly what Daiyu's "refined intention" is, by associating Daiyu's flower burial with *The Peony Pavilion* (Mudan ting), the most famous play to celebrate qing, and with historical female figures such as Wang Zhaojun and Su Xiaoxiao, he extends the meaning of qing beyond personal love and elevates it to a form of affirming and preserving the self so that could remain uncontaminated by a world of vulgarity and corruption.

As Daiyu's double, Skybright shares Daiyu's beauty, her flower identity (hibiscus flower), her deep but unfulfilled love for Baoyu, her purity, and her intense qing that lingers on even after her death. In Cao Xueqin's novel, Skybright's death spurs Baoyu to write the most touching elegy to express his everlasting sorrow. In the ballad script "Lady Wang Dismisses Skybright" (Qian Qingwen), the author Jiaochuang (pseudonym, The Window under the Plantain) also reveals why Skybright's story moves him deeply and inspires him to rewrite a zidishu piece for her. The second stanza of his opening poem reads: "I am saddened that the young master sees Skybright's things after she dies, and in memory of her, writes 'An Invocation to the Hibiscus Spirit;' I sigh that the beautiful girl's fragrant soul has left this world just like a jade broken into pieces and a pearl sunk into deep water" (哀公子物在人亡填詞作誄, 歎佳人芳魂豔魄玉碎珠沉) (Hu 1983: 198). Jiaochuang is attracted to Skybright as a fictional character not only because of her superior beauty and character and her most undeserved tragic fate, but also because of Baoyu's (actually Cao Xueqin's) writing that celebrates and commemorates her as a flower fairy. As an incarnation of Hibiscus Fairy, Skybright is described as "in worth value more precious than gold or jade, in nature more pure than ice or snow, in wit more brilliant than the sun or stars, in complexion more beautiful than the moon or than flowers" (Cao 1980: 3: 576). To Jiaochuang, Skybright is forever memorialized by Baoyu's (Cao Xueqin's) most touching and marvelous poem, and she is someone who not only embodies but also elevates the poet's (Baoyu's/Cao Xueqin's, and of course, in turn, Jiaochuang's) *qing* to its most sublime level. The celebration of *qing* and its two female personifications are more fully displayed in the longer and better written *zidishu* pieces such as "The Invocation to the Hibiscus Spirit" (Furong lei), "Daiyu Laments the Autumn," and "The Destiny of Dew and Tears," which will be discussed in detail in the latter sections of this study.

If modern critics consider *Honglou meng zidishu's* emphasis on Lin Daiyu and Skybright as representatives of *qing* is consistent with Cao Xueqin's original, they feel less certain about the *zidishu* writers' fascination with Grannie Liu, a very minor character from the novel. The *Honglou meng zidishu* writers devote almost the same amount of attention and textual space to this character as they do to Daiyu and Skybright. Hu Wenbin's collection contains a total of nine rewrites of Grannie Liu, and these stories are taken from chapters 6, 39, 40, 41, and 42 of *Honglou meng*, covering every detail of Grannie Liu's first two visits to the Rong Mansion and the Prospect Garden. In addition, the piece on Baochai giving birth to Baoyu's son in Lin Junjia's collection adds the plot of Grannie Liu coming back to help with Baochai's delivery based on chapter 120 of Gao E's continuation. As a way of explaining the Bannermen's great interest in this old country woman, some scholars claim that they were "lower class intellectuals" and presume that, as lower class intellectuals, they would be more interested in a poor old country woman's life (Geng 1983: 8). Others attribute such an interest to the Manchu Bannermen's change of lifestyle in the mid-Qing, particularly when some of them were relocated to Shenyang to cultivate virgin land under the Qianlong Emperor's imperial edict (Chiu 2007: 234–236). While the former argument may be inconsistent with most scholars' views about the class status of the *zidishu* writers, without specific dates of publication and accurate information about the authorships to support it, the latter theory is speculative.[118] I would argue that the strong interest in Grannie Liu demonstrated by the *Honglou meng zidishu* writers reflects their profound understanding and appreciation of Cao Xueqin's intentions and the underlying messages endowed to this character in *Honglou meng*—namely, the artistic value of contrast, the Confucian concept of "having compassion for the old and poor" (*xilao*

---

[118] According to Guo Xiaoting (3013: 105), among the 404 extant *zidishu* texts, there is not a single work reflecting the lives of peasants, merchants, or artisans. This means that the writers were not familiar with these people's lives. This further indicates that the suggestion that the Bannermen writers might have experienced the harsh life of peasants is speculation.

lianpin), and the irony and inversion of the fates of rising and falling under-scored throughout the whole novel.

Although she is a minor figure unrelated to the Jias, Grannie Liu plays a significant role in the narrative structure of Cao's original novel. Her famous "three visits" to the Rong Mansion and the Prospect Garden occur at the most crucial points of the Jia family fortune and become indicators of her hosts' prosperity and decline. In addition, Grannie Liu's country life and farming experience present a striking contrast to the Jias' extravagant and pampered lifestyle and their boredom turned to idleness. The two chapters (40 and 41) about her visit to the Prospect Garden are considered the noisiest and liveliest episodes in the novel; to provide a foil to them, they are sandwiched between quieter scenes and events. Even the rustic and hilarious flavor of Grannie Liu's language contrasts with that of the young garden residents whose talks are elegant and reserved.

When Patience tries to convince Grannie Liu to meet Grandmother Jia, she describes Grandmother Jia as someone who has "compassion for the old and poor." Although this seems to be a passing comment in the novel, it is actually a time-honored theme in Chinese literature and a subject that Cao Xueqin attended to in dealing with the episodes of Grannie Liu and of Bailiff Wu Jinxiao sending New Year gifts to the Ning Mansion in chapter 53. "*Min nong*" (having compassion for farmers) is a well-established theme in Chinese poetry; Li Shen (772–846) and Yang Wanli (1127–1206) are famous for writing poems on this subject. In fact, Jia Baoyu recites one of Li Shen's "*min nong*" poems in chapter 15: "Each grain of rice we ever ate/ Cost someone else a drop of sweat." (誰知盤中餐, 粒粒皆辛苦) (Cao 1973: 1: 292). Building a "village"—"Daoxiang cun," or The Village of Fragrant Rice—in the Prospect Garden should not be considered as unintentional by Cao Xueqin, but rather his pur-poseful design for artistic contrast as well as a resonance of the old "*min nong*" theme (or a mockery of this theme if we take seriously Baoyu's remarks about the unnaturalness of the Village of Fragrant Rice).

Finally, but probably most importantly, the story line of Grannie Liu re-veals the irony and inversion of fates that seems to toy with human life. While the Jias journey downward in power and fortune, Grannie Liu's star is on the rise, even though her fortune is modest in comparison with that of the Jias in their better days. However, the role reversal between Wang Xifeng and Gran-nie Liu cannot be more poignant, for the former turns from being the rescuer of the latter into being rescued by her. In turning the wheel of fortune here, Cao Xueqin's message probably lies more in how low a family of power and wealth can fall than in anything else. This is where we can sense his profound personal loss, sadness, and helplessness as the heir of a fallen house, who had witnessed, with open eyes, the inevitable and irredeemable downward course of his family and his life.

A close reading of the Grannie Liu series in *zidishu* reveals that all of the above three aspects—the artistic value of contrast, the Confucian concept of "having compassion for the old and poor," and the irony and inversion of rising and falling—are reaffirmed and serve as the motives for reworking the respective *zidishu* texts. In the piece entitled "Faithful Makes Three Calls on Wine Games of Dominoes" (Sanxuan yapailing), the anonymous author starts his piece by indicating the contrastive function of Grannie Liu's episodes and the freshness that they bring to the fictional characters and the readers of Cao's novel as well as to those of *zidishu* ballads:

> Bitter greens will bloom when the spring comes,
> They could surpass the most beautiful flowers in decorating the wilderness.
> The rich will tire of rouge and powder,
> So that they do not mind talking about raising silkworms and weaving hemp.
> Seeking joy, there's no harm in being "vulgar and disgusting,"
> Now savoring [the episodes of Grannie Liu], I would say that they can be compared with
>   those that are "flowery and resplendent."
> In accompanying the wine, Faithful makes three calls on the wine game of Dominoes,
> She orders about the old country woman who makes funny jokes.

> 苦菜逢春亦放花，
> 點裝野景勝奇芭。
> 應嫌胭脂還嫌粉，
> 重問蠶桑複問麻。
> 快意不妨俗且厭，
> 追思敢比麗而華。
> 金鴛鴦牙牌佐酒三宣令，
> 支使那惹笑的村婆費齒牙。
> (Hu 1983: 127)

It is very clear here that the author of this piece appreciates the aesthetic value of the Grannie Liu series, as he discusses and anticipates the impact of these episodes on three different groups of readers/audiences. The first group of readers is the rich Jias who are entertained by Grannie Liu's rustic and refreshing stories and jokes in Cao Xueqin's novel. The second group comprises the readers of *Honglou meng*, those like the author himself. The author admits that he was drawn to the Grannie Liu sections, thinking that they could be compared to the most refined parts of Cao's novel. Such artistic excellence and effect obviously stimulated the author's interest in retelling these episodes to his audience/readers in his *zidishu* rewrite, and in so doing, he hoped to reproduce the same artistry that Cao had achieved in his original.

In the Grannie Liu series, "Granny Liu Visits the Rong Mansion a Second Time" (Er ru Rongguo fu) is the longest of the Granny Liu pieces, containing twelve chapters. Both the date and authorship are unknown. This piece has drawn the attention of many scholars because of its *"min nong"* theme: the author holds great sympathy, not only for Grannie Liu, but for farmers in general, and seems to be knowledgeable about farming life. In fact, chapter 10 of this piece mainly focuses on the hardships of agricultural labor and livelihood:

This old woman finds a stool and sits beside the bed;
She recounts farmers' various kinds of hardships.
She says that a farmer needs to repair his plough as early as the second day of the
    second month;
She says that at the time of the vernal equinox the farm cattle will break the earth.
She says the spring rain is as precious as "Holy Water,"
She says one cart load of manure is as valuable as gold.
She explains that one plants seeds of gourds at the time of the Tomb-sweeping Festival;
She explains that the seedlings of autumn crops will be thinned out in the season
    of Grain Rain in the third month.
A farmer's livelihood depends on the autumn harvest;
It would be disastrous if there were a drought that lasted over half a month.
She then points out that there should be no rain when the wheat is harvested,
However, the land of autumn crops longs for rainy weather.
She afterwards talks about how to grow sesames and soya beans,
And how to cultivate broomcorn millets, wheat, and sorghums.
She describes how tough it is for the wife and son to send meals to the field;
And how diligent one needs to be to watch melons in a thatched shed.
She subsequently turns to the work of spinning thread, fluffing cotton, and weaving
    cloth,
And to the matters of taking crops to the market and of paying taxes.
She complains about the year of a big drought when no single drop of rain fell,
And the burning sun spat out clouds of fire.
She resents the year when a storm flooded crops,
As a result not a single grain was harvested and farmers had to eat grass roots.
She finally mentions milling crops, winnowing, and stacking grass and beanstalks,
As well as killing chickens, making pancakes, and meeting fellow villagers.
She concludes that farming is like people begging for food from the Heaven,
That all work of cultivating, growing, and harvesting relies on the will of the gods.

這婆子又尋杌凳挨床坐,
訴說那田家的萬苦與千辛。
因說道龍抬頭後修犁杖,

又說道耕牛劃地等春分。
又說道三月的春雨難如聖水,
又說道一車的糞土貴似黃金。
又說那清明節種下了葫蘆籽,
又說那穀雨時分定了軟秋根。
全仗著秋麥收了才吃飯,
倘若是半月的晴旱就害死人。
又說那麥子登場不要雨,
又說那大田六月盼連陰。
又說那芝麻黃豆如何種,
又說那糜麥高粱怎的耘。
又說那田間送飯妻兒的苦,
又說那棚下看瓜日夜的勤。
又說那紡線彈棉織大布,
又說那糧食上市納租銀。
又說是那年大旱無滴雨,
赤日炎炎冒火雲。
又說是那年大雨淹莊稼,
顆粒不收咽草根。
又說那壓碾揚場堆草豆,
又說那殺雞打餅會鄉親。
總說罷人和天年把飯討,
這耕種收割是仰仗著神。

(Hu 1983: 106–107)

Some modern scholars are very impressed by this writer's familiarity with farming and attribute this knowledge to life experience related to agriculture. Without completely ruling out this explanation, I would argue that a writer could gain such knowledge through reading about and observing farming. A well-versed literatus would certainly be familiar with and influenced by the time-honored literary theme of *min nong*. A piece of good *min nong* literature might induce an imitation, both in writing and in action, thereby displaying compassion for farmers. We see such imitation by Grandmother Jia and Jia Zheng in *Hongluo meng*. While Grandmother Jia's compassion toward Grannie Liu is probably more genuine than Jia Zheng's embrace of country life, both look at farming and country life from the perspective of outsiders, and their "connoisseurship" in this respect, particularly in the case of Jia Zheng, is ridiculed by Cao Xueqin through the character of Baoyu.

A set of forty-six paintings by the Yongzheng Emperor (re. 1722–1735) on the theme of farming and weaving that are preserved in the Palace Museum in Beijing has recently been made available on the Internet. These paintings, depicting various agricultural activities, are accompanied by poems that celebrate the joys of farming. In these paintings, it is the emperor who assumes the role of a farmer who works at farming. There are two points of releveance here. First, the Yongzheng Emperor had done his share of doubly imitating the *min nong* theme in both art and action (or maybe simply an act of *min nong* in the art or the painting). Second, if a Qing emperor showed such great interest in and paid homage to the subject of *min nong*, it is not remarkable that the subject would be so popular and used so frequently by the Manchu Bannermen ballad writers who lived only a generation or two later.

To many *Honglou meng zidishu* writers, the Grannie Liu series, particularly in the irony of fate and the untenability of power and wealth revealed in these episodes, mirror their own lives, thus stimulating their sympathy and providing lessons for their own situations. Several pieces in this series express an ironic or sarcastic viewpoint in commenting on the original fictional characters and events in *Honglou meng*, in turn revealing the authors' opinions about life in general and their own lives in particular. For example, in "Wang Xifeng Says Good-bye to Grannie Liu" (Fengjie'r songxing), the author laments the uncertainty of life and sighs: "Look at the pathetic end of Fengjie'r; she could not even provide the kind of security for her family that Grannie Liu did for hers" (試看鳳姐兒終身後, 還不及劉姥姥的身家保的牢) (Hu 1983: 143). In "Grannie Liu Adopts Qiao Jie'r" (Guoji Qiaojie'r), the writer warns those who desire wealth and honor and attach themselves to the rich and powerful by saying: "Smart birds would be tired by now and want to return to their bird-nests; [they] should not perch on high branches for long" (好鳥知還已倦飛, 高枝不必久棲遲) (Hu 1983: 139). Moreover, the author of "Grannie Liu Samples the Sleeping Accommodations at the House of Crimson Joy" (Zuiwo Yihong yuan) delivers the most interesting and ingenious irony in his "opening poem," which reads:

[Grannie Liu's] old eyes are blurred and cannot see things clearly,
The large quantity of wine makes her mind even more confused.
Although she refuses to admit that she is already drunk after countless cups,
She falls into a deep slumber dreaming "the dream of Handan."
"The House of Silk and Brocade" now adds to this country woman's day-dream,
She, the rustic one, is pleased in this "Home of Tenderness."
Why not enjoy a good sleep after a satisfying meal and wine?
I envy her as an outright person who adapts herself to circumstances.

老眼模糊看不真,
更兼多酒亂神魂。
千觴醖釀休辭醉,
一枕邯鄲已睡沉。
錦繡場添村婦夢,

溫柔鄉樂野人心。
酒余飯飽何妨睡,
可羨他是隨遇而安的爽快人。
(Hu 1983: 135)

Here, this poem has two literary allusions. First, in the fourth line, when mentioning Grannie Liu's sleep, the poet evokes the story of "the dream of Handan" told in a Tang tale entitled "The Story Inside the Pillow" (Zhen zhong ji) by the Tang writer Shen Jiji (c.759–800). The story tells of a young scholar Lu Sheng who, on his way to take the civil service examination, meets a Taoist priest at an inn in Handan. He falls asleep on the porcelain pillow given him by the priest while the priest starts to cook a pot of millet porridge. In Lu's dream, he enjoys over ten years of wealth, honor, and splendor. When he wakes up, the millet porridge is not yet done. The story is a Taoist allegory that reveals the illusive nature of the world of Red Dust and warns those who desire wealth and power that everything one gains in this life could turn into a dream in the blink of an eye. This story was adapted as an opera script by the famous Ming playwright Tang Xianzu (1550–1616), and a Chinese idiom "beautiful dream of the yellow millet" (*huangliang meimeng*) is also based on it.

The second allusion occurs in the fifth and sixth lines where the phrases "the House of Silk and Brocade" and "the Home of Tenderness," or "Sweet Home," are used in reference to the Jia family and the Rong Mansion in *Honglou meng*. In chapter 1 of *Honglou meng*, the Jia household is described as "a powerful clan that produces cultured men and court officials; a splendid place decorated with flowers and willows; and a sweet home full of riches and honor" (诗礼簪缨之族, 花柳繁华之地, 温柔富贵之乡) by a Buddhist monk. The clerical figure makes this comment when he is about to take the magic Stone on an earthly journey, which is obviously considered to be a dream. Those who are familiar with Chinese literature would certainly not miss the connection between "the dream of Handan" and *Honglou meng*, as the same warning about the illusive nature of the world of Red Dust is delivered to Jia Baoyu, the fictional dreamer, and through him to the readers of *Honglou meng*. Like Lu Sheng in the story of Handan, the Stone/Baoyu's journey to the material world is only a "beautiful dream of the yellow millet," and he eventually awakens when he finally renounces the world and severs all of his ties with it.

The poet in question, by associating *Honglou meng* with Shen Jiji's Tang tale, has already demonstrated his profound understanding and appreciation of the underlying message of Cao Xueqin's novel. He creates two ironic twists on this theme by linking it to the episode of the drunken Grannie Liu napping in Baoyu's chamber. First of all, by referring to the story of Handan and commenting that the wealth and power of the Jias are nothing but a dream, the poet seems to indicate that the real dreamers here are the Jias. Grannei Liu's episode only serves as a metaphor or a vehicle for this dream theme and the allegorical meaning behind it. As a poor country woman, Grannie Liu's trip to the Rong Mansion and Prospect Garden is like a beautiful dream, and she will wake up from it shortly when she returns to her old country life. The irony is that those who willingly or unwillingly remain unenlightened are the Jias, who have been dreaming this "beautiful dream of yellow millet" with their eyes wide open. A further ironic twist occurs in the last two lines of the poem when the poet expresses his envy of a simple and unworried character like Grannie Liu. Such envy could be explained in two ways—the poet advises his readers/audience to take a hedonistic attitude towards life, which is fleeting and illusory, or he envies those who are at ease and worry-free because they can enjoy whatever life offers them. Whichever the explanation, the poet is highly sensitive to the uncertainty of life and the irony of fate.

In discussing *Honglou meng zidishu*, scholars tend to bypass the group of rewrites that focus on the *yunshi*, or "tasteful" episodes/events, from *Honglou meng*. I have identified seven texts from both Hu's and Lin's collections in this category. The expression "*yunshi*" is taken from the opening poem designated for the piece called "A Tipsy Xiangyun Sleeps on a Peony-Petal Pillow" (Xiangyun zuijiu), in which the author uses this word to praise Shi Xiangyun, who eats deer meat with wine in chapter 62 of *Honglou meng*. Other tasteful episodes share with this piece a sense of spontaneity and innocence and all of them are tastefully done, which means that either the young female characters' and Baoyu's genuine feelings about love are revealed or expressed without the restrictions of Confucian rituals and protocols, or that some literary or artistic activities, such as writing poems, playing wine games, and playing or listening to the zither, are performed. *Yunshi* therefore can be interpreted as having a twofold meaning: one is related to the expression of "*fengliu yunshi*" (a romantic affair or a love affair); another is associated with the so-called elegant and cultured activities favored by Chinese literati of all periods.

In the group of "romantic affairs," for instance, we find the story of Aroma's entertaining Jia Baoyu at her humble home; it is categorized as such because Aroma is portrayed in this narrative as naturally sweet and genuinely loving toward Baoyu. In the same vein, the episode of Xue Baochai's helping Aroma work on a piece of embroidery for Baoyu is selected possibly because it sheds a light on this rather reserved girl who, in other parts of the novel, frequently restrains herself according to the Confucian rules of conduct for women. The other three pieces in this group also involve romantic sentiments in one way or another; they are: "Charmante Scratches a 'Qiang' and Mystifies a Beholder" (from chapter 30 of *Honglou meng*), which relates the infatuation of the young actress, Charmante, with Jia Qiang; "Baoyu and Adamantina Listen to Daiyu Play the Zither" (from chapter 87), which reveals the beautiful nun Admantina's feelings towards Baoyu; and lastly, "Baoyu Thinks of Daiyu and Shows Affection to Fivey" (chapter 109), which focuses on Baoyu's continually thinking of and longing for Daiyu and Skybright after both have died.[119]

Only two pieces from Hu Wenbin's collection are classified as dealing with literary activities, and they are: "A Tipsy Xiangyun Sleeps on a Peony-Petal Pillow" and "Forming of the Crab-Apple Poetry Club" (Haitang jieshe) from chapter 27 of Cao's novel. These two pieces are the most revealing of the literati tastes of the *zidishu* writers. It is unlikely that semi-literate itinerate storytellers or an audience that mostly consists of illiterates or those with minimal education would appreciate ballads like these. "Forming of the Crab-Apple Poetry Club," for instance, not only revolves on the establishment of a poetry club by the youngsters from the Prospect Garden, it also includes all of the poems written by the main protagonists, including Daiyu, Baochai, Tanchun, and Baoyu. Understanding and appreciating this piece require a highly educated ballad writer/singer who is well-versed in classical Chinese poetry and an audience that shares with him a similar-educational background and artistic tastes. According to Suet Ying Chiu (2007: 283), when *zidishu* was taken up by blind professional singers in Tianjin in the early Republican era, "A Tipsy Xiangyun Sleeps on a Peony-Petal Pillow" was not included on the list recommended for performance. Although it was thought to be "not fit for social education" (283), I suspect that its elitist and literati tastes, little understood and appreciated by the common populace, would also be reason to eliminate it from the list.

In summarizing this part of the discussion, I want to emphasize that the themes and characters that *zidishu* writers chose from *Honglou meng* and the ways they reworked these selected materials attest to their profound understanding and appreciation of Cao Xueqin's novel. While the *zidishu* authors can be regarded as the "faithful" rewriters of *Honglou meng*, their rhymed and cantabile rewrites reveal their elite status and taste as well as their privileged socio-cultural backgrounds. In many ways they are a group of readers-turned-rewriters familiar with Cao Xueqin in terms of their shared Bannerman culture, a cross-cultured learning in both Han and Manchu traditions, a leisured lifestyle that could afford spending time on literature and art, and likely a similar fate of family and personal declines caused by both the drastic political and social changes of the Qing court and the constant historical turmoil witnessed at the turn of the twentieth century.

---

119 This story also reflects Baoyu's deep love and devotion to Daiyu and Skybright. However, since such a sentiment is indirectly dealt with here and Baoyu's showing his affection to Fivey is at the center of the episode, I classified this piece in the category of *yunshi*.

CRITIQUING BY REWRITING: THE CASES OF "THE INVOCATION TO THE HIBISCUS SPIRIT" AND "THE STORY OF THE STONE"

Like all rewritings or derivative literature, the *Honglou meng zidishu* have become a vehicle of their writers' views and criticism of the original and they mainly respond to and critique the philosophical foundation and literary endeavor of *Honglou meng* in ways afforded by the genre. Here, despite some fundamental differences, a parallel can be drawn between the *zidishu* rewrites and of *Honglou meng* sequels, a genre that also surged right after the publication of the Cheng-Gao edition. More than a dozen *Honglou meng* sequels were produced during the second half of the Qing dynasty and the early Republican era. Intending to "redress" the "resentment of separation" (*lihen*) or the tragic ending of the original, most of them rewrite the novel's conclusion or reverse the fates of the characters from either chapter 98 (where Daiyu dies) or chapter 120 (where Baoyu renounces the world and returns to the celestial realm). This group of writings has long been ignored or dismissed mainly for their philistinism and conventionality. Recently, however, some scholars in China and the West have indicated that, although most *Honglou meng* sequels are mediocre and disappointing in their conservative ideologies and lack of artistry, they deserve scholarly attention because they are an important form of commentary on the novel.

Lin Chen (1985), for example, characterizes the *Honglou meng* sequels as "collections of criticism" devoted to the original novel. Similarly, Wang Xuchuan states that:

> The appearance of a good number of *Honglou meng* sequels in the Qing dynasty was a special literary phenomenon reflecting the *Honglou meng* craze of the time, and was also a unique way of critiquing *Honglou meng*. By using this particular form of criticism, the authors of sequels not only expressed their appraisals of the fictional characters in *Honglou meng*, and their judgments of the ideological and moral values underscored in the novel, but their own ideals and philosophies of life as well. Through these sequels, we are able to learn a great deal of the ideological beliefs and moral judgments of intellectuals during the period from the end of the Qianlong Emperor's reign (1735-1795) to the end of the Guangxu Emperor's reign (1875-1909).

> 清代大量《紅樓夢》續書的出現，是當時《紅樓夢》熱的一種特殊表現，是对《红楼梦》的评论的一种特殊形式。續作者們通過這種方式表達他們對《紅樓夢》中人物的褒貶，表達他們對《紅樓夢》中所表現的思想精神與價值判斷的看法，表達他們的生活理想。我們可以通過這些續書看到在清乾隆末到光緒末這一段時期我國知識份子中間一般的價值判斷與精神狀態。(Wang 2004: 293)

Echoing Lin and Wang, Martin Huang (2004) writes that "how to read (or interpret) the parent novel and how to interpret the other 'interpretations' (the sequels) of this same work became a prominent issue for the characters as well as the 'readers' of these sequels. It is in these *Honglou meng* sequels that we are compelled to confront the 'interpretative' nature of *xushu* as well as the endless possibilities of 'competing interpretations'" (38-39). The issue of interpretation had become the major subject of the narrative in the *Honglou meng* sequels. In other words, they were written in an interpretative or commentarial mode, with their authors trying to express their own opinions and desires as readers.

Character alteration is a prominent feature of the fictional sequels. As Keith McMahon notes, with the intention of eliminating traumatic antinomies and redressing the resentments left by the original, the sequels worked hard on the improvement of Baoyu, the vindication of Daiyu, and the resolution of the love affair between Baoyu and Daiyu (McMahon 2004: 98-115). The sequel writers were not subtle in this regard, and they did everything to change the main fictional characters to their liking. As a result, most of the unconventional characters, including Lin Daiyu and her double, Skybright, are changed beyond recognition. To use the female commentator Shen Xiangpei's (1808-1862) words, in order to vent Lin Daiyi's grievances, the sequels "invert her ill fate, and impart wealth and rank to this descending immortal plant. [In their sequels, the authors] make the dead come back to life, and the pure become impure (翻薄命之舊案, 將紅塵之富貴加碧落之仙珠。死者令其複生, 清者揚之使濁) (in Zhao 1997: 97).

Although similarly using their rewrites as channels for their appraisal and critique of Cao Xueqin's novel, the *zidishu* writers differ greatly in two respects. First of all, except for a couple of pieces that can be considered written in an interpretative or commentarial mode, most of the *zidishu* rewrites of *Honglou meng* focus on the transformation of genre and tend to faithfully follow the fictional original. In other words, instead of trying to eliminate traumatic antinomies and redress the resentments left by the original as the sequel authors, the *zidishu* writers faithfully kept the tragic mode and ending intact but worked to successfully retell the same story in the genre of ballad singing. Second, the thorough makeover of the characters that is so common in the sequels is rarely seen in the *Honglou meng zidishu* texts, although minor changes were frequently made according to the authors' personal tastes, beliefs, and lifestyles. The kind of vulgarization, which so disgusted Shen Xiangpei, of Lin Daiyu or someone like her (such as Skybright) is almost never found in the *zidishu* texts. Rather, when changes are made to the characters of Daiyu and Skybright, they tend to enhance the idealization and romanticization. One scholar puts it this way:

The *zidishu* writers are all very good at characterization. They are able to grasp the essences of the fictional characters in the original: not only keep them in the same shapes and manners, but also display their romantic sentiments and emotions more fully and transparently by using the genre of ballad singing.

子弟書作家都是塑造人物的高手, 他們巧妙地抓住了原著人物形象的性格精髓, 不僅沒有使人物性格走樣, 反而將人物飽滿的情思通過吟唱 "透明" 地展現于聽眾面前。(Cui 2005: 42)

It seems that the *zidishu* underwent a different form of "popularization" than did the sequels to *Honglou meng*: whereas the former broadens the artistic forms of the original, the latter engages in a radical ideological makeover.

The following discussion deals with two *zidishu* pieces that appear more critical of *Honglou meng* than do some others: "The Invocation to the Hibiscus Spirit" and "The Story of the Stone." Whereas the former works to improve Skybright's character, the latter challenges Gao E's handling of Baoyu's marriage to Baochai and tries to return to Cao Xueqin's original design for the way Daiyu's life should end.

"The Invocation to the Hibiscus Spirit" is one of the six *zidishu* texts by Han Xiaochuang included in Hu Wenbin's collection. It is also the best and most elaborate piece on Skybright. The whole text is divided into six chapters that retell stories taken from chapters 52 to 78 of *Honglou meng*. Despite his being one of the most influential and prolific writers of *zidishu*, the personal life of Han Xiaochuang remains unknown to us. To this day, scholars dispute some basic but important biographical questions about Han, including: Was he a Manchu or Han Bannerman? What exact period did he live in during the Qing? Where was he born? Which city, Beijing or Shenyang, was the main place where he worked and was artistically active?[120] Judging from his contributions to the *Honglou meng zidishu* repertoire, two things can be discerned about him. First, since Han wrote "The Destiny of Dew and Tears," a piece based on Gao E's part of the 120-chapter version, he must have lived during the period after the publication of the Cheng-Gao edition (1791). This is confirmed by De Shuoting's description of performing "Daiyu Laments the Autumn" (also believed to be written by Han) in his *Caozhu yichuan* in 1817. Second, Han's writings surpass those of other writers in artistic quality and poetic expression, and this seems consistent with the belief that he

---

120 For instance, while Geng Ying thinks that Han Xiaochuang was born in Shenyang during the Qing Jiaqing (1796–1820) and Daoguang (1820–1850) periods, Cui Yunhua believes that Han was from Beijing and lived during the Qianlong (1735–1795) and Jiaqing periods. Some scholars such as Hu Guangping even claim that Han was born in 1840 and died in 1896, passing the majority of his life during the Guangxu Emperor's (1874–1908) reign. For detailed information on this, see Geng 1983: 3 and Cui 2005: 27–128.

was well versed in the literary classics and that he had attempted (though unfortunately failed) the civil-service examination (Yao 2007: 178). These two discernments are relevant to my analysis: that Han lived after the publication of Cheng-Gao edition would have meant that he was familiar with the surge of the *Honglou meng* sequels; and his conventional training for and pursuit of the Confucian career path would have impacted his views and appreciation of *Honglou meng* and its characters.

The six chapters of "The Invocation to the Hibiscus Spirit" are respectively entitled: "Mending the Woolen Cloak" (Bu ni); "Being Slandered" (Chan hai); "Bitterly Parting from Baoyu" (Tong bie); "Leaving Her Nails for Baoyu" (Zeng zhi); "Baoyu's Meeting of Skybright's Sister-in-law" (Yu sao); and "Baoyu's Memorial Elegy for Skybright" (Lei ji). This piece obviously focuses on the highlights of Skybright's emotional drama and the most touching and tragic parts of her story. In addition to some minor restructuring of the order of the narrative, Han Xiaochuang made four major changes to the original in terms of characterization, narrative plot, and artistic representation: (1) the moralization of Skybright as a character; (2) ascertaining a love relationship between Baoyu and Skybright; (3) changing the plot about Baoyu's meeting of Skybright's sister-in-law; and finally (4) completely rewriting the "Invocation to the Hibiscus Spirit."

By moralization of Skybright, I mean that Han Xiaochuang has made an effort to improve her character according to his moral beliefs, which are obviously more Confucian and conservative than those of Cao Xueqin. In Han Xiaochuang's writing, not only is Skybright still the pure, noble, loyal, and righteous character that she is in Cao's novel, but she also acquires a strong sense of Confucian morality. No longer the carefree and clever maid who finds an excuse for Baoyu to avoid attending school and seeing his strict father, the remodeled Skybright now constantly worries about Baoyu neglecting his study. In chapter 1, for instance, Han Xiaochuang describes how, while Skybright is mending the peacock patterned woolen cloak for Baoyu, her thoughts repeatedly turn to his study:

I can see that you know all kinds of things under heaven,
But you show the whites of your eyes when people talk about [the Eight-legged] essays.
Why waste your intellect on petty things?
You might as well make a firm resolve to study books.

我看你天下的事兒全知曉，
就只是談起了文章翻眼睛。
你與其把那聰明兒來零用，
何妨去憤志把書攻。
(Hu 1983: 158–159)

In chapter 4, even on her deathbed, Skybright still encourages Baoyu to strive for *"gongming"* (scholarly honor and official rank by taking the civil-service exams): "My dear Second Master, you have a bright future and should work hard for it. It is a pity that I cannot live to see the day when you gain your honor and fame" (二爺呀, 你前程遠大須努力, 可惜我不能看你把名成) (Hu 1983: 183). Furthermore, in her farewell to Baoyu, Skybright cautions him to be filial to his parents and show fraternal love to his brother, while expressing her own wish to die for the purpose of preserving her chastity. Evidently, Han Xiaochuang has turned Skybright into a Confucian paragon whose behavior can be summarized as "certainly never speak in words outside of the Confucian books; and never behave in a way that is against the Confucian rituals" (非禮的話兒決不講, 非禮的事兒決不行) (Hu 1983: 193). In idealizing Skybright, Han Xiaochuang has endowed her with Confucian feminine virtue that was not part of her character in the novel. Such a change seems to be consistent with Han's education and aspiration and is reflective of his ideological makeup. Han impresses us as someone who desired to pursue the Confucian dreams and live a life according to the Confucian teachings, although he was obviously not very successful in his pursuit of honor, rank, and fame.

In Cao Xueqin's original, the relationship between Baoyu and Skybright is a bit ambiguous and shifts between genuine mutual appreciation and devotion as friends and an infatuated attraction between a romantic young master and his beautiful maid. Although Grandmother Jia chose Skybright to be a potential "chamber maid" or even concubine for Baoyu, such a relationship is neither confirmed nor broached. Unlike Aroma, who seems quite eager to secure the official status to share Baoyu's bed, Skybright is an innocent soul who is very happy and content that Baoyu genuinely cares for her and treats her with equality, sincerity, and respect. It seems that Cao Xueqin intentionally keeps Skybright in her position as Baoyu's maid, since, in Baoyu's eyes, an unmarried maid is so much more precious than a married woman, as the latter can be easily contaminated by the filth and corruption of men.

Han Xiaochuang is not satisfied with the ambiguous relationship Cao Xueqin designs for Baoyu and Skyright. Although he does not alter such an arrangement in terms of plot, Han makes both Skybright and Baoyu express the mutual wish that if they cannot be husband and wife in this life, they would be so in death or in their next lives. In chapter 4, after giving her nails and garment to Baoyu as mementoes, Skybright expresses her eternal love for Baoyu by saying, "I wish that we could continue the old love between you and me in our next lives" (但願來生再續舊盟) (Hu 1983: 181). In the final chapter, when Baoyu recites his "Invocation to the Hibiscus Spirit," he also expresses a wish to join with Skybright as a couple in death and declares, "I only want to share the same quilt with you and be together forever; I simply desire to meet you in death and share the same tomb with you" (我為你只想同衾常聚首, 我為你惟求共穴兩相逢) (Hu 1983: 196). In affirming a definitive love relationship between Baoyu and Skybright, Han Xiaochuang, as a reader-cum-rewriter of *Honglou meng*, has done at least two things. First, he further idealizes Skybright, making her a perfect lover for Baoyu, and romanticizes their relationship to that of an eternal love. Second, he intensifies Baoyu's everlasting sorrow at losing Skybright and poeticizes their love tragedy. Han's remake is reminiscent of some famous love tragedies in Chinese literature, including the love between Emperor Xuanzong (685-762) of the Tang ydnasty and his beloved imperial concubine, Yang Yuhuan, portrayed in Bai Juyi's (772-846) "Song of Everlasting Sorrow" (Changhen ge) and the devoted but doomed husband and wife in the Han folk song, "Southeast Fly the Peacocks" (Kongque dongnan fei). Whereas in the former, the male protagonist longs for his dead consort and expresses his everlasting sorrow, in the latter, after being forced to separate, the wife drowns herself and the husband takes his own life by hanging. Since we know that Han Xiaochuang was well versed in the literary classics, it is not surprising that, in reworking the characters from *Honglou meng*, he was drawn to other literary models of the past, particularly to some influential narrative poems, which share some generic features with the *zidishu* ballads.

The third change that Han Xiaochuang makes is also quite deliberate and evident, and that is to delete the bizarre sexual attack on Jia Baoyu by Skybright's sister-in-law. Although a whole chapter is dedicated to Baoyu's meeting with Skybright's sister-in-law, who is portrayed as coquettish and skittish, the part that describes her brutal attack on Baoyu is removed. Instead, she mainly chats with Baoyu, using her seductive manners and words—though this conversation is interrupted by Skybright's brother. Han Xiaochuang obviously did not feel comfortable representing this incident in his *zidishu* text, and this reluctance suggests several things. First, the woman's sexual aggression appalled Han the Confucian moralist and, for moral reasons, he intentionally purged it from his rewriting. Second, the sexual detail was inconsistent with the romantic and lyrical style of this piece and keeping it would degrade the artistic aesthetic of the work. Third, his audience might not appreciate having such a story enacted in their households, which were the main venues where *zidishu* were performed. In fact, as a rule, *zidishu* writers were not inclined to include pornographic details. When they did write about sexual matters, they tended to play word games and use euphemisms rather than providing graphic descriptions and details.[121]

---

121   The second chapter of "Yuxiang huayu" deals with the sexual affair of Baoyu's servant Tealeaf and a maid Wan'er. However, the text is sanitized in the way that no graphic description or detail is included. See Lin Junjia 2012: 424-426.

In this *zidishu* text, chapter 6, entitled "Baoyu's Memorial Elegy for Sky-bright," stands out as the most refreshing and impressive. Although the narrative event is taken from *Honglou meng*, the text of "The Invocation to Hibiscus Spirit" is completely Han Xiaochuang's creation. Cao Xueqin's original "Invocation" is written in classical Chinese in the form of a lengthy elegy. As one of the most beautifully written and moving pieces, this elegy demonstrates Baoyu's deep and sincere feelings for Skybright and his profound loss and sorrow at her death. With its elegant diction, rich imagery, and literary allusions, this piece also showcased Cao Xueqin's talents as a writer. Given the nature of Cao Xueqin's original "Invocation," particularly since it is written in classical Chinese, a form unsuitable for speaking or singing, it is no surprise that Han wanted and needed to completely rewrite the piece. Therefore, Han's decision was determined by artistic invention and the demands of the *zidishu* genre.

The chapter starts with Baoyu hearing of Skybright's death and deciding to conduct a memorial ceremony for her and ends with the ceremony itself. The elegy, containing a total of 144 sentences, occupies the central textual space of this chapter and presents an emotional climax to the entire six-chapter work. Structurally, the elegy can be divided into seven parts: Part 1 (thirty-two lines) deals with the fact that death has forever separated Baoyu and Skybright. A series of poetic contrasts suggests that although sharing their unchangeable love and mutual longing, Baoyu and Skybright are now in different realms. Part 2 (thirty-two lines) generally eulogizes Skybright's personality and character. She is described as someone who possessed all of the Confucian virtues as a feminine paragon, a moralization that permeates the whole text. Part 3 (sixteen lines) relates Skybright's love and caring for Baoyu, describing in detail how, in their past times together, she tirelessly served him in every possible way and urged him to study hard. Part 4 (sixteen lines) pities Skybright's tragic fate and expresses indignation toward the slander and injustice inflicted on her. The theme of "talent wasted" that is underscored in *Honglou meng* is also emphasized here. Part 5 (sixteen lines) recapitulates the best times and the most memorable occasions Baoyu and Skybright spent together. However, the nostalgic memory is presented in a negative future tense by repeatedly using the phrase "*zai buneng*" (I no longer can), lamenting the impossibility of repeating these beautiful experiences. Part Six (sixteen lines) declares Baoyu's love and devotion to Skybright and describes how he mourned her death. Part 7 (sixteen lines) ends with Baoyu's eternal love and longing for Skybright by repeating the expression "*xiang de wo*" (I miss you so) sixteen times. Since this section is the most intensely emotional, it is worth translating here in its entirety:

I miss you so that I stare blankly and act like a puppet every day,
I miss you so that I am depressed and as if shocked by thunder from morning to night.

I miss you so that my two ears are booming and cannot hear,

I miss you so that my eyes are dim and cannot see.

I miss you so that I am absent-minded and restless,

I miss you so that I am mumbling and cannot express myself clearly.

I miss you so that I behave anxiously and am unable to sit still,

I miss you so that I am confused between what is a dream and what is not, and unable to sleep well.

I miss you so that I am tortured by my tender feelings and filled with pain,

I miss you so that I produced thousands of drops of blood tears and they are bright red.

I miss you so that I rack my brains and the pain is like a knife carving out a piece of my gallbladder,

I miss you so that I turn my mind back and forth and it hurts like a dagger stabbing my chest.

I miss you so that I have lost my spirit, my looks, and my mood,

I miss you so that I am out of my mind like a drunk—stupefied, mute, and deaf.

I miss you so that I am tired of thinking of you in the human world,

I miss you so that I want to go to the nether world to consummate our unfulfilled love in this life.

想得我每日發呆如木偶，
想得我終日納悶似雷轟。
想得我兩耳轟轟聽不見，
想得我二目昏昏看不明。
想得我精神恍惚神不定，
想得我話語模糊語不清。
想得我舉止慌張坐不穩，
想得我夢魂顛倒睡不甯。
想得我柔腸九轉滿腹兒痛，
想得我血淚千行一色兒紅。
想得我左思右想刀剟膽，
想得我想後思前刃刺胸。
想得我無精無采無情緒，
想得我如醉如癡如啞聾。
想得我懶在人間將你想，
想得我要到陰曹續前盟。
(Hu 1983: 196)

The language style and artistic techniques of *zidishu* sampled here seem very close to those of traditional Chinese operas, particularly the operas originating in the south, such as *kunqu* and Yue opera (*yueju*) that have elaborate arias and emphasize lyricism and romance. This part is reminiscent of the famous duet called "Shi xiangsi" from the Yue opera, *The Butterfly Lovers* (Liang

Shanbo yu Zhu Yingtai). The duet contains ten sentences, each starting with the same expression "I was thinking of you" (*wo xiang ni*), and describing through various figurative expressions and vivid depictions how the lovers long for each other. A more detailed discussion of the influence of *zidishu* on other types of performing arts is provided in the final section of this study.

Another *zidishu* piece that critiques the Cheng-Gao edition of *Honglou meng* is "The Story of the Stone," by an anonymous writer. This piece specifically challenges Gao E's treatment of Baoyu's marriage and Daiyu's death by restoring Cao Xueqin's original design in these two important narrative developments. It seems odd that the author uses the title "Story of the Stone" for his *zidishu* text, which reworks chapters 96 to 98 of the Cheng-Gao edition in four chapters. Further scrutiny, however, reveals that the author may have had a dual purpose in adopting the title that Cao Xueqin originally used for his manuscript versions of the novel. First, the author intends to hint to his readers/audience that his rewrite is based on Cao's original design, not Gao E's. It is well known that, although "*Honglou meng*" is one of the alternative titles included in chapter 1 of Cao's text, it was not used as the name of the book until the publication of the Cheng-Gao edition in 1791. Cao's manuscript versions were consistently circulated with the title "Story of the Stone." It is common knowledge that those (scholars and rewriters alike) who wanted to demonstrate their faithfulness to Cao's original tended to retain the title "Story of the Stone," and David Hawkes's English translation is a case in point. Han Xiaochuang's "Destiny of Dew and Tears" provides a counter example: it mainly employs narrative events from Gao E's part of the novel, and has an alternative title "*Honglou meng*," suggesting its close relationship to Gao's continuation. Therefore, we should not treat the "Story of the Stone" author's choice of title as arbitrary, but rather as a meaningful gesture of his allegiance to Cao's original.

The second purpose of adopting this title may lie in the focus of this *zidishu* rewrite. Although retelling the events that unfolded in chapters 96, 97, and 98 of Gao E's part of the novel, this particular *zidishu* completely eliminates Baoyu's wedding ceremony, or the part called "the good marriage of jade and gold" (*jinyu liangyuan*), and revolves only on the doomed love and failed marriage between Baoyu and Daiyu and Daiyu's tragic death. In other words, the focal point the story is "the destiny of the stone and wood" (*mushi zhi yuan*), and its title "Story of the Stone," in emphasizing Baoyu's pre-incarnation as a magic stone and his predestined bond with Daiyu, whose previous existence was that of a celestial plant, would focus his readers/audience's attention on this theme.

The author's effort to restore Cao's original design can be seen in the following three aspects: first, it is Yuanchun, the imperial concubine, not Grandmother Jia and Wang Xifeng, who chooses Baochai to be Baoyu's wife and takes the initiatives to arrange their wedding; second, Daiyu is profoundly saddened to hear Yuanchun's edict, and she dies from emotional exhaustion but does not hold grudges against Baoyu and Baochai; third, Daiyu dies before, not at the same time, as Baoyu's wedding.

The theory that Cao Xueqin probably wanted Yuanchun to be the advocate for the "good marriage of jade and gold" is well known to *Honglou meng*'s readers and critics. Many believe that Cao Xueqin had provided clues for this design. The first clue is in chapter 18 where Yuanchun changes Baoyu's inscription of "red fragrance and green jade" (*hongxiang lüyu*) into "crimson joy and green delight" (*yihong kuailü*). Some critics think that the "*lüyu*" or green jade refers to Daiyu, and Yuanchun's dropping of "*lüyu*" suggests that she does not favor Daiyu as Baoyu's potential wife. In commenting on this detail, the famous Qing *Hongou meng* critic Zhang Xinzhi (*f*.1850) states: "'red fragrance and green jade' refers to Daiyu, the imperial concubine does not want to see Daiyu marry Baoyu. This means that 'heaven'[122] does not give its consent to Daiyu's marriage to Baoyu but favors the marriage of gold and jade. This is particularly indicated by Baochai [who reminds Baoyu that the imperial concubine does not like the word 'green jade']" ("紅香綠玉" 乃黛玉也, 貴人不喜見此段姻緣, 天所不許而許在金玉姻緣也, 故特用寶釵提白) (Feng 2000: 373). The second clue appears in chapter 28. When Yuanchun sends home gifts, she gives only Baochai gifts that exactly match Baoyu's—a meaningful detail that has also drawn much readerly attention. Yuanchun's gesture is intended to be "meaningful," because Cao Xueqin even uses Baoyu's comment (and that of Aroma's, for that matter) to draw the reader's attention to it. Baoyu is obviously disturbed by the fact that Baochai, not Daiyu, has received exactly the same kinds of presents from his older sister and wonders what it means. He "hopes" it is merely a mistake. Aroma, however, seems to be very pleased and reassured that such a "match" is exactly what the imperial concubine intends. Zhang Xinzhi explains the implication of this detail: "Yuanchun represents the will of heaven. In the chapter of her homecoming, she symbolizes the heavenly spell of good fortune. In this chapter, she has turned into an authority on the 'marriage of gold and jade'" (以元春為天, 在歸省, 以為氣數之天, 在此回: 金玉姻緣所由定也) (Feng 2000: 613).

Evidently, the author of "Story of the Stone" was aware of the aforementioned theory and he attempted to redress Gao E's deviant treatment. In chapter 1 of the text in question, Yuanchun proposes the marriage with an imperial edict and her proposition pleases the family elders, including Grandmother Jia, Lady Wang, and Aunt Xue. Unlike Gao E's version in which the true nature of the wedding is hidden from both Baoyu and Daiyu, here,

---

[122] "Heaven" means Yuanchun because she is an imperial concubine who represents the emperor, son of heaven.

the marriage proposal is known to all the parties involved: Xue Baochai bashfully hides herself away; both Daiyu and Baoyu are extremely disappointed and sad, although they can do nothing about it. As Zhang Xinzhi indicates, the proposal comes from Yuanchun who represents "the will of heaven," and her authority cannot be challenged or even questioned. Yuanchun's supreme authority produces a decisive effect to the development of "Story of the Stone" *zidishu*: What else could Baoyu and Daiyu do but resign themselves to their fates? Although they are unable to alter what fate has designed for them, it cannot change how they feel about each other:

> It is pitiful that she is depressed at realizing that she cannot marry Baoyu,
> But [she] cannot even open her heart to Nightingale despite having thousands of words to say.
> She continuously pretends to be at leisure and carefree, forcing herself to eat and drink,
> Contrary to her old self, she now puts on a smiling and joyful face when she sees Baoyu.
> Seeing her in this way, Baoyu becomes more worried and vexed,
> His depression worsens every day and turns into despondence.
> He stays in the House of Crimson Joy day in and day out,
> Staring blankly, his belly full of bitterness, he cannot tell anyone.

> 可憐他好事無成芳心失望，
> 向紫鵑總有那萬句衷腸也難話明。
> 他依舊的假作安閒強餐茶飯，
> 見寶玉時倒添了些笑語共歡容。
> 寶玉他見此神情更添了愁悶，
> 漸漸的積成憂鬱似癲瘋。
> 終朝只在怡紅院，
> 乜呆呆一腔心事倩誰憑。
> (Hu 1983: 226)

This is how the author represents the states of Baoyu's and Daiyu's minds as he understands them to be in Cao Xueqin's original design, though of course he contributes his share of artistic imagination and creativity. Baoyu and Daiyu meet and open their hearts to each other before Daiyu dies quietly. Daiyu, seeing the situation cannot be altered, persuades Baoyu to make peace with fate, saying: "From now on, 'the precious jade' (meaning Baoyu) will be married with the fine-looking girl; Let's resign ourselves to this fate for the rest of our lives" (從此後頤眷通靈成大禮，且將這跟前的因果了今生) (Hu 1983: 229). Before her death, Daiyu also calmly transmits her last wishes to Nightingale, including giving Tanchun a portrait of herself and several poetry collections to Caltrop. Unlike the manner of Daiyu's death in Gao E's continuation, here Daiyu dies without resentment towards Baoyu and Baochai. Although she dies knowing that Baoyu still loves her, she does not hold Baochai responsible for separating her and Baoyu. It is hard for us to judge whether this ending would be close to Cao Xueqin's original conclusion, but this *zidishu* author offers a critique of Gao E's treatment and at the same time projects an alternative finale. His reworking of Baoyu's and Daiyu's characters is actually reminiscent of the modern fictional writer Ba Jin's (1904–2005) treatments of his tragic hero and heroine, Gao Juexin and Cousin Mei, in *Family* (Jia), a novel often thought to be a modern *Honglou meng*. As suggested by Ba Jin through his alter ego, Gao Juehui, both Juexin and Cousin Mei are perceived as extremely weak and lacking in rebellious spirit. Ba Jin obviously imitated Baoyu and Daiyu in writing his two romantic but hapless characters. Such an imitation, in a way, also reflects the similar views that many modern scholars and writers probably shared with this *zidishu* author in terms of how Cao Xueqin could have ended the doomed love between Baoyu and Daiyu.

POPULARIZING BY GENERIC REFORMALIZATION: THE THEMATIC AND ARTISTIC INFLUENCE OF "THE DESTINY OF DEW AND TEARS"

Although *zidishu* clearly played a significant role in disseminating and popularizing the stories of *Honglou meng*, it is not easy to evaluate this role. After one and a half centuries of existence, *zidishu*, as an oral performing art, disappeared from the stage at the turn of the twentieth century, and its art, including both melodies and singing scripts, was appropriated by or incorporated into other oral performing arts or operas. According to Chen Jinzhao, four types of existing oral performing arts—Beijing drum songs (*jingyun dagu*), plum blossom drum songs (*meihua dagu*), wharf-style tunes (*matou diao*), and monochord, the performer sings accompanied by the three-stringed lute (*danxian*)—have borrowed from *zidishu* and used or reworked as many as fifty-two *zidishu* stories/singing scripts (Cui 2005: 33). On Chen's list, there are three pieces of *Honglou meng zidishu*, and they are: "The Complete Ballad of Lin Daiyu Laments the Autumn" (Quan beiqiu), aka "Lin Daiyu Laments the Autumn," "Baoyu and Adamantina Listen to Daiyu Play the Zither," and "Destiny of Dew and Tears." The *Honglou meng zidishu* obviously also influenced different types of Chinese operas. For instance, while the Grannie Liu series has been adopted by *pingju* from Beijing and Hebei, the tragic love between Baoyu and Daiyu and Skybright's stories have become popular themes in various operas such as Yue opera from Zhejiang and Shanghai, *kunqu* from Suzhou, and *huangmei xi* from Anhui. It is hardly a coincidence that these are the same themes and stories that were selected by the *zidishu* writers. This part of my study probes the relationship of one particular *zidishu*'s relationship with the Yue opera version of *Honglou meng* in an attempt to investigate specifically how the former influenced the latter. The *zidishu* piece in question is none other than "Destiny of Dew and Tears" by Han Xiaochuang, a work that is considered the most influential among the *Honglou meng zidishu* rewrites.

Taking episodes mainly from chapters 96, 97, 98, 104, 113, and 116 of the Cheng-Gao edition of *Honglou meng*, "Destiny of Dew and Tears" recapitulates Gao E's version of the doomed love between Baoyu and Daiyu. It contains thirteen chapters, starting with Wang Xifeng's plotting of the "pockets exchange scheme" (*diaobaoji*) and ending with Baoyu's second trip to the Land of Illusion and his effort to open his heart to Nightingale after Daiyu's death. Modern critics have either praised this work's superior artististry in comparison with Gao E's original (Cui 2005: 41) or emphasized its successful generic transformation from a fictional text to a script of ballad singing (Qu 1989: 257–260). For me, "Destiny of Dew and Tears" might not necessarily be the best of Han Xiaochuang's works, but it is certainly the most inspirational piece in terms of the generic transformation from written literature to oral performance and for the dissemination and popularization of *Honglou meng*. Several scholars have recognized and indicated the close relationship of "Destiny of Dew and Tears" with the Yue opera version of *Honglou meng* (Geng 1983: 7; Cui 2005: 33). However, thus far, the discussion of this issue is limited to pointing out some shared lines.

As Linda Hutcheon indicates, "seen as a formal entity or product, an adaptation is an announced and extensive transposition of a particular work or works. This 'transcoding' can involve a shift of medium (a poem to a film) or genre (an epic to a novel), or a change of frame and therefore context" (Hutcheon 2006: 8). Obviously, *zidishu* deals with at least the first two aspects of transposition from the parent novel to a ballad form and may involve all three. The successful transposition or transcoding of *zidishu* from a written text to that of a performing art laid a good path for further theatrical adaptation in Yue opera. The following analysis suggests that the influence of "Destiny of Dew and Tears" on the Yue opera *Honglou meng* extends far beyond linguistic borrowing. The Yue opera *Honglou meng* as well as other operatic adaptations of *Hongluo meng* followed the model of *zidishu* in at least three aspects of generic transformation or transcoding: (1) thematic refinement and structural reconfiguration; (2) transposition of narrative strategies; and (3) language versification.

One of the most daunting tasks in adapting *Honglou meng* to a form of the performing arts, whether ballad singing or opera, is that of thematic refinement and reconfiguration. This is due not only to the length of novel (120 chapters) and its multitude of characters (over 400 of them), but also because of the complexly interwoven and multilayered subject matter and character relationships. In addition, *Honglou meng* has a much more integrated and organic narrative structure than some of its predecessors, such as *Water Margin*, a text that may be easily broken into smaller sections or cycles according to its focus on different fictional characters. This is not surprising because the textual history of *Water Margin* is very different from that of *Honglou meng*: it was first circulated in segments of oral performing arts before being reconstructed into a complete fictional text (Ge 2001).

Earlier in this chapter, I touched on the issue of thematic selection. To reiterate and recapitulate, there are three main subjects, including *qing* (love between Baoyu and the two female characters, Daiyu and Skybright), the stories about Grannie Liu, and a group of episodes considered to be tasteful events, which were chosen from *Honglou meng* for reworking into *zidishu*. The *zidishu* writers made these choices based on their own literary tastes and their understanding and appreciation of the fictional original.

In addition to the thematic selection, a heavy retailoring of material needs to be accomplished to fit them into the *zidishu* genre. On the one hand, as a type of oral performing art, *zidishu* anticipates a different type of communication between writer/performer and reader/audience than that of a fictional text. While in the former the communication of a performer/storyteller with his audience is more strictly linear and time restricted, the writer's interaction with his reader in the latter can be cyclical, can allow or demand the reader to reread or retrace, for instance, and not restricted by time. On the other hand, ballad singing shares some commonalities in this respect with another type of narrative art—theater. The way that *zidishu* writers retailored *Honglou meng* materials is reminiscent of Li Yu's (1611–1680) discussion on establishing a subject and tailoring the materials to write a theatrical script:

> [When] our forefathers wrote their essays, [they] must have had an essential point in their minds. The essential point is none other than the real intention of the author. This holds true for theater as well. There are many characters in an opera, but most of them are foils after all. If we investigate the playwright's original intention, these characters are all designed as a foil for one person. For this one person, from the beginning to the end of the play, [the playwright] designs all sorts of partings, reunions, sorrows, and happiness, [that in turn, generate] numerous causes and related circumstances. But most of these events are derivative, and they are again designed only for a single event. This "one person and one event" should be the essential point of the theater.

> 古人作文一篇, 定有一篇之主腦, 主腦非他, 即作者立言之本意也。傳奇亦然。一本戲中有無數人名, 究竟俱屬陪賓, 原其初心, 止為一人而設; 即此一人之身, 自始至終, 離合悲歡, 中具無限情由, 無窮關目, 究竟俱屬衍文, 原其初心, 又止為一事而設; 此一人一事, 即作傳奇之主腦也。(Li Yu 1992: 8)

This choice of "one person and one event" seems to be a guiding principle in the *zidishu* writers' practices of retailoring *Honglou meng* materials. "Destiny of Dew and Tears" is a case in point.

In "Destiny of Dew and Tears," Han Xiaochuang obviously intends to re-tell the doomed love tale of Jia Baoyu and Lin Daiyu portrayed in the fictional original, but his *zidishu* rewrite turns Daiyu into the central figure and her death into the main story. This essential point is evident not only by the foiling function of the dozen characters involved in this piece, but also by how the narrative events and emotional dramas are used to serve and highlight this main theme. For instance, in Han's piece, whereas important characters in the fictional original such as Grandmother Jia and Lady Wang are transformed into "names" merely dropped to fill in narrative gaps, a very minor character, Simple, occupies a whole chapter, because she plays a crucial role in revealing to Daiyu the secret of Baoyu's marriage to Baochai. Xue Baochai and Nightingale form another pair of contrasts in terms of their support or as foils to Daiyu: while the former appears only in chapter 11 as a foil to both Daiyu and Baoyu in her persuading Baoyu to follow the Confucian career path and to deal with Daiyu's death, Daiyu's loyal maid Nightingale becomes Daiyu's double in valuing *qing* and loyalty.

Nightingale's case is worth probing further, because, in order to support the main theme of "Destiny of Dew and Tears," Han Xiaochuang intensifies the character's emotional drama and adds narrative details to his work. Chapter 7 appropriates the narrative detail of Nightingale's refusal to help with Baoyu's wedding from chapter 97 of *Honglou meng*. In the fictional original, when Daiyu lies on her deathbed fighting for her life, the Jia family elders ask Nightingale to leave Daiyu and accompany Baochai to the wedding. This is part of Wang Xifeng's plot to fool Baoyu and make him believe that he is marrying Daiyu. Nightingale's emotional state is described as "lying on the empty bed, her face a ghastly green, her eyes closed, tears streaming down her cheeks" (Cao 1982: 4: 357). Her rejection of the elders' request clearly reveals her anger and indignation, but her words are held in check and restrained. Here is the paragraph from the novel describing her words and action in detail.

> Before Li Wan could say anything, Nightingale spoke up herself: "Mrs. Lin, will you be so kind as to leave now? Can't you even wait until she is dead? We will leave her then, you need not fear. How can you be so..." She stopped short, thinking it ill advised to be so rude, and changing her tone somewhat, said: "Besides, after waiting on a sick person, I fear we would not be fit for such an occasion. And while Miss Lin is still alive, she may ask for me at any time." (Cao 1982: 4: 358)

This brief detail is developed in Han's rewrite into a whole chapter with one hundred lines of singing. It begins with an introduction of Nightingale's character as a capable and loyal maid with a close relationship to Daiyu, moving to her sorrow and anxiety over Daiyu's tragic fate and her illness, and lastly to Nightingale's indignation and resentment toward the wedding plot. When she is asked to provide her services at the wedding, Nightingale's response is elaborate and unyielding. She even declares that she would rather die than betray Daiyu:

To be honest with you, I am determined not to leave here today,
I will not wrinkle my brow even if this means that I will be smashed to pieces.
I do not know how to float on the top of water,
I care even less about "adding brilliance to one's present splendor."
I am not interested in the other place's wealth and prosperity,
But would rather stay in this lonely fragrant chamber.
Imagine that everyone in the wedding chamber is happy and jolly,
Someone unlucky like me can hardly be good company.
I would rather die if you force me to go the wedding chamber,
For that would suit me, as I could be with my mistress forever.

實說罷! 今朝斷不肯離此地,
就把我粉身碎骨也不皺眉。
我一輩子不會浮上水,
錦上添花更覺不肯為。
別處的繁華富貴由他去,
我情願守這冷香閨。
想那邊洋洋高興人人樂,
加上這不吉利的人兒也難奉陪。
要再相逼破著一死,
正好和姑娘往一處歸。
(Hu 1983: 263)

Here, the intensification of Nightingale's emotional drama, her deep sympathy, and her extraordinary loyalty to Daiyu not only further highlights Daiyu's character and her tragic love, but also contrasts with the coldness and heartlessness of the other Jia family members and condemns fickleness and snobbery in human relationships. In "Destiny of Dew and Tears," Nightingale is given a much more important role than that of any other character, with the exception of Daiyu and Baoyu.

As the central figure of "Destiny of Dew and Tears," Daiyu mainly appears in five of the thirteen chapters, including chapter 2, "Simple Discloses the Secret" (Sha xie); chapter 3, "Daiyu Verifies the News in Her Deranged State" (Chi dui); chapter 4, "Daiyu is Heartbroken" (Shen shang); chapter 5, "Daiyu Burns her Poems" (Fen gao); and chapter 9, "Daiyu Bids Her Final Farewell to

Nightingale" (Jue bi). If chapter 2 and 3 chiefly appropriate narrative events and episodic details from the novel, chapters 4, 5, and 9 may be considered Han Xiaochuang's addition to or his improvement of Gao E's characterization in *Honglou meng*. For instance, chapter 4 is entirely Han's creation, portraying Daiyu's inner feelings—her shock, despair, resentment, and anguish—after hearing the news of Baoyu's wedding. The episodes of both chapters 5 and 9 are taken from the fictional original, but they have been significantly embellished and enhanced by Han Xiaochuang to fit the theme of the piece in question and into the genre of *zidishu*. For example, Daiyu burning her poems is a detail depicted in chapter 97 of the novel. It is a symbolic gesture by Daiyu to demonstrate that she now wants to leave the loveless world without any yearning for the past. This symbolic gesture is mainly consistent with a series of "acts" or "orders" that Daiyu initiated—asking her maids to find the poems and bring them to her, ordering the maids to make a fire in the brazier and, finally, burning the poems in the brazier. Daiyu's emotional state is indirectly reflected in this series of acts rather than openly expressed in words. In "Destiny of Dew and Tears," however, Han Xiaochuang has Daiyu reveal her state of mind openly at the moment of each action through the singing of a song of fifty lines. This part begins with Daiyu relating how poetry has been part of her—her "soul mate" and her "flesh and blood"—in her short and lonely life, then turns to her nostalgia for the poetry club and the good times of the past in Prospect Garden, and finally ends with her resentment that Baoyu's love token (the handkerchief on which her poems are written) is still in her hands despite Baoyu's betrayal of her.

In "Destiny of Dew and Tears," although an equal number of chapters (five) is dedicated to Baoyu, he also serves as Daiyu's foil. Even in these so-called Baoyu chapters, Daiyu is the soul or "essence" of the narrative and emotional drama. Whether during the wedding, from which she is absent, or later when she is dead, Daiyu is constantly mentioned, thought of, and terribly missed by Baoyu and the *zidishu* narrator. Particularly in Baoyu's three key chapters—chapter 6, "Baoyu Is Misinformed about the Wedding" (Wu xi); chapter 8, "Baoyu Is Surprised at the Wedding" (Hun cha); and chapter 10, "Baoyu Cries for Daiyu" (Ku yu), Baoyu has become a vehicle through which Daiyu's character is idealized and her tragic fate further dramatized. If, in the novel, Jia Baoyu can be seen as an alter ego of the novel's author, Cao Xueqin, the Baoyu remake in "Destiny of Dew and Tears" takes Han Xiaochuang's perspective in reevaluating, improving, and lyricizing the female protagonist of *Honglou meng*.

The thematic refinement and reinforcement, retailoring of material, and structural reconstruction that Han Xiaochuang produced in his "Destiny of Dew and Tears" successfully transforms a fictional text into a balladic singing script. Such a generic transformation was probably guided by Li Yu's principle of "one person and one event," which could be employed in both the theater and the oral performing arts. Han Xiaochuang's successful rewrite undoubtedly provided a good model for later theatrical adaptation of *Honglou meng*. In fact, the Yue opera *Honglou meng* has appropriated many artistic strategies from "Destiny of Dew and Tears." For instance, the opera similarly has the tragic love of Baoyu and Daiyu as its central theme, and it changes the significance of supporting characters. More specifically, the Yue opera *Honglou meng* transforms Simple and Nightingale into figures of greater importance than they were in their fictional original.

Even more important, "Destiny of Dew and Tears" provided a ready-made structure for the Yue opera. Except for the last three chapters, the main part of the *zidishu* is included in the Yue opera, forming the five acts of the second half of the play: (1) an act about Wang Xifeng's scheming, corresponding to chapter 1 of "Destiny of Dew and Tears"; (2) an act about Simple disclosing the wedding secret, corresponding to chapter 2 of the *zidishu*; (3) an act about Lin Daiyu burning her poems, condensing chapters 4, 5, and 9; (4) an act about Baoyu's wedding, condensing chapters 6 and 8; and (5) an act about Baoyu mourning for Daiyu, corresponding to chapter 10. In addition to such thematic and structural innovations, the Yue opera version of *Honglou meng* has also borrowed from "Destiny of Dew and Tears" in terms of its narrative strategies and language versification. A brief analysis of these aspects is in order.

As a group of enthusiastic and sophisticated opera fans, *zidishu* writers were well versed in traditional Chinese opera; the fact that there are 165 pieces (41% of the extant works) of *zidishu* adapted from theater speaks volumes of the writers' familiarity with the art. In adapting the stories of *Honglou meng* to the form of *zidishu* ballad, they also borrowed some narrative strategies from theater and these strategies, in turn, fit perfectly in the Yue opera performance. Guo Xiaoting, for instance, summarizes that in *zidishu*, the narrative strategies appropriated from theater include the "bead string" narrative structure, the scene-oriented narration, the narrative transition through stage entering and exiting devices, characters' internal point of view, and characters' soliloquy (Guo 2013: 188–199). All of the aforementioned strategies except for the stage entering and exiting devices are employed in "Destiny of Dew and Tears." Since the "string" or the "essential point" of the narrative structure and the character's soliloquy are dealt with in other parts of this study, no further analysis is needed here.

The scene-oriented narration means that in theater no narrator can appear on stage to tell the audiences what will unfold in terms of the dramatic plot; the story's development has to be shown and propelled from one scene/act to the next by characters' interactions and actions. Although *zidishu* is a storytelling art and a third-person omnipresent narrator does appear in it from time to time, the most prevalent narrative strategy in *zidishu* is the scene-oriented narration.[123] Most *zidishu* are structured by one or two main story lines, which threads all of the chapters or scenes together. In other words, the chapter divisions in *zidishu* are actually scene divisions. The narrative development and transition, including the temporal and spatial alterations, rely on the change and action of the characters. "Destiny of Dew and Tears," for example, is divided into thirteen chapters/scenes, and the story line moves forward by a particular character's principal action or interaction with others in each of the chapters/scenes. As indicated earlier, the main story line is Daiyu's death after hearing the news of Baoyu marrying Baochai. Thus, the story starts with Wang Xifeng's scheming to make Baoyu wed Baochai (scene 1), then moves to that of Simple revealing the secret to Daiyu (scene 2), then to the three acts where Daiyu questions Baoyu, digests the news, and burns her poems (scenes 3, 4, and 5). The middle four scenes (Scenes 6, 7, 8, and 9) switch back and forth between Baoyu's dwelling, where the wedding is taking place, and Daiyu's deathbed in order to contrast Baoyu's and Daiyu's (and Nightingale's) actions and emotions. The following two acts (scenes 10 and 11) deal with Daiyu's death: Baoyu cries for Daiyu and Baochai advises him to restrain his grief. The last two scenes are very much like a stereotypical theatrical *shousha* (closure) in which there is a kind of catharsis over the pain of Daiyu's tragic death: while scene 12 allows Baoyu to meet Daiyu again in the celestial realm, scene 13 has Baoyu beg forgiveness of Nightingale. Notably, the naming of the thirteen chapters/scenes is also similar to the titling of theatrical scenes, with a two-character verb-object expression indicating the main action of the scene. Because in its process of generic transposition *zidishu* borrowed the so-called scene-oriented narrative strategy from theater, it set a successful model for further adaptation: the ballad was so close to the treatment of theater in terms of its narrative structure and strategy that the major scenes were, as indicated earlier, retained without much change in the Yue opera *Honglou meng*.

Theatre often emphasizes soliloquy. It does so partly because of the absence of an omniscient narrator. Most of traditional Chinese theater was operatic in form and used singing to reveal the inner thoughts and feelings of a character. Like Chinese opera, *zidishu* often turns to the perspective of a character's inner self and uses elaborate and lengthy singing to reveal what is on his or her mind. In "Destiny of Dew and Tears," three characters' inner perspectives dominate: those of Daiyu, Baoyu, and Nightingale.

---

123 According to Guo Xiaoting (2013: 190), there are only forty-seven pieces of *zidishu* from 404 extant works that do not use this form of narration. The overwhelming majority (88%) of the ballad texts have employed the scene-oriented narrative strategy.

Chapter/scene 10, "Baoyu Cries for Daiyu," is not only a good example of turning to the inner perspective of a character but also convincing evidence of *zidishu*'s creativity and its impact on later performing arts. The story is taken from chapter 98 of *Honglou meng*, narrating Baoyu's revisit of the Naiad House (Xiaoxiang guan) after Daiyu's death. Gao E added this part of the story, writing it in just a few lines:

> As Baoyu arrived, his thoughts went back to the days before Daiyu had fallen ill, before things had taken this turn. The sight of the familiar room was too much for him and he started howling wildly. How close they had once been! What a gulf death had put between them! His passionate display of grief began to concern them all. (Cao 1982: 4: 381)[124]

In the fictional original, we get only a glimpse of Baoyu's thoughts, leaving some readers dissatisfied, given the deep love shared by Baoyu and Daiyu. In "Destiny of Dew and Tears," Han Xiaochuang dedicates a whole chapter/scene and seventy-two lines/stanzas to deal with Baoyu's inner feelings at the loss of his love. For example, he elaborates on the idea of the "the familiar room" missing its hostess in the following rhymed lines:

> Entering the gate I see no familiar sight,
> Overwhelmed by pain, my tears fall like rain.
> In my eyes, the tips of Bamboo drip green teardrops,
> The pine woods are shadowed by bloody evening glow.
> In the courtyard, "love peas" are planted in vain,
> By the steps, blooming flowers appear heartbroken.
> Old trees are heartless, floating fallen leaves,
> Dark forest must be resentful, crying with cawing ravens.
> The twelve balustrades are still here,
> But where can I find the one who leaned against them?

> 進得門來哪裡還像當時景，
> 由不得百感交集淚似麻。
> 但只見竹梢滴露垂青淚，
> 松影濃蔭帶晚霞。
> 庭前空種相思豆，
> 砌邊都是斷腸花。
> 老樹無情飄落葉，

幽林有恨噪啼鴉。
欄杆十二依舊在,
倚欄的人兒在哪一搭。
(Hu 1983: 273-274)[125]

Here, Han Xiaochuang uses a variety of personified images to describe Baoyu's psychological state—after Daiyu is gone, everything in her former dwelling becomes sorrowful and seems to grieve (or triggers the emotion of grief) in Baoyu's eyes and mind. Evidently, Han does a much better job than Gao E in reflecting how Baoyu felt after Daiyu's passing. However, Han's success is partly the product of the genre he is working in, because ballad singing demands the lengthy elaboration of emotion. In any case, "Destiny of Dew and Tears" provided an effective artistic bridge for Yue opera to fill a gap left by Gao E in dealing with Baoyu's sorrow. Indeed, the Yue opera *Honglou meng* includes an independent scene called "Baoyu Cries at Daiyu's Tablet" with a lengthy soliloquy for Baoyu.

Scholars of *zidishu* have recognized its artistic lyricism, realized mainly through its narrative strategies and its linguistic versification. As Cui Yunhua says, instead of creating a plot climax, *zidishu* writers intentionally generate a "climax of emotion" or an emotional drama in their works by employing the two narrative devices of "directly expressing inner feelings" (*xinyu hua*) and "indirectly expressing inner feelings through the use of similes and imagery" (*wuyu hua*). The example I analyzed above could be cited here as a good case of both devices. What I want to emphasize here is that the *zidishu* writers are extremely frugal in plot, but quite extravagant in developing characters' inner feelings and the "climax of emotion." As for language versification, *zidishu* has adopted the thirteen most popular rhymes of northern China, and its rhymed lines are flexible enough to contain from seven to more than a dozen characters. The diction of *zidishu* is both elegant and easy to understand, having been influenced both by the traditions of Chinese poetry and by the popular oral performing arts (Cui 2005: 72-76, 82-91).

In terms of narrative strategies and linguistic features, *zidishu* obviously have more in common with Chinese opera, such as Yue opera, than they do with fiction. Thus, it is not surprising that the Yue opera *Honglou meng* appropriated many linguistic devices from Han Xiaochuang's "Destiny of Dew and Tears" and that some of Han's lines were even taken verbatim. The following is a translation of Lin Daiyu's climax of emotion in chapter 5 of "Destiny of

---

125 The last two lines allude to the familiar image of a lonely and longing woman in classical Chinese poetry. "Twelve" is a number implying many, used in this allusion to suggest that the woman spends hours and days leaning against balustrades waiting for her man. Here, the image is used to describe Daiyu's failed longing and waiting for Baoyu.

Dew and Tears" (the underlined sections are included in the singing part of the Yue opera *Honglou meng* with minor changes):

I remember that my poems on catkins were praised for their exceptional creativity,
<u>I remember that my verse for the Crab-Apple Poetry Club competed with others for freshness.</u>
I remember that Xiangyun and I wrote about the bright Moon in front of Concave Pavilion,
I remember that I played the zither in Green Bower Hermitage.
<u>I remember that we competed in creating new wine games in House of Crimson Joy,</u>
<u>I remember that we discussed old essays in Autumn Cool Studio,</u>
I remember that we drank wine and made *fu* to celebrate the Double Ninth holiday,
I remember that I commemorated the ancients by composing the verse for five fair women.
Now that I will return to the "Yellow Earth" in a short while,
All of my poems will also turn into dust with me.
I summon Nightingale to pass me the "poetry handkerchief,"
Seeing the handkerchief is like seeing the person from whom I got it.
<u>Baoyu used to carry this handkerchief on his person,</u>
After he made me a present of it, I wrote poems on it to express my feelings.
My deep love for him is expressed by the twenty-eight words,
The stains surrounding the characters are the traces of my tears.
<u>Now though the handkerchief is still the same, its donor has already changed his heart,</u>
I recall my old dream and it is really like a floating cloud.
I ask Nightingale to add more charcoal to the brazier,
I want to burn the handkerchief and the poems together.

曾記得柳絮填詞誇俊逸,
<u>曾記得海棠起社鬥清新</u>。
曾記得凹晶館內題明月,
曾記得攏翠庵中譜素琴。
<u>曾記得怡紅院裡行新令</u>,
<u>曾記得秋爽齋頭論舊文</u>。
曾記得持樽把酒把重陽賦,
曾記得吊古攀今《五美吟》。
到如今奴身不久歸黃土,
它也該一律化灰塵。
又叫紫鵑將詩帕取,
見詩帕如見當初贈帕人。
<u>想此帕乃是寶玉隨身帶</u>,
贈與我珍重題詩暗寫心。
無窮心事都在二十八個字,

圍著字點點斑斑是淚痕。
至如今綾帕依然人心變，
回憶舊夢似浮雲。
命紫鵑火爐之內多添碳，
把詩帕詩篇一概焚。
(Hu 1983: 256)

Here Lin Daiyu's act of "burning her poems" is transformed into an emotionally charged drama of commemorating *qing* and her poeticized life and love and condemning the loveless world that has destroyed her hope, her beloved, and her purpose for living. A similar treatment can be found in the Yue opera version of *Honglou meng*, and the act in which "Lin Daiyu burns her poems" has become one of the most memorable and touching parts of the whole operatic adaptation.

CONCLUSION

Generally speaking, the *Honglou meng zidishu* tend to faithfully retell the stories of the fictional original, and they are able to accomplish this by selecting the most representative materials from the novel and skillfully using the generic forms of *zidishu* to heighten the lyrical quality of their reworked characters.

Nevertheless, as rewrites of *Honglou meng*, the *zidishu* texts inevitably became a means by which their authors (who were first and foremost readers of *Honglou meng*) expressed their views on the ideology and artistry of their parent work. For various reasons, some of the *zidishu* rewrites, such as "The Invocation to the Hibiscus Spirit" and "The Story of the Stone," take a more critical stance toward the Cheng-Gao edition of the novelistic text. Their efforts to remake the characters and narrative events, as well as to restore Cao Xueqin's original design, reveal their own moral beliefs and literary tastes as a group of elite Manchu Bannermen.

Han Xiaochuang's "Destiny of Dew and Tears" presents a convincing case that *Honglou meng zidishu* was instrumental in the dissemination and popularization of Cao Xueqin's eighteenth-century masterpiece in the mid and late Qing. *Zidishu*'s successful strategies in reworking the fictional original's subject matter, narrative strategies, language, and means of artistic representation provided an exemplary model for operatic adaptations such as the Yue opera *Honglou meng*. For this reason, *zidishu* are an important part of the *Honglou meng* repertory, and should be subject to further scholarly scrutiny and more extensive investigation.

APPENDIX 1: THE TABLE FOR HU WENBIN'S *HONGLOU MENG ZIDISHU*

	The Title of the Work	Chaps	Chaps. in HLM	Author
1	《會玉摔玉》Lin Daiyu Meets Jia Baoyu and Jia Baoyu Casts His Jade	2	3	
2	《一入榮國府》Grannie Liu Visits the Rong Mansion for the First Time	4	6	韩小窗 Han Xiaochuang
3	《玉香花語》The Jade is Fragrant and the Flower Talks	2	19	叙庵 Xu'an
4	《雙玉埋紅》Baoyu and Daiyu Bury Flowers	1	23	
5	《葬花》Daiyu Buries Flowers	5	26–28	
6	《悲秋》Lin Daiyu Laments the Autumn	1	27–29	韩小窗 Han Xiaochuang
7	《椿齡畫薔》Charmante Scratches a "Qiang" and Mystifies a Beholder	1	30	
8	《晴雯撕扇》Skybright Tears the Fan	1	31	
9	《寶釵代繡》Xue Baochai Helps with the Embroidery	1	36	韩小窗 Han Xiaochuang
10	《海棠结社》Formation of the Crab-Apple Poetry Club	1	27	
11	《二入榮國府》Granny Liu Visits the Rong Mansion for the Second Time	12	39	
12	《議宴陳園》Discussing the Banquet and Displaying the Garden	2	40	符斋 Fuzhai
13	《兩宴大觀園》Having Two Banquets in the [Prospect] Garden	1	40	
14	《三宣牙牌令》Faithful Makes Three Calls on the Wine Game of Dominoes	1	40	
15	《品茶櫳翠庵》Jia Baoyu Tastes Some Superior Tea at the Green Bower Hermitage	1	41	
16	《醉臥怡紅院》Grannnie Liu Samples the Sleeping Accommodations at House of Crimson Joy	1	41	
17	《過繼巧姐兒》Grannie Liu Adopts Qiao Jie	1	42	
18	《鳳姐兒送行》Wang Xifeng Says Good-bye to Grannie Liu	1	42	
19	《湘雲醉酒》A Tipsy Xiangyun Sleeps on a Peony-Petal Pillow	1	62	

20	《芙蓉誄》 The Invocation to the Hibiscus Spirit	6	52–78	韩小窗 Han Xiaochuang
21	《遣晴雯》 Lady Wang Dismisses Skybright	2	74	蕉窗 Jiaochuang
22	《晴雯換襖》 Skybright Exchanges Her Undergarment with That of Baoyu	2	77	云田 Yuntian
23	《晴雯齎恨》 Skybright Harbors Resentment	1	77–78	
24	《雙玉聽琴》 Baoyu and Adamantina Listen to Daiyu Play the Zither	1	87	韩小窗 Han Xiaochuang
25	《石頭記》 The Story of the Stone	4	96–98	
26	《露淚緣》 The Destiny of Dew and Tears	13	96–98, 104, 113, and 116	韩小窗 Han Xiaochuang
27	《思玉戲環》 Baoyu Thinks of Daiyu and Shows Affection to Fivey	1	109	

APPENDIX 2: THE DIFFERENCES BETWEEN LIN JUNJIA'S EDITION AND HU WENBIN'S COLLECTION

1. "Changchun zanghua" 傷春葬花 (Daiyu Laments Spring and Buries Flowers) is listed in Lin Junjia's collection; the same piece is called "Zanghua" 葬花 (Daiyu Buries Flowers) in Hu Wenbin's collection.
2. "Daiyu zanghua" 黛玉葬花 (Daiyu Buries Flowers) is included in Lin's edition, but not in Hu's collection.
3. "Yuxiang huayu" 玉香花語 (The Jade is Fragrant and the Flower Talks) has four chapters in Lin's collection, but the first and second chapters are missing in Hu's.
4. "Quan Beiqiu" 全悲秋 (The Complete Ballad of Lin Daiyu Lamenting the Autumn) is divided into five chapters in Lin's edition. In Hu's collection, the same piece is not divided into chapters and it is entitled as "Beiqiu" 悲秋 (Lin Daiyu Laments the Autumn).
5. In Lin's collection, the two-chaptered "Tanbing" 探病 (Baoyu Visits the Sick Daiyu) is taken from "Beiqiu"in verbatim, and maybe used as a separate piece only for performance. Hu's edition has no entry of such a piece.
6. "Haitang jieshe" 海棠结社 (Formation of the Crab-Apple Poetry Club) is divided into two chapters in Lin's edition. In Hu's collection the same piece is not divided into chapters.
7. "Shuangyu tingqin" 雙玉聽琴 (Baoyu and Adamantina Listen to Daiyu Play the Zither) is divided into two chapters in Lin's edition. In Hu's collection, the same piece is not divided into chapters.

8. There are two different versions of "Eryu lunxin" 二玉論心 (Baou and Daiyu Exchange Their Internal Feelings) included in Lin's edition that are absent in Hu's collection.

9. "Baochai chanyu" 寶釵產玉 (Baochai Gives Birth to Baoyu's Son) is included in Lin's but not Hu's collection.

8 SHI TUO'S NARRATOR AS CENTRAL CONSCIOUSNESS: SHORT-STORY CYCLE *RECORDS FROM ORCHARD TOWN*

DUŠAN ANDRŠ

The appeal of literary works by Chinese writers of the Republican period often derives from the daring or conflicting values and ideas they impart, as well as from the remarkable diversity of techniques and methods they employ. Literary works emerging from confluence between tradition and modernity can vary in value, but they are generally marked by a considerable degree of creative diversity. This is particularly true for the modern Chinese short story, a genre distinctive for its "great complexity and evident concern for technique" (Huters 1990a: 3).

In this chapter, I draw attention to the artistic achievements of Shi Tuo (1910–1988), an important but still understudied writer of the 1930s and 1940s. As has been observed by several scholars, two novels by Shi Tuo are noteworthy in their experimental and unconventional style, *Ma Lan* (Ma Lan, 1948) and *Marriage* (Jiehun, 1947) (Gunn 1980: 84, 88; Hsia 1999: 464–465; Slupski 1973: 21, 27). The two novels, composed in the 1940s, were preceded by a series of notable short stories penned during the author's experimental period in the late 1930s and early 1940s. As aptly articulated by Zbigniew Slupski (1973: 12), one of the first western students of the writer's work, "Shih Tuo's stories, or to be more exact, his short prose pieces, have no fixed form, and the line drawn between sketch, story, essay or mere report tends to disappear." Similarly, Theodore Huters (1990b: 76) locates in Shi Tuo's short story "A Kiss" (Yi wen) "characteristics of a prose essay," such as the "sketchiness of the plot" or the "predominance of static description," concluding that the piece "falls into a nebulous area somewhere between story and essay." The generic peculiarity of the writer's work had already been perceived by some contemporary critics of the period. Meng Shi in his comment on Shi Tuo's short stories "The Valley" (Gu) and "Light of the Setting Sun" (Luori guang) observes that the writer "likes more depicting sceneries and people than telling stories. When writing short stories, he is unable to extricate himself from his inveterate habit of writing descriptive or travel prose pieces" (1937: 235). Indeed, the author himself, when looking back on his literary oeuvre, highlighted a lack of generic purity as a distinctive feature of most of his short stories. In a foreword to the collection of his short stories published in 1980, Shi Tuo (1980: 165) comments on their form as follows: "Among these so called short stories, there is no single one that conforms to the standard of the short story; even less do they conform to the standard set by the 'practice of writing of short stories.' At most they can be called stories, but some of them even do not deserve to be called stories, for example 'Orchard Town' ... can only be regarded as an inferior essay."

Despite an apparent tendency toward blending diverse writing styles and generic strategies, many short pieces from Shi Tuo's experimental period bespeak a high degree of thematic unity. This is especially true of the three series of stories set in a specific setting and included into the collections *Sketches Gathered at My Native Place* (Limen shiji, 1937), *Shanghai Correspondence* (Shanghai shouzha, 1941) and *Records from Orchard Town* (Guoyuan cheng ji, 1946). According to students of Shi Tuo's work, *Sketches Gathered at My Native Place* comprises satiric-melancholic snatches from the lives of inhabitants in the writer's native town (Ma 1988: 179), *Shanghai Correspondence* reflects the author's experience with gloomy sides of life in the Shanghai area of the late 1930s (Gunn 1980: 78-9), and *Records from Orchard Town* "portrays the decay and stagnation of life in a small town just prior to the war" (Gunn 1980: 80).[126]

This essay focuses on the stories that constitute the collection *Records from Orchard Town*[127] and draws attention to the structural unity that governs not only the collection's motifs and themes, but also its narrative modes and strategies. In the essay, I discuss the complexity of the collection's semantic structure as Shi Tuo's major artistic achievement and an important characteristic of *Records from Orchard Town*. I argue that among the key constituents of the "textual poiesis"[128] employed by the writer should be counted a distinctly individualized narrator. Looking at *Records from Orchard Town*—generally read as an evocative rendering of lives of petty characters, inhabitants of a small town in China's interior—from this perspective opens up the text to a new interpretation. I read selected pieces from the collection as narratives communicating experiences, recollections, and visions of an

---

126 For a synopsis of the collection *Sketches Gathered at My Native Place*, see Ma 1988. Gunn (1980: 78-80) briefly discusses the collection *Shanghai Correspondence*. *Records* has been touched on by Hsia (1999: 463), as well as by Gunn (1980: 80-82) and Yingjin Zhang (1996: 39-58).

127 I subscribe to the David Malcolm's (2012: 42-47) view that short stories (even though they are originally published individually) when taken together more often than not present a remarkably coherent and cohesive vision of their author.

128 I am using Lubomír Doležel's (1998: 23) term defined as an activity producing fictional worlds of literature.

individualized narrator who occupies a central position not only within the individual stories but also on the level of the collection as a whole. By extension, in scrutinizing the narrator's peculiar voice, I hope to provide an avenue for a possible clarification of the problem of the generic ambiguity of the writer's early short prose pieces.

ORCHARD TOWN AND ITS INHABITANTS

In his preface to the collection's first edition, Shi Tuo provides information about the inspiration for and circumstances under which he wrote the stories in *Records from Orchard Town* (hence, *Records*).[129] The author opens his preface with a recollection of a trip he undertook in 1936. On his way from Beiping to Shanghai, he visited a friend living in an undisclosed small town and spent two weeks in his friend's crumbling family estate and on lanes marked by a strangely stagnant atmosphere. Shi Tuo connects his decision to write with his fascination for the place he visited; at the same time, however, he points out that since he had no intimate knowledge of his friend's town, the town depicted in *Records* is in principal a product of his personal experience with life in small rural towns.

At first reading, the collection of eighteen prose pieces, written between 1938 and 1946, offers a series of portraits of typical inhabitants of small Chinese towns: the landlord, the landlady, the postman, the gardener, the maiden, the teacher, the revolutionary, the storyteller, the tinsmith, etc.[130] As a result, many readers and critics have valued primarily the representational character of the stories and typicality of their protagonists.[131] As observed by Yingjin Zhang (1996: 57), by unfolding an array of lives and personalities the writer created "a certain set of mentalities" embodying life in a small county

---

129   *Records from Orchard Town* was published in 1946 by Shanghai chuban gongsi. Most of the individual stories appeared prior to 1946 in various literary journals. By the time of publication of the collection, Shi Tuo had already published five collections of short stories and four collections of essays. As a primary source, I am using the third reprint of the first edition from 1952. All citations from this text give page numbers only. The second edition of the collection published by Shanghai xin wenyi chubanshe in 1958 has been considerably modified. For the details and a complete list of the author's works, see Liu Zengjie 1982: 391–407.

130   As enumerated in the writer's postscript to the 1958 edition of the collection, Shi Tuo originally planned to compose even more stories conceived as portrayals of representative characters, or representatives of different occupations or walks of life. He intended to write also "a story of a donkey-man," "a story of an actor," "a story of a handicraftsman," "a story of a shop assistant," "a story of a county official," and even "a story of a Nationalist Party official" (Shi Tuo 1958: 98–101).

131   Such an approach appears to be a common denominator of several Chinese language studies devoted to the collection. See, for example, Zhang Zhonghui 2002: 21–22 and Bai Chunchao 2000: 39–42.

town. Shi Tuo's evocative portrayal of the spirit or the essence of small towns has to be acknowledged as an important artistic quality of *Records*. Seen from this viewpoint, *Records* reads as a series of stories linked to a central concept of the small town, preconceived as an embodiment of all backwoods places in China of the day.[132]

An appreciation of its key representational element—individual portrayals of small town dwellers—gives one a sense of the collection's unity. However, the stories in the collection should be appreciated for their mutual interrelatedness on other levels. A deeper understanding of the structural unity and originality of the collection entails analysis of the collection's complex structure on motific and thematic levels.

"Orchard Town" (Guoyuan cheng), the opening story in the collection, mentions some of the characters that people the fictional space of Orchard Town and foreshadows small portions of their life stories. The fragmentary nature of the information—which also serves to frame and give unity to the collection—hints at an important characteristic of many of stories to follow.[133] Although in most cases main characters' names or appellations serve as titles of the stories—highlighting thus their "biographical" format,[134] protagonists' fates are usually depicted in a conspicuously fragmentary and indirect manner. The lives of protagonists are often rendered in the process of remembering or reconstructing events of the past. Even though Shi Tuo's first-person narrator—who identifies himself in the opening story as a visitor to the town—is able to "cross spatial and temporal boundaries" (Yingjin Zhang 1996: 41), he is by no means an omniscient source of knowledge of the protagonists' lives. When tracking their fates, Shi Tuo's narrator focuses on fundamental patterns that govern the town dwellers' lives. However diverse they appear, accounts of life stories of individual protagonists serve primarily to layer integral motifs and unfold unifying themes, such as the inexorable passage of time, the cycles of rise and fall, the prevalence of sadness and evil in the world, or the alternation between encounters and partings, leaving and returning.

---

132   Yingjin Zhang (1996: 36) points out the uniqueness of *Records* "in Chinese literature in featuring a small town as the central protagonist, endowed with its own life, character, thought, opinion, feeling, and fate, exactly like a living person."

133   The opening story can be read as both an introductory text and one of the collection's stories. As an introductory text, it can be seen as the key element of the collection's "external structure," an indication that *Records* should be read as a story cycle. For a definition of "external structure" of short story cycles, see Ingram 1971: 20.

134   The writer even uses—apparently for satirical purposes—the traditional term *liezhuan* or "biography" in the title of the story "Biographies of the Various Masters Liu" (Liuye liezhuan) which tells a story of the youngest son of Liu family: the "pet" of the family, an excellent pupil and favorite with teachers and schoolmates, gradually becomes a bankrupt and opium addict.

SPACE AND TIME

An overview of the topographic layout of Orchard Town shows that, in many stories, it is marked by a limited number of places laden with symbolic meanings. Consisting of a number of private places (dwellings, courtyards, and gardens) and public places (lanes, market streets, and busy intersections), the town is enclosed by walls. The sealed space of the town can be entered only through guarded gates.[135] The most prominent sight of the town and also one of the most important constituents of its spatiotemporal dimension is an ancient pagoda built on the top of the city wall. Serving as a recurrent motif, the pagoda contributes significantly to the structural cohesiveness of the collection: it is repeatedly imagined by the narrator as an imposing structure looking down unconcerned on the endless stream of human lives below.[136]

These limited places create a highly distinctive, self-contained space of Orchard Town governed by cyclical time. The special temporal quality of the town can be articulated with Mikhail Bachtin's (1975: 396) words: "Here are no events, but merely a constantly repeating 'existence.' The time differs from linear, historical time. It moves in cycles: there are cycles of the day, of the week, of the month, of the whole life. Day by day, the same actions of existence are repeated, the same themes of conversations, the same words." For example, the stories "Mr. Postman" (Youchai xiansheng), "Lamp" (Deng), or "Ge Tianmin" (Ge Tianmin)" offer portrayals of the fates of Orchard Town dwellers ruled by the cyclical time; the narrative voice reflects a bitter-sweet nostalgia for the place seemingly untouched by the outer world as well as a fascination for old ways of life. Although in other stories, such as "Garden Balsam," "The Storyteller" (Shuoshuren), or "A Pigment Box" (Yanliao he), motifs of decline and the disintegration of what used to be an idyllic place prevail, characters' fates are still largely determined by cyclical time.

An important place in the layout of the fictional space in the collection is the railway station, situated outside the town walls. The narrator establishes the space of the railway station in "Orchard Town," the opening story of the collection, where he tells the reader that it is ten *li* distant and separated from the town by a river and that it serves as an interface between two mutually alien territories; it is the most distant "outpost" of the town, which is peacefully enclosed not only by its walls but by its numerous orchards as well. Distinct from the quiet and uneventful atmosphere of the town, the railway station is a place teeming with activity and enterprise, and a space where two diverse kinds of time—the cyclical and the linear—clash. For characters

---

135 See, for example, the stories "Pagoda" (Ta) (Shi Tuo 1952: 129) and "Awaiting" (Qidai) (154).

136 The tower serves as leitmotif in the story "Pagoda," and it appears as an important motif also in other stories of the collection, for example in "Orchard Town."

leaving or returning to the town, the railway station and its vicinity are not a mere stopping over place; rather, it is often where they suddenly awake to the impact of time concerning their fates.

Characters whose stories unfold outside Orchard Town are mostly subject to the reign of linear time. "Biographies of the Various Masters Liu" (Liuye liezhuan), "Three Insignificant Persons" (Sange xiao renwu), "Meng Anqing's Cousin" (Meng Anqing de tangxiongdi), or "Lofty Character" (Aogu) can serve as examples of stories of Orchard Town natives whose fates accentuate linearity of time; some of them leave the town forever, while others make futile attempts to return. Nevertheless, most of them resemble wanderers or expatriates who feel alienated from their home. The pace of the stories is typically marked by an accelerated flow of time, disconnection from the past, and uncertainty about the future.

Most stories in the collection are interconnected by the prominent motif of time. Protagonists of the stories may experience various predicaments and be involved in various affairs but crucial moments in their lives are usually associated with an awareness of the inexorable flow, the repetitiveness, or the motionlessness of time. In order to highlight the impact of the flow of time on lives of his protagonists, Shi Tuo repeatedly uses sudden jumps in time or a juxtaposition of past and present. For example, Sister Liu, the protagonist of the story "A Kiss," after having completed her visit to Orchard Town, the place where she spent her childhood, realizes the futility of her attempt to recover remnants of her own past. Questions raised by a voice that can be attributed to the narrator (but clearly speaking for Sister Liu) highlight the protagonist's abrupt awakening to the crushing power of an inexorable flow of time: "But why had she been in such a hurry to come here? After having left this small town for ten, fifteen, or even almost twenty years, with Mother Liu probably long since dead, her husband possibly dead even before her mother, she herself entering middle-age, what could this little town have that she could not forget?" (204).[137]

Other Orchard Town dwellers may experience uneasiness at the absence of change in their lives. Whereas the sudden awareness of the irreversible passage of time teaches Sister Liu about life's transience, the repetitiveness of time reveals to other Orchard Town dwellers the meaninglessness of their existence. The efforts of protagonists whose lives are governed by the linear flow of time are often doomed to failure because the irreversible flow of time destroys all their hopes; the efforts of protagonists whose lives are enmeshed in the web of repetitive or cyclical time are similarly hopeless: they can only endlessly replay their pasts.

---

137 All translations are mine. Similarly powerful juxtaposition of the past and the present serves as the basic configuration in the story "Hunt" (Shoulie) (173–181).

The motionlessness of time that makes a protagonist's life empty and absurd appears, for example, as the key motif in "Garden Balsam" (Taohong).[138] The protagonist of the story, maiden Sugu, lives with her widowed mother. After her father's death, the house seems to descend into silence and apathy. A clock whose hands don't move and the ever-recurring calls of street vendors suggest the end of time and its crushing impact on the heroine:

> "What's the time, mum?" Suddenly, as if something stirred in Sugu's mind, she couldn't help raising her head and asking. Madam Menglin had been awake already for a long time. Happily and without any yearning, she was enjoying lounging around after her noontime nap. "Have a look." This was her usual answer. The clock on the dressing table— you should have known already long ago, there was no use of a clock for this family— they have forgotten to wind the spring, it stopped no one knows how long ago. (61–62)

Seen from the viewpoint of time, Sister Liu and maiden Sugu represent two character types in Shi Tuo's *Records*. Active and striving heroes experiencing a linearity of time, like Sister Liu, tend to leave (and sometimes return to) Orchard Town. They attempt to establish themselves as independent, often progressive individuals. Passive and inert protagonists obeying the law of cyclical time, like Sugu, stay in Orchard Town and accept their fates. The life stories of the two character types outlined above represent two opposite and, at the same time, complementary motivic configurations. Their recurrence in *Records* contributes significantly to the structural unity of the collection.

DYNAMIC PATTERNS

As is apparent from the above discussion of its key configurations of characters, space, and time in the collection, *Records* reads as a self-contained whole marked by a high degree of structural unity. The structural unity of the collection can also be observed on the deeper level of its dynamic patterns—that is, in the recurrence and development of motifs shared by the majority of stories in the collection. Seen from the viewpoint of the collection's whole, individual stories in *Records* perform an important structural role—they build the collection's "internal structure," understood as a product of the tension between each individual story and a set of stories to which the individual story belongs.[139]

---

138 Taohong is a local name used by Orchard Town dwellers for "garden balsam." The garden balsam fading in the courtyard symbolizes the lifelessness and spiritlessness of the main protagonist.
139 As observed by Ingram, the presence of an "internal structure" should be seen as the fundamental characteristic of cycles of stories (1971: 19).

The opening story, "Orchard Town," for instance, plays a central role in forging the collection's internal structure. By introducing the theme of an intricate interrelationship between the town dwellers and the place they inhabit, by providing a glimpse into the life stories of several prominent characters, and by showing the web of characters' mutual relationships, this first story foreshadows recurrent dynamic patterns that are central to the collection as a whole. Similarly, later stories in the collection, which not only develop motifs hinted at in the opening story, but also open new designs, may be identified, in Ingram's (1971: 20) terms, as components of the collection's "internal structure" endowed with "dynamic patterns of recurrence and development."

As already observed, despite the centrality of characters and their stories, *Records* draws readers' attention not to characters' fates per se, but rather to patterns that underlie the destinies portrayed in individual stories. In fact, recurrence and development of certain motifs and themes belongs to the key dynamic structural devices of the stories. As an example of the writer's technique of building dynamic unity in the collection, we can observe the recurrent pattern of parting and returning, which is highlighted as a leitmotif in at least six stories in the collection.

"Lofty Character" presents the life story of a teacher with a leftist inclination who leaves his hometown for political reasons. His attempt to settle among his revolutionary peers in Shanghai fails, and he returns to Orchard Town. But locals hold the returnee in contempt despite his sincere concern for the plight of his neighbors. The protagonist ends up becoming a disillusioned, apathetic loner. A variation on this particular pattern can be found in "The Storyteller." Presumably after many years of separation, the narrator-protagonist returns to the town of his childhood where he used to listen to a local storyteller. While on a stroll through the town searching for the storyteller, the protagonist encounters the storyteller's funeral procession. As a result, the protagonist experiences a painful feeling of inner emptiness; he realizes that tales and heroes once brought to life by the storyteller have disappeared forever. The two stories employ an analogous pattern of parting and returning with the aim of articulating the sense of disillusionment and emptiness that is an unavoidable consequence of the clash between lofty youthful ideals and a reality marked by indifference and misunderstanding (the former story) or between emotional attachment to traditional culture and the reality of its unstoppable decline (the latter story).

"Hunt" (Shoulie) is another example of Shi Tuo's variations on the theme of parting and return. The protagonist decides to leave his beloved cousin and the narrow space of his hometown to start a new life in the wide world. After many years, dissatisfaction and hollowness in his life drive him to return home. Back in Orchard Town he learns that his cousin is married and that he—a "puzzling" person who traded the comfort and safety of home for the precariousness of the world outside, has become an object of his neighbors' reprobation. The disheartened protagonist leaves for the railway station, where he is confronted with "all those hostels and boarding houses hired on a month by month basis" (181).

In "A Kiss," a boy from the neighborhood kisses seventeen-year-old Sister Liu. Fearing that her maturing daughter is in danger of losing her virginity, her mother promptly sells her as a concubine to an older wealthy man. After many years, aged Sister Liu returns to Orchard Town. She hires a rickshaw that takes her from the railway station to the town without knowing that the man pulling the cart is the boyfriend of her girlhood. In the final scene, when Sister Liu presents the rickshaw driver with an unusually large tip, she has a sudden recognition of her erstwhile boyfriend and his present predicament. Only then does Sister Liu realize the futility of her visit to Orchard Town.

As with "Lofty Character" and "The Storyteller," "Hunt" and "A Kiss" can be read as variations on the theme of parting and return by drawing prominence to an awakening to the ephemerality of emotional bonds and the volatility of human fortune when confronted with the merciless passing of time. Other examples of the dynamic pattern of parting and return can be found in the collection's opening and closing stories, "Orchard Town" and "Three Insignificant Persons," which take on a particularly strong structural role for the collection as a whole. While the first story serves, among other things, to foreshadow the collections central pattern of parting and return, the closing story not only adds a new layer of meaning to this recurrent motif, but also rounds off—by means of presenting the last variation on the pattern—an important component of the "internal structure" of *Records*.[140]

"Orchard Town" introduces the narrator-protagonist as a visitor to Orchard Town; it has been seven years since he last visited this his second home. Significantly, the story opens with the narrator's arrival at the railway station. While slowly approaching and finally entering the town, the narrator is attracted and repelled simultaneously by the place. For the most part, his encounter with Orchard Town unfolds on the level of recollection and imagination—only the closing part of the story portrays the narrator's encounter with his relative, Madame Menglin. An important moment in the process of the narrator's reunion with Orchard Town is his hesitation while standing in front of Madame Menglin's door. For a while he contemplates leaving the town, but in the end he knocks on the door and enters. The narrator's homecoming experience foreshadows the centrality of the pattern of parting and return for the whole collection; at the same time, his apprehension that he

---

140 As observed by Ingram (1971: 22–23), the concluding part of a cycle of stories often rounds off the themes and patterns recurring and developing throughout the cycle by drawing them together.

will eventually regret his decision not to leave Orchard Town introduces disillusionment about return as one the collection's central motifs, creatively developed in several of its stories.

In "Three Insignificant Persons," Shi Tuo's narrator tells stories of the turbulent lives of three Orchard Town natives, two siblings from a wealthy family and a son of their family gatekeeper. The lives of the family heir and his pretty sister end in disaster: the extravagant and bankrupt heir is murdered and his spoiled sister ends up in a brothel; the destitute son of the gatekeeper becomes involved in a rebellion and flees the town. The story culminates in a scene where the gatekeeper's son, now an underground revolutionary, returns to Orchard City. When setting off from the railway station to the town, he passes a house in which the spoiled sister, his childhood sweetheart, sings a lewd song. The story ends with the narrator questioning the meaning of the protagonist's return: "Even if they chanced to meet, what good outcome could they achieve?" (238).

Apparently, the recurrence and development of the pattern of parting and return serve—by deepening and broadening of one of the collection's underlying themes—as important constituents of the collection's overall meaning; at the same time, the dynamic pattern of parting and return should be seen as one of the most prominent unifying aspects of the collection's semantic structure.

INDIVIDUALIZED NARRATOR

Although Shi Tuo's creative use of recurrent motivic patterns serves as an important source of structural unity for *Records*, other essential sources of such a unity can be found as well. Seen from the viewpoint of its deeper structure, unifying elements in the collection operate not only on the level of the plot; they also work at the level of narration. In other words, the source of artistic unity of the collection can be sought not only in the dominant principle governing its motifs and themes, but also in its narrative modes.

When scrutinizing individual stories in *Records*, a variety of narrative modes can be found. In more than one-third of the stories, the narrator not only tells the stories of Orchard Town natives, he is also a protagonist who stays in the town. In "Orchard Town," the collection's opening story, the narrator named Ma Shu'ao enters Orchard Town and establishes himself as a visitor to Orchard Town who observes and listens. The narrator—as a voice with a body—is present also in the stories "Ge Tianmin," "A Pigment Box," "A Ti," "Pagoda" (Ta), "Awaiting" (Qidai), and "The Storyteller." In the rest of the collection's stories, the source of narration appears to be a disembodied narrative voice; in most cases, however, this narrative voice can be attributed to a limited omniscient narrator implicitly situated within the fictional world of Orchard Town. Seen from the viewpoint of the whole collection, Shi Tuo's narrator—despite the above outlined variability—speaks with an unmistakably individualized voice.

Throughout the collection, the narrator's discourse is marked by frequent subjective statements, comments, and questions. Shi Tuo's narrator repeatedly airs his personal attitudes toward protagonists, events, and scenes recounted in his own narration.[141] For example, when the main protagonist of "A Kiss," Sister Liu, learns the sad destinies of several of her erstwhile neighbors, the narrator leaves her sighing and adds the following personal comment:

> She sighed deeply over this—to tell the truth it really is worth sighing over. Without the slightest bit of concern, people fight, shout, cry, and laugh, their minds busy with habitual calculations; until they suddenly open their eyes and realize that, when confronted with iron-faced and impersonal time, they are so insignificant, empty, pitiful, that they are so weak! (200)

Similarly, in "Hunt" the narrator does not hesitate to insert his own appraisal of the turnaround in the mind of the story's protagonist, Meng Anqing:

> It seems that the matter should have ended at this point. But what did I say earlier? Right, in the whole world, no other seed can be pulled out with greater difficulty than that planted into our hearts at the very beginning of our lives. After the initial excitement had vanished […], his mind gradually became hollow, and in the end he became disheartened and desolate; unexpectedly, one day he returned suddenly to Orchard Town. (176)

Another element that strengthens the narrator's individual voice is the frequent use of a rhetorical mode of narration. Shi Tuo's narrator repeatedly makes use of the first- and second-person personal pronouns in order to establish a certain degree of intimacy or familiarity with the reader. For example, In "Biographies of the Various Masters Liu," Shi Tuo's narrator presupposes familiarity an the part of the reader with fates typical for characters he is going to talk about: "You have probably already heard this kind of story before ..." (73). When reproaching one of the protagonists' for his

---

141 Apparently, the narrative modes employed by Shi Tuo in his *Records* oscillate between the rhetorical Ich-form narrator and rhetorical Er-form narrator. Besides being the medium of the narration and the producer of the narrative text, Shi Tuo's narrator is marked by a tendency toward evaluating and interpreting the reality of the fictional world. For the functional delineation of the two types of rhetorical narrator, see Doležel 1973: 3-13.

opium addiction, the narrator draws attention to the fact that he shares values and opinions with those of the reader: "Maybe you find it strange; why is it that they like this stuff? You don't understand—we, too, don't understand what benefit it brings" (79). A few lines later, the narrator addresses the reader again. This time he envisages the reader's hypothetical reaction in case he would meet the impoverished and seedy protagonist of his story: "You would be greatly surprised, when looking at him; you wouldn't even recognize him" (80).

In "The Master of the Town" (Chengzhu), the life story of Mater Kui, Orchard Town's celebrity, the narrator offers readers the opportunity to share his memories, inviting them for a "guided tour" through the mansion of the wealthy landlord:

> Nowadays—no, all this luxury and mightiness is already a thing of the past. Let us go back—as we did before—to the time of ten years ago, let us go to the mansion of Master Kui! Master Kui lives inside the town near the Western Gate; the moment we enter Orchard Town's Western Gate, we will see the wide Western Gate street, often with pigs or dogs roaming it, covered by a thick, always so thick layer of dust; in the distance, we will see a tall gate decorated with animal ornaments, a gate indicating official rank. (42)

At another point, Shi Tuo's narrator even makes a long digression and appeals to readers, trying to persuade them toward his scornful view of Master Kui's toadies:

> He took his most capable flunkies—you are probably fed up with this word, but I can't find a more appropriate and beautiful expression for these people. They are of different kinds, rascals, local ruffians, landlords; most of them belong to the second-class gentry. If you had such a position, you would solicit them; these people are always prepared, for the sake of their own status and for their prestige in the eyes of poor peasants, to swarm your parlor like flies that cannot be swatted away—it was precisely these people Master Kui installed into various offices. (41–42)

An important aspect of the rhetorical repertoire surrounding the narrator's individualized voice is frequent occurrences of storyteller-like passages. In "Three Insignificant Persons," for example, Shi Tuo's narrator introduces his account of one of the characters' life with a formula evoking the manner of oral storytelling: "Now allow us to tell you about our third protagonist, Miss Hu Fengying" (224). In a similar vein, in "Lofty Character" the narrator asks the reader to recognize the protagonist's exceptional personality: "In fact, isn't it exactly so? Please, open your eyes and look around you as closely as you can. Is there another real talent besides him in this place?" (109–110). Similarly, the narrator closes a lengthy depiction of the sorrows of the local teacher in "He Wenlong's Manuscript" (He Wenlong de wengao) with an appeal to the reader to assess the heaviness of the protagonist's predicament: "Then, take this under consideration please; if he has to get up tomorrow as early as before half past five, what else will he be able to undertake?" (88). An example of the storyteller-like self-reference is poignant in the narrator's exclamation from "A Pigment Box," a tragic story of a free-thinking female teacher who, by swallowing colors from her pigment box, commits suicide after one of her colleagues gets her pregnant during a wild drinking party: "I, too, want to pack up my pigment box, why should we depict these painful portrayals?" (103).

Instead of presenting himself as a self-assured, persuasive storyteller in the manner of traditional fiction, Shi Tuo's narrator doesn't conceal his uncertainty, hesitations, or limited knowledge of the events and characters he depicts. For example, the narrator of "A Kiss" frequently utters such phrases as "do not know in complete detail," "or maybe it was," "we don't know how," or "perhaps we should say." One of the characteristics of Shi Tuo's narrative voice is that it oscillates between a "self-assured commentator" and an "uncertain narrator," as Huters puts it (1990b: 81, 86). Approached from this angle, the apparent predilection for a rhetorical mode of narration—which draws on, and simultaneously revolts against, the tradition of authoritative storytelling—represents another prominent aspect of the individuality of Shi Tuo's narrator.

Still another materialization of the narrator's individuality can be discerned in the occurrence of numerous speeches, dialogues, and conversations. Despite their brevity, they often serve as essential building blocks of the semantic structure of the stories in the collection; utterances and conversations are carefully distributed through the individual stories where they execute important structural functions. Typically, the narrator listens to questions, utterances or fragments of conversations of Orchard Town's dwellers; in some instances he merely "quotes" overheard voices, in others he ponders their meaning, responds to them, or elaborates on them in his narration.

In "Orchard Town," the narrator-protagonist, while leaving the railway station, remembers the question put to him by an old man a few minutes earlier: "'Where are you going, sir?' He asked me right at the moment the engine was giving a long whistle. Where am I going? His question awakened my childhood memories; it awakened me from the weariness caused by my journey, from the hubbub of travelers, from my anxieties" (1). Later, when already in town, the narrator overhears fragments of conversation, which, despite their fragmentary quality, mark important moments in his wandering through the town: "'Is it late already?' 'It is.' Meeting on a dark street, two men are greeting each other" (9). Here the narrator immerses himself in the pitch-dark and strangely quiet space in order to gather information of the town dwellers. Several pages later, while considering the possibility of a hasty retreat from the town, the narrator relates the following: "Two Orchard Town dwellers' greetings or maybe parting voices reaching him from far away, 'Late already?' 'Already late'" (14). As implied by the closing part of the story, the careful distribution of anonymous voices serves to adumbrate the narrator's awakening to the fact that it maybe be too late to recapture bygone times.

Rather than narrated in a straightforward manner, the fates of protagonists in individual stories are often retraced or remembered with the help of recorded dialogues or conversations. On the one hand, Shi Tuo's narrator frequently lets other voices speak for him; as we have seen, he sometimes even casts doubts on his ability to provide a faithful depiction of events or an accurate characterization of persons. On the other hand, these voices are only rarely given the final word; more often than not, it is the narrator who offers a concluding judgment.

A good example of such a strategy can be found in "The Master of the Town." The story opens with a short conversation between two anonymous voices discussing a 'big-wig' of Orchard Town, Master Zhu. The dialogue is followed by the narrator's comment that ten years earlier Orchard Town dwellers often used to hear discussions like this one not only in the town's public places, but also in the "inns one-day-walk distant from town" (37-38). Similarly, later in the story, when retracing the life and deeds of the town's big shot, the narrator quotes a series of brief utterances attributed to town dwellers. Apparently, these voices serve as an important source of knowledge for the narrator on the fates of Master Zhu and his ilk. At the same time, however, the narrator—who is clearly knowledgeable about the place and people—corrects assertions of characters, supplies missing information, or provides his own interpretation of events and happenings. As in the story's opening, a quotation of a person's utterance plays an important role in the story's ending. The narrator, depicting a desolate scene that underscores Master Zhu's final decline, sees a visitor knocking at the gate of the big shot's house. After waiting a long time, the visitor leaves the closed gate, murmuring: "Ah! After all, good times must pass. If there was that day, so there is also this day!" (57) This exclamation by an anonymous Orchard Town resident sets the stage for the narrator's own assessment of the end of Master Zhu's life story: "He meant that the fortune of humans is just like morning and evening tides, it flows and ebbs. Just like a fool's formula in a theatre: 'Entertainment is over, ladies and gentlemen, the performance ends'" (57).

"Lamp" and "Awaiting" also show Shi Tuo's predilection for the use of dialogue and utterances as well as his inventiveness in employing them as important structural components. In the former story, important episodes from the life of a kerosene hawker are rendered in the form of a series of sketchy, as if overheard, conversations between the hawker and his customers. The latter story is notable for its passages relating a "conversation" between the narrator-protagonist and the father of his deceased friend. The empathetic narrator addresses his saddened host only in his thoughts and even hears words the father never utters. Significantly, the closing part of the story offers another fragment of peculiar conversation: the narrator listens to questions uttered by the mother of his friend, but he answers them, for the most part, only in his thoughts.

As a recurrent pattern of the narrator's discussions with locals, his passion for reliving personal memories emerges. For example, in the story "Ge Tianmin," the narrator-protagonist visits the house of a landlord, Mr. Ge Tianmin. Instead of depicting the appearance of the place or the situation of its inhabitants, the narrator's account consists mostly of his memories and recollections. Also in his conversation with the landlord, the narrator clearly prefers the search for the past: "What would be the most suitable topic for our discussion now? 'Do you remember where it was we met the last time?' [...] 'Let me think, was it in the shipyard?' 'I don't think so.' 'So was it in the orchard?' [...] He has probably forgotten about it. The last time I saw Ge Tianmin was seven years ago, at that time he was younger than today, his whiskers were sparser, he was on his farm instructing his workers" (24–25). The short conversation is interrupted by the narrator's lengthy discussion of the differences in attitude toward past events between the narrator and his host. The closing part of the conversation between the narrator and his counterpart introduces a new point of departure for the narrator's final remarks: "There was nothing important we needed to discuss, so I reminded him in passing. 'I remember how we two once crossed the river!' 'Crossed the river together?' A contended smile appeared on Mr. Ge Tianmin's face; it was as if he had all of a sudden fished from the ocean some thing lost long ago. He has now remembered the event. Is there anything one should rejoice more than this?" At this point, the narrator closes the conversation by highlighting the pleasures of remembering (26).

CENTRAL CONSCIOUSNESS

In *Records*, the narrated world and the narrating subject are constantly competing for the reader's attention. Shi Tuo's narrator acts not only as a voice creating a distinctive fictional world and its inhabitants but also as a central consciousness of both the individual stories and the collection as a whole. His absorption in remembering the town's past and in re-imagining bygone people and events lends a conspicuously lyrical character to the most stories in the collection. The protagonists who people the world of Shi Tuo's stories seldom appear in direct personal interactions; the complex, dynamic relations that typically mark the existence of fictional characters in fictional worlds are often of little importance in the world of Orchard Town. Most developments unfold not on the level of an interaction between characters,[142] but on the level of the narrator's reflections, musings, recollections, or conversations. As a result, stories in *Records* are often marked by the predominance of rambling talk over narrated action.

Shi Tuo's narrator may depict places he visits or scenes he witnesses, portray people he meets or quote conversations he holds, record utterances he hears or retell stories he listens to, but a substantial portion of what he narrates originates is his memory or is shaped by his imagination. In other words, though he depicts the fates of Orchard Town dwellers, the reader learns more about the narrator's attitudes, opinions, and emotions because of the prominence of his unique voice.

Looked at from the perspective of individual stories, Shi Tuo may be seen as a sustainer of the May Fourth literary tradition marked simultaneously by the lasting influence of traditional modes of narration and a penchant for probing new narrative modes and techniques. A number of prominent aspects of the stories under scrutiny bespeak a conjoined influence of the storytelling tradition and modern Chinese writers' experimentation with the manipulation of narrative time or such techniques as abrupt openings, open endings, static plot, and a focalized narrator.[143] Looked at from the perspective of the collection as a whole, *Records* represents a cycle of lyrical short prose pieces that are not easily placed into a strictly delineated generic category. In this sense, Shi Tuo's collection may be viewed as a predecessor of several short story cycles or novels shaped as strings of motif-based short narratives by root-seeking writers of the 1980s.[144]

Shi Tuo's narrator, who serves as the central consciousness of most of the stories in *Records*, should be seen not only as an important unifying force for the collection's semantic structure, but also as the very source of the collection's most prominent characteristics—its lyrical character and generic ambiguity.

---

142 My discussion refers to Doležel's (1998: 96–112) model of "multi-person" fictional world and his nomenclature of modes of interaction between fictional characters.

143 For a discussion of these aspects of the May Fourth fiction, see, for example, Zhao 1995: 97–99; 154-157; 167–170.

144 I am referring to short story collections and novels by Jia Pingwa, Zheng Wanlong, Li Rui, or Mo Yan. For the comparable characteristics, see Leenhouts 2005: 109–110.

PART II:
IDENTITIES
AND SELF-REPRESENTATIONS

9 MULTICULTURAL HISTORY IN A MULTIPARTY TAIWAN: THE NATIONAL MUSEUM OF TAIWAN HISTORY

KIRK A. DENTON

In this chapter, I analyze the permanent exhibit at the National Museum of Taiwan History (Guoli Taiwan lishi bowuguan). Opened in the fall of 2011, it is the first museum in Taiwan dedicated to the history of the island. My approach to the museum is generally narrative, and I analyze the complex politics and ideology driving the museum's story of the history of Taiwan. To appreciate the implications of this story, some understanding of the contestation over historical memory that has erupted in Taiwan since the lifting of martial law in 1987 is necessary.

CONTESTED HISTORICAL MEMORY

Since the end of martial law, Taiwan has undergone a dramatic political transformation from a single party dictatorship to an open, multiparty democracy. Like the post-Mao liberalization on the mainland, the process of political liberalization in Taiwan was spawned by a death—in this case the death of Chiang Kai-shek in 1975. Unlike on the mainland, however, the liberalization quickly evolved from the cultural arena into the political: Chiang Ching-kuo's reforms, which recognized political elements "outside the Party" (the "Party" referring to the Nationalists, aka KMT), or *dangwai*, and ended martial law; the reforms of Lee Teng-hui in the 1990s that led to Taiwan's first ever presidential election in 1996 and eventually to the election of the opposition Democratic Progressive Party (DPP) in 2000, the first time a party other than the KMT controlled the nation's political apparatus.

History and historical memory have been particularly sensitive topics in post–martial law Taiwan. During its single-party rule over Taiwan from 1947 to 1987, the Nationalist Party sought to control the representation of history in ways that are akin to those of the Chinese Communist Party (CCP) on the mainland. The KMT government suppressed local Taiwan history and upheld a Sinocentric view of the past, a cultural policy serving the political platform that Taiwan was part of China and that the Nationalists had an *in abstentia* dominion over the mainland. In the KMT cultural rhetoric, Taiwan was the bastion for the preservation of traditional Chinese culture, which was being destroyed on the mainland through successive political and cultural campaigns. In the process, Taiwan's "local" culture and history were ignored or radically downplayed, and the history of Taiwan was reduced to little more than a chronicle of its 300-year interaction with the mainland. Of course, the KMT also suppressed memory of more recent history, including that of the Japanese occupation and the "white terror" imposed on Taiwan from the late 1940s to the late 1970s.

The KMT propagated its historical and cultural vision in museums and memorial sites throughout Taiwan, particularly in Taipei. Exhibitions in the 1950s promoted an anti-communist agenda and the national fantasy of "restoring the country" (*fuguo*). Typical of museums and memorial sites in the Nationalist era were the National History Museum (Guoli lishi bowugan; 1955), the National Palace Museum (Guoli gugong bowuyuan; 1965), the Sun Yat-sen Memorial Hall (Guofu jinianguan; 1972), and the Chiang Kai-shek Memorial Hall (Zhongzheng jiniantang; 1980). These sites reflected the Nationalist political agenda and the its Sinocentric view of history, or they contributed to the propagation of cults surrounding KMT leaders and father figures.[145]

With the political liberalization of the 1980s, many intellectuals, writers, and political figures started questioning KMT narratives of the past and its monopoly on the meaning of that past. A literature movement of the late 1970s and 1980s drew attention to Taiwan's "nativist" (*xiangtu*) culture and society. The Taiwan consciousness movement of the early 1980s suggested there was a uniquely Taiwanese "subjectivity" (*zhutixing*) that was an accumulation of Taiwan's particular history of multiple occupations. Taiwan nationalists began calling for "de-sinicization" (*quhanhua*)—that is, the decoupling of Taiwan's history and identity from China—and for the promotion of Taiwan's unique history and culture.

As a product of and response to these trends, new museums and new kinds of museum exhibitions have since the 1990s gradually displayed facets of that unique history. These museums tend to focus on four aspects of Taiwan's past: (1) prehistory (that is, the history of Taiwan prior to written records and well before the arrival of ethnic Chinese to the island); (2) the history of Taiwan's interaction with non-Chinese cultures, in particular during the Dutch and Japanese colonial eras; (3) the trauma inflicted on Taiwan

---

145   For an interesting discussion of the "cult of Chiang Kai-shek," see Taylor 2006.

by the Nationalists during the Chiang era; and (4) Taiwan's aboriginal cultures. In what follows, I look briefly at examples of each category.

First, the most prominent museum in the "prehistory museum" category is the National Museum of Prehistory (Taiwan guoli shiqian bowuguan; opened 2002) in Taitung.[146] To appreciate the significance of this museum, one should recall that in the KMT era Taiwan's history was thought to begin only in the Ming dynasty—in other words, the history of Taiwan corresponded with the history of Han Chinese immigration from the mainland. By contrast, this museum and others like it draw attention to a much earlier history of Taiwan. In displaying the archaeological discoveries of Taiwan's pre-historical past, the museum forges an historical origins for Taiwan, an origins that is independent from that of the mainland. The museum suggests that the people of Taiwan today are connected to those who lived here millennia earlier and connected to the land that yielded the artifacts from these ancient civilizations. A museum placard in the introductory hall of the museum makes this idea of "roots" to the past explicit: "Facing the future, we treasure the past, for without history we have no roots, and without roots, we have no future."

Taiwan's long history of interaction with the world has been stressed in a variety of exhibitionary contexts. "Ilha Formosa: The Emergence of Taiwan on the World Scene in the Seventeenth Century," an exhibit held in 2003 at the National Palace Museum, marked a radical move for an institution that had always been associated with "Chinese" culture and the Sinocentric vision of the past.[147] The cover of the museum exhibition catalogue shows a map of Taiwan from the Dutch era with Taiwan "on its side" (the east at the top) and the mainland absent.

---

146 Unlike the Shihsanhang Museum (Shisanhang bowuguan), which focuses solely on the Shihsanhang culture, this museum is broad in its scope and, as its name suggests, is a "national" museum. The museum opened officially in 2002, though planning had begun as early as 1990. The museum is located in Taitung, on the southeastern coast of Taiwan, near an archaeological site of the prehistoric Peinan culture (Peinan wenhua). The site was first discovered by Japanese scholars in the early part of the occupation period, but was not fully excavated until the 1980s. The Peinan people are sometimes said to be the ancestors of the present-day Puyuma aboriginal group. Peinan is a late neolithic culture, whose origins are Austronesian. Archaeologists see it as a manifestation of a larger Austronesian cultural arc that extended from the south Pacific islands to Southeast Asia. One of the most remarkable features of this culture is the huge slate vertical slabs it used for memorials and coffins.

147 The exhibition catalogue's foreword, written by then museum director Du Zhengsheng, who later became the DPP's minister of education, puts it this way: "The National Palace Museum is home to one of the finest collections of Chinese art from archaic times to pre-modern days. While the holdings are Han Chinese in nature, not of any pertinence to Taiwan, the Museum as a national institution has as its unwavering goal of assuming a more active stance to introduce its audiences to the island's historical and cultural past. The staging of exhibitions such as this one, to be sure, is an effective approach; yet, it should reach beyond the mere installation and presentation of artifacts to arrive at the realm of cultural and historical interpretation" (Shi Shouqian 2003: 3).

Figure 1: Cover of the exhibition catalogue *Ilha Formosa: The Emergence of Taiwan on the World Scene in the Seventeenth Century* (Taipei: National Palace Museum, 2003)

The introduction to the catalogue puts Taiwan at the "center of the East Asian maritime traffic" and stresses the history of Taiwan's "emergence on the world scene." The exhibit expresses a global cultural attitude that is at the heart of Taiwan's new self-identity in the post–martial law era, an attitude that contrasts sharply and ironically with Taiwan's decreasing political position in the world. This does not mean that the museum is projecting a fantasy in which Taiwan is somehow a major player in global politics; rather, its stresses a cultural attitude that looks boldly to the world rather than timidly over its shoulder at the mainland.

In 2005, the National Museum of History, another bastion of the Sinocentric historical narrative, mounted its first permanent Taiwan-related exhibit titled "Oceanic Taiwan: A Dialogue between the People and the Island." Like

Figure 2: Map of Taiwan entitled "Looking at Taiwan from Another Angle." Source: http://www.taiwantt.org.tw/tw/index.php?option=com_content&task=view&id=5474&Itemid=5

the "Ilha Formosa" exhibit, this exhibit emphasizes Taiwan's history of contact with the world beyond its shores. This reorientation of Taiwan away from the mainland and toward the ocean and other parts of the world is embodied in the map above, entitled "Looking at Taiwan from a Different Angle." The mainland is still present, but Taiwan's relation to the islands of East Asia and Oceania is now forefronted. The cartographic disorientation is intended to get the viewer to radically rethink Taiwan's geopolitical position.

Other museums stress Taiwan's interaction with the world by depicting the Japanese colonial era—a period when the mainland influence in Taiwan was slight—as the birth of Taiwanese modernity. Somewhat predictably, in the February 28 Memorial Hall (Ererba jinianguan) in Taipei, the history of Japanese colonialism in Taiwan is presented more positively than that of the KMT period. This is a discursive strategy to make the KMT look bad, and this procolonial historiography, as both Jeremy Taylor (2005) and Yoshihisa Amae (2011) argue, is part of the process of "de-sinicizing" Taiwan's history and culture by emphasizing the Japanese social and cultural influence there. This positive representation of Japan's colonial control of Taiwan contrasts sharply with the horror and atrocity emphasized in mainland museums dedicated to the War of Resistance Against Japan (Denton 2014: 133–152).

The third category of historical representation consists of memorial sites exposing the wounds and trauma inflicted on Taiwanese during the Nationalist era and includes, most famously, the February 28 Memorial Hall in Taipei, which was ushered into being by DPP politician Chen Shuibian when he was mayor of Taipei.[148] But many other memorial sites have opened in the past decade or so that focus on human rights abuses—for example, the ChingMei Human Rights Culture Park (Jingmei renquan wenhua yuanqu), which is on the site of a former detention center for political prisoners in Taipei, and the Green Island Human Rights Culture Park (Lüdao renquan wenhua yuanqu), where leftists, Taiwan nationalists, and dissidents were incarcerated more long term. There is at present a preparatory committee, established by the Administrative Yuan, assigned to begin the process of joining these two sites into a single entity called the National Human Rights Museum (Guoli Taiwan renquan bowuguan). With the "national" designation, it will have a new political significance in defining Taiwan's support of human rights—a tactic that is at least partially motivated by a desire to contrast Taiwan's democratic identity with the mainland's repressive single-party regime, which abuses human and civil rights.[149]

The fourth and final category comprises museums and exhibitions that detail the history and cultures of Taiwan's aboriginal peoples. Taiwan has two major museums (Shung Ye Museum of Aborigines [Shunyi Taiwan yuanzhumin bowuguan] and the Ketagalan Cultural Center [Kaidagelan wenhuaguan]) and two theme parks [one near Sun-Moon Lake and the other outside of Gaoxiong] devoted to indigenous peoples. Since the 1980s, aboriginal cultures have been put on display in the service of de-sinification and the forging of a unique Taiwan cultural identity. Museums that focus on aboriginal peoples, as well as on the prehistoric origins of Taiwan, contribute to creating a "national imaginary" founded on a sense of rootedness in the physical landscape of Taiwan. Representation of aboriginal cultures contributes to the construction of new national identities for Taiwan as a multi-ethnic, multicultural nation.

Some of these museums go so far as to suggest that because of intermarriage between Han Chinese immigrants and Taiwan's indigenous peoples—in particular the coastal flatlander Pingpu people—a new ethnic group has emerged. A placard in the Ketagalan Culture Center exhibit is labeled: "Looking for the shadow of our Pingpu brothers," and the inscription reads: "What

---

148 Of course, *dangwai* and then DPP politicians, many of who had suffered various forms of KMT repression, sought to draw attention to the long history of KMT totalitarianism and violent political repression of Taiwan's people. During his tenure as mayor of Taipei (1994–98) and then president of the Republic (2000–08), Chen Shuibian embarked on a program of promoting museums and memorial sites that served his more radical form of Taiwan identity politics.

149 See: http://www.nhrm.gov.tw/nhrm/code/.

is the Pingpu ethnic group? Where are they? Who are they? ... The folk saying 'have a Tangshan father, but not a Tangshan mother' (*you Tangshan gong, wu Tangshan ma*) best reflects the indisputable fact that the Taiwan Pingpu ethnic group has nearly fused into a single blood lineage with the Han." The institute's website makes its political intentions rather explicit:

> The Ketagalan Institute embodies President Chen's vision of democracy becoming deep-rooted in Taiwan. The name 'Ketagalan' pays tribute to Taiwan's tribal ancestry and recognizes the country's ethnic heritage while highlighting the diversity of its modern culture—one whose character is interwoven with indigenous ancestry and historical remnants of Spanish, Dutch, Japanese, Chinese influence. Through its advocacy for democratic ideals, the Ketagalan Institute seeks to promote harmony in Taiwan and to integrate Taiwan's voice of democracy with the world.[150]

This discourse has all the elements of the vision the DPP has sought to display through the four types of museums I have been introducing: desinicization; historical rootedness in Taiwan; ethnic diversity and interaction with the world; and democratic pluralism. All four types of museums and memorial spaces have contributed to forging a Taiwanese identity that is different from the kind of essentialized notions of Chinese identity that dominated under the KMT.

Even as the DPP and Taiwan nationalists appropriated exhibitionary spaces for their cultural and political causes, the KMT and those sympathetic to its cultural vision have not stood idly by. Indeed, in some cases, the KMT has sought to tame the excesses of Taiwanese cultural consciousness in some museums and memorial sites and to assert Taiwan's cultural ties to China and downplay the horrors of KMT rule in others. In short, the struggle over the past in Taiwan has become embroiled in the oppositional politics of Taiwan's multiparty system, and Taiwan's two main political parties have both actively used museums and memorial sites to promote their cultural agendas.

That museums and memorial sites are stages for tugs-of-war between the Nationalists and the DPP over historical memory and cultural identity is seen most dramatically in the example of the Chiang Kai-shek Memorial Hall.[151] The site was conceived as a paean to the Nationalist leader after his death in 1975. Since 1980, the grand Ming-style memorial has stood in the heart of Taipei as testimony to Nationalist rule and to their benevolent leader.

---

150 See http://www.ketagalan.org.tw/. According to a *Taipei Times* article, "The institute was Chen [Shuibian]'s brainchild and was founded to allow future leaders of the country from all backgrounds to have a forum in which to discuss issues in Taiwanese society, map out strategies for the nation's future, and consider how to promote Taiwan to the international community." See: http://www.taipeitimes.com/News/taiwan/archives/2004/03/30/2003108404.

151 For a detailed discussed of the memorial site and the recent controversy, see Chu-Jen Wu 2009.

Figure 3: Statue of Chiang Kai-shek in the Chiang Kai-shek Memorial Hall

In 2007, when the DPP was in power and Chen Shuibian was president, DPP politicians co-opted the space and converted it into the Taiwan Democracy Memorial Hall, which exhibited human rights abuses under the Nationalist regime, thus boldly challenging the hagiographic legacy of Chiang's rule embodied in the memorial itself. With the return to power of the KMT in 2008, the original name of the memorial hall was restored.[152] This is not just a squabble between two political parties; it marks a real contestation over how the Nationalist era should be remembered and how Taiwan should be defined. What is remarkable about Taiwan, compared to the mainland, is that such contestation takes place openly in the public sphere. The problem faced by the National Museum of Taiwan History was how to reconcile such competing visions of the past into a coherent narrative that would speak to all Taiwanese.

NATIONAL MUSEUM OF TAIWAN HISTORY

In the fall of 2011, not long after Beijing unveiled its new National Museum of China, the National Museum of Taiwan History celebrated its grand opening in Tainan, in southern Taiwan. The idea for the museum can be traced back

---

152   As Jeremy Taylor (2009) puts it, "For the first time since its arrival on Taiwan, the KMT is acting to protect the heritage of its own past—thanks, in large part, to DPP efforts to relegate the KMT to 'history.'"

Figure 4: The National Museum of Taiwan History, with a bank of solar panels to the right

to 1992, during the Lee Teng-hui presidency, after martial law had been lifted and the KMT's grip on power was loosening. However, it took more than seven years for a preparatory committee to be formed and almost twenty years for the museum to finally open to the public, suggesting serious problems in reaching consensus as to what kind of "story" to tell of Taiwan's history and of "constructing a shared historical memory of the Taiwan people," as the museum's mission statement puts it.[153]

Though conceived during the Lee Teng-hui era, which saw the rise of the Taiwanese consciousness and the identity politics movement, and formulated and built when the DPP was in power, the National Museum of Taiwan History opened after the KMT had regained control of the presidency and the legislature in 2008. In this sense, the museum reflects a mish-mash of politic interests and perspectives. To the objection of many who wanted the museum to attract the numerous visitors that only the capital Taipei could offer, the southern city of Tainan was chosen as the site because of its historical importance: Tainan had been the center of Taiwan politics and culture until Taipei displaced it in the latter part of the Qing dynasty, and this history was justification enough for supporters to build the museum there.[154]

---

153   See GLTWLSBWG 2011 for a general overview of the museum, its development, and its exhibits.
154   Tainan is also home to Anping Fort and Chikanlou, two sites associated with the Dutch colonization of Taiwan in the seventeenth century.

The museum is in a remote area well beyond the bustle of Tainan proper, in a district called Annan that had once been a center for trade and commerce. The museum building is environmentally friendly, and the first thing greeting the visitor is a massive wall of solar panels, in which appear the words—in English—"National Museum of Taiwan History." To the back of the building is a park, with wetlands that attract numerous species of birds. The grounds around the museum are referred to as the "Taiwan History Park," a term that stresses the interrelationship between the land and the social history of the people who lived/live on that land. This relationship between natural history and the "people's history" is an overarching framework for the museum site (GLTWLSBWG 2012: 4–5).

The grounds around the museum also boasts meeting rooms and an outdoor learning space for school children called the Happy Kaleidoscope, which includes a hopscotch game called the 24 Histories of Taiwan (Taiwan ershisi shi). The game allows the user to skip happily through the entire chronology of Taiwan history, each square highlighting a key moment in Taiwan's historical development. The museum is actively involved in a variety of outreach programs aimed at children and adults alike. The eco- and child-friendly quality of the museums lends it a welcoming atmosphere that seems self-consciously designed to make Taiwan history accessible and open, a stark contrast to the kind of intimidating monumental starchitecture that characterizes many state museums on the mainland. The inviting atmosphere of the museum and its grounds is consistent with some of the themes conveyed through the permanent exhibit itself, to which I now turn.

INCLUSIVENESS

The main exhibit in the museum is called Our Land, Our People: The Story of Taiwan (Situ simin: Taiwan de gushi).[155] The exhibit is divided into seven parts, organized in chronological order, beginning with ancient times and ending with the democratization of the post–martial law era.

One enters the exhibit by going up an escalator from the main floor lobby to the second floor. As you get off the escalator, and look up ahead, you see a huge video screen next to a sign that reads "Who Is Taiwanese?" The video screen is connected to a live camera that feeds images of people getting off the escalator—if you are alert, you will see yourself projected onto the screen. The large placard beneath the screen reads: "Thus the term 'Taiwanese' is a form of self affirmation impossible to define with a particular language or

---

155 An earlier name for the exhibit was "Taiwan Story: Confusion, Transformation, and Rejuvenation" (Taiwan de gushi: kunhuo, bianhua, yu chongsheng). I learned this from pdf outlines of early designs for the museum exhibit kindly shared with me by the museum director, Lü Lizheng.

ethnicity. All those who identify with and are concerned about Taiwan, who love and accept Taiwan, and who wish to live together in this land can declare with a loud voice 'I am a Taiwanese.'"

The entrance to the exhibit and the video display suggests that everyone whose image appears there (including, for example, a foreign visitor like myself) is Taiwanese, or potentially Taiwanese. From the outset, then, the exhibit raises the question of what it means to be Taiwanese and of who can lay claim to that identity. The openness and inclusiveness of the category of citizen presented in this museum is unlike anything I have ever seen on the mainland, where notions of "Chineseness" are more rigidly defined or simply a normative given. Whereas in some Taiwanese nationalist discourses in the 1980s the Hoklo were positioned as uniquely Taiwanese, this museum takes a post-identity politics view of Taiwanese identity that emphasizes not language or ethnicity but rather one's ties to the land and to the culture. The exhibit is still strongly "nationalist" in the sense of defining belonging not in purely ethnic terms but in terms of one's emotional and experiential attachment to the nation.

The museum's slogans are "Everyone's Museum" (*dajia de bowuguan*) and the "People's Museum" (*renmin de bowuguan*), which capture this sense of trying to make the museum speak to all Taiwanese, whatever their ethnicity, social class, age, or gender. The museum has a Facebook page that seeks to reach out to as broad (and as young) an audience as possible.[156] The museum promotes the notion that history is not some transcendent idea disconnected from real people, but intimately connected to their lives and identities. It seeks to de-politicize history—that is, from narrow agendas driven by political parties or ethnic identity movements—and recognizes that history can be viewed from multiple perspectives. As Chen Jingkuan (2011), one of the members of the museum's research team, puts it:

> Research on Taiwan history was, in its early phase, heavily influenced by politics. Recently, because of the opening up of political democracy, the study of history has become more and more pluralized (*duoyuan*), and the interpretations of Taiwan history have become more open, no longer limited by the historical view of the rulers. The research on Taiwan history has thus become richer and no longer in the service of politics.

When history is freed from political control, it can be seen from multiple perspectives and interpreted in multiple ways. In this sense, the museum exhibit itself is the product of the historical trajectory—from cultural diversity to democratic pluralism—it narrates.

---

156 http://www.facebook.com/NMTH100.

ETHNIC DIVERSITY AND IMMIGRATION

Like other museums and exhibitions in Taiwan, this one stresses the multiple cultural forces that shaped Taiwan. And these multiple cultural forces are part and parcel of the sense of openness and inclusiveness discussed in the previous section. Because it is an island that sits on important ocean trading routes, Taiwan has experienced multiple cultural influences from Austronesia (Polynesia), Southeast Asia, Japan, Western trading powers such as Spain and Holland, and of course mainland China.

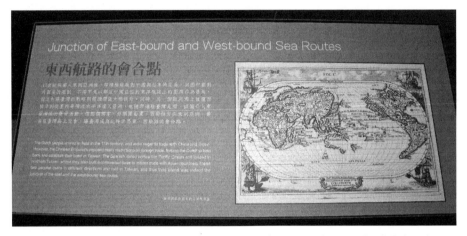

Figure 5: A placard in the exhibit emphasizing Taiwan's strategic location for global trade routes

Taiwan has also been politically occupied multiple times: (1) by the Dutch (1624–62); (2) the Ming loyalists under Zheng Chenggong (1662–83); (3) the Manchus (1683–1895); (4) the Japanese (1895–1945); and (5) the KMT (1945–2000) (with a strong American cultural influence due to Cold War ties between Taiwan and the US). With those occupations came waves of immigration and new cultural influences. In addition, of course, Taiwan has a diverse population of indigenous peoples, who make up, at present, around 2 percent of the total population of the island.

The museum's recurring leitmotif is "diversity" (*duoyuan*)—geographical diversity, ethnic diversity, and cultural diversity.[157] One placard on ethnic diversity reads:

---

157 A 2009 travelling exhibit prepared by the museum, even before the museum opened to the public, was called "Taiwan: A Multicultural Island" (Yujian Taiwan: yige duo wenhua de daoyu). The exhibit travelled to Germany.

Before Han Chinese crossed the sea and immigrated to Taiwan, indigene of the greater Austronesian linguistic group were already living there. Located at a major node in the maritime networks of East Asia, this treasure island attracted Chinese, Japanese, Dutch, and Spanish visitors to its shores, leading to various degrees of agitated encounters with indigenous cultures on the island, and leaving their traces there. Today, communities of Atayal, Seediq, Saisiyat, Bebalan, Amis, Taroko, Sakizay, Puyama, Tao, Bunun, Paiwan, Rukai, Tsou, Thao, Pingpu peoples, Hoklo, Hakka and mainlanders, as well as new immigrants from the Chinese mainland and Southeast Asia live together in this land, writing the new history of Taiwan together.

Displays through the exhibit emphasize in positive ways the cultural contribution of the Dutch, the Spanish (who controlled parts of northern Taiwan from 1626 to 1642), the Chinese, and the Japanese, as well as Taiwan's aboriginal tribes.

In emphasizing diversity, the museum reflects a post–identity politics recognition of the multiple ways of looking at Taiwan's past and a new emphasis on ethnic harmony and healing the wounds of ethnic discord, particularly that between mainlanders and Taiwanese. At the same time, its discourse of diversity clearly asserts Taiwan as a modern nation. Former museum director Wu Mi-cha, who was closely involved in the development of the museum and

Figure 6: A display depicting the various visitors and immigrants to Taiwan

its exhibits in its early phase, has acknowledged that the museum constructs a politicized story of the "nation," in particular through a "multicultural" embrace of the various ethnicities and cultures that make up Taiwan (Wu Mi-cha 2009; Vickers 2013). As on the mainland, ethnic and cultural diversity are made to serve an idea of national unity—that is, beneath the multicolored heterogeneity of Taiwan's cultural and ethnic make-up, there is a shared sense of national belonging. As a whole, the exhibit's narrative offers a neat telos of national formation: Taiwan's culturally diverse past leads inevitably to its "march toward democracy" in the present. The museum's emphasis on ethnic and cultural diversity is part of its positioning of Taiwan's national identity in opposition to an imagined identity for the Chinese mainland: if the mainland is homogenously Han and has a conservative continental culture and an autocratic state, Taiwan is ethnically diverse, interconnected with the world, and democratic.[158]

To be sure, the section on Chinese immigration constitutes the largest part of the exhibit, so in no way does the museum constitute a radical de-sinicizing mode of remembering the past—immigration from the mainland and Chinese culture are portrayed as key elements in Taiwan's national narrative. At the same time, the second longest and most detailed display in the exhibit is that on the Japanese colonial period, entitled "Transformations and the New Order" (Jubian yu xin zhixu). In this sense, the Japanese colonial era gets almost equal billing to the history of Chinese immigration.

With its displays on local police, mapping, land surveys, household surveys, and the like, "Tranformations and the New Order" does not skirt the issue of the Japanese military, political, and cultural control over Taiwan. But it also emphasizes, as the introductory placard puts it, the "allure" for Taiwanese of the modernity brought to Taiwan by the Japanese. The exhibit has displays on: the positive contributions of Japanese anthropology, which offered the first systematic ethnographic surveys of Taiwan's aboriginal groups; the building of the Sun-Moon Lake Power Plant, which when completed in 1934 "deeply influenced the development of industries and lives in Taiwan," as a placard puts it; the modernization of agricultural production and the refinement of sugar; and the formation of modern health and educational systems, the latter of which "opened a window to the world for members of the Taiwanese elite [who] absorbed elements of modern Western civilization while developing a specifically Taiwanese ideology."

---

158 It should be said that on the mainland, ethnic and cultural diversity are also made to serve an idea of national unity (see Denton 2014: 199–213). Although the appropriation of ethnic minorities for the construction of a multi-ethnic nation state is similar in the PRC and Taiwan, the Taiwan narrative seems to place these minorities in a more central position in the construction of national identity, reflecting a greater sense of inclusiveness.

In much Taiwan nationalist discourse, the colonial era has become the period that, ironically, gave birth to a Taiwan identity or a Taiwan consciousness (often referred to as "subjectivity," *zhutixing*). In this museum, for example, there is a large display on the Taiwan Cultural Association (Taiwan wenhua xiehui) and the journal it published, *Taiwan minbao*. The organization was principally cultural—it advocated for vernacularization of the Chinese language and for the "new literature" that was being promoted on the mainland—but it also had a political agenda and promoted "self-rule" for Taiwan. The Taiwanese consciousness promoted by the organization filtered down to the popular level as well, with the appearance of hit Taiwanese language songs such as "Our Taiwan," to which the exhibit devotes a display. The colonial era is also depicted as the beginning of Taiwan democracy, with a display on Japanese government-sanctioned elections in Taiwan.

Rather than a period of oppression, Japanese colonization is depicted as contributing significantly to the material, educational, cultural, and political modernity of Taiwan, as well as to the formation of a Taiwanese conscious-

Figure 7: A display shows Taiwanese going to vote in an election held during Japan's colonial rule

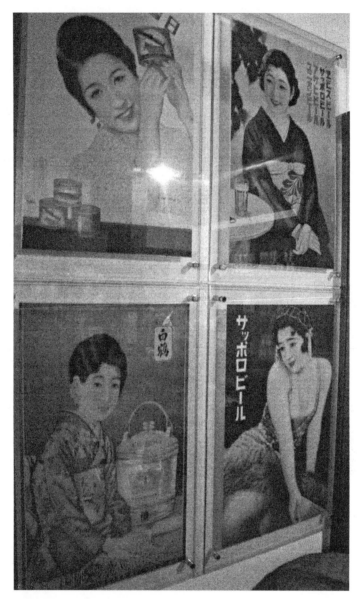

Figure 8: Japanese-language advertising posters of the colonial era

ness among the people. The displays in this part of the exhibit also suggest a nostalgia for this facet of Taiwan's past, as seen in near-life size dioramas of a Japanese-era phonograph store or in Japanese-language poster advertisements, as pictured above. This kind of representation is starkly at odds with the representation of the horrors of Japanese occupation in mainland Chinese museums (Denton 2014: 133–152).

DE-TRAUMATIZATION OF HISTORICAL TRAUMA

The picture of ethnic diversity presented in the museum belies a history of ethnic strife and violence. The indigenous peoples' encounter with a parade of outside occupiers was far from a happy one, involving at worst violent suppression campaigns and at best a range of "civilizing policies." The museum downplays this more negative side of the story. Ethnic tensions between mainlanders and Hoklos are also downplayed, and relations between Japanese and Taiwanese during the Japan period are generally portrayed in positive ways. All of this seems to be motivated by a post–identity politics desire for ethnic harmony; rather than drawing attention to ethnic conflicts, the museum seems to be interested in healing the wounds of the past and forging a notion of "unity" in diversity.

Just as the repression of the Japanese colonial era is whitewashed in the museum, so too is the violence of the KMT era downplayed. As mentioned earlier, in some other exhibitionary contexts, the 2–28 Incident is the defining historical event in the shaping of a Taiwanese identity and consciousness, something along the lines of Taiwan's holocaust. In the National Museum of Taiwan History, however, 2–28 and other facets of KMT white terror occupy

Figure 9: A KMT-era classroom

a relatively minor position: one small display, consisting of a single enlarged photograph and two small placards, one on the incident and the other on the repression that followed. The display simply states the facts, without lingering on the trauma or reflecting on the significance of the event to Taiwan national consciousness.

Rather than a time of political repression, the exhibit conveys a nostalgic feeling for the martial law era. One display (pictured above) is a recreation of a KMT-era classroom. Beneath a photo of Sun Yat-sen, a video screen projects images related to the promotion of Chinese (Guoyu, or the National Language) under the KMT. The display stresses the positive, unifying effects of promoting the national language. Although there is also a small display case devoted to "banned Taiwanese songs," the promotion of the national language and the Taiwan educational system in general do not come across as forms of hegemonic KMT brainwashing. Similarly, a placard about the military residential compound culture (*juancun wenhua*) is presented without any reference to military dictatorship or intellectual repression.

POLITICAL PLURALISM

The cultural and social pluralism that is the main narrative thread in the exhibit also serves to lay the discursive foundation for a narrative of the emergence of Taiwan as a democratic society in the 1980s and 1990s. The sixth chapter in the exhibit is called "Striding Toward a Diverse Democratic Society" (Maixiang duoyuan minzhu de shehui). It makes an explicit link between Taiwan as a multicultural society with a multicultural history and the emergence of democracy. One display, entitled "An Era in Which Everyone Can Have a Say" (Zhongsheng zhengyan de niandai), shows various groups protesting against such things as nuclear power and nuclear waste disposal; political oppression and white terror; and the limiting of academic freedom.

The exhibit is careful not to demonize the KMT for inhibiting the development of democracy in Taiwan. The focus of this part of the exhibit is less on the KMT as an authoritarian force that imposed martial law and sent dissidents to prison camps than on the gradual emergence of democratic forces, which the KMT was at least partly responsible for unleashing and fostering. The museum presents a rosy picture of democratic pluralism and the idea that people's voices matter.

Figure 10: The "An Era in Which Everyone Can Have a Say" display

CONCLUSION

The museum's mission statement lists one of its goals as to "construct common historical memories for the Taiwan people" (*jiangou Taiwanren gongtong de lishi jiyi*). Given the multiple political, social, and ethnic constituencies in Taiwan, it is no easy task to come up with "common historical memories," but it is clear that prioritizing memories that serve the interests of one constituency or that make another look bad are to be avoided in the name of creating a sense of common investment in the national narrative. A narrative of diversity leading to democratic pluralism serves this purpose nicely, as does a nostalgic mode of representation that downplays historical trauma, political repression, and ethnic conflict.

A special exhibit entitled Taiwan Memories: A Century of Life (Bainian shenghuo jiyi tezhan) appears immediately after the end of the permanent exhibit and nicely conveys the nostalgic tenor of the museum as a whole.[159] Al-

---

[159]   This special exhibit was present when I visited the museum in the fall of 2012.

though it presents artifacts of historical, political, and cultural significance to Taiwan, it also personalizes historical memory by displaying everyday objects related, for example, to the "sentimental days of campus life" or advertising and movie posters from the 1950s. In this museum, people's everyday lives are taken seriously as part of history, an approach to the past that is seldom seen in national museums in mainland China. Paralleling this sentimental nostalgia for a happy past, is the final display of the permanent exhibit, which includes a video entitled "A Letter to Taiwan" that shows a series of children reading letters they had written to Taiwan expressing their good wishes for the future of the island. The children are adorable and their hopes for Taiwan are endearing, but the view of the future presented here is as whitewashed as the museum's representation of the past. Visions for a bright future are built on images of a happy past.

The museum's permanent exhibit avoids the polemical and confrontational approach to historical memory that characterizes some of the museums and exhibitionary spaces developed during periods of more radical Taiwan nationalism. In the process, the past becomes a happier place to visit. The National Museum of Taiwan History marks an attempt to construct a past that is a reflection of ethnic and cultural good will, one that does not rile up ethnic differences so much as it seeks to harmonize them in a multicultural mosaic.

10 EMPOWERED MOTHERS IN AN ALIEN LAND: THREE CHINESE-CANADIAN WOMEN WRITERS

XUEQING XU

In this chapter, I compare representations of motherhood in fictional works by three Chinese-Canadian women writers, Edith Maud Eaton's (1865–1914) "The Wisdom of the New," written at the beginning of the last century, SKY Lee's *Disappearing Moon Café* (1990),[160] and Ling Zhang's *Aftershock* (Yu zhen; 2007).[161] Separated by more than a century in their time of publication and representing three distinct generations of Chinese-Canadian cultural life, all three works nonetheless share a common motif, a mother's love causing her child's death. In Edith Eaton's story, the mother kills her son; one of the daughters in SKY Lee's novel commits suicide; and in Ling Zhang's novella, the mother chooses to save her son at the cost of her daughter's life. To provide some transnational cultural context, I compare the treatments of these three mothers with those created by women writers in mainland China during the 1980s and 1990s, examining their different perspectives on and approaches to mother-child dynamics. The essay concludes with my discovery of a riveting pattern in the relationships between mothers and children in Chinese-Canadian works of fiction, one that challenges the traditional representations of motherhood generated by the patriarchal cultures within which these writers both operate and set their works.

For over one and a half centuries, traditional Chinese culture has been a primary guide for Chinese immigrants in Canada struggling to survive in an alien land. It is a culture that emphasizes the process of educating children through an ideology anchored in the Chinese way of mothering and motherwork, since mothers act "as cultural bearers and tradition keepers" (O'Reilly 2004a: 11). Situated in different historical and cultural settings,

---

160 *Disappearing Moon Café* was nominated for the Governor General's Award and the Ethel Wilson Fiction Prize. "SKY" is an acronym for Sharon Kwan Ying.

161 *Aftershock* was ranked among the top ten novellas of the year and was adapted into the movie *Aftershock* (Tangshan dadizhen; dir. Feng Xiaogang) in 2010. It has had the highest box-office in the history of the Chinese film industry.

these three works of fiction illustrate from different angles the complexity of Chinese motherhood and the cultural values that shape relationships between mother and children. As Andrea O'Reilly (2004a: 29) writes in her *Toni Morrison and Motherhood: A Politics of the Heart*, "Motherhood is a cultural construction that varies with time and place; there is not one essential or universal experience of motherhood." Motherhood in China, however, is governed overwhelmingly by patriarchal traditions. While necessarily sharing some cultural attributes associated with motherhood in other countries, Chinese motherhood stands out for its heavy stress on devotion to country and cultural heritage, so that motherly love is often transformed into an impersonal and collective passion.

Andrea O'Reilly summarizes Sara Ruddick's model of maternal practice this way: "Ruddick argues that motherwork is characterized by three demands: preservation, growth, and social acceptance" (2004a: 27). To preserve and protect a child's life is the first responsibility of a mother, while to raise a child with careful nurture is the second. The last but the most important demand practiced in many cultures is to educate her child to be socially acceptable. The Chinese motherwork portrayed in the three fictional works I discuss align with these demands. Pau Lin in Eaton's "The Wisdom of the New," Fong Mei in SKY Lee's *Disappearing Moon Café*, and Li Yuanni in Ling Zhang's *Aftershock* are all portrayed as typical loving mothers in their total devotion to raising and protecting their children, dutifully meeting societal expectations. They are rewarded with their children's love. Raising their children as if they were their servants, the mothers are nonetheless empowered by cultural practice whenever concerns with "social acceptance" become an issue: Pau Lin stops at nothing to prevent her son from being contaminated by Western culture; Fong Mei does everything she can to prevent her daughter from entering a "shameful" marriage; and Li Yuanni, forced to choose between her son and her daughter, prefers her son, for in the Chinese tradition only a son can carry on the family line.

The transformation from motherly love to impersonal collective passion can be a painful process, and sometimes a very cruel one, because in many cases the choice made under the pressure of social necessity goes against the mother's nature. In the conflict between personal feeling and "social acceptance," Chinese mothers were taught to submit to the latter, but that submission did not come without struggle. Pau Lin's mental collapse after killing her son in Eaton's "The Wisdom of the New" exemplifies the disturbing and destructive outcome of a mother exercising her power in order to maintain her son's cultural purity.

Edith Maud Eaton was born in England in 1865 to a Chinese mother and an English father. Eaton's father often traveled to China on business, where he fell in love with a Chinese woman, whom he married in Shanghai. At age seven Eaton and her parents immigrated to the United States, then in the early 1870s moved to Montreal. Eaton started her career working for the Montreal *Daily Star* at age eighteen. From then on she worked not only as a reporter but also as a creative writer under the pseudonym Sui Sin Far, which means "water lily" (*shuixian hua*) in Chinese. Her story "The Wisdom of the New" focuses on a one-year period during which the protagonist Wou Sankwei's wife Pau Lin brings their son with her from China to San Francisco to join her husband, only to experience one culture shock after another.

As hinted at by the title "The Wisdom of the New," the story presents the clash of cultures, the mother's resistance, and how the child is caught between Western modernity and Chinese tradition. When Pau Lin arrives, she finds her husband has changed into a different person, speaking a language she does not understand, dressing in a way her former fellow villagers could hardly imagine, and speaking to her about many things of which she cannot approve. She sees her husband becoming lively and talkative whenever they are visited by white ladies, but remaining very quiet when the two are left together. Worst of all is that her son is now undergoing a similar change, beginning to speak English and becoming fascinated by new things in the new country. Fearing her son's rapid acculturation to American "wisdom," Pau Lin decides to exercise her mothering as a site of power to stop its process.

Pau Lin's resistance against Western culture, nourished by her cultural training, is backed up by the fellow country women in her neighborhood, a community that conservatively cherishes the values of Confucian ideology. The balconies where Chinese wives meet and chat daily serve as a cultural front that informs Pau Lin of battles between Chinese and Western cultures. The negative comments that abound in her community targeting westernized Chinese girls and young men solidify her beliefs and teach her what kind of person her son ought to become. The news "that the good old mother of Chee Ping—he who was baptized a Christian at the last baptizing in the Mission around the corner—had her head secretly severed from her body by the steadfast people of the village" (Sui Sin Far 1995: 49) further confirms her determination to use all her power to maintain her son's genuine Chinese identity and to protect herself against the shame of having "lost face" (49). Close to the end of the story, terrified by the idea that her son will, like his father, become a westernized stranger, thereby betraying the Chinese beliefs of his ancestors, Pau Lin kills her joyfully forward-looking son with drugs the night before his first day of school, for the sake of saving him "from the Wisdom of the New" (60)—that is, America's culture.

A mother murdering her own child and thinking it in the child's best interests does, of course, happen both in life and in literature. "The Wisdom of the New" reminds us of *Beloved* (1987), the Pulitzer Prize–winning novel by Toni Morrison, in which the protagonist Sethe kills her daughter "out of desperate love, wanting to keep her safe from the horror of slavery" (Jeremiah 2004: 63). In this novel, Morrison shows her great concern "with how oppression distorts maternal love" (64), which as a result becomes destructive. Her character's murder "signifies rupture, disturbance, but Sethe's act is also one of resistance and love" (65). So, in both Edith Maud Eaton's "The Wisdom of the New" and Toni Morrison's *Beloved*, the act of murder represents the mother's attempt to protect her child, trying to "put [her] babies where they'd be safe" (Morrison 1987: 190). The difference between the two works is that Sethe does not want her daughter to suffer as a slave, while Pau Lin acts as an agent of a certain cultural ideology to protect her son and family against the stigma of a shame she has been culturally conditioned to feel.

The violent images of the murderous mothers in these two works are disturbing, clashing with the discursively dominant representations of idealized mothers. To understand how a mother could kill her children, one needs to examine the impulse within its cultural context. In her analysis of Toni Morrison's theory on motherwork, Andrea O'Reilly differentiates Morrison's maternal standpoint of mothering from the conventional one as "a site of power" and as a "profoundly a political act with social and public connections and consequences ... Morrison foregrounds the importance of preservation in her theory of mothering as empowerment" (30). Her view reflects the Chinese kind of motherwork that is ideologically and politically bound with sets of cultural values and assumptions. In cultural discourse, the Chinese mother is one of the most loving and devoted yet also one of the most brutally tough-minded mothers in the world. Whichever side she shows comes from her deep love for her children, and is for the sake of her children's wellbeing. Yet different from Morrison, whose empowered mothers aim to save their children from suffering, Chinese mothers wield power over their children only when their children are not meeting the expectations that they and society have designed for them. If the honor of a family or community collective is at stake in the conduct of a child, it is the mother's duty to carry out the verdict of the invisible "institution" (2010: 571).[162] The traditional story of Mencius' mother moving three times to save her son from the wicked influence of his neighborhood exemplifies the Chinese mother's role as a guarantor for her children becoming culturally acceptable.

Almost a century later, second generation Chinese immigrant SKY Lee in her 1990 novel *Disappearing Moon Café* portrays another Chinese mother whose exercise of power drives her beloved daughter to commit suicide. In its

---

162 According to Adrienne Rich, author of *Of Women Born*, "as an institution, motherhood has specific social, cultural, and political goals that work to benefit and perpetuate patriarchal society." See *Encyclopaedia of Motherhood*, ed. Andrea O'Reilly, Vol. 2 (Los Angeles: Sage Publications, 2010), 571.

gradual revelation of a Chinese immigrant family's secrets, the novel shows how a traditional male-centered culture can suppress and eventually destroy a mother's own nature. Significantly, however, it is the women in this novel who, having been brought up in China in accordance with traditional cultural values, do the suppressing in the name of preserving the family's and community's honor. The story, told by Kae, its chief narrator, is partly about her aunt Suzanne, who had been a girl of great beauty and her mother's favorite daughter. Fong Mei, the mother of Beatrice and Suzanne, transforms into a heartless and unyielding person after learning of Suzanne's pregnancy and her engagement to a younger man, a relationship she fears will stigmatize her whole family. Slapping her on the face and dragging her by the hair, Fong Mei shouts at her, "Have you no shame—no shame at all?" (202) and "I'll see you dead first. You will never marry him" (203). Her words, more than her beating, break Suzanne's heart.

Fong Mei's own life follows a typical pattern of victimization by a male-centered culture. Suppressed and bullied by her mother-in-law, Fong Mei gradually changes into an oppressor after she becomes a mother, succeeding her mother-in-law as the family's bearer of culture and keeper of tradition. Although Fong Mei does not kill her daughter as Pau Lin kills her son, the outcome is no different. Her actions in locking Suzanne up in an institution for Wayward Girls and taking away her baby serve a similar function, suffocating Suzanne's life. The tragedy of Suzanne's death bears all the bitterness that three generations of women in the family have suffered.

In the exercise of her power over her daughter, Fong Mei's conduct clashes with what Sara Ruddick in her *Maternal Thinking* regards as the "constitutive, invariant aim of maternal practice": "preserving the lives of children" (1989: 19). Instead, it exemplifies what Ruddick proposes as the third "demand" of motherwork: that it should shape "children's growth in 'acceptable' ways" (21), in accord, that is, with traditional social order. It is this last demand that determines whether or not a mother's practice meets community and cultural expectations and empowers her to correct her children's behavior, preventing them from acting in ethnically unacceptable ways. Her enforcement can be manipulative, abusive, and even destructive. Fong Mei is doing what she was taught and what is rooted in her mind, a tradition passed on by numerous generations.

Some critics have argued that the novel presents a stereotypical mother who appeals to Western readers' fantasies of Oriental mother images. Yet strong support for Lee's representation can be found in the biography of another Chinese-American writer, Amy Tan's "confession" in her *The Opposite of Fate: Memories of a Writing Life*, in which she recalls horrifying experiences of her youth, when her mother yelled at her, "I rather kill you! I rather see you die" (Tan 2002: 231). Worse is her memory of how her mother, with a meat cleaver in hand, pushed her "to the wall and brought the blade's edge within an inch of my throat. Her eyes were like a wild animal's, shiny, fixated on the kill" (213). The motive for this violent outburst is similar to Fong Mei's: Amy Tan was dating a man the mother believed would bring stigma to the family, since maternal practice in Chinese convention is overwhelmingly governed by cultural designs and sets of values.

The third work I discuss, the contemporary novella *Aftershock* by Chinese-Canadian writer Ling Zhang, traces back thirty years the suppressed traumatic memory of a freelance writer named Shirley that has caused her to suffer a major depression. Shirley is a survivor of the deadly Tangshan earthquake in China in 1976. The earthquake caused both herself and her seven-year-old twin brother to be buried under the weight of a heavy cement floor. Their rescuers faced the problem of which child to save, for the other would inevitably be crushed when the cement slab was lifted to save the one. The rescuers waited for the mother to make the grim choice. On the verge of death, Shirley heard her mother utter her brother's name to the rescue workers. Though it seemed like a mere murmur, Shirley felt as if she had been struck by a hammer. In the end, though, she did not die. She was awakened by the rain, miraculously rescued, and eventually adopted by another family. Yet Shirley defines herself as a victim of gender bias rather than as a survivor of a natural disaster. After being rescued and adopted, she never returns home to see her mother, who does not even know she has survived. In her unconscious, the sense of having been abandoned by her mother develops into a psychological complex, creating a deep wound in her mind that does not heal until the end of the story. Trapped in the past, her recurrent fragmented memory of the horrifying earthquake only connects with her mother's uttering of her twin brother's name, which results in her complete rejection of her mother. This traumatic experience increasingly plagues her while she is pursuing her Ph.D at the University of Toronto, developing a chronic headache into an insomnia that gradually turns into a deep depression, because of which she tries to commit suicide three times.

Shirley's paranoid schizophrenia in some way resembles that of the female narrator without name in *Surfacing* (1972), a novel by Margret Atwood. Though the two works of fiction narrate completely different stories in different social and historical settings, their female protagonists share a similar development of frustration, depression, mental disorder, and psychosis, which is the result of a cultural practice that devalues women. Both feel abandoned by their parent(s), and both internalize their feelings and become alienated from others, including the boyfriend in Atwood's novel and the husband in Shirley's case. The narrator of Atwood's novel rejects her lover's marriage proposal, and Shirley divorces her husband. Their attempt to retreat from society, Atwood's narrator by escaping to the wilderness of nature and Zhang's Shirley by committing suicide, signifies their desperate struggle with a male culture in which they feel powerless.

Unlike the two works discussed earlier in which a mother's prohibition causes her child's death, Ling Zhang tests the mother, forcing her to choose in an extreme circumstance between one of her twin children's lives and interrogating her valuation of gender. In traditional male-centered China, a son's wellbeing represented the axis of the family and a wife's position in the family largely depended on whether she gave birth to a son or not. "Giving birth to sons," as Adrienne Rich (1976: 193) puts it, "has been one means through which a woman could leave 'her' mark on the world." As the mother Li Yuanni observes to her younger brother with unconcealed pride, her father and mother-in-laws doted on their grandson as if he was a little deity. Although there have been significant advances in gender equality, this cultural heritage is still a strong presence in many parts of China. It is not without painful struggle that Li Yuanni finally chooses to save her son's life, a struggle between a mother's nurturing nature and patriarchally oriented motherhood.

For comparative purposes, let us now briefly look at how writers of contemporary fiction in mainland China have tended to depict mothers in their work. In general, with rare exceptions, mothers until twenty years ago were eulogized, portrayed as loving, devoted, altruistic, and even sacred, with emphasis on their submission and self-sacrifice. In these writings the mother's sufferings from patriarchal oppression are hidden completely in the praise showered on her deeds. The mother is presented as goddess-like, without personal feelings or frustrations, flawless and perfect. This was the case in works by both male and female writers. The only major exception I am aware of is Eileen Chang's novella "The Golden Cangue" (Jinsuo ji) of the 1940s, in which the female protagonist gradually falls into the trap of accepting her life in a "gold cangue,"[163] a symbolic term for the money, power, and agency of male-centered culture: she consequently transforms from a naïve and carefree girl into an evil mother.

In the late 1980s, there was a further development called forth by a search for women's independence, in that several leading women writers presented mother figures not only as mentally stronger but also spiritually superior to men. In their continual battle for greater independence in a male-dominated society, they idealized mothers who had been abandoned by their husbands. While praising the mothers for not relying on their husbands, these women writers also show them as being deprived of a normal life, forced as they are to raise children alone without any kind of support from the father, and as clearly victimized. Often, their children would die from an accident or disease, depriving them still further of the chance to experience a happy

---

163 A cangue is a device of punitive constraint used in ancient China.

motherhood. These fictional works set up all sorts of hardships for mothers to endure, while the fathers continue to enjoy life without any concern for their wives.[164] These works emphasized motherly virtues—patience, tolerance, and forgiveness—but not their rights as women. As Andrea O'Reilly and Marie Porter observe fittingly: "to be a good woman, one must be a mother and to be a good mother one cannot be a woman—that is, have a self outside of motherhood" (2005: 11). Inadvertently, such treatment confined mother figures to the traditional code of female conduct, idealizing them in such a way as to serve the rhetoric of a male-centered ideology, exactly as Adrienne Rich, American poet, essayist, and source of inspired research on mothering, points out in her famous book *Of Woman Born*: "Institutionalized motherhood demands of women maternal 'instinct' rather than intelligence, selflessness rather than self-realization, relation to others rather than the creation of self. Motherhood is 'sacred' so long as its offspring are 'legitimate'" (Rich 1976: 42).

But then after 1990 came a strong reaction. Several prominent Chinese women writers began to deconstruct idealized mother images and present mothers of malicious character who either spoil their sons or victimize their daughters.[165] Since then, the emphasis in the portrayal of mothers has been not so much on being victims of patriarchal culture as on their victimization of their children. In these works of fiction, daughters are without exception compelled to desert their mothers, running away for freedom and independence, while sons all end up disappointing. One critic laments this sudden change: "I feel pain in my heart when I am writing about 'the collapse of the mother myth'" (Sheng 1999: 102). Xu Kun, a woman writer and critic, goes so far as to state that contemporary Chinese women writers "have been marching together along the matricidal road" (Xu 2003: 90). Yet Danya Lin highly praises the shift in fiction by Chinese women writers from portrayals of goddesses to disgraceful mothers. She sees this transition as marking a rupture from the traditional design for mother characters: "The merciless rebellion against the traditional role model of mother in the Chinese women's literature of the 1990s ... has crushed cultural and historical norms that had standardized Chinese women images" (Lin 2003: 326). She regards this shift as a self-revolution by women writers, who split females' cultural and

---

164 The 1980s witnessed a surge of fiction by leading Chinese women writers that focused on women's motherly devotion to both their [ex]husbands and children, such as "Emerald" (Zumu lü; 1984) by Zhang Jie, "Oriental Females" (Dongfang nüxing; 1985) by Hang Ying, "Love in a Small Town" (Xiaocheng zhi lian; 1986) by Wang Anyi, and "Haystacks" (Maijie duo; 1986) by Tie Ning.

165 Representative works are Fang Fang's "Landscape" (Fengjing), Chi Li's "You are a River" (Ni shi yitiao he), Xu Kun's "Nü Wa," and Chen Ran's "No Way to Say Goodbye" (Wu chu gaobie). The mothers in these novellas bear similar characteristics of suffering from the male-defined tradition of motherhood, resulting in ambivalent emotional conflicts and psychological instability. They vary only in the degree to which they change from victimhood when they themselves become the victimizers of their daughters.

biological attributes into a binary of mother and daughter. The former ex-emplifies one side of woman that embodies the tradition; the latter, the new generation, represent the other side of woman who fights for gender equality.

Yet, in my view, these women writers, while portraying mothers' rejection of victimhood and their rebellion against the mainstream rhetoric of motherhood, became confused in their search for a type of woman that stands outside of "the oppressive patriarchal institution of motherhood" (O'Reilly 2004b: 160). As a result, the mothers they present ironically become cold and cruel executives of male-centered agencies, now less victims than victimizers. While uprooting the idealized mother image, these writers condemned the mother figure for her submission to patriarchal ideology, thus failing to create a new image worthy of replacing the old one. Their writings reflect the fact that China still remains a male-dominated kingdom, in which truly independent yet happy mothers are rare and in which feminist movements have never actually taken place and feminism is regarded as a derogatory term.

It is then, I think, of great interest that the three works of fiction I have been discussing here display in their deep structure a new path that has been missing in China's own fiction during the 1980s and the 1990s. Edith Maud Eaton's "The Wisdom of the New" ends with Wou Sankwei taking his wife to China for treatment—her killing of her son is regarded as an illness that needs treatment. In other words, killing is not her nature, and she herself is a victim of a certain ideology, of "'the violence of the institution of mother-hood,' whose love for her children was warped by despair" (Jeremiah 2004: 61), imprisoned by her cultural conditioning. Among the three mothers, Pau Lin appears the most loving and devoted one. Her tranquil singing and smiling beside her son's body tragically contrast with the violence she has just committed. The irreconcilable clash between a mother's nature and her cultural imprints brings about her collapse. Pau Lin's mental breakdown testifies to her victimization.

The narrator Kae in SKY Lee's *Disappearing Moon Café* realizes that she gets "sucked into criticizing" her grandmother and great-grandmother, who "were ungrounded women, living with displaced chinamen, and everyone trapped by circumstances" (Lee 1990: 145). While describing how Suzanne's mother changed from a victim of male-centered culture to a victimizer of her own daughters, Lee also presents another type of mother—Suzanne's sister Beatrice, the narrator Kae's own mother. Like her sister Suzanne, Beatrice was also oppressed and her marriage interfered with by their mother. Yet, she becomes stronger in her fight against her mother to assert her rights, and grows in understanding and tolerance in the upbringing of her own daughter. Though not idealized, Kae's mother's conflicts with Kae always end in reconciliation. Meanwhile, Kae constantly brings new ideas to her family, defiantly challenging conventional norms. The whole process of investigating secrets of the family history leads to Kae's discovery of her own identity. In order to become a truly independent woman, Kae finally decides to live with her girlfriend and raise her baby in an environment that is free of patriarchal culture, an action that shows her feminist manifestation as an individual, not "one of a series of individuals—someone of whom come before her, some after her" (189).

Focusing on Shirley's reflection of her mother's favouritism for son over daughter, which has tortured her psychologically throughout her life, Ling Zhang's *Aftershock* depicts her gradual understanding of her mother's perspective through the ordeal. Shirley's mysterious headache is symptomatic of her mental state after having been abandoned. Her own mothering experience and the tension in her relationship with her daughter Suzie cause her to carefully scrutinize the nature of motherhood. When her daughter runs away from home, rebelling against her strict rules and prohibitions, Shirley begins to realize that she has been transmitting her own rage toward her mother to her own daughter. The rules and prohibitions Shirley set for her daughter are what Elizabeth deBold calls the "wall": "The wall is our patriarchal culture that values women less than men … . To get through the wall girls have to give up parts of themselves to be safe and accepted within society" (12). When Shirley punishes Suzie for not diligently playing piano, Suzie responds by just crying; when Shirley does not allow her to attend a sleepover, Suzie plays rock music as a protest; and when Shirley secretively peruses Suzie's online chatter, spying into her privacy to discover whether she is dating, she revolts. Shirley's failure to apply conventional norms when raising her daughter reflects her inheritance of the "wall" she has struggled against in her psychic relationship with her own mother. In Shirley, this "wall" is allegorically presented in numerous dreams of windows, which she tries to push open one after another, but always failing to succeed with the last one.

Advised by her psychiatrist, Shirley determines to clear out the "rust" covering the last "window" (Zhang 2007: 43), thereby seeking to go beyond the confines of her mind. The "window," symbolizing the "institutional" norm of motherhood shaped by society, had been further fostered by Shirley herself. It remains closed as long as she is not willing to confront it. She does so when, after four months of psychological treatment, Shirley finally decides to go to China to meet her mother for the first time since the dreadful earthquake. Refusing to be a victim of the tightly closed "window," she then is able to go on with her life beyond "institutionalized, sacrificial, 'mother-love'" (Rich 1976: 246) and becomes a daughter who recognizes the social construct of motherhood and is ready to work with her mother to break the "wall" and push open the "window" that has separated them for so many years; as a consequence, she will become a mother who will help her daughter grow into an independent, free, and self-sufficient woman. Her feeling for her mother revives as soon as she sees her in their hometown, and for the first time in thirty years tears come to her eyes. The narrator in Atwood's *Surfacing* similarly ends the novel by refusing "to be a victim" (Atwood 1972: 222) and fighting her way back from the wilderness of self-exile to society; her "search for the father leads to reunion with the mother," as Rich puts it (Rich 242). Switching from interrogation of the mother to introspection of the daughter, Ling Zhang challenges the rightness of such interrogation, examining the daughter's position in the relationship between a mother and her children.

Contrary to most works by Chinese women writers, the mothers in these three works are neither idealized nor demonized. While portraying the oppressive side of mothering, the three writers delve into the role patriarchal ideology plays in that oppression, and reveal how the daughter and thus the reader judge the mother. Instead of applying male-centered ideology for such a judgment, daughters stand side by side with their mother in their fight for equality, identity, and women's rights.

11 SUSPENSION OF IDENTITIES: THE CASE OF HONG KONG

GILBERT C. F. FONG AND SHELBY KAR-YAN CHAN

PREAMBLE

> [S]omething unique has been emerging from Hong Kong's cities: it is Hong Kong Man. He is go-getting and highly competitive, tough for survival, quick-thinking and flexible. He wears western clothes, speaks English or expects his children to do so, drinks western alcohol, has sophisticated tastes in cars and household gadgetry, and expects life to provide a constant stream of excitement and new openings. But he is not British or western (merely westernized). At the same time he is not Chinese in the same way that the citizens of the People's Republic of China are Chinese. (Baker 1983: 469)

Ever since Hugh Baker's definition of the "Hong Kong man," there have been numerous attempts to study the people in the former British colony. History has bestowed on them ambiguity and flexibility, which have become almost a trademark. With the territory's 1997 "re-unification" with China, its statelessness and sense of superfluity should have been replaced by a sense of belonging to the mother country, yet a definitive Chinese citizenship, under the arrangement of "One Country, Two Systems" whereby Hong Kong maintains its capitalistic society within a socialist China, is still as evasive as ever. Some scholars have pointed out that "One Country, Two Systems" creates a barrier against total identification with China (Leung 1998: 193) by reinforcing the differences between Hong Kong and the mainland. Hong Kong identity, it appears, is still in a state of flux. That is why it has been a subject of intensive study and monitoring ever since 1985 when the Sino-British Agreement on the handover of Hong Kong was signed.

SURVEYS

Ethnic or national identity, often conditioned and regulated by birth or law, has not been in doubt since 1997. Even though many Hong Kong Chinese hold foreign passports, they are still considered Chinese by the People's Republic government because of their Chinese blood. What the polls survey is cultural identity and identification with conceptualities created less by geopolitics than by affiliation, a kind of emotional narrative people create of themselves.

Thus not only do the percentages fluctuate, the "strength of identification" also varies from time to time according to contemporary socio-political conditions. Stuart Hall argues that there are two ways of thinking about cultural identity. The first defines it "in terms of one shared culture, a sort of collective 'one true self,' hiding inside the many other more superficial or artificially imposed 'selves,' which people with a shared history and ancestry hold in common" (Hall 2003a: 8). Here we may apply the concepts of Chinese traditional culture, history, and geographical features, which have through the ages been given authenticity through literature, art, myths, and other narratives. This kind of Chineseness, dubbed "cultural China," is non-controversial and readily acceptable by most, despite the fact that it is indisputably a social construct. The constructedness brings us to the second point mentioned by Stuart Hall—cultural identity is "not an essence but a *positioning*." It is "a matter of 'becoming' as well as of 'being'. It belongs to the future as much as to the past" (Hall 2003a: 10–11). This reminds us of Wei-ming Tu's cultural China project, which is an attempt to wrestle the power to define Chineseness from a geopolitical authoritarian China to the periphery, the diasporic communities abroad (Tu 1994). And some zealous and more radical scholars even advocate dispensing with China altogether and making the periphery as the center (Ang 1998: 2; Chow 1997). What is apparent is that identification can be changed, made into a "project," and that authenticities can be rendered unstable. The center, obviously, cannot hold. When changeability is established, identification and what it entails become interrogatable.

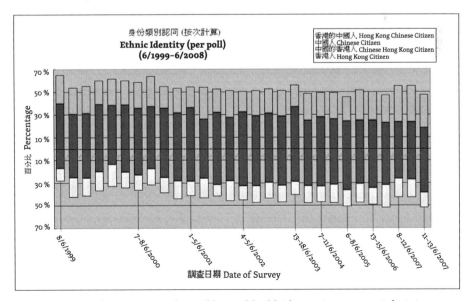

Figure 1: Ethnic Identity. Source: http://hkupop.hku.hk/chinese/popexpress/ethnic/

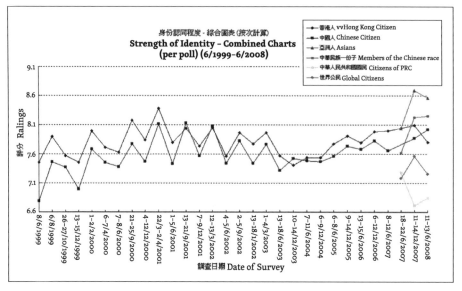

Figure 2: Strenght of Identity. Source: http://hkupop.hku.hk/chinese/popexpress/ethnic/

None of the surveys above makes a distinction between identification with a geopolitical China and a cultural China. One would assume that there is a bit of both in the categories. Writing in 2001, pollsters Wong Kar-ying and Wan Po-shan observed that:

1. There is no apparent difficulty for Hong Kong people in choosing between being a Chinese or a Hongkonger.
2. The percentages of respondents identifying themselves as Chinese or Hong Kongese have been relatively stable. This is also the case after the 1997 handover.
3. Throughout the years, the percentages of respondents identifying themselves as Hongkongers exceed those identifying themselves as Chinese by 20 % or more. (Wong/Wan 2001: 434)

Recent figures, though, tell another story. With increasing Chinese presence and acceptance of Chinese rule, the trend has been for the Hong Kong people to identify themselves more as Chinese. Current events may also sway the populace, evoking their nationalist fervor and gravitating them toward awareness of their Chinese identity. For example, the disastrous earthquake in Sichuan Province in May 2008 and expectations about the Beijing Olympics led to significant increases in the number of respondents identifying themselves as Chinese. According to a survey done by the Public Opinion Program of the University of Hong Kong in June 2008, one month after the

Sichuan earthquake and less than two months before the Beijing Olympics, the percentage of Chinese identification surged to 38.6 %, a 40 % increase over six months earlier (at 27.2 %) and more than double the percentage in August 1997 (at 18.6 %). At the same time, Hong Kong identification dropped from 23.5 % to 18.1 %, nearly half of what it was in August 1997 (at 34.9 %). A reasonable guess would be that nationalistic feelings skyrocketed with the successes of Chinese athletes at the Beijing Olympics in August 2008.

Another interesting feature in the polls is the creation of the new categories of "Hong Kong Chinese" and "Chinese Hong Kong." This reflects a new development that further demonstrates the growing complexity of the identity question and the inadequacy of exclusive categorization. Whereas "Chinese Hong Kong" emphasizes Chineseness over the local, "Hong Kong Chinese" underlines Hong Kong and at the same time downplays Chinese citizenship. The figures of these two new categories roughly parallel those of "Hong Kong" and "Chinese," revealing a trend toward recognizing China as the mother country. And starting in June 2007, four new categories have been added to the survey. Interestingly, the highest in terms of "strength of identity" is "Asians," followed by "Members of the Chinese race," "Chinese," "Hongkonger," "Global citizens," and "Citizens of the PRC" in descending order of percentages. These data indicate the emergence of multiple Hong Kong identities, a complexity that is tangible and measurable in numbers. The trend appears to be that the more generic the category, the easier it is for people to identify with it. One exception is "Global citizens," which might have been considered too vague and far-fetched. Importantly, identification with the People's Republic of China is the lowest among all the categories.

Given the government's drive to promote patriotism and the rapid growth of the Chinese economy, it may very well happen in the future that Hong Kong identity will be absorbed into the great tide of Chinese nationalism as interpreted by a hegemonic central government. And the Hong Kong-ness may decline into a regional variety like Shanghai-ness or Nanjing-ness, defined by and allowable within the confines of state ideology, but perhaps still defiantly independent. The "two systems" policy will certainly prevent Hong Kong from being totally absorbed into "one country" in the next few decades.

NATIONALIZATION

There are historical reasons for Hong Kong's unstable identity. Ever since its concession to Great Britain in 1841, Hong Kong has undergone three major periods of fluctuation and change in terms of its relationship with China and the world. It is our contention that the swing between nation and de-nationalization, the inward and outward pull of cultural and socio-political orientations in terms of the center, has resulted in the particular make-up of Hong Kong-ness today.

When the British first came to Hong Kong in 1841 after the Opium War, they were only looking for a deep-water port as a logistical base in their trade with China. There were no natural resources to exploit in the new colony, and the indigenous population (about 5,000) was too small to make it an attractive market for British goods. The colonial government adopted a two-tier system whereby the European and Chinese communities were governed separately, and the Chinese were left to their own devices in social and commercial affairs, with taxation and the military still in the hands of the British. The two communities were also physically segregated—the Chinese, no matter how wealthy they were, were forbidden to live on Victoria Peak. The Chinese and the British regarded the other with "supreme indifference," each holding onto the notion of their own superiority (Baker 1983: 469).

The border between Hong Kong and China was open and people and goods could move freely in and out of the colony. With economic expansion, more and more Chinese came to settle in Hong Kong, and ties with the mainland were strengthened with increasing trade and movement of goods. Hong Kong also became a haven for Chinese people fleeing wars and other disasters. In the 1850s, the anti-Manchu Taiping Rebellion drove many wealthy Chinese to Hong Kong, and later, the rebels themselves also sought refuge in Hong Kong after their defeat. Around the turn of the twentieth century, Dr. Sun Yat-sen and his revolutionaries gained a lot of financial support from overseas Chinese through Hong Kong, which was used as a base for revolutionary activities to overthrow the Manchus on the mainland. In fact, from that time on, Hong Kong became a breeding ground for Chinese political activities—for instance, the protest against the colonial government when it banned the use of Chinese coins, support for the May Fourth Movement and the boycott of Japanese goods in 1919, and the Seamen's Strike in 1922. The most devastating was the Canton-Hong Kong General Strike against British Imperialism in 1925 and 1926, which paralyzed the colony and threatened to destroy British trade and business in South China. Nationalistic fervor was at its zenith with the onset of the Anti-Japanese War. In 1937, the Japanese embarked on a large scale invasion of China, and as Chinese cities fell one after another, many Chinese, including businessmen and cultural workers, fled south to Hong Kong, transforming the colony into a teeming cultural center until it, too, fell into Japanese hands in December 1941. When the British regained Hong Kong in 1945, it became a battleground for a propaganda war and spy activities between the Communists and the Nationalists on the mainland, who would soon be involved in a protracted civil war.

From 1841 to 1949, Guangzhou (Canton City), Hong Kong, and Macau (a Portuguese colony) were the most important cities in the Pearl River

Delta in southern China. There was free-flowing traffic in population, trade, and cultural and political activities. To the general populace, they were all "Chinese" cities, though under different jurisdictions, and there was no ambiguity as to the identity of the residents and where their allegiance lay. Vis-à-vis the fervent patriotism in Hong Kong in the early twentieth century, it is interesting to note that fifty years later in 1998, one year after the handover to China, less than 20% of the population considered themselves Chinese.

DE-NATIONALIZATION

The period from 1949 to 1997, which witnessed a decline in nationalistic identification, has to be considered pivotal in molding the contemporary Hong Kong identity. In relation to China, the Self-Other dichotomy became focalized in trade and culture increasingly as Hong Kong grew more prosperous in lifestyle. Traffic between Hong Kong and the mainland was restricted when the border was closed in 1950 after the Communists took over China. The distance between the Hong Kong Chinese and the mainland was also widened by political happenings on the world stage. The Cold War between the Soviet block and the West and China's involvement in the Korean War cut off China from the rest of the world—by what was at the time known as the Bamboo Curtain—and Hong Kong as a British colony had to follow the foreign policy of Great Britain and take part in the embargo against China. Hong Kong was thus cut off from its roots; it was now confronted with a hostile Other. Reports coming out of China, embellished by the propaganda machine of the U.S. and other "free world" countries, of the killings of landlords during the land reform movement, the atrocities of the Anti-rightist campaign, the famine caused by the failure of the Great Leap Forward, all painted a picture of an erratic and inhuman evil empire ready to jump on the tiny colonial enclave with its massive People's Liberation Army. There were still some young people who went north to participate in the construction of a "New China," but the number dwindled as returnees brought back reports of disappointment and failures. Of course, those refugees fleeing the terror of communism were fiercely anti-communist.

With the onset of the Cultural Revolution (1966–1976), China abandoned its role as spokesman of a cultural China by radically repudiating all Chinese traditions. The irrational behavior of its leaders, the ruthlessness of the young Red Guards, and the destruction of cultural artifacts were all inconsistent with the image of a peaceful and contemplative Chinese scholar in the popular imagination. Most of all, reports of the cruel struggle meetings, the fighting among Red Guard factions, and the dead bodies floating into Hong

Kong waters from the nearby Pearl River all imbued the Hong Kong population with a feeling of terror.

For a time in the 1950s, in Hong Kong and abroad, the void of a cultural China, with its rich tradition of philosophy, literature, and the arts, was filled by Chinese intellectuals who had escaped from the mainland and who were once staunch communist fighters. They were helped, financially and ideologically, by the Nationalist government in exile in Taiwan, which called itself "Free China." But their activities were checked and monitored carefully by the Hong Kong government, which did not want to take sides in order not to offend China, but maintained in the colony a delicate balance between Communist and Nationalist politics. Traditional China, representing a "cultural China" antithetical to the People's Republic, is an important part of being a Hong Kong Chinese. It represented authenticity—"we are the real Chinese" who carry on the traditions and values of ancient China—and a reinforcement of the Self defined by a rejection of the Other China on the mainland.

The Self-Other chasm was further widened during and after the riots of 1966 and 1967. In early April 1966, a protest against the 10-cent fare increase by Star Ferry, at the time the major cross-harbor route between Hong Kong Island and the Kowloon peninsula, developed into protest marches and riots involving labor unionists. The leftists in the colony seized upon the opportunity to instigate the populace to challenge British occupation of Hong Kong, aiming to bring the colonial government to its knees and re-claim Hong Kong as Chinese territory. Waving the little red book of Chairman Mao's quotations in the style of the Cultural Revolution, they held demonstrations and strikes, planted homemade bombs and confronted the police. The final tally was fifty-one dead, 800 injured, and 5,000 arrested (Ma 1999: 27). In the beginning, participation in the protests was not limited to Communist supporters, but it quickly turned into an insurgence, and when the riots, with their violence and bombs, threatened the livelihood of the people, whatever sympathies the Communists supporters had generated before dissipated quickly. Many started to regard Hong Kong not as a refuge or stepping stone but rather as their home, in which they were to remain permanently. To some scholars, the 1966-1967 demonstrations constitute the conception of a distinctive Hong Kong identity, proof of the maturation of the locally-born generation during the postwar baby boom who for the first time found a voice to express their concerns (Tsang 2004: 183; Mathews/Ma/Lui 2008: 32).

The Cultural Revolution in China and the ripples it created alienated the Hong Kong people from China and widened the gulf between the two. The demonstrations in Hong Kong had the effect of galvanizing, if only temporarily, the people and the colonial government, which became aware of the urgency to respond to their needs. A fundamental change in governance could be seen in the narrowing of the gap between "we" and "they" in a series of reforms, the so-called "consultative democracy" or "government by consent" (Mathews/Ma/Lui 2008: 34); professionals and representatives were invited to participate in government affairs, replacing the old elite and corrupt bureaucrats (corruption was rampant until the Independent Commission Against Corruption was established in 1974).

A similar tendency toward less "colonial" governance could also be seen in the official policy on translation. For example, the official Chinese translation of the names of Hong Kong's governors became increasingly localized over the years. Not only did they follow local naming customs (using a surname followed by a name of one or two Chinese characters), auspicious Chinese characters were often used in the translations, for example, Tai Lun-chi 戴麟趾 (Trench), Mak Lei-ho 麥理浩 (MacLehose), You Tak 尤德 (Youde), Wei Yik-shun 衛奕信 (Wilson), and Pang Ting-hong 彭定康 (Patten). These names functioned like camouflage, as if to conceal the British origin of the colonial rules. The Hong Kong Chinese also give themselves English names, probably to appear less Chinese (Fong 1998). The last colonial governor, Chris Patten, went out of his way to make special efforts to localize himself: he refused to put on the colonial governor uniform at his inauguration, made frequent visits to local shops to mingle with the grassroots, and made himself a fan of the traditional herbal tea and Hong Kong-style egg tarts; he did almost everything to attempt be a native, except to speak Cantonese. His behavior could be described as an "almost but not the same" form of mimicry. Obviously, his efforts were intended to improve relations between the colonizer and the colonized—a relationship that itself was affected by global politics—so as to facilitate his rule. This transposition of roles, or mimicry by the colonizer instead of the colonized, demonstrates the ambiguity of colonial governance, which consequentially had an impact on the Self-Other division between the colonizer and the colonized.

Besides practicing "reverse mimicry," the government also adopted measures directed at the young postwar generation, such as building new community playgrounds and facilities and providing better education and other forms of social infrastructure. The reforms and changes in policy by no means constituted a democratic system in the making. The colonizer still held on to power, but it became more responsive and responsible. It was to an extent a government for the people, though not of the people or by the people. And as the economy began to grow, opportunities existed for most people to be upwardly mobile (legends of the from-rags-to-riches Hong Kong dream abounded), and they consequently were comfortable with the status quo of living in a British colony. All this created a feeling of belonging ("home in Hong Kong"), taking the place of the nostalgia for the Chinese homeland. What the British colonial government did in Hong Kong from the late 1960s onward was to an extent de-colonization. The process was not complete, because it was impossible for the British to abandon sovereignty over Hong Kong lest the Chinese would take over, nor was it possible to put in place a democratic style of government for the same reason that China would intervene if there were any hints of the colony evolving into an independent state.

During the Sino-British talks from 1982 to 1984, the Hong Kong people were not represented, perhaps deliberately excluded from the proceedings; only the two "masters" were present. The feeling of being abandoned soon transmuted into a strong awareness of the Self, which "othered" both China and Britain, reinforcing the burgeoning Hong Kong identity that was already being manifested emphatically in popular culture. For a while, local history was the vogue: people tried to dig deep for their roots in the pre-colonial days of fishing and farming and the evolution of Hong Kong into a mega city. But these nativist days were short-lived, soon giving way to the market reality of doing business with China and the economic necessity of aligning with the Chinese nation.

RE-NATIONALIZATION

Significantly Hong Kong did not partake in any mainland-based political movements after the 1967 riots, a signal that the Hong Kong people were content to be mere observers of Chinese political upheavals, such as the fall of the Gang of Four in 1976. The disinterest lasted until June 1989 when Chinese students occupied Tiananmen Square in Beijing demanding democracy and government reform. In support of the democracy movement, more than one million people marched on the streets of Hong Kong, only to have their hopes for a new style of government in China shattered when the PLA troops violently drove students and other demonstrators out of the square. There were reasons for the show of fervent passion in Hong Kong: sympathy for the students' demand for democracy and good government and fear for their own fate under an authoritarian government after the handover. The crackdown on the students sparked another wave of emigration to foreign countries; even the British government, in order to stamp out the brain drain, had to offer British passports with rights of abode in Britain to some 50,000 families.

However, Chineseness was (and is) still very important to the Hong Kong people. When a tremendous flood hit East China in 1991, they donated huge amounts of money to help the victims. The slogan for the donation campaign was "Blood is thicker than water." And as the 1997 handover became imminent, popular culture, always market-oriented, paid homage to the discourse of the state. Instead of criticizing or lampooning the backwardness of mainland China, television programs and movies began to paint a more positive picture of the future master (Ma 1999; Chu 2003). Popular music, with titles such as "Be a Brave Chinese," "Descendants of the Dragon," etc., lauded the virtues of the Chinese race and co-sanguinity.

Has this race consciousness made it easier for Hong Kong in its transition from a colony to a Special Administrative Region of China? The answer is yes and no. Yes in the sense that Hong Kong people are also Chinese, and with the handover a national shame of 150 years ago was rectified. At the same time, the Communist state, with its espousal of Marxist-Leninism and its many cultural icons, such as the five-star red flag and the People's Liberation Army (with its less than glamorous image after the Tiananman Incident), are considered un-Chinese and even uncivilized (Mathews/Ma/Lui 2008: 104). There have been visible signs of change: the growing use of Chinese and Putonghua in everyday and government affairs, the push to make English language schools teach in Chinese, the broadcast of the national anthem before prime-time news every evening, etc. All these appear to many as nationalistic hard sell. The incompetence of the Tung Chee-hwa administration (he was the first Chief Executive of the Hong Kong Special Administrative Region "elected" with Chinese support), which led to an economic downturn, and the SARS epidemic in 2003, also did not endear China to Hong Kong. The heavy-handed Chinese People's Congress's interpretations of Hong Kong's Basic Law (the Hong Kong constitution) and the proposal to enact Article 23, the subversion law which would have criminalized many political activities, created the impression that Hong Kong would be overwhelmed by Chinese presence and interests, further aggravating the latent doubts and antagonism of the "we-against-they" variety. This was despite the fact that the government was vigorously promoting nationalism, and the media, which were mostly owned by tycoons with huge business interests in the mainland, turned around and depicted China, mainlanders, and things Chinese in a more positive light than before (Mathews/Ma/Lui 2008: 95–107).

In the first decade after the handover, jingoistic propaganda appear to have created a change in people's attitude. With the surge of China as a world economic power and the success of the 2008 Beijing Olympics, more and more Hong Kong people are identifying themselves as Chinese (see survey above). Even though one may still argue that the former is due to the prospects of economic gain and the latter to the feeling of pride for the Chinese athletes as individuals, it may well happen that Hong Kong-ness will eventually become a regional sub-category of Chinese citizenship, totally subsumed within the great tide of a geopolitical China out of emotional necessity, self-interest, and economic contingency.

OF IDENTITY AND IDENTITIES

TRANSIENCE

There are a few observations we can make about the rollercoaster process that shaped Hong Kong's identity. First, a feeling of transience has evolved. A catch phrase for both the government and the people has been "going forward with the times" (*yushi bingjin*). An adage rendered almost meaningless by its tautology, it nonetheless underlines the desire for change, especially in the social, economic, and political spheres. This was a legacy of Hong Kong being regarded as a stopover for mainlanders doing business or taking refuge in the colony. Former governor Alexander Grantham (1947–1958) wrote about the situation before the War:

> The majority of Chinese in the Colony ... had little loyalty to Hong Kong. Like the Europeans, they came to Hong Kong to work until they retired home to China, just as the Europeans returned home to Europe. Not inaptly Hong Kong has been likened to a railway station, and its inhabitants to the passengers who pass in and out of the gate. (Grantham 1965: 112; in M. K. Lee 1998: 159)

Writing in 1965, Grantham also believed, with prescience, that the "railway station" situation would change and that a Hong Kong consciousness would develop among the populace. "The picture is changing since China went communist, as few Chinese in Hong Kong now intend to return to the country of their birth. They are becoming permanent citizens" (Grantham 1965: 112; in M. K. Lee 1998: 159). The heyday of British colonial rule was in the late 1960s and 1970s, when the economy surged and a local popular culture began to assert itself in songs and movies, which also became the rage in overseas Chinese communities and many parts of Asia. Pride and confidence led to a sense of belonging and the idea of "Home in Hong Kong." However, this feeling of permanence was short-lived, lasting only until the Sino-British talks on the future of Hong Kong started in earnest in 1982, and the urge to move re-emerged.

Thus with the news of Hong Kong's imminent handover to China in 1997, many people chose to emigrate. With their newly acquired money and skills, they swamped foreign consulate offices for visas to foreign countries, especially English-speaking countries like the U.S., Canada, Australia, and New Zealand. The annual number of emigrants rose from around 20,000 in the early 1980s to 60,000 in 1992, almost one percent of the population. (Skeldon 1995: 57; in Mathews/Ma/Lui 2008: 44). Stories abounded of Hong Kong people's penchant for collecting foreign passports. A rough estimate would be that about 300,000 to 350,000 people in Hong Kong, or 5 to 6 % of the population, hold foreign passports.

MARKET MENTALITY

The British rule in Hong Kong did not, for obvious reasons, encourage identification with any state. It did not want to see a repeat of the 1967 riots or any association with Chinese politics, nor did it advocate Britain as the mother country, lest the Hong Kong people might swamp Britain with their demand for right of abode (which was taken away from locally born Chinese in 1962). A market mentality soon emerged to dominate Hong Kong society in the absence of state ideology. Under the circumstances, it was natural that "the discourse of the state was the market" (Mathews/Ma/Lui 2008: 17). Economic success, which had been phenomenal for Hong Kong, could only lend legitimacy and strengthen British rule. This "put your allegiance where the money is" philosophy had the effect of defining the Hong Kong character, in addition to the awareness of transience of place and loyalty.

Those with money and the means tend, with only slight exaggeration, to choose their nationality in the same manner that they choose merchandise in a store; it is a matter of choice, convenience, and utility rather than loyalty. As Mathews says, "Hong Kong identity itself may be defined, in part, as loyalty to the global market over any state" (Mathews/Ma/Lui 2008: 15). As a commercial city, the rules and demands of the market are familiar to the Hong Kong people. The uniqueness of this market mentality is that it is allowed to rule people's personal lives, business, and even matters of the state. Profit is the focus of all decisions, from investment to personal relations and being the first in line for everything, and loyalty to a nation or a place is less a moral than a strategic decision to maximize returns.

SELF VS. OTHER

In our discussions of the negotiations with the Other—the nationalization and internationalization process—it is apparent that there is a readiness among the Hong Kong people to abandon their Self, just as many of them have been willing to abandon their residency, to acculturate themselves, and engage the Other "on their own terms." (We return to this point later.) At the same time, there is a side of the Hong Kong character that is self-bound, sometimes almost to the point of xenophobia. During British colonial rule, foreigners were referred to as "foreign devils" (*kwei-lo*, a term which has been used so often and commonly that it has lost its derogatory overtone and become a generic term), and there are still reports of racial discrimination against people of colored skin, such as South Asians, Filipinos, and blacks. And the Hong Kong people often use the label "Hongkonger" to distinguish themselves from the Mainland Chinese, who are considered backward country bumpkins. The Self-Other split has not developed into any racial conflict in society, and certainly has not prevented Hong Kong from engaging other cultures. Conversely, it has strengthened the Self, which serves as the foundation for all dealings with the Other.

There are three presences in the making of Hong Kong identity: China, Hong Kong, and Britain/Foreign. Hong Kong is the space, the territory where the process is acted out, and it has been through the particular geography of place, i.e., a deep-sea harbor, and development stages from a fishing village, to an entrepôt, and finally a world financial service center (DeGolyer 2007: 23-25). But it is also a place where power is allowed to play out to the tunes of transience, hegemony, and one-upmanship.

We mentioned the dominance of the Self-Other negotiation in the Hong Kong identity project. In fact, self-consciousness was also largely a result of geopolitical events such as the Communists' takeover of China, the border closing in 1950, the Korean War, and the Vietnam War. While these developments led to a temporary cutoff with mother China, which of course proved to be more prolonged than expected, colonial rule was also instrumental in promoting a Self-Other division, or a moving away from the historical Self. One of the most insidious aspects of colonial rule is burying the Self and transforming it into the Other through adoption of the colonist's gaze of contempt and condescension. The Self becomes silenced and loses its power to speak, and empowerment has to be re-acquired, perhaps at times of decolonialization. Stuart Hall calls this "the inner expropriation of cultural identity" that "cripples and deforms" (Hall 2003a: 11). And to Fanon, it produces "individuals without an anchor, without horizon, colorless, stateless, rootless—a race of angels" (Fanon 1963: 176). Stories abound of confused Hong Kong people trying to figure out what to put down as their citizenship when going through foreign customs, or trying to find an anthem to represent themselves and the colony. The famous writer Xi Xi once wrote a story titled "Floating City" in which Hong Kong is allegorized as a city floating in midair like a balloon, rootless and dangerously precarious (Xi 2008)

The "floating" metaphor of course carries with it the feelings of rootlessness and disorientation, but such a Self is also afforded freedom disconnected form history or even power. For a brief period in the late 1960s and 1970s, the Hong Kong people were allowed the freedom to build up economic and cultural capital, both personally and territory-wise. Spurred on by economic growth and the need for external trade, internationalization started to pick up speed, with American popular culture, such as Hollywood movies, popular music, and fast food, spearheading another round of imperialistic invasion. Displacement and appropriation were the order of the day and were internalized as being normal and automatic. The phenomenon of "yellow face, white mask" could be seen in speech, personal behavior, and commodities. Seen from an extremely nationalistic viewpoint such as that of Fanon, such happenings ought to be condemned, for they could be deemed betrayals of the authenticities of the Self. But we should not be too quick in our judgment of what has been happening in Hong Kong. Morality and history can be strange bedfellows.

As a site of ruptures, discontinuities, and displacements, Hong Kong has weathered its trials extremely well. All these have left their marks on the land and its people. So has internationalization, which has transformed not only Hong Kong into a "world city," but also its citizens into cosmopolitans. History makes indelible changes, and identity is not merely built on archeology but on the process of becoming. The myths, collective memories, and narratives represent the shared attributes making up a common origin, the authenticity, the "unity" underlying all the continuities and discontinuities, and the flowering and suppression. Distinctions have been made between the nation and the state: the nation is the abstract receptacle of the elements of history and oneness, whereas the state is the government with its everyday functions and manifestations (Mathews/Ma/ Lui 2008: 4-6). With Hong Kong's "return" to or "reunification" with the motherland, the appeal was to history—a rectification of past national shame, and to the more ancient sense of shared origins. Even though allowance was made to the capitalist fun and games of "dancing" and "horse racing"—acquired tastes under colonial rule—the state still insists on intervening with a strong show of legitimacy and power. "Stability and Prosperity" became buzzwords during the first few years after the handover, and the Chinese government prefered to view the change of sovereignty as a "quiet revolution" that nobody would notice. It was to be "business" as usual. And the history of the Hong Kong people and its representations were ignored, smoothed over in the celebration of the triumphant return to the motherland to the marches of the People's Liberation Army. Whereas during the last years of British rule the government and the people enjoyed a close relationship in community building, the Chinese takeover actually dramatized the Self-Other split between Hong Kong and China, and the feeling of the Hong Kong people being ruled by a master from the outside predominated—to them, the handover was a transition from one colonialism to another.

OTHERING OF THE SELF

From the 1950s to the 1970s, before the rise of Hong Kong and other Asian countries as economic powers, wealth, culture, and progress were to be found in the West. As an exporting economy, Hong Kong had to aspire to the style and thinking of the exporting countries in Europe and North America. Thus in their pursuit of wealth, the Hong Kong people also developed an outward-looking philosophy. During the same period, things Western, especially

American, were all the rage. American-style jukeboxes blaring hit songs by Elvis Presley, Pat Boone, and later the Beatles were found everywhere on the streets; Hollywood and foreign movies were considered high-end entertainment, beating out locally produced Mandarin and Cantonese movies in the fight for audience share; and American-subsidized "Greenback Culture" produced Chinese translations of American novels, plays, and poetry, etc. Coupled with the high status given to the English language in the government and in society in general, the West was considered superior and the object of imitation. Later when Japan became an economic powerhouse, Hong Kong was inundated with Japanese goods and departmental stores, and Japan became another sought-after model of style and fashion. Under the circumstances, China, at the time mired in endless political upheavals and considered an economic backwater, was the alienated Other, whereas the West and Japan were the admired Others, lending defining qualities to shaping the Hong Kong character and way of life.

The readiness to accept things foreign speaks volumes of the adaptability so vital to Hong Kong's survival and continued prosperity. Hong Kong has little by way of indigenous culture, and thus so-called cultural baggage does not generally get in the way. The absence of nationalistic discourse also preempts the problem of national pride. However, this is not to say that Hong Kong was a totally unmarked and neutral territory devoid of Chineseness. Even though Communist China may be categorized somewhat dubiously, when it comes to "the good of the Chinese race" (i.e., ethnic China), many Hong Kong people are still fervent and staunchly nationalist. This can be seen in the demonstrations and expeditions to the Diaoyu Islands condemning Japanese occupation—the claim of Chinese sovereignty was perceived as a serious matter of territorial integrity and the dignity of the Chinese race.

In many ways, Hong Kong society, before and after the handover, could be defined as a "diaspora" within one's nation—"a transnational group of emigrants living in a host country but maintaining economic, political, social and emotional ties with their homeland and with other diasporic communities of same origin" (Lim 2000). When it was a colony, the population was "transnational," in that the people were official British subjects and were living in the "host country" of Britain (i.e., a British colony). After China took over the colony, the people have become a "national group" living in their own country but considered different as residents of a Special Administrative Region ("One Country, Two Systems"). Throughout its history, Hong Kong has been a diaspora looking back at cultural China and negotiating with two "host countries"—China and Britain. More important, diasporic identities, "living with and through, not despite, difference ... are those which are constantly producing and reproducing themselves anew, through transformation and difference" (Hall 2003a: 21). The legacy of 150 years of colonial rule, with its memories, indifference, absences and presences, and constant new additions, bestows on Hong Kong an indelible cosmopolitanism, outward-looking and unafraid of change, and at the same time rendering its identity unstable and overdetermined.

Capitalism has a tendency toward de-sublimation. Standing before the gate of globalization, a person of any nationality has to be ready to stash cultural differences away in a box, forget about them and give up his own cultural traits temporarily in exchange for an admission ticket (Wang 2000: 96, 101). In Hong Kong's capitalist society today, everyone is a potential consumer, and identity is based on what one possesses or will possess, instead of who he or she is. Hence, there is no stability to this identity. The formation of identity is a ceaseless performative process, constantly becoming and dependent on how the narrative of the Self is rewritten over time. Differences in language and culture are manifested in impossibilities in cultural transfer and untranslatability in the translation process. From a strategic perspective, parts of the in-the-flux identity can be given up or appropriated to make up for the vacancy resulted from differences, thus facilitating the process of cultural transfer and reception. Simultaneously, the high malleability of the subject means that it can easily adapt to different situations.

Hong Kong has gone through the periods of nationalization, de-nationalization, and re-nationalization, as discussed earlier in this chapter. Internationalization, which came into being with the closing off of contacts with the mainland, first moved in to fill the void of nationalism; it later became an important counter-balancing force between the onset of Chinese politics and culture and Hong Kong's westernization. The Chinese government frequently accused the Hong Kong liberals of "bad-mouthing" Hong Kong in foreign countries and making local issues (which China considers internal affairs) matters of international diplomacy. One has to admit that without internationalization and the concerns of foreign countries for Hong Kong affairs, Hong Kong would just be another Chinese city like Shanghai or Beijing, and it would have lost its raison d'etre.

SUSPENSION OF IDENTITIES

In the othering process, authenticity becomes suspect, and origins, or the historical, are liable to be overwhelmed. Binary oppositions, such as "colonizer vs. colonized," "source text vs. target text," "foreign vs. local," etc. run the risk of becoming essentialized clichés that misrepresent the reality of multiplicity. The postmodern colonial space, consisting of different compositions and intermixing identity elements and processes, cannot be generalized by any mechanical dialogism. To Stuart Hall, cultural identity is undoubtedly a kind of hybrid, the result of the process of social transformation through which ideas, worldviews, and other forces interact with one another and are rewritten until they replace past conditions (Hall 1988: 5). Such hybridization is not based on sheer confrontation, but is a process of continuous negotiation, identification, and interaction. Homi Bhabha, by contrast, feels that hybridity cannot be likened to a melting pot, but rather to a mosaic painting, for identification mainly occurs in a place between displacement and reinvention, and its power resides in the separateness of its different constituent parts. At the same time, these "stubborn chunks" contain incommensurable elements that form the basis of cultural identification, and among these mutually resistant parts occurs the "Third Space," in which meaning and cultural signs have no primordial unity or fixity. As there is no absolute authenticity, cultural identity and meaning mainly exist in the in-betweenness so as to elude the politics of polarity and emerge as "the others of ourselves" (Bhabha 1994: 219; Bhabha 1995).

Rey Chow also points out the existence of a "Third Space" in Hong Kong's negotiation of identity, a site away from the two "aggressors": the colonizing culture and the dominant Chinese culture. She believes that Hong Kong possesses a unique in-betweenness and an awareness of its "impure origins" and "origins as impure"; its cultural productions are "often characterized by a particular kind of negotiation in which it must play two aggressors, Britain and China, against each other, carving out a space where it is neither simply the puppet of British colonialism nor of Chinese authoritarianism" (Chow 1998: 157). Chow's conception of the Third Space as in-betweenness, a fighting spirit asserting itself between two colonizing "aggressors" for survival, effectively places the Self and the hybridizing elements apart from each other. We can certainly assume that a degree of separateness, revealed in confrontation and interrogation, exists between the parts in the negotiation of identity, as Bhabha insists in his notion of "stubborn chunks."

It has been observed that Hong Kong's cultural development is characterized by an "add-on" quality. This is most clearly seen in its urban landscape, which is a dense mixture of the most fashionable and the most old-fashioned, and the most commercialized and the most indigenous. "These vernacular forms of cultural hybridity provide the real motive force behind Hong Kong's accepted fragmentation." (Leo Lee 2008: 240). To a large extent, the development of Hong Kong identity is no different, in that it tends to add on what it already possesses and keeps on building its fragmentary multiplicity. Even though the two "aggressors" of China and Britain have been viewed negatively (or "mutually resistant") at times, they have undeniably played important roles in shaping what Hong Kong is. In fact, they have been internalized and become rather important components in what we understand as Hong Kong identity.

In the reception process, the constituting parts, which are of different or contrasting characters, play the role of familiarizing agent, i.e., providing points of entry for the new to be absorbed into the Self. What are not serviceable at the time are temporarily suspended to make way for the part deemed most receptive, and which are then made prominent. In other words, the unfamiliar is made familiar, the foreign becomes local, and the Other becomes the Self. The idea is similar to wearing masks, but the mask is concealment and has a false ring to it, and with the suspension of identities, the part that is not suspended actually belongs to and resides in the Self. Thus in viewing a Hollywood movie, the Hong Kong audience, because of their familiarity with the language and culture of the movie, manage to reduce the foreignness in watching it—they may not even feel the foreignness at all. In a translated play, because the language has been localized, receptibility is enhanced. This is even more so with adaptations, in which characters, settings, and stories are domesticated.

To suspend is to put things on hold, "to stop or cause to be not active, either temporarily or permanently" or "to delay it or stop it from happening for a while."[166] With the suspension of identities, the key is contingency, the ability to adapt and change depending on the situation and the position of the Self in relation to the external Other. While an identity has been made prominent and is put in operation, resulting in a temporary stabilization of subject positions, others are placed in a hold pattern, dormant but not obliterated, waiting to be put into use when the situation arises. Hong Kong is no stranger to such contingent actions: when after being a British colony for one and half centuries, it suddenly found itself a Special Administrative Region of China, and this was accomplished and accepted with apparent equilibrium and resignation, without a whimper, a sense of regret or (much) celebration. Nationalism demands a centering pull toward the powers that be, an unquestionable and monopolizing allegiance that eliminates others in its path. Having been baptized by periods of fluctuations between nationalization, de-nationalization, and re-nationalization, the people of Hong Kong have become maladjusted to the demands of nationalistic devotion, a constancy anathema to the choice of the market. This is not unlike Aihwa Ong's concept of "flexible citizenship"—"the strategies and effects of mobile managers, technocrats, and professionals seeking to both circumvent and benefit from different nation-state regimes by selecting different sites for investments, work, and family relocation" (Ong 1999: 112). To such a homo economicus, a sense of loyalty is superseded, having been turned over to concerns for security and profits, and the discourse of the market successfully overcomes that of the state.

---

166 See the two dictionary entries listed in the bibliography under "Suspend."

Hong Kong has been effectively de-centered, in that it tends not to recognize a center and prefers to be in the periphery. In fact, the center-periphery hierarchy may have lost its relevance in the face of a faithless market mentality. While this may bring about a feeling of loss, it also allows picking and choosing a position to best manage the situation at hand. As Stuart Hall says of the postmodern subject: "The subject assumes different identities at different times, identities which are not unified around a coherent 'self'. Within us are contradictory identities, pulling in different directions, so that our identifications are continually being shifted about" (Hall 1992: 277; Barker 2005: 224).

We all speak and perform according to a specific history and culture—that is, we do our tasks in context. By temporarily adopting certain identities and suspending others, one is creating one's own context to take advantage of the situation—in the same manner a Hong Kong person with a collection of passports would select a most suitable one for ease of entry into or exit from a country. An identity, to pursue the same metaphor, is like a passport, a mere traveling document, and there need not be any compunction or feeling of betrayal in using it.

In cultural reception, the appropriation of the identity of the incoming culture will essentially lessen the impact of strangeness, making it easier for absorption. A large majority of translated plays in Hong Kong have been translated from English. When watching the performances of these plays, the audiences are able to lower their resistance caused by cultural differences—with the foregrounding of their "English identity"; the power of the source text is neutralized and the need for acculturation is kept to a minimum. Even with translations of non-English plays, the audience's open-mindedness, long conditioned by routine inclusiveness, facilitates reception while retaining the awareness of exoticism. Identities are characterized by instability, and the suspension of identities is a strategy for social, political, cultural, or other purposes. And for this strategy to work, one has to put in place what may be labeled "strategic essentialism"—that is, "the recognition that we act as if identification were stable identities for specific political and practical purposes," marking a temporary closure of meaning (Barker 2005: 245). The idea is to be both flexible and fixed in shaping identities, not to be bound by nationalistic or hegemonic beliefs, but to act with agency in self-contextualizing one's actions. With the Hong Kong situation, pragmatism is the key.

Faced with western influences over the years, the eclectic Hong Kong drama has displayed little resistance to foreign languages, stories, and performance styles; instead, it has absorbed these elements and remolded them into a myriad of styles. In contrast, the disputes in Mainland China concerning nationalistic forms in drama in the 1950s were in fact caused by the introduction of Stanislavsky and Brecht onto the Chinese stage. Such acts of resistance never occurred in Hong Kong, and it would thus be extremely difficult if not impossible for one to come up with a definition of a nationalistic drama for Hong Kong.

The positive aspect of hybridity is that it acknowledges identity as constructed through a negotiation of differences, and that the presence of fissures, gaps, and contradictions is not necessarily a sign of failure. In its most radical form, the concept also stresses that identity is not the combination, accumulation, fusion, or synthesis of various components, but an energy field of different forces, the coexistence among them, the encounters between them, and their own transformations (Papastergiadis 1997: 258). Hybridity should not be regarded as a panacea for the questions and issues brought forth by the problems of identity. While abandoning nativist purity and authenticity, hybridity also embraces internationalism and neglects the disasters and agonies that colonialism has brought to the colonies. For this reason we should treat hybridity as a descriptive concept rather than a normative one. Hong Kong's colonial and postcolonial experiences are unique in that they are characterized not by resistance or defiance, but rather by absorption, acceptance, and tolerance. Because these are the motivating forces behind the territory's various manifestations, it is appropriate to apply the concept of hybridity to generally define its identity. As a strategy for survival and self-transcendence, Hong Kong went from binary opposition to postmodern ambivalence and postcolonial pluralism, and from the opposition of differences to their coexistence as a strategy to transcend oneself.

It is only normal for one to be skeptical of and resistant to foreign forces. How then has Hong Kong been able to adopt a tolerant and embracing attitude? And how does it deal with its identity? We have already mentioned that Hong Kong is situated in a gap, a Third Space that is "neither here (British) nor there (Chinese)." Under the political, historical, and social-cultural circumstances, its subjectivity is inherently weak and thus inadequate to contend with the two masters. The only solution is to make use of its existing unique temporal and spatial characteristics and foreign cultural elements, and transform them into positive forces for constructing and then strengthening self-identity. As a colony, Hong Kong has long been baptized by colonial rule, which is a unique temporal factor; in a geopolitical context, it is situated on the periphery of a dominating and nationalistic China, which is a unique spatial factor. The absence of these temporal and spatial factors would have made the creation of a "hybridizing" environment impossible. Mutual mimicry between the colonizer and the colonized as well as confusion of the Self with the Other rule out typical binary oppositions. All these factors have, more or less, weakened the fixity of identity and facilitated the process of cultural transfer. Hong Kong's identity is therefore impure and diversified, similar to Bhabha's Third Space; it is a place that consists of co-existing incommensurable elements and different identities. At the same time these identities, upon their contact with foreign cultures, can be temporally suspended or appropriated into use. This flexibility is Hong Kong's motivating and driving force to rewrite and reinvent its identity through the years. Such being the case, we should not describe Hong Kong as the intersection of Chinese and foreign cultures, but rather a set of building blocks of various cultural elements ready for use in the reception of foreign cultures and construction of the Self and the Other. This space is at the same time a productive one, giving rise to new cultural sites and productions.

POSTSCRIPT: TRYING NOT TO BELONG TO A NATION

In the wake of the Umbrella Movement, which lasted seventy-nine days, from September 26 to December 14, 2014, there have been marked changes in the territory's political vista. Whereas the Hong Kong public had been indifferent or apathetic towards politics, especially during the pre-1997 era of British colonialism, now many people have found themselves engaged, perhaps involuntarily, in the affairs of the city, some even to the point of fanaticism. The feelings are far from uniform; as a matter of fact, the talk of a fractured society appears to be rampant, as protests and counter-protests have become everyday happenings. Vying for public and media attention, these groups include those from the pro-democracy camp, the pro-Beijing establishment, nativists, the independence movement (though voicing their demands subtly), and those nostalgic for the old days of British colonialism. The polarization testifies to our presumption of the multiplicity of Hong Kong identity, as if some Hongkongers have chosen to suspend some of their identities while others opt to put them to use for their own purposes.

The big shift has been towards localism, especially among the young. Hong Kong has had a long tradition of identifying itself with fighting for democracy on the Mainland. Patriotism reached its apex during the June Fourth Incident in 1989 when millions of Hongkongers marched on the street to lend their support to the students who were camping out at Tiananmen Square. This kind of long-distance moral support has since continued uninterrupted, as every June 4 anniversary has been marked with marches and protests demanding the reassessment of the incident as an insurgency. But there are signs of change in direction. This year the June 4 slogan of the University of Hong Kong Student Union was "Guard and Protect Hong Kong; Don't Forget June 4." This begs the question: Protect Hong Kong from what? The answer is obvious. The outcry is a call to preserve indigenous values, life-style, language, and culture, lest they be marginalized and eventually dissolved into the vortex of an all-consuming China. The slogan also did not call for a repeal of the June 4 verdict, as many old democrats have been doing over the years; instead, it reminded people of the disastrous consequences of mainland Chinese political policies and the iron-handedness of the Chinese government.

The 2014 Umbrella Movement was mainly a war cry for localism. Its slogans and writings, prominently displayed on social media and yielding tremendous mobilizing power, were written in Cantonese, not the standard Mandarin, and the concerns were mainly aimed at wresting power—the right to freely choose the Chief Executive—from Beijing. With this trend was born, much to the chagrin of the Hong Kong Government and Beijing, a small but vocal independence movement. In fact, the Umbrella Movement has been considered "the flowering of localism, the awakening to the fact that any democracy must be local democracy" (Yee Lee 2015). The latest identity poll (June 15-18, 2015) reports that six months after the Umbrella Movement, Hong Kong people's localism has somewhat subsided. The percentage of respondents who considered themselves Hongkongers had a slight drop from 42.3 to 36.3%, which is still considered high. The percentage of those who identify as Hongkonger in China" rose from 24.3 to 27.4 %, which shows that there remain feelings that just refuse to go away. During a protest march on May 31, 2015, one of the banners loudly proclaimed "I'm not Chinese."

Date of survey	Total Sample	Sub-sample	Hong-konger	Hong-konger in China	Chinese in Hong Kong	Chinese	Mixed Identity	Other	Don't know/ Hard to say
15–18/6 /2015	1003	678	36.3 %	27.4 %	13.1 %	22.1 %	40.5 %	0.3 %	0.8 %
10–16/12 /2014	1016	660	42.3 %	24.3 %					

Figure 3: Identity Poll (June 15-18, 2015). Source: http://hkupop.hku.hk/english/popexpress/ethnic/eidentity/poll/datatables.html

The Hong Kong University Public Opinion Programme describes the survey as follows:

POP [Public Opinion Programme] interviewed 1,003 Hong Kong people between 15 and 18 June by means of a random telephone survey conducted by real interviewers. According to our latest survey, whether in terms of absolute rating or dichotomous contrast, pe of 0–10 measuring the absolute strength of identity, the identity rating of "Hongkongers" stands at 7.95, that of "members of the Chinese race" stands at 7.02, "Chinese" 6.70, and "citizens of PRC" 5.87. When importance ratings are incorporated to generate "identity indices" between 0 and 100 (the higher the index, the stronger the positive feeling), Hong Kong people's feeling is still the strongest as "Hongkongers", at 77.6 marks, followed by "Asians" 72.3, then "members of the Chinese

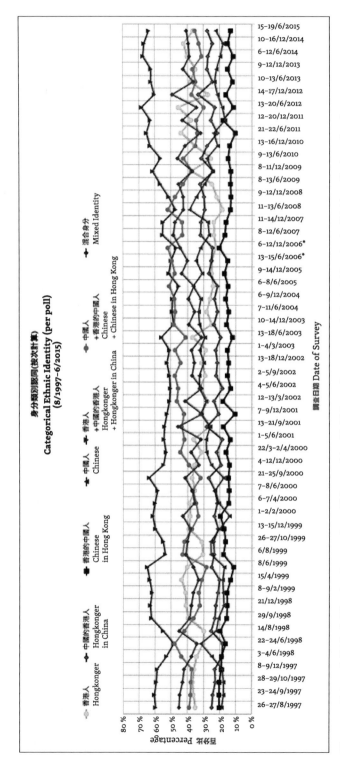

Figure 4: Categorial Ethnic Identity. Source: http://hkupop.hku.hk/chinese/popexpress/ethnic/eidentity/poll/eid_poll_chart.html>>

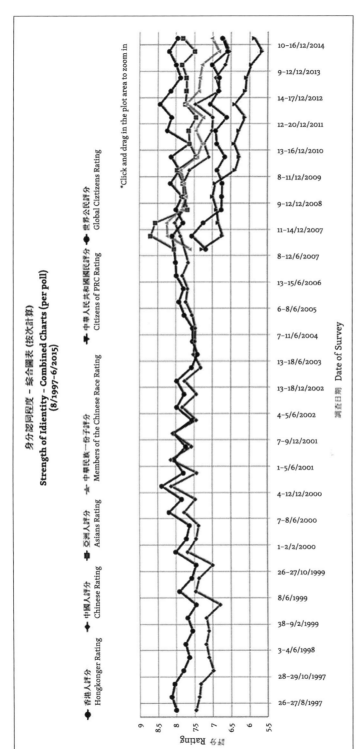

Figure 5: Strength of Identity – Combined Charts. Source: http://hkupop.hku.hk/chinese/popexpress/ethnic/overall/poll/overall_poll_chart.html

race" 67.3, "Chinese" 65.3, "global citizens" 64.1, and finally "citizens of the PRC" 55.9. If we follow the usual study method of using a dichotomy of "Hongkonger" versus "Chinese" to measure Hong Kong people's ethnic identity, the proportion of people identifying themselves as "Hongkongers" outnumbers that of "Chinese" both in their narrow and broad senses by 14 to 29 percentage points. All in all, Hong Kong people feel the strongest as "Hongkongers", then followed by a number of cultural identities. The feeling of being "citizens of the PRC" is the weakest among all identities tested. ("HKU POP releases latest survey")

It has been said that in the years immediately following 1997 the entire Hong Kong population had to embark on an education of "learning to belong to a nation" (Mathews/Ma/Lui 2008: xiii). Many people, especially the young, are keen on "trying not to belong to a nation." Some are still drawn toward being Chinese and espouse political Chineseness, but more prefer multiple identities, gravitating towards a Hong Kong identity of many faces.

Before political discourses dominated society, Hong Kong identity was largely defined by lifestyle—capitalistic hedonism, with a work-hard-play-hard attitude toward life. Or, as Deng Xiaoping put it, Hong Kong people after 1997 would be allowed to continue to "dance their dances and race their horses." Now a new ideology of awareness has been developing with more and more urgency and cogency in the form of an antagonistic ideology against Chinese socialism and communism, concentrating on the topics of Hong Kong's core values of the rule of law, fair competition, good governance, and, most important, freedom and democracy. These characteristics are, as some argue, the result of years of creolization and then internalized and assimilated into Hong Kong society, and now they are being used as ammunition directed against the deficiencies on the Mainland; as such, they are considered worth preserving as protection against the onset of Chinese encroachment.

Despite the economic integration in trade and the stock market with China in recent years, the tendency has been to move away from the center and to denationalize, so much so that talks of establishing of a city-state have become more frequent and noticeable. One of the more vocal separatists is Chin Wan in his best seller *On the Hong Kong City-State* (Chin Wan 2011). Hong Kong people should adopt "Hong Kong First" and "Hong Kong-China separation" positions, and not the "China First" and "China-Hong Kong integration" as promoted by the so-called democrats keen on fighting for democracy on behalf of the Chinese people. On June 18, 2015, the Hong Kong Legislative Council voted twenty-eight to eight against passage of the Election Reform Bill—this is despite the tremendous pressure exerted by Beijing and the SAR government. This could be interpreted as a move on the part of Hong Kong away from the central government and political Chineseness. Whether the experiment of "One Country, Two Systems" will continue or suffer an utter failure remains to be seen. But with the awakening of the Hong Kong people to the values of their language and culture, it is foreseeable that their allegiance and identity will be more restive and further fracture.

12 FLUID GAZES: NARRATIVE PERSPECTIVES AND IDENTITY CONSTRUCTION IN STORIES BY CHINESE CANADIAN WRITERS

HUA LAURA WU

In his seminal study on cultural identity, Stuart Hall presents two different ways of construing cultural identity. The essentialist position thinks about cultural identity "in terms of one, shared culture, a sort of collective 'one true self,' hiding inside the many other, more superficial or artificially imposed 'selves,' which people with a shared history and ancestry hold in common. Within the terms of this definition, our cultural identities reflect the common historical experiences and shared cultural codes which provide us, as 'one people,' with stable unchanging, and continuous frames of reference and meaning, beneath the shifting divisions and vicissitudes of our actual history" (Hall 2003b: 234). If we were to apply this notion of identity to a particular diasporic group, it would refer to their ethnic and cultural commonalities. For instance, the Chinese people residing around the world would be seen to form a homogeneous group because of shared ancestry, place of origin, historical experiences, cultural codes and practices, skin color, physical features, etc. "This 'oneness,' underlying all the other, more superficial differences, is the truth, the essence" of "Chineseness" and of the Chinese experience. It, therefore, defines "who we are." However, this essentialist "who we are" can "just as well be a strait-jacket" (Ang 2002: vii), confining, limiting, and reductive. Diasporic Chinese intuitively sense that we are "one people," but we are also different from other Chinese living elsewhere because "the cultural context of 'where you're at' always informs and articulates the meaning of 'where you're from'" (Ang 2002: 35), and those "critical points of deep and significant *difference*," due to changes in time and place, "constitute 'what we really are', or rather... 'what we have become.'" So identity is "a matter of 'becoming' as well as of 'being'" (Hall 2003b: 236).

To contemplate this "becoming" in identity construction, Hall puts forward a second conception of cultural identity. "In this perspective, cultural identity is not a fixed essence at all, lying unchanged outside history and culture. It is not some universal and transcendental spirit inside us on which history has made no fundamental mark. It is not once-and-all. It is not a fixed origin to which we can make some final and absolute return" (Hall 2003b: 237). Accordingly, Hall believes that identities are "'framed' by two axes or vectors, simultaneously operative: the vector of similarity and continuity; and the vector of difference and ruptures ... . The one gives us some grounding in, some continuity with, the past. The second reminds us that what we share is precisely the experience of a profound discontinuity" (237). And "difference ... persists in and alongside continuity" (238), therefore, identity construction is actually an ongoing process of "positioning and repositioning" (240).

So, as Hall and many other scholars of diaspora claim, identity is never transparent and fixed; on the contrary, it is projected and "grounded in the shifting space between the past and the future through the subject's present agency" (Walter 2003: 26), and thus "interrogative, shifting, unstable, and heuristic" (Davis 2002: 174). Identity construction, in theory as well as in reality, is an involving and evolving process.

This chapter examines two Chinese Canadian writers' fiction about the diasporic experiences of Chinese immigrants in North America since the 1980s. The stories under study are Yuanzhi's novel *Of Different Skies* (Bu yiyang de tiankong; 2003) and short story "Jia Na Da/Canada" (Sheng ge Jianada; 2008) and Zeng Xiaowen's novellas "The Kilt and Clover" (Sugelan duanqun he sanyecao; 2012a) and "Deportation" (Qiansong; 2012b). Yuanzhi's and Zeng's stories try to explore the life of Chinese immigrants at various stages in their cross-cultural and transnational migration. Changes in time and status engender different constructions of identity, and so the stories under analysis present a trajectory of identity changes. Through the representations of shifting identities, these literary texts also delve into how migrating subjects perceive the host country and how dominant social groups in the host country treat newcomers.

A SELF-GAZE AT THE CHINESE ENCLAVE AND A HESITANT GAZE AT THE HOST COUNTRY: YUANZHI'S STORIES

Let us first examine Yuanzhi's stories. The novel *Of Different Skies* is autobiographical in nature. The author herself acknowledges it, stating:

In *Of Different Skies*, I tell the stories of about twenty wives of Chinese students and their families. The names and families are fictionalized, but 99% of these stories are based on real events that took place in the recent past [i.e., the 1980s and 1990s]. Let me use a simile: if *Of Different Skies* were a necklace, the stories of these twenty or so wives were the individual pearls of the necklace and the female protagonist Lin Mengyu were the thread that linked up those pearls. Chapter Twenty-five is one of those pearls and this story is a fusion of life stories of a few real persons.[167]

The novel's subtitle, *An Account of the Ten Year Experiences of a Chinese International Student's Wife* (Peidu shinian jishi), also confirms the autobiographical essence of the work. Consequently the novel is intended as a thinly veiled, faithful record of real life experiences.[168] Here we witness a curious phenomenon of what Betsy Huang (2010: 11) calls the "autobiographic imperative"—that is, "an interpretive disposition of readers who habitually read fiction by ethnic writers as autobiography, as testimonies to lived experiences, typically assumed to be those of immigrants." This "autobiographical imperative" reflects "the popular audience's fetishization of 'the true story' and preference for an 'authentic' sociohistorical account," and so "[e]ven in a work of fiction, then, the ethnic writer is expected to 'tell the truth,' to posit her own perspective as an authentic and reliable episteme for individual *and* collective ethnic identities" (Huang 2010: 13). Huang further postulates that in contrast to "autobiography of Americanization," the "immigrant autobiography" is "indifferent to the 'mythos'" of Americanization and "attends instead to the autobiographer's place within a particular community or social sphere, whether that community is the culture of origin or destination" (15). Yuanzhi's *Of Different Skies* is typical of the "immigrant autobiography" in the sense that in this work the "mythic individual" who exemplifies the "conversion from alien to American" is "*not* the narrative object of desire" (15); to the contrary, the novel devotes its entire narrative space to a Chinese enclave in Canada. The enclave is inhabited by international students from China and their families, and since the stories are told by the female protagonist, wife to a Chinese international student whose social sphere is mostly confined to her family and the community of fellow Chinese students and their spouses, especially the latter, the "alien" Canadian society and its members seldom make an appearance in the novel. The fictional characters that populate this Chinese enclave live out their daily lives, interact with one another, and believe in and behave according to Chinese cultural codes, just like ordinary people back in China.

Take Chapter 25, "The Scientific Way to Cultivate the Land," as an example. In this chapter, Lin Mengyu, the female protagonist, gives birth to a baby daughter and is recuperating in the hospital and then at home. Many of her friends, especially female ones, visit her, bring her gifts, and help

---

167 Cai Yuanzhi 2013. Yuanzhi is Cai Yuanzhi's pen name. Translations are mine unless otherwise identified.
168 In this particular case, the author confesses that the publisher actually urged her to strengthen the autobiographical elements and suggested the title. This information comes from a private conversation with the author.

her out with tips for how to nurture the new-born. Chapter 25 also communicates typically Chinese cultural values and social codes, especially in the character of Lu Ruixue, Lin's new acquaintance from her hospital stay. Lu has also given birth to a daughter, her second one. Lu and her husband represent the Chinese culture of the past. Although trained scientists, they believe in fortune-telling, *fengshui*, and other traditional practices, some of which verge on being superstitious. First and foremost, they firmly believe in the value of a male child to carry on the family line. The primary purpose for them to come to Canada is, reportedly, to have the opportunity to give birth to a son. Lu informs Lin that they have named their daughters Jiajia/Jessica and Nana/Liana, and are determined to have a son. They have already chosen a name for that yet-to-be conceived son: Dada/Davie. With all three children, they will have given birth to "Jia Na Da/Canada." The stories narrated in the novel demonstrate that members in this enclosed community of wives of Chinese students seem to have very little contact beyond their own small, and somewhat isolated, social sphere. The only "foreign" element that manages to infringe upon this Chinese enclave is the exchange of Christmas gifts, and this foreign practice is deemed by the protagonist incomprehensible, stressful, and thus extremely frustrating.

If *Of Different Skies* offers an inward gaze that directs its attention unswervingly toward a Chinese enclave in a foreign land, Yuanzhi's short story "Jia Na Da/Canada" switches to an outward glance at the social environs beyond the Chinese community. "Jia Na Da/Canada" is actually a rewrite of Chapter 25 of *Of Different Skies*. The basic storyline remains: a Chinese couple relocate to Canada so that they can have a son. Important motifs and details are also kept but further developed in the rewrite: the couple are under pressure from their relatives back in China and by their neighbours to produce a son for the extended family (Yuanzhi 2008: 753, 755); they also name their daughters, one born in China and one in Canada, Jiajia/Jessica and Nana/Liana, and the husband is keen on having a Dada/Davie so that they can give birth to "Jia Na Da/Canada" (Yuanzhi 2008: 755). To get that precious son, they have tried various "scientific" methods, including a special, low-sugar diet, a daily soda rinse of the wife's private parts before going to bed, or the so-called "scientific way to cultivate the land," and the "comprehensive scientific way to cultivate the land" that combines the diet, the soda rinse, and a chart that takes into account the couples' birth days and the wife's monthly days of ovulation to dictate "the most opportune dates to conceive a boy" (Yuanzhi 2008: 753-754, 756). However, the author makes a number of skillful narrative maneuvers that bring the protagonists into contact with the outside world—that is, non-Chinese groups in the host country. Such narrative twists enrich the theme of identity construction in this diasporic story.

One of the maneuvers is to give the fictional characters a new status. Instead of casting them as international students and their wives from China, as in the source story, Yuanzhi makes Feng Jian and Sheng Jiqi, the couple in "Jia Na Da/Canada," immigrants to Canada. This change in social status is significant because, as immigrants who voluntarily relocate to Canada, Feng and Sheng are no longer sojourners like their prototypes in *Of Different Skies*. They are settlers, and Canada is now their chosen home and homeland, and so to give birth to Jia Na Da/Canada in this story is not just a joke, as it is in the source story, but indicates a strong intention to figuratively "own" Canada. Another narrative transformation is to remove this new immigrant couple from the closely-knit, homogeneous Chinese community. In "Jia Na Da/Canada," the narrative focus is on Feng and Sheng, and their Chinese friends make fewer appearances than in the source story; Chinese characters are, moreover, outnumbered by characters who are either clearly marked as non-Chinese or whose ethnicity is not specified. These characters tend to be professionals, for instance, police officers, doctors, and Feng's colleagues at a high-tech company. Obviously "Jia Na Da/Canada" positions its protagonists in an in-between space so that they can interact not only with their fellow Chinese but also with people outside the Chinese community.

From these interactions with people outside the Chinese community, we can detect meaning about how the Chinese characters see themselves and other ethnic groups in the host country—that is, how the story both draws a self-image of Chinese immigrants and images of the "Other" in identity construction. The Chinese in this story are portrayed as family-centered, hard working, fiscally responsible, very conscious of saving money, and highly respectable. Sheng Jiqi worries about the family's wellbeing and the impact of having a third child on the family's fragile financial security. She twice voices her concerns: when Feng tries to persuade her to have a third child, she bursts out: "Look at you. You have been in Canada more than a year, and you still don't have a permanent job, just part-time jobs or contract work. Your income is as meagre as a labourer's and we have to use our savings to pay bills. And you still want another child!" (Yuanzhi 2008: 755). When she is informed that she is carrying twins, "she began to feel weighted down again. Feng Jian was still doing contract work and since he was certainly not a giant with three heads and six arms, how could they manage to raise so many children?" (759–760). In contrast to the Chinese family as "a model of productivity, savings, and mobility" (Lee 1999: 11), some ethnic groups in Canada are perceived in a more negative light. Feng Jian, the male protagonist, says:

As for our life here, we can manage. Even if we did not work, our savings could still support us for a year or two. Haven't you heard the saying that Canada (Jia-na-da) means "da-jia-na," "na-da-jia," and "da-na-jia"?[169] That is, "everyone dishes out from the big communal pot." If you have more children, you are entitled to more benefits; if you have fewer, you are entitled to fewer; and if you have none, you are entitled to nothing. So why not have more? If we have another child, we are simply taking a bit more from the big pot! *Look at those refugees from all over the world. They all seem to have a big brood of kids, and are they poorer than we? No. They can eat and drink until their bellies are full, and they can have whatever fun they fancy. Remember what our Prime Minister Jean Chrétien once said about those people: they just take welfare money and drink beer at home. They felt offended and went out to protest. That is truly "na-da-jia," the big takers!* (755; emphasis added)

The contrast between the diligent and conscientious Chinese and the shameful and shameless advantage-takers from some other ethnic groups reveals that "Jia Na Da/Canada" presents a self-image of Chinese people as the "model minority"[170] and that, although the story has the Chinese begin to look beyond their own community, their gaze is a very tentative and condescending one that is directed mostly at other under-privileged ethnic groups in the host country. Moreover, this ethnic Other is caricatured stereotypically.

"Jia Na Da/Canada" also has its male protagonist come into contact with the dominant group in the host country. In the beginning and end of the story, the author introduces two episodes that are thematically similar but that mirror each other. The opening episode has Feng Jian speed back home to prepare food for his wife who has just given birth to a daughter; he is pulled over by a white police officer and gets a speeding ticket. In the closing episode, Feng is on his way to his wife who just informed him that she was pregnant with twins, a boy and a girl. He is elated and fails to notice he is speeding again. He is pulled over by a black police officer and is about to receive another speeding ticket. In the first episode, the white officer expresses his envy because he is the father of three sons and really wants a daughter, whereas Feng, who is very much disappointed with the birth of another daughter, cannot understand why the other man would be envious. In the second episode, both the policeman and Feng are puzzled: the former feels perplexed by why Feng is so excited with the news of the twins, whereas the latter simply cannot understand how the officer isn't jealous.[171] This framing device, to me, actually throws into bold relief the theme of misunderstanding and lack of under-

---

169 Literally "da-jia-na" means "everybody takes"; "na-da-jia" means "taking from others"; and "da-na-jia" means "the big takers," terms that pun on Jia-na-da/Canada.

170 For studies on "model minority myth", see Lee 1999, Palumbo-Liu 1999, Cheung 1993, and Khoo/Louie 2005.

171 See Yuanzhi 2008: 753, 760. Even though the second police officer is black, I still put him as a member of the dominant group or the "mainstream" society because of his profession in the police force.

standing between the Chinese and other ethnic groups embedded in the main body of the story. It also emphasizes that this lack of understanding is mutual and widespread.

A RECIPROCAL EXCHANGE OF GAZES AND THE GAZE OF THE OTHER: ZENG XIAOWEN'S STORIES

Zeng Xiaowen, a prolific Chinese Canadian fiction writer, develops the theme of lack of understanding and scrutinizes it in her stories. Moreover, in her works, she does not stop at exposing the lack of mutual understanding between ethnic minorities and the dominant mainstream but also tries to explore the possibility of reaching out for understanding and acceptance through interracial romance. The two stories penned by Zeng and analyzed here, "The Kilt and Clover" and "Deportation," both feature a love relationship between a Chinese woman and a white man and both begin with the female protagonist in a position of inequality and disadvantage, progress into an uneasy mutual identification of the Chinese woman and her white lover, and end with the underprivileged woman evolving into a survivor and savior.

The female protagonist in "The Kilt and Clover" is Lei, a new immigrant from China. At the beginning of the story, she is an alien "Other" in Canada. As a newcomer, she tries very hard to make a meagre living, first in Toronto and then in small town St. Catherines, so she is literally twice uprooted, first from her home country and then from the Chinese community in Toronto. Although she was a university instructor teaching psychology back in China, in Canada she has to work as a laborer in a factory and then as a cleaning lady in a retirement home because of her weak English and lack of training at Canadian universities. In St. Catherines, whose residents are predominantly white middle-class, Lei is doubly alienated because of race and poverty. Lei starts doing cleaning jobs for Sean, a white sailor, and gradually the two develop a romantic relationship as they discover their selves in the other—or it is more appropriate to say that it is when Lei starts to see herself in Sean that she begins to identify with him (Zeng 2012a: 146–166). Leslie Bow (2001: 59), drawing from Diana Fuss, adeptly points out the importance of this kind of identification in identity formation:

> Psychoanalysis has theorized identification as a means of restoring a lost love-object and … it is a process intrinsically tied to the formation of identity, "the detour through the other that defines a self." Identification … is "the play of differences and similarities in self-other relations" that brings identity into being, the point "where I become other." …Identification is … "a question of *relation*, of self to other, subject to object, inside to outside."

Indeed, Lei goes through a detour of identifying the "Other" in Sean to know herself. When she first meets him, she notices some odd features that set Sean apart from the archetypical hero in romantic fiction:

> Sean was far from the image of a sailor that I had been entertaining. He was not tall and slim, with blue eyes and blond hair. Rather, he had brown hair and brown eyes. The arms sticking out of his blue-grey T-shirt were not really sinewy. His skin was not tanned a radiant bronze, it was just dark because of his olive complexion. For whatever reason, he avoided looking squarely into my eyes. His expression was hard to read, a mixture of humility and shyness.
>
> Right away I smelled loneliness in him. Perhaps loneliness transcended borders and cultures (Zeng 2012a: 148–149).

Intuitively, Lei senses that, just like herself, Sean is a loner. Later Lei also discovers more similarities between her and Sean. They both love reading books and enjoy literature. They are both, to a certain degree, "social outcasts" and have uneasy relationships with their own families, particularly with their mothers. Lei suffers from offspring's "feeling of guilt, rejection, and doubt" (Ghymn 1995: 24), and her mother takes advantage of the daughter's guilty feeling to squeeze hard-earned money out of Lei.[172] Sean's feeling toward his mother is more of bitterness, resentment, and rebellion. His mother expects him to go to university to become a lawyer or a doctor, but Sean never enjoyed school. He chooses to be a sailor, and an unconventional one who loves to comb through second-hand bookstores wherever the ship docks. He believes that in his mother's eyes, he is "forever a loser, a pathetic drowning dog" (Zeng 2012a: 152). More important, Lei and Sean both suffer setbacks in love relationship. With her "long and narrow eyes, low and flat nose, thick lips ... not a single feature met the conventional, Chinese idea of beauty," Lei is a homely woman, who is neglected by Chinese men. The only romantic relationship she had back in China ended in failure; now she is in her thirties, still unspoken for (153, 155). When the relationship between Lei and Sean becomes physical, Lei is willing to nurture it. She reaches out to Sean but he withdraws into an emotional cocoon; to Sean, Lei's gestures of intimacy represent a threat and he reacts with "the fear of an intruder" (159). On the surface, Sean's fear of intimacy seems to come from his failed marriage; however, it is only after his death that Lei learns the more profound trauma Sean is inflicted with. Sean is obsessed with his unfaithful ex-wife

---

172 Lei tells Sean: "When I save money, I save one dollar at a time. When I send money back home, I send by the hundred." She takes up the new job of cleaning at a retirement home because the job pays $15 an hour, almost twice as much as the wage of her previous job in Toronto. She needs the money since her mother has asked her to send more money home (Zeng 2012a: 154, 146).

and his obsession has developed into a phobic fascination with pornography "featuring beautiful women of blond hair and blue eyes, of huge breasts and wide hips" (164), or blond beauties who resemble his ex-wife. Lei and Sean both realize that they are the "Other" not only to each other but also among their own people, and this sense of "Otherness" makes them click and become emotionally attached.

What is also significant about "The Kilt and Clover" is that it contests the literary, as well as social, convention of making the ethnic "Other," especially the non-white woman, the object of the white gaze. In an interracial romance between a white man and a Chinese woman and its literary representations, the relation between the gazer and the object of the gaze highlights a power structure. The Chinese woman is usually the passive object of the white man's sexual fantasy and the romantic courtship is more a quest for subjugation and conquest. A more radical critique of the literary norm calls it a sell-out that "turns the Chinese woman into a prostitute for the voyeuristic gaze" of the West.[173] Zeng Xiaowen turns the gaze in her story into a mutual scrutiny of the "Other" and of the different worlds the female and male protagonists inhabit. Lei's gaze discloses "Sean's self-confined emotional world and his pathetic/pathological obsession with his ex-wife while Lei's 'obsession' with sacrificing herself to please her family is exposed through Sean's gaze. They are both fully aware of the other's weakness that originates from their respective cultural upbringing but do not see their own cultural vulnerability" (Xu Xueqing 2010). The reciprocal gaze favoured in "The Kilt and Clover" indicates a new positioning in identity construction: the normally and normatively underprivileged Chinese woman is no longer cast as the absolute suppressed or weaker sex and race. Instead of being the helpless object gazed at, fantasized over, pitied, or despised, the Chinese woman begins to look back at the Western gazer. Or we can say that the subject position of the Chinese woman in the power structure embedded in the interracial romance discourse has switched from absolute subjugation to reciprocity and equality, or even triumph.[174]

"Deportation," another story authored by Zeng Xiaowen, contains many thematic similarities with "The Kilt and Clover," though it differs in being set in Texas. It also narrates a love relation between a Chinese woman, Xia Han, and an American man, Benjamin. Like their counterparts in the earlier story, both Han and Benjamin have emotional burdens. Han was jilted by her first lover and then separated from her husband, while Benjamin was first abandoned by his father and then by his wife. But the story has a happy end-

---

173 See Kong Shuyu's (2012) insightful analysis of the gaze in Yan Geling's *Fusang* (*The lost daughter of happiness*) and Pan Wen's (2012) discussion of "miscegenation" in American popular literature.
174 For studies on this change, see Wang Lieyao/Li Peipei 2011 and Wang Lieyao. 2009.

ing: Han and Benjamin, after going through some seemingly insurmountable obstacles, are reunited (Zeng 2012b: 176–207). But, unlike the earlier story, which focuses on Lei, the Chinese woman, "Deportation" is told entirely from Benjamin's perspective and thus is more about his quest for self. It is also from Benjamin's eyes that Han as the "Other" is presented and represented.[175] To use the author's own words,

> Han does not look like any of the Chinese women in American movies: she does not accept humiliation compliantly, nor does she plea and beg humbly. However, she certainly isn't the dragon lady in *gongfu* movies who fights with a sword or a spear and who flies to the rooftop or runs on the high walls. Han completely changes the image of the Chinese woman Benjamin held, and through her, he understands better Chinese culture. (Zeng n.d.)

So "Deportation" represents the curious case of a Chinese writer writing about Chinese through the eyes of the Western "Other."

If Han does not fit the stereotypes of Chinese, especially Chinese women, created by the white popular culture, then what is the new image she conjures up? Benjamin recalls his first sight of Han:

> Benjamin arrived at the former 88 Chinese Restaurant. He saw a pretty and graceful Chinese woman walking back and forth on the weed-infested lawn in front of the restaurant. She did not seem to be contemplating the business prospects of the property but was savoring the desolate milieu.
>
> She tied her hair into a casual ponytail, wore an off-white tank top and a pair of beige khaki shorts, and her hands were in her pockets. She looked serene yet aloof, surprisingly compatible with the Texas desert. Benjamin recalled seeing a painting in Tedgeton's Chinatown; that painting was titled "Spring of the Lower Yangzi Valley" and the girl featured in the painting looked just like Han, of fine complexion, pretty, a character who seems to have lived in a remote place and remote time; yet she had big and beautiful eyes, eyes that could bewitch a man in a blink of the eye and make him lost in them … . Han smiled, and her smile immediately added a touch of intimacy and intelligence that the Chinese girl in the painting lacked. (Zeng 2012b: 182).

To Benjamin, Han is a young woman of graceful demeanor, refined taste, and with an innate melancholy. She looks extremely distant yet very intimate all at once, and so she poses an enigma. This sense of unfathomable mystery deepens when they meet again:

---

175 I have examined the narrative mode (narrative perspective and focalization) in a previous essay. See Wu Hua. 2010.

Han told him that the Chinese character *han* stood for water lily, a flower that became purer and prettier when growing out of filthier water... He noticed that Han had a pair of lovely and delicate hands. She wrote one stroke after another and surprisingly a flower emerged; he felt intrigued. Apparently writing *han* was much harder than spelling out "water lily." How could the Chinese invent a writing system that was so complicated? Their scripts were not the only mysterious thing, there were many other mysteries about the Chinese.

"The four dots, what are they?" He asked out of curiosity.

"The buds, rain drops, dew droplets, tears ... whatever you take them for." Han replied.

What did the four dots stand for? Benjamin still wondered. (177)

Han embodies the mysterious Chinese, but she is also knowledgeable of the West and seems to have an innate appreciation of the true spirit of Texas and the Texans, who, Benjamin believes, "more than the New Yorkers, are the true embodiment of the American Spirit" (181). However, it is Han the foreigner who recommends *Paris, Texas*, a quintessential Texan film to Benjamin the proud Texan. Strangely, both Han and Benjamin, culturally apart, identify with Travis the character in the film and the images of Texas, the lonely wanderer and the bleak, dry, alien landscape of the Texas desert. Benjamin finds "his shadow merged into that of the male protagonist. After his wife disappeared, he often dreamed the same dream: wandering aimlessly in the desolate desert." And Han believes, "Flowers and grasses will wither while the desert will not; intimacy is a flighty sentiment while alienation is forever; roaming, wandering, and trying to escape ... these are eternal." She also tells Benjamin, "I have been trying to escape ... I feel I am like a little mouse, with a cat, a white one or a black one, lurking behind it and chasing it ... I thought that if I fled to the desert, the chase would end and I'd be safe" (185–186).

In decoding the enigma of Han, Benjamin comes to identify with her. "Blue-eyed Benjamin" (177), who is a US immigration officer in the process of deporting Han, is made into the "Other." To the diasporic and under-privileged races, Benjamin is the "Other." Socially, he is a member of the mainstream society and the power establishment. Politically, he is a right-wing conservative. The idol he lives up to is his immediate boss Charles, a bureaucrat who believes in iron-fisted policies in immigration and is a descendent of Old South plantation-owner lineage. Ideologically, Benjamin supports most of Charles' dogma and views. He thinks that he is "the son of the lone star" representing the real Texas and the true American Spirit. He holds the kinds of prejudices a "pure-blood" American has against non-whites, so when coming across a young woman of Chinese descent who speaks non-accented English, Benjamin alleges that she "must be an ABC (American born Chinese). She just assumes she has all the rights an American citizen enjoys since she was born here" (189). This comment suggests that he believes ABCs are second-class citizens, not deserving of all the rights an American citizen is entitled to. For the Chinese immigrant workers he deals with in his investigation of human trafficking, he is convinced that they are all members of a human smuggling ring, though his wife Jennifer, who is the only non-Chinese staff member in the restaurant that Benjamin investigates, knows that her co-workers "work fifteen or sixteen hours a day and seven days a week in the restaurant. How could they find the time to commit the crime they are charged with?" (196). So Jennifer's misgivings contest the objectivity, reliability, and impartiality of Benjamin and his views.

Benjamin is one of "them," but he is also the "Other" among "them." In racial terms, "Blue-eyed Benjamin" is the son of a white father and a Latino mother, so according to the American rules of the racial game, he is a "colored person," yet to the non-white people, including his partner, who is of Mexican descent, he is white.[176] In terms of social belonging, he is an agent working for the immigration bureau, thus a member of the power establishment and a protector of "law and order"; however, he is the son of a father who rebels against the social and political establishments, the son of a single mother who herself is a person of color, and the husband abandoned by his wife. In terms of political beliefs, although he idolizes President Bush and "the Spirit of Texas" that Bush and Benjamin's boss Charles represent and is truly proud of his profession and an excellent officer, he does not fully believe in the effectiveness and legitimacy of deporting people who for various reasons live in the United States "illegally." Consequently, his boss doesn't fully trust him (178). "Deportation" lays bare the complexity and ambiguity of social belonging found in Benjamin. Such complexity and ambiguity highlight the themes of a person's personal identity in conflict with his social identity and the resultant crisis: the deporting agent is the deported and the abandoned at metaphysical and emotional levels.

As Zeng Xiaowen adeptly points out:

> Immigration police officer Benjamin and Han are "perfect strangers." Racial prejudices dividing whites and visible minorities, gaps in social status separating a law enforcing policeman and a prisoner, and cultural differences between the West and East necessarily cause tensions between the two protagonists. Such tensions can lead to conflicts and they can also create mystery.... Because of the constant and subtle transformation in the two protagonists' positions and postures, the two "perfect strangers" become "perfect soul mates." Benjamin is the agent who executes the deportation act and the person who suffers from acts of abandonment (first by his father and later by his wife) all at once ....The deportation agent sends himself into [spiritual] exile when he carries

---

176 "Blue-eyed Benjamin" is the nickname his non-white colleagues give him (Zeng 2012b: 177–178).

out the very act of expulsion … . Han is the character who is being deported, yet at the very end of the story she becomes Benjamin's spiritual salvation. (Zeng n.d.)

Zeng Xiaowen calls the reader's attention to the multiple roles Benjamin and Han play, the frequent switches of their roles, the inherent power structure in their respective roles, and the displacement of the power balance. Thus, "Deportation" not only examines but also complicates and enriches literary representation of and reflection on identity construction in ethnic literature.

CONCLUSION: FLUID GAZES

All four stories under discussion here deal with identity construction in their individual ways; however, when they are examined together, a pattern begins to emerge. These stories present a continuum of evolving positions of identity formation. In *Of Different Skies*, Chinese students and their spouses are portrayed as a closely-knit and ethnically-homogeneous group of people who are in transit. They live temporarily in Canada and are aware of the temporality of their stay, so they pay very little attention to the host country and its social and cultural practices. The Chinese are portrayed as sojourners, ever ready to return to the homeland. As settlers in Canada, characters in "Jia Na Da/Canada" begin to show interest in "Others" in the country they choose to live in, but they look "up" to the dominant "mainstream" and look "down" at other ethnic groups. Their biased look at "Others" engenders perplexities and prejudices. "The Kilt and Clover" features an intense look at the "Other" and an equally intense look-back at oneself; moreover the two gazers, one from the underprivileged Chinese race and the other from the dominant "mainstream," are positioned on a relatively equal footing. Consequently, their examination of the other and their self-inspection are reciprocal and not hierarchical. "Deportation" adopts an external perspective, having an outsider look at the Chinese. Moreover this external viewer does not take the usual orientalist stance that fantasizes, pities, or demonize the Chinese "Other," so this new point of view reflects a change of self-positioning in the character, as well as in the ethnic writer, who is more comfortable and also confident in her in-between status and can withstand the focused gaze of the "Other," even when the "Other" is a member of "mainstream" society and the power establishment.

The four stories posit different gazes of the migrating subjects: a self-gaze completely directed to the Chinese themselves; a hesitant gaze of Chinese immigrants looking at the host country; a reciprocal exchange of gazes between the Chinese and members of "mainstream" society; and an external gaze zeroing in on the Chinese diaspora. These evolving and fluid gazes also embody a continuous process of identity constructions, and thus reveal that identity is unstable, evolving, and always "somewhere-in-between" (Bromley 2000: 3). Moreover, identity does not only define "who we are" but also projects "who we have become" and "who we are to become." So identity construction is essentially a self-journey that leads to wider and widening horizons.

13 REVISITING SHEN FU'S *SIX RECORDS OF A LIFE ADRIFT* (FUSHENG LIUJI)

GRAHAM SANDERS

Over forty years ago, Milena Doleželová-Velingerová identified the Qing dynasty memoir *Six Records of a Life Adrift* (Fusheng liuji) by Shen Fu (1763–ca. 1811) as "a telling example of an historical paradox that can be often observed in the development of literature and of art in general: a work of art, crowning and closing an old tradition, finds a new life in a quite different historical context because by its artistic originality it anticipates the aspirations and ideals of a new age" (1972: 160). My illuminating experience as a student studying the work with Prof. Doleželová-Velingerová led to my decision decades later to prepare a new English translation of it (Shen 2011). It was during this translation work, that I discovered this slim volume from China at the turn of the nineteenth century still has much to teach us regarding the "aspirations and ideals" of our "new age" in terms of how we might structure and record experiences—or more precisely, our memories and feelings of our experiences—at a time when multiple modes of self-presentation threaten to fragment our identities.

The very title of Shen Fu's memoir—*Six Records of a Life Adrift*—subverts the notion of a stable subjectivity that can be pinned down by a single master narrative; instead, multiple iterations are needed to build up a story with layers of meaning. The locus classics for the phrase "life adrift" can be traced back to a passage in Chapter 15 of the classic of Daoist philosophy *Zhuangzi*, which says of the sagely man, "he lives his life as though adrift and dies as though coming to rest."[177] The Tang dynasty poet Li Bai (701–762) later echoes this sentiment: "For in this cosmos we are but sojourners among all things in creation; in time we are but passing travelers through the ages. So in this life adrift as in a dream, how much joy will we find?"[178] Shen Fu himself notes that Li Bai happened to be the favorite poet of his wife Chen Yun. How does one organize a life that is spent adrift? How will it be remembered after the subject has come to rest? In the pages of his records, Shen Fu gives us an answer that is at once playful and profound; full of both joy and melancholy.

---

177 Translations from the Chinese are my own.
178 From a "preface" written by Li Bai for his poem "A Spring Evening Banquet with My Cousins in the Peach Garden" (Chunyeyan congdi taohuayuan xu).

In discussing the unusual structuring principles of *Six Records*, Doleželová-Velingerová (1972: 147) points out: "Mood determines the distribution of episodes among the chapters; as a result, particular chapters are unified by a specific mood. Chronology is secondary and is subordinated to the basic plot structure principle, determining only the sequence of episodes within the particular chapters." For instance, the years of Shen Fu's life from the ages of 18 to 40 are recounted four times using four different moods or lenses to select and focus on different events in each iteration. In her article, Doleželová-Velingerová (1972: 151) identifies an overall movement from joyful and idyllic in the first two records, to tragic in the third, and neutral in the fourth. The dominant mood and topic for each record is identified in its title (following my translations):

I.   Delights of Marriage
II. Charms of Idleness
III. Sorrows of Hardship
IV. Pleasures of Roaming

In my introduction to *Six Records of a Life Adrift*, I explain Shen Fu's innovative organization of chapters as follows:

The rhythm of each record depends on its topic—marriage, idleness, hardship, roaming—and its dominant mood—delight, charm, sorrow, pleasure. Extended scenes describing Yun's illnesses in the third record, "Sorrows of Hardship," are glossed over in a few words or omitted altogether in another record. Shen Fu spends pages in the fourth record, "Pleasures of Roaming," describing a trip that is mentioned elsewhere in one sentence. The individual records work together to produce a multilayered collage of Shen Fu's memories; the very structure of the book mimics the shape and behavior of human memory itself. Our memories are selective, inconsistent, recursive, colored by mood; we both recall and forget as a way of finding reasons and patterns in the welter of chaotic particulars and emotional associations that are left behind in the wake of our daily experiences. Shen Fu is remembering his life for the reader (and for himself) in four different but complementary ways that end up producing a more satisfying and genuine account together than any single, linear narrative might on its own. He does not try to reconcile the competing versions of his life into a tidy package that would show the artificial "chisel scars" that he detests so much. Instead, he lays out each record side by side and invites the reader to be the fashioner of his life story. (Sanders 2011: xiv)

But a closer examination reveals that, apart from the four dominant moods, the entire set of records is shot through with conflicting impulses that form a pattern of setting up an ideal, and then compromising it repeatedly through incompletion. It is this pattern of incompletion (reflected in the very fact that only four of the original six records are extant) that I explore further here.

BROKEN IDYLL

In the first record—"Delights of Marriage"—Shen Fu paints a picture of an ideal marriage, but the realities of poverty, illness, and infidelity often break into that idyll. The following passage frames Shen Fu's marriage to Chen Yun when they were still teenagers with an intimate account of their wedding banquet:

> On February 26, 1780, in the forty-fifth year of the Qianlong reign, I could see by the flickering light of our wedding candles that Yun's figure was just as delicate as before.
>
> When her bridal veil was lifted, she looked at me and smiled warmly. After we had sipped wine together from the wedding cups, we sat down next to one another at our banquet table with our shoulders touching. I secretly took her hand into my own beneath the table, and her warm, smooth, delicate touch set my heart to thumping wildly within my chest.
>
> I invited her to eat first, but she had just started her vegetarian fast, which she had been doing at regular intervals for the past several years. I did a mental calculation and realized that the first time she went on one of these fasts was when I had chickenpox, so I laughed and teased her, "Now that my skin has cleared up without a spot left, surely you can give up your vow of abstinence?"
>
> Yun smiled at my request with a glance of her eyes and assented with a nod of her head. (Shen 2011: 4)

The description succinctly evokes the private (often wordless) communications between the lovers (who have known each other since childhood) even in the midst of the wedding ceremony in front of their family.

This idyllic beginning continues in the early years of Shen Fu's wedded life with Yun:

> At home, if we met each other in a darkened room or bumped into one another in a narrow hallway, we would clasp hands and ask each other, "Where are you off to?" Our secretive hearts would be aflutter as though we feared someone might see us at any moment. The truth is that we started out not letting anyone see us walk together or sit side by side, but after a while it did not concern us anymore. If Yun happened to be sitting down to chat with someone and she saw me come into the room, she would always

stand up and move over to let me sit down next to her. Neither of us really thought about why we were acting this way, and we were even sheepish about it at first; but after a while it just seemed to happen naturally. I have always found it odd when older couples look upon each other as sworn enemies and have never understood the thinking behind it. Some people say, "If they didn't act like that, how could they last until they were old and white-haired together?" I wonder if this is really true. (12)

The whole tenor of the "Delights of Marriage" is highly lyrical; explicit references to poetry, quotations from poems, discussions of poetry and poets appear repeatedly throughout, as do lyrical moments told in prose, such as the following:

On August 6, 1780, during the Seventh Night Festival of that year, Yun set up a small altar with incense sticks and pieces of melon and fruit in My Choice Hall, where we made our obeisance to the Weaving Girl star.

...

That night the moonlight was particularly lovely and we turned our eyes down to the river, where we saw the light shimmer upon the waves like fine white silk. We sat there together in that small window overlooking the water, dressed in summer robes, fanning ourselves gently. Then we raised our eyes to see scudding clouds break into countless shapes as they crossed the sky.

...

Before long, the candles burned low, the moon sank in the sky, and we cleared away the plates of fruit and went to bed. (12–13)

One gains the sense that Shen Fu and Chen Yun lived their married life as poetry; or, at least, Shen Fu wanted to remember and portray his married life as a form of poetry.

Despite Shen Fu's attempts to corral misfortunes into the third record—"Sorrows of Hardship"—the threats of illness, poverty, family strife, and infidelity still lurk behind the scenes of the first record, occasionally coming to the surface. The following episode immediately follows the one above and makes an illuminating contrast with that night of wedded bliss.

August 14, 1780, was the full moon in the middle of the month, known as the Ghost Festival, so Yun prepared a small tray of wine and snacks to invite the moon to drink with us. But the sky suddenly grew overcast and as dark as a moonless night. Yun's face looked troubled and she said, "If I'm meant to grow old and white-haired with you, then the full moon should show itself!"

...

While we were chatting, the water clock had advanced to midnight. Slowly, much to our delight, we saw the wind sweep away the clouds to reveal a full moon. We leaned on the windowsill and drank to the moon, but before we finished our third cup, we suddenly heard a great splashing noise from beneath the bridge as though someone had fallen into the water. I thrust my head out the window and scanned the waters carefully, but they were as flat and bright as a mirror in the moonlight and I could not see anyone. All I heard was the sound of a duck scurrying away on the sandy shoals. I knew that the area around Azure Waves was the favorite haunt of ghosts of people who had drowned, but I did not dare to mention this to Yun for fear of her timid constitution.

"Oh!" Yun cried. "That noise! Where did it come from?"

We could not stop ourselves from trembling, so we hurriedly shut the window and brought the wine back into the room. The oil lamp was sputtering, casting spooky shadows on the bed curtains that made it hard for us to calm down. I cleaned the lamp wick to make it brighter and brought it into bed, but Yun was already having an attack of feverish chills. I fell ill soon after, and the two of us suffered for almost three weeks. It was truly a case of disaster arriving at the height of delight as well as an omen that we were not destined to grow old and white-haired together. (14–15)

These two episodes form counterpoints of joy and fear in the marriage of Shen Fu and Chen Yun, following the principle he mentions explicitly of "disaster arriving at the height of delight." The first episode, on the night of the Seventh Night festival dedicated to lovers, is the portrait of an ideal night of conjugal bliss, seen to its natural conclusion. The second episode, during the Ghost Festival, casts their relationship as something that can easily go awry, ending as a night of illness rather than sexual intimacy. Every lyrical moment of romance is but one turn away from a premonition of tragedy.

Intimations of illness and early death appear elsewhere in the first record. Yun's incomplete poems, which she worked on as a teenager, are an omen of a life that will not be lived to completion—she dies at the age of 41, after twenty-three years of marriage to Shen Fu. He makes the omen all too explicit when he carelessly inscribes her poetry notebook with the title "Brocade Pouch of Fine Verses," alluding to the work of the Tang poet Li He, who died at the age of 27. Shen Fu often reveals himself to have less literary sensitivity than his wife, who seems to have an innate affinity for the emotional and ephemeral qualities of artistic expression. As Shen describes her:

Yun did, however, treasure all sorts of tattered books and damaged paintings to an almost excessive degree. She would gather up all kinds of loose pages from old books, sort them out into separate categories, collate them, and then bind them into new covers. She referred to these books as her "bits and pieces" of literature. When it came to torn scrolls of calligraphy and paintings, she would look for some matching old paper on which to remount them, then ask me if I might restore the missing places with my brush before she rolled them up again. She called these scrolls her "scraps of appreciation." Whenever she had time off from her sewing and cooking, she could spend an entire day working diligently at these pastimes without feeling tired in the least. When she was lucky enough to find a piece of paper with something worthwhile on it in a worn out chest or between the pages of a moldering book, it was as though she had acquired a priceless treasure. Old Woman Feng next door was always collecting an assortment of old books and scrolls to sell to her. (20)

Yun's obsession with rescuing fragments of "tattered books and damaged paintings" is at once a testament to her literary sensibility, but also a powerful image of her attempt to arrest and restore the inevitable deterioration and loss brought on by the passage of time. Her pastime is a figure for how Shen Fu himself constructs his memoirs: as a patchwork of memories pieced together and filled in with his writing brush in an attempt to capture that which has been irretrievably lost.

Shen Fu occasionally acknowledges explicitly the discrepancy between an ideal marriage and its lived reality. His greatest regrets are of his inability to make enough money to support a stable and healthy household that might have secured a longer and more enjoyable life for his beloved Yun:

Yun said to me happily, "One day you and I should pick a spot here to build a home and buy an acre or two of land around it for gardens. We would have our servants plant melons and vegetables for us to live on. You could paint and I could do my needlework to keep us in wine and poetry. We'd be able to live out our days in delight with humble clothes and simple food and never have to think about leaving again." I had deeply hoped to make all this come true. Now the place is still there, but the one who knew me is gone and I can do nothing but sigh deeply. (24)

Shen Fu's response to his feelings of impotence take shape in the next record in his obsessive impulse to fight back against the disappointments of his life by controlling reality on a miniature scale.

CONTRIVED NATURE

In the second record, "Charms of Idleness," Shen Fu lovingly describes pastimes—gardening, growing bonsai trees, arranging flowers, writing poetry, painting—that are based on a love of nature, but also on his impulse to contrive natural scenes. He opens the record with his childhood memories of seeing the miniature world as something larger in his mind's eye:

I would often crouch down in the ditches by the earthen walls or among the thickly growing plants in flower beds, my eyes level with the ground. I would watch patiently until the plants appeared to me as a forest, insects as great beasts, small mounds in the gravel as mountains, dips as ravines—I would let my spirit roam over all of them without a care in the world.

One day, I saw two insects struggling among the blades of grass; I was observing them intently when a gigantic monster suddenly arrived on the scene, pulling up mountains and knocking over trees in its path. It was actually a toad, and it gulped down both insects with a flick of its tongue. I was still young at the time and had been so enrapt in the scene that my mouth fell open in shock. Once I calmed down, I caught the toad and gave it a good thrashing before banishing it from the yard. Now that I am older, I think back on that battle of the two insects and realize that it was likely an act of rape in progress. The old saying has it that "rape is close to killing." Could this be true for insects as well? (35)

Even these small worlds are subject to the chaos of sex and violence, over which the young Shen Fu attempts to exert some influence through punishment and banishment.

The child, who used the power of his imagination to create a world larger than life, grows into a man, who in reaction to his larger life spinning out of control in terms of finances and relationships turns to miniature pastimes in which he is able to calibrate every variable. Virtually the entire second record is taken up with lists of various rules for flower arranging, growing bonsai, designing gardens, staging mock poetry examinations, hosting picnics, even offering tips on frugality in home decorating and fashion. In every case, the goal is to produce the appearance of things being exactly as you want them to be:

Then you push pins up through a thin slip of copper and affix it to the inside of a pot using the hot glue. After the glue cools down, tie up a bundle of flowers with fine wire and stick them onto the pins at the bottom of the pot, making sure that they are at angles for maximum effect and not just sitting in the middle. Then spread the stems apart and ensure that the leaves are clearly separated and not all crammed together. Finally, add water and a small amount of decorative sand to cover up the copper slips at the bottom. The ideal effect has been achieved when the viewer mistakes the arrangement for live flowers actually growing in the pot. (38)

The degree and frequency of Shen Fu's attempts to keep up the appearance of a serene and elegant life of leisure are so relentless in "Charms of Idleness" that the artifice soon wears thin. As happens in the first record on "Delights of Marriage," reality eventually breaks through.

Shen Fu enlists his wife Yun in fashioning miniature scenes; she even provides him with invaluable advice on how to increase the realistic quality of his creations. Together they spend countless hours designing and planting a tiny natural idyll in a ceramic basin, then they proceed to label everything in it, imbuing their creation with the value that comes from the power of naming:

> We placed the basin outside under the eaves, where Yun and I could appreciate and comment on various spots: here we would build a waterside pavilion; here was perfect for a thatched gazebo; here was a nice spot for an inscription reading, "Betwixt falling blossoms and flowing water"; here we could make our home; here we could fish; and from here we could survey it all. We harbored these mountains and ravines in our hearts as though we might actually be able to move there one day. (43)

Reality intrudes in the shape of two stray cats:

> But one night a pair of worthless cats slipped from the eaves while fighting over some food and smashed the basin and stand to pieces in the blink of an eye. I sighed and said to Yun, "Even this small effort of ours has made the Fashioner of Things jealous!" The two of us could not hold back our tears. (43)

Shen Fu interprets this incident as nature itself asserting its dominance, rebuffing his attempts to build something shielded from the external forces constantly dogging his and Yun's efforts to lead a happy existence together. It is the forces of disorder—largely a lack of money—that constantly threaten the most fundamental relationships in Shen Fu's life, those with his family, friends, and even with his beloved Yun. All the misery that was held in check for the first two records bursts onto the page in the third.

FAILED RELATIONSHIPS

In the third record, "Sorrows of Hardship," Shen Fu reveals that his relationships with his family and friends are tragically compromised by his constant need for money. The familiar pattern of being unable to completely attain an ideal reasserts itself, but this time as the relentless and explicit theme of the record, rather than something to be kept at bay.

> When my wife, Yun, and I were living at home we were sometimes forced to pawn something when the need arose. At first we were able to make ends meet, but it became more and more difficult to go on in that fashion—as the saying goes, "Without cash one soon finds both house and home in decline." What started out as petty gossip among nobodies eventually brought us the ridicule of our own family.

...

Although I am the senior son in my family, I am the third child, so everyone used to call Yun Third Lady. One day someone happened to call her Third Madam in jest and though it began as a joke it became a habit until everyone, of every station and age, was calling her Third Madam. Sometimes I wonder if this was when all our troubles began. (55)

"Madam" (Taitai) was a title reserved for the wives of high officials and was inappropriate for the wife of a commoner such as Shen Fu. The "Third" designation also implied that he had at least two other wives. The term "Third Madam" was being used as a form of ironic mockery that violated the basic Confucian principle that everyone should occupy a properly defined role in a society. A lack of money brings about a lack of respect, which brings about a lack of etiquette, signaling a breakdown in the proper order of the world.

In "Sorrows of Hardship," a toxic mixture of poverty, class insecurity, and perceived slights to family honor poisons the relationship between Shen Fu and his parents and brother (Qitang), particularly in relation to his spouse Yun. This breakdown comes to a head in an episode when Shen Fu's father intercepts a letter from Yun meant for Shen Fu, in which she mentions his family's financial troubles and his mother's anger over his father taking a concubine. Shen Fu's father threatens to banish Yun from the family:

When my father saw all of this in the letter, he was enraged. He questioned Qitang about the matter with the neighbor, but Qitang said that he knew nothing about it. So father wrote to set me straight, chastising me. "Your wife borrowed money behind your back and put the blame on her brother-in-law," he said. "And then she referred to her mother-in-law as 'your mother' and even called me, her father-in-law, 'your old man'—this is all simply disgraceful! I have already dispatched someone to Suzhou with a letter dismissing your wife from the family and if you have the least bit of human sentiment left, you will acknowledge the error of your ways!" (57)

Violations involving money and etiquette over familial appellations are at the heart of Yun's crimes, but she becomes even worse in her father-in-law's eyes when she starts consorting as a sworn sister with a courtesan, whom she wishes to procure as a concubine for Shen Fu. Even this false family relationship based purely on money, which Yun is naive enough to mistake as one based on genuine affection, is not seen to its completion: the courtesan, Hanyuan, is snatched up by a wealthy man who is able to offer her a better life than Shen Fu and Yun ever could.

Money manages to compromise the central relationship of the book: the twenty-three year marriage between Shen Fu and Chen Yun. Shen Fu's inability to make enough money to support his family places an ultimately fatal strain on Yun's mental and physical health:

Alas, my poor Yun! She had all the breadth of mind, ability, and talent of a man but was born a woman. After she came to live with me as my wife, I was rushing about every day to keep us fed and clothed, and even though we often ran short of money, Yun was always careful not to be resentful. Whenever I was at home, we would pass the time with nothing more than our discussions and debates about literature. That she should end her days in illness and poverty and die with a heart full of pain—who brought this about? It was I who betrayed my true companion among women; is there anything more that I can say? I have some advice for the husbands and wives of this world: while you must not hate one another, nor should you love one another too much. They say that "a loving couple never makes it to the end"; the path I took could certainly serve as a lesson to others. (73)

Poverty forces them to give up their children when they can longer support them, and compels Shen Fu to constantly travel in search of work. (It is during a trip to sell merchandise in Guangzhou that Shen Fu takes up with a prostitute who reminds him of Yun, living a temporary life of ease with her that he was unable to attain with his wife.) The debilitating lack of money that is a constant refrain in the third record causes one to reevaluate the happy moments described in the other three records. How real can the "Delights of Marriage," "Charms of Idleness," and "Pleasures of Roaming" be when the "Sorrows of Hardship" are so powerful and insistent? One is reminded of a passage in D. H. Lawrence's famous story "The Rocking Horse Winner" in which he describes a middle-class family struggling to maintain appearances: "There was always the grinding sense of the shortage of money, though the style was always kept up … . And so the house came to be haunted by the unspoken phrase: *There must be more money! There must be more money!* The children could hear it all the time though nobody ever said it aloud" (Lawrence 1995: 230).

Shen Fu is reduced to fighting with his brother over their inheritance as their father lies unburied in his casket just inside the house. He is forever sending his daughter to pawn goods; he lives off the generosity of friends, even staying with them for long stretches; and he frequently calls on distant relatives to borrow money. It is his unceasing need for more money that drives much of the traveling he recounts in the final record of his book.

TRANSIENT TRUTHS

In the fourth record, "Pleasures of Roaming," Shen Fu seems torn between his desire to roam freely in a transient state, and his need to constantly label and explain everything, to try to pin down a permanent truth value for his experiences. He opens the record with a short disquisition on the variability of opinions:

> In all matters I enjoy forming my own opinion rather than blindly following what others say is good or bad. Especially in discussing poems or judging paintings I am always of a mind to reject what others treasure while choosing what others reject. So too with famous scenic sites: whether I esteem them or not is found in my own heart. There are some famous spots that I do not feel are particularly beautiful, and there are others not so famous that I personally feel are quite superb. So here I have made a record of all the places that I have visited over the course of my life. (85)

This opening passage establishes Shen Fu's prerogative to form his own opinions, even as it undercuts the truth value of opinions in general as nothing more than subjective interpretations. Throughout the record, Shen Fu obsessively names and dates the places he visits, contextualizes them with references to history and literature, then passes judgment on them. Just as Sima Qian, the Grand Historian, corralled the myriad episodes of China's long history into a systematic form and appended his interpretations to them in the *Historical Records* (Shiji), so too does Shen Fu attempt to bring order to his peregrinations. Being a literary man, he cannot help but read the landscape as a form of writing to be delineated and evaluated:

> After crossing the bridge, you see a three-story building with painted ridgepoles and upturned flying eaves in all sorts of brilliant colors. There are mounds of decorative rocks from Lake Tai and the whole place is ringed by a balustrade of white stone. It is named the Abode of Many Splendid Clouds and it is positioned in the park like the climax at the height of a literary composition. Just past it is a spot called Sunny Slope of Shu Ridge, a flat place of no particular interest that has been stuck on as a kind of forced addendum to the main work. (95)

It is in this final record that one gains a true sense of Shen Fu's yearning for a stable place where he might build the foundations for a happy life away from the demands of reality. He seems to find it briefly when he accompanies his friend, Xia Yishan, to collect rent from a rural community of farmers in in the undeveloped county of Chongming (near modern-day Shanghai):

> The tenant farmers lived scattered between the fields like a constellation of stars, but Ding could gather all of them with a single shout. They all addressed the owner of their property as "Landlord" and were very compliant in listening to his orders with a charming unaffected sincerity. Yet if they were stirred by an injustice, they could be wilder than any wolf or tiger. Fortunately, one word of fair treatment would quickly

return them to a proper attitude of respect. They lived by the wind and rain, in the darkness and the light, as the ancients used to do.

I would lie in my bed at night and look out my window to watch the billowing waves. From my pillow the sound of the surging tide sounded like singing gongs and booming drums. One night I caught sight of a red light as big as a wicker basket, floating in the ocean about ten miles offshore. Then I saw red rays of light illuminating the sky so brightly it seemed to catch fire. Shichu told me, "When divine lights and fires appear in this region, it means that a new sandbar will soon emerge from the waters."

Yishan always had a bold and carefree spirit about him, but when he came to this place he was even more liberated. I too was more unbridled in my behavior and took to singing out wildly from atop an ox and dancing drunkenly on the beach. I just followed my impulses wherever they might lead, and it truly was the most unrestrained, delightful trip that I have made in my entire life. It was already November by the time we wrapped up our affairs and returned home. (124)

In this primitive land, which is still literally being born out of the ocean, Shen Fu finds a place free of the constraints of marriage, family, and money. It is, nonetheless, the financial task of rent collection that takes him there, and his own need for money that compels him to leave. The brief respite he finds in Chongming echoes his frequent allusions elsewhere in his records to the famous account of Peach Blossom Spring by the poet Tao Qian (365–427). The story tells of a fisherman who follows a stream lined with peach trees to its source behind a cliff, where he finds a hidden village that has been cut off from the outside world for centuries and still follows a simple way of life. The villagers are astonished by his arrival and treat him with great hospitality during his stay. After he returns home he reports his discovery to the local officials but is never able to find his way back again.

Anytime Shen Fu thinks he has found an ideal spot for a garden and a home, his need to pursue income draws him away:

I lived in the south part of the garden in a small boat-shaped building with an earthen mound in its courtyard. Atop the mound was a small gazebo I could climb to take in the whole layout of the garden. It was enclosed by cool green shade on all sides and provided respite from the summer heat. Zhuotang wrote the words "Unmoored Boat" on the lintel for me. In all my travels in search of employment this was the most pleasant place to live. Several dozen varieties of chrysanthemum had been planted on the earthen mound, but sadly they did not even have a chance to bud before Zhuotang was transferred to the post of Provincial Surveillance Commissioner in Shandong Province. His family moved to live at Tongchuan Academy and I went with them to take up residence there. (132–133)

When Shen Fu's employer, Zhuotang, chooses the phrase "Unmoored Boat" as the title for Shen Fu's abode, he is making a double-edged selection. It comes from a well-known passage in Chapter 32 of *Zhuangzi*: "A skillful man toils, a wise man worries, but a man without ability seeks nothing and is happy to roam about with a full belly; adrift as an unmoored boat, he roams without purpose." Interpreted in an ideal light, the quotation is a reference to a Daoist state of ease in transience, a recognition that the ultimate truth cannot be captured with the mundane qualities of skill or wisdom. In a more realistic light, the allusion could be seen as a biting characterization of Shen Fu as "a man without ability" who "roams without purpose"—though, unlike a Daoist sage living a life "adrift as an unmoored boat," Shen Fu's belly is seldom full.

Reading the final record on "Pleasures of Roaming" directly after the previous record on the "Sorrows of Hardship" produces a painful contrast between the happy face Shen Fu puts on his itinerant lifestyle and the relentless financial urgency that the reader now knows drives him ever onward. What makes Shen Fu a literary genius is that he is fully aware of this contrast and exploits it for artistic effect, making it the centerpiece of his powerful third record of suffering, while still letting it show through briefly in the ostensibly happier records that surround it. He acknowledges the illusory nature of his happiness, but cherishes it all the more for its ephemerality. It can be no accident that he chooses to end his fourth record with the following episode:

> In March of the following year I took up my assignment at Laiyang in Shandong. In the autumn of 1807 Zhuotang was demoted to the Hanlin Academy and I also went to the capital. As for what is known as the Ocean Mirage of Dengzhou, I never did find a way to see it in the end. (135)

The ocean mirage of Dengzhou is a Fata Morgana type of mirage that occurs seasonally off the coast of Shandong, producing the illusion of an entire city floating over the water. The Song poet Su Shi (1037–1101) wrote a poem on the phenomenon called "Ocean City" (Haishi): "Swirling and tossing, this world adrift gives rise to myriad forms, / could those palaces of pearl, behind cowry gates, really be there?" Shen Fu could not have chosen a more appropriate image than a missed opportunity to witness an unreal apparition to close his records of a life based on ideal aspirations meeting repeatedly with failure. "I never did find a way to see it in the end."

The enduring literary value of *Six Records of a Life Adrift* is that it is able to capture multiple facets of Shen Fu's life—his happy memories and his sad realities, his fondest dreams and his crushing disappointments—placing them side-by-side without choosing between them. Shen Fu's literary technique holds out a way to reconstitute a sense of self in a modern age that constantly seeks to fragment our self-presentation over a broader array of media channels—emails, blogs, status updates, tweets, keywords—all are short and discrete, and often unrelated. Shen Fu shows us how to embrace fragments and weave them into a meaningful whole, but one that still retains the rough, real edges of the pieces from which it is fashioned—just as Yun liked to do with her pastime of compiling "bits and pieces" of old books and "scraps of appreciation" from old paintings. In an age when many people feel increasingly alienated and isolated despite being more connected, perhaps we can look to Shen Fu's records of his life centuries ago to find a way of being more lyrical and poetic about our own lives, by paying attention to the emotional tenor of our memories and experiences, and not working too hard to reconcile the dissonant strands of our stories.

GLOSSARY

A Cheng	阿城
"A Ti"	阿嚏
"Aogu"	傲骨
Ba Jin	巴金
bai	白
Bai Juyi	白居易
Bai Xianyong	白先勇
Bainian shenghuo jiyi tezhan	百年生活記憶特展
banhu	板胡
bao	報
"Baochai chan yu"	寶釵產玉
"Baochai daixiu"	寶釵代繡
Bei hai de ren	背海的人
biji	筆記
bieji	別集
binzhu	賓主
"Bing che xing"	兵車行
Bing Xin	冰心
Bingxin wenxue jiang	冰心文學獎
"Bu ni"	補呢
buyifa	步移法
Cai shi	蔡氏
Cai Yuanzhi	蔡遠智
Cao Cao	曹操
Cao Ren	曹仁
Cao Xueqin	曹雪芹
Caozhu yichuan	草珠一串
"Chan hai"	讒害
"Changhen ge"	長恨歌
chaoran	超然
"Che lin"	車鄰
Chen Gong	陳宮
Chen Jinzhao	陳錦釗
Chen Kaige	陳凱歌
Chen Pingyuan	陳平原
Chen Ruoxi	陳若曦
Chen Shuibian	陳水扁
Chen Yun	陳芸
"Chengzhu"	城主
chi cun qian li	尺寸千里
"Chi dui"	癡對
Chitu ma	赤兔馬
Chiang Ching-kuo	蔣經國
chong	衝

Chongming	崇明
Chuci	楚辭
"Chunling huaqiang"	椿齡畫薔
"Chunyeyan congdi taohuayuan xu"	春夜宴從弟桃花源序
ci	詞
cu	鼛
da najia	大拿家
Dahong denglong gaogao gua	大紅燈籠高高掛
Dajia de bowuguan	大家的博物館
Dajia na	大家拿
Datian	大田
Daxue yanyi bu	大學演義補
"Daiyu zang hua"	黛玉葬花
Dai Yuan	戴員
danxian	單弦
dangwai	黨外
Dao	道
Daoguang	道光
Daoxiang cun	稻香村
De Shuoting	得碩亭
"Deng"	燈
di	坻
diji/yudizhi	地記/輿地誌
diaobaoji	調包計
Diaochan	貂蟬
die	坒
Ding Yuan	丁原
Dong Yue	董說
Dong Zhuo	董卓
Du Fu	杜甫
Du Zhengsheng	杜正勝
duan qianbai zhi gong'an	斷千百之公案
Dulü peixi	讀律佩觿
Duo Guniang	多姑娘
duoyuan	多元
Erchen zhuan	貳臣傳
Ererba jinianguan	二二八紀念館
erhu	二胡
"Er ru Rongguo fu"	二入榮國府
"Eryu lun xin"	二玉論心
"Fen gao"	焚稿
Feng Jian	冯建
Feng Xiaogang	馮小剛
"Fengjie'r songxing"	鳳姐兒送行
fengliu yunshi	風流韻事
fengyue baojian	風月寶鑒
fuguo	復國
Fusheng liuji	浮生六記
Fuxi Fuxi	伏羲伏羲
ganjue	感覺
gankai	感慨
ganshi youguo	感時憂國
ganshou	感受
Gao E	高鶚

Gao Juehui	高覺慧
Gao Juexin	高覺新
Gaoyou	高郵
"Ge Tianmin"	葛天民
Ge You	葛尤
gemingde dawutai	革命的大舞臺
gongming	功名
goulan wasi	勾欄瓦肆
"Gu"	谷
guci	鼓詞
Guan Yu	關羽
Gui Lan	嫣覽
Guo Xi	郭熙
"Guoji Qiaojie'r"	過繼巧姐兒
"Guxiang"	故鄉
Guofu jinianguan	國父紀念館
Guoli gugong bowuyuan	國立故宮博物院
Guoli lishi bowuguan	國立歷史博物館
Guoli Taiwan lishi bowuguan	國立台灣歷史博物館
Guoli Taiwan renquan bowuguan	國立台灣人權博物館
Guoyu	國語
"Guoyuan cheng"	果園城
Guoyuan cheng ji	果園城記
"Haishi"	海市
"Haitang jieshe"	海棠結社
Han Shiqi	韓士奇
Han Xiaochuang	韓小窗
Han Huandi	漢桓帝
Han Lingdi	漢靈帝
Han Xiandi	漢獻帝
Hanyangfu	漢陽府
Hanyuan	憨園
Haohan	好漢
he	合
"He Wenlong de wengao"	賀文龍的文稿
Helü shi	鶴侶氏
Hong gaoliang jiazu	紅高粱家族
Honglou meng	紅樓夢
hongxiang lüyu	紅香綠玉
Hu Guangping	胡光平
Hu Shi	胡適
Huguang	湖廣
"Hua shanshui xu"	畫山水序
Hua Xiong	華雄
huaben	話本
huaju	話劇
huangliang meimeng	黃粱美梦
Huang mao	黃毛
huangmei xi	黃梅戲
Huazong shijie huawen wenxue jiang	花踪世界華文文學獎
Huang Lizhen	黃麗貞
Huang tudi	黃土地
Huang Shuning	黃恕寧
"Hun cha"	婚詫

Huozhe	活著
huiyi zi	會意字
ji	記
ji	積
Jia Baoyu	賈寶玉
Jia bian	家變
Jia bian liu jiang	家變六講
Jianada	加拿大
Jia-Na-Da	嘉-娜-达
jian xiong	奸雄
Jiaqing	嘉庆
Jia Qiang	賈薔
jiangou Taiwanren gongtong de lishi jiyi	建構臺灣人共同的歷史記憶
jianghu yiren	江湖藝人
Jiaochuang	蕉窗
jie menfan	解悶煩
Jiehun	結婚
Jin Shengtan	金聖嘆
Jinqiao	金橋
"Jinsuo ji"	金鎖記
jinyu liangyuan	金玉良緣
jing	景
Jingmei renquan wenhua yuanqu	景美人權文化園區
Jin Ping Mei	金瓶梅
jingyin zidishu	京音子弟書
jingyun dagu	京韻大鼓
Jubian yu xin zhixu	巨變與新秩序
Judou	菊豆
juancun wenhua	眷村文化
"Jue bi"	決婢
kai	開
Kaidagelan wenhuaguan	凱打格籃文化館
kan	崁
Kangxi	康熙
"Kongque dongnan fei"	孔雀東南飛
"Ku yu"	哭玉
kunqu	昆曲
kwei-lo	鬼佬
lamei	臘梅
langzhong	郎中
Lao She	老舍
"Laoshu peng cha qing renke"	老鼠捧茶請人客
Lee Teng-hui	李登輝
lei	累
Lei	蕾
"Lei ji"	誄祭
Leiyu	雷雨
li	理
li	里
Li Bai	李白
Li Dian	李典
Li He	李賀
Li Oufan	李歐梵
Li Shen	李紳

Li Su	李蕭
lihen	離恨
lishi fansi	歷史反思
Liang Shanbo yu Zhu Yingtai	梁山伯與祝英台
Liangshi	亮士
liao	繚
Lienü zhuan	列女傳
Lin Daiyu	林黛玉
Lin Jingjie	林靖傑
Lin Mengyu	林梦雨
Limen shiji	里門拾記
lingchi	凌遲
Liu Bei	劉備
Liu Biao	劉表
Liu Shaoming	劉紹銘
Liu Zhenyu	劉振玉
"Liuye liezhuan"	劉爺列傳
linchuan gaozhi	林泉高致
Lingling	零陵
Liu Zongyuan	柳宗元
liushu	六書
Lü Bu	呂布
Lü Lizheng	呂理政
Lu Ruixue	魯瑞雪
Lu Sheng	盧生
Lu Xun	魯迅
Lüdao renquan wenhua yuanqu	綠島人權文化園區
"Lulei yuan"	露淚緣
Luo Guanzhong	羅貫中
Luo Songchuang	羅松窗
"Luori guang"	落日光
Ma Lan	馬蘭
matou diao	馬頭調
"Maixiang duoyuan minzhu de shehui"	迈向多元民主的社会
Mancheng jindai huangjin jia	滿城盡帶黃金甲
Manshu zhenjun	曼殊震鈞
Mao Lun	毛綸
Mao Zonggang	毛宗崗
meihua dagu	梅花大鼓
"Meng Anqing de tangxiongdi"	孟安卿的堂兄弟
miaoxie	描寫
miaoxie jingguan/shanshui zhi xie	描摹景觀/山水之寫
min nong	悯农
Mo Yan	莫言
Mudan ting	牡丹亭
"Mulan ci"	木蘭辭
mushi zhi yuan	木石之緣
na dajia	拿大家
Nahan	吶喊
Nanbei chao	南北朝
Nanhua Laoxian	南華老仙
Nüwa	女媧
Ouyang Zi	歐陽子
Peinan wenhua	卑南文化

pifu lanyin	皮膚濫淫
piaoyou	票友
pingju	評劇
Pingpu	平埔
qi	其
Qi Baishi	齊白石
"Qi wang"	棋王
"Qi wu"	齊物
"Qidai"	期待
Qiqie chengqun	妻妾成群
Qitang	啟堂
Qianlong	乾隆
"Qian Qingwen"	遣晴雯
Qian Zhongshu	錢鍾書
qianliang	錢糧
qin	嶔
Qin Keqing	秦可卿
Qin Zhong	秦鐘
qing	情
qing	清
Qing Shi Gao	清史稿
qingmi Zhongguo lun	情迷中國論
qingshu	清書
qingyin zidishu	清音子弟書
qingyu	清語
Qiu Jun	丘濬
Qu Yuan	屈原
quhanhua	去漢化
"Quan beiqiu"	全悲秋
ren	人
"Rensheng gewang"	人生歌王
Rulin waishi	儒林外史
sandian toushi	散點透視
"Sange xiao renwu"	三個小人物
Sanguo zhi	三國志
Sanguo zhi yanyi	三國志演義
sanwen	散文
sanxian	三弦
"Sanxuan yapailing"	三宣牙牌令
san yuan	三遠
"Sha xie"	傻泄
Shan Fu (Xu Shu)	單福 (徐庶)
Shanshan de hongxing	閃閃的紅星
shanshui fu	山水賦
shanshui shi	山水詩
shanshui yishi	山水意識
shanshui youji	山水遊記
Shanghai shouzha	上海手札
Shen Congwen	沈從文
Shen Fu	沈復
Shen Jiji	沈既濟
"Shen shang"	神傷
Shen Xiangpei	沈湘佩
Sheng Jiqi	盛季琦

shi	事
shi	勢
Shi Tuo	師陀
"Shi xiangsi"	十相思
Shi Yukun	石玉昆
"Shiba sui chumen yuanxing"	十八歲出門遠行
shihua tongyuan	詩畫同源
Shiji	史記
Shijing	詩經
shipian	詩篇
Shisanhang bowuguan	十三行博物館
Shitou ji	石頭記
"Shoulie"	狩獵
shousha	收煞
"Shouye"	守夜
Shu	蜀
shufa ganshou	抒發感受
shuqing	抒情
"Shuangyu maihong"	雙玉埋紅
"Shuangyu tingqin"	雙玉聽琴
Shui Jing	水鏡
Shuihu zhuan	水滸傳
shuixian hua	水仙花
Shunyi Taiwan yuanzhumin bowuguan	順益台灣原住民博物館
Shunzong	順宗
shuoming	說明
"Shuoshuren"	說書人
sijiu	四舊
Situ simin: Taiwan de gushi	斯土斯民: 台灣的故事
"Siyu xihuan"	思玉戲環
Su Shi	蘇軾
Su Tong	蘇童
Su Xiaoxiao	蘇小小
Sun Quan	孫權
Sun Yikui	孫一奎
"Ta"	塔
Taitai	太太
Taiwan de gushi: kunhuo, bianhua, yu chongsheng	臺灣的故事: 困惑, 變化, 與重生
Taiwan ershisi shi	台灣二十四史
Taiwan guojia wenyi jiang	台灣國家文藝獎
Taiwan guoli shiqian bowuguan	台灣國立史前博物館
Taiwan minbao	台灣民報
Taiwan wenhua xiehui	台灣文化協會
Tan Hong	譚洪
"Tanbing"	探病
tanci kaipian	彈詞開篇
Tang Xianzu	湯顯祖
Tangshan dadizhen	唐山大地震
Tao Qian	陶潛
"Taohong"	桃紅
"Tong bie"	慟別
tonggan	通感
tongqingde muguang	同情的目光

wa	洼
wanhua	萬化
Wang Kentang	王肯堂
Wang Mang	王莽
Wang Mingde	王明德
Wang Qiao	王樵
Wang Shuwen	王叔文
Wang Wei	王維
Wang Wenxing	王文興
Wang Wenxing shougao ji	王文興手稿集
Wang Xinzhan	王心湛
Wang Yongji	王永吉
Wang Yibu xiansheng Lüli jianshi	王儀部先生律例箋釋
Wang Yun	王允
Wang Zhaojun	王昭君
Wang Zhenhe	王禎和
"Wangshi yu xingfa"	往事與刑法
Wei	魏
wei zidishu	衛子弟書
Wei-Jin	魏晋
wen	文
wenhua fansi	文化反思
wo xiang ni	我想你
Wolong Nanyang (Zhuge Liang)	臥龍南陽
wu (thing)	物
Wu (state of)	吳
wu (military)	武
Wu Jinxiao	烏盡孝
Wu Jingzi	吳敬梓
"Wu xi"	誤喜
wuyu hua	物語化
Xi Xi	西西
Xi Xiangji	西廂記
xilao lianpin	惜老憐貧
Xiyuan lu	洗冤錄
Xiyou bu	西游補
Xiyou ji	西遊記
xia	岈
Xia Han	夏菡
Xia Zhiqing (C.T. Hsia)	夏志清
Xia Ji'an	夏濟安
Xia Xiaohong	夏曉虹
Xia Yishan	夏揖山
xian mu	賢母
xian xiaoqian	閑消遣
Xiandai wenxue	現代文學
"Xiandai Zhongguo wenxueshi sizhong heping"	現代中國文學史四種合評
xiang de wo	想得我
xiangtu	鄉土
"Xiangyun zuijiu"	湘雲醉酒
xiao	孝
xiaoshuo jiayan	小說家言
Xiaoxiang guan	瀟湘館

xin wenxue	新文學
xinwenxue de chuantong	新文學的傳統
xinyu hua	心語化
xingji/youzongji	行記/遊踪記
xingsheng zi	形聲字
Xu shi	徐氏
Xu Shu	徐庶
xushi	敘事
xushi	虛實
Xuanzong	玄宗
xue	穴
Xue Baochai	薛寶釵
xungen	尋根
Yazhou zhoukan	亞洲周刊
yan	岩
Yan Yuanshu	顏元叔
"Yan'an wenyi zuotanhui shang de jianghua"	延安座談會上的講話
yancheng	演成
yanleide kuanguang	眼淚的寬廣
"Yanliao he"	顏料盒
Yang Wanli	楊萬里
Yang Yuhuan	楊玉環
Yangzhou qingqu	揚州清曲
"Yao"	藥
Ye Weilian	葉維廉
yi	佾
"Yi wen"	一吻
Yige he bage	一個和八個
yigui	縊鬼
yihong kuailü	怡紅快綠
yijue	移覺
yilun	議論
yisheng tuoyi	以聲托意
yixing biaoyi	以形表意
yiyang	弋陽
yiyin	意淫
yin	淫
yinsheng	蔭生
yinsheng	廕生
yingxi	影戲
yin-yang	陰陽
ying	縈
Yongzheng	雍正
Yongzhou	永州
Yongzhou baji	永州八記
you Tangshan gong, wu Tangshan ma	有唐山公, 無唐山媽
"Youchai xiansheng"	郵差先生
youzong jishu	遊踪記述
yu	嶼
yu	欲
Yujian Taiwan: yige duo wenhua de daoyu	遇見台灣一個多文化的島嶼
"Yu sao"	遇嫂
yushi bingjin	與時並進
"Yuxiang hua yu"	玉香花語

Yuan Shao	袁紹
Yuanchun	元春
yuanwen	原文
Yuanzhi (Xu Shu)	元直
yue ju	越劇
Yun	芸
yunshi	韵事
zai buneng	再不能
Zeng Xiaowen	曾曉文
"Zeng zhi"	贈指
zha	猹
Zhang Ailing	張愛玲
Zhang Fei	張飛
Zhang Jue	張角
Zhang Junzhao	張軍釗
Zhang Tianyi	張天翼
Zhang Xinzhi	張新之
Zhao Yun	趙雲
"Zhen zhong ji"	枕中記
Zheng Chenggong	鄭成功
Zheng Hengxiong	鄭恆雄
Zheng Zhenduo	鄭振鐸
zhiguai	志怪
zhonglie zhuan	忠烈傳
"Zhongsheng zhengyan de niandai"	眾聲爭言的年代
Zhongwen da cidian	中文大辭典
Zhongzheng jiniantang	中正紀念堂
Zhou Guozheng	周國正
Zhou Houyu	周厚堉
Zhuge Liang	諸葛亮
zhugongdiao	諸宮調
zhutixing	主體性
zhuzhi ci	竹枝詞
zhuyin fuhao	注音符號
"Zhuangshi jiangxiang"	莊氏降香
Zhuangzi	莊子
zi	字
zichuangzi	自創字
zidishu	子弟書
"Ziditu"	子弟圖
zi buyu guai	子不語怪
Zong Bing	宗炳
zuan	攢
"Zuiwo Yihong yuan"	醉卧怡红院

BIBLIOGRAPHY

Allen, Joseph. 2011. *Taipei: City of Displacements*. Seattle: University of Washington Press.

Amae, Yoshihisa. 2011. "Pro-colonial or Postcolonial? Appropriation of Japanese Colonial Heritage in Present-day Taiwan." *Journal of Current Chinese Affairs* 40, no. 1: 19–62.

Ang, Ien. 1998. "Can One Say No to Chineseness? Pushing the Limits of the Diasporic Paradigm." *Boundary 2* 25, no. 3 (Fall): 223–242.

———. 2002. *On Not Speaking Chinese: Living between Asia and the West*. London: Routledge.

Anonymous. 1977. "Mulan shi" 木蘭辭 (Ode of Mulan). Tr. Han H. Frankel. In Frankel, *The Flowering Plum and the Palace Lady: Interpretations of Chinese Poetry*. New Haven: Yale University Press. URL (last accessed 4/29/13): http://www.chinapage.com/mulan.html.

Atherton, Carol. 2005. *Defining Literary Criticism: Scholarship, Authority and the Possession of Literary Knowledge, 1880-2002*. Houndmills: Palgrave Macmillan.

Atwood, Margret. 1972. *Surfacing*. New York: Popular Library.

Bachtin, Mikail. 1975. *Voprosy literatury i estetiki*. Moscow: Chudozestvennaia literatura.

Bai Chunchao 白春超. 2000. "Shi Tuo xiaoshuo de xiezuo celüe" 師陀小說的寫作策略 (Strategy in Shi Tuo's fiction writing). *Zhoukou shifan gaodeng zhuanke xuexiao xuebao* 17: 39–42.

Bailey, C. D. Alison. 2009. "Reading Between the Lines: The Representation and Containment of Disorder in Late Ming and Early Qing Legal Texts." *Ming Studies* 59 (May): 56–86.

Baker, Hugh D. R. 1983. "Life in the Cities: The Emergence of Hong Kong Man." *The China Quarterly* 95 (Sept.): 469–479.

Barker, Chris. 2005. *Cultural Studies: Theory and Practice*. London: Sage.

Bawden, C. R. 2009 [1968]. *The Modern History of Mongolia*. London: Routledge.

Bhabha, Homi K. 1994. *The Location of Culture*. London: Routledge.

———. 1995. "Cultural Diversity and Cultural Differences." In Bill Ashcroft, Gareth Griffiths, and Helen Tiffin, eds., *The Post-colonial Studies Reader*. London and New York: Routledge, 206–209.

Bergonzi, Bernard. 1990. *Exploding English: Criticism, Theory, Culture*. Oxford: Clarendon Press.

Besio, Kimberly. 1997. "Zhang Fei in Yuan Vernacular Literature: Legend, Heroism, and History in the Reproduction of the Three Kingdoms Story Cycle." *Journal of Sung-Yuan Studies* 27: 63–98.

Besio, Kimberley and Constantine Tung, eds., 2007. *Three Kingdoms and Chinese Culture*. Albany: State University of New York Press.

Bloom, Harold. 1973. *The Anxiety of Influence*. New York: Oxford University Press.

Bow, Leslie. 2001. *Betrayal and Other Acts of Subversion: Feminism, Sexual Politics, Asian American Women's Literature*. Princeton: Princeton University Press.

Bradford, Richard. 1994. *Roman Jakobson: Life, Language, Art*. London: Routledge.

Bromley, Roger. 2000. *Narrative for a New Belonging: Diasporic Cultural Fictions*. Edinburgh: Edinburgh University Press.

Brooks, Cleanth. 1940. "Literary History vs. Criticism." *The Kenyon Review* 2, no. 4: 403–412.

Brown, Melissa J. 2004. *Is Taiwan Chinese? The Impact of Culture, Power, and Migration on Changing Identities*. Berkeley: University of California Press.

Bush, Susan. 1971. *The Chinese Literati on Painting*. Cambridge, MA: Harvard University Press.

Bush, Susan and Shih Hsio-yen, eds. 1985. *Early Chinese Texts on Painting*. Cambridge, MA: Harvard University Press.

Cai Yi 蔡儀. 1952. *Zhongguo xinwenxue shi jianghua* 中國新文學史講話 (Talks on new Chinese literary history). Shanghai: Xinwenyi.

Cai Zhenzhang 蔡振璋. 2012. *Liu Zongyuan shanshui wenxue yanjiu* 柳宗元山水文學研究 (A study on landscape literature by Liu Zongyuan). In Zeng Yongyi, ed., *Gudian wenxue yanjiu jikan*. Xinbei: Huamulan wenhua, vol. 14.

Cao, Xueqin [曹雪芹]. 1973, 1977, and 1980. *The Story of the Stone*. Tr. David Hawkes. 3 vols. New York: Penguin.

———. 1982 and 1986. *The Story of the Stone*. Tr. John Minford. 2 vols. New York: Penguin.

Chan Kwok Kou 陳國球. 2004. *Wenxue shi shuxie xingtai yu wenhua zhengzhi* 文學史書寫形態與文化政治 (The modes of writings and cultural politics of literary histories: studies on Chinese literary historiography). Beijing: Beijing daxue.

Chang, Eileen. 1981. "The Golden Cangue." In Joseph S. M. Lau, Leo Ou-fan Lee, eds., *Modern Chinese Stories and Novellas 1919–1949*. New York: Columbia University Press, 530–559.

Chang, Bi-yu and Henning Klötter, eds. 2012. *Imaging and Imagining Taiwan: Identity Representation and Cultural Politics*. Wiesbaden: Harrassowitz.

Chang, Han-liang [張漢良]. 1992. "Graphemics and Novel Interpretation: The Case of Wang Wen-hsing." *Modern Chinese Literature* 6: 133–156.

———. 1973. "Qian tan *Jia bian* de wenzi" 淺談《家變》的文字 (A brief discussion of the language of *Family Catastrophe*). *Zhongwai wenxue* 1, no. 12: 122–139.

Chang Qie 昌切. 2006. "Qimengshi Liu Heng" 启蒙师刘恒 (Liu Heng, the enlightener). In Liu Heng, *Liu Heng jingxuanji* 刘恒精选集 (Selected works of Liu Heng). Beijing: Beijing Yanshan, i–x.

Chang, Shelly Hsueh-lun. 1990. *History and Legend: Ideas and Images in Ming Historical Novels*. Ann Arbor: University of Michigan Press.

Chang, Sung-sheng 張誦聖. 2001. "Xiandai zhuyi yu Taiwan xiandai pai xiaoshuo" 現代主義與臺灣現代派小說 (Modernism and modernist fiction from Taiwan). *Wenxue changyu de bianqian* 文學場域的變遷 (Changes in the field of literature). Taipei: Lianhe wenxue, 7–36.

———. 1993. *Modernism and the Narrativist Resistance: Contemporary Chinese Fiction from Taiwan*. Durham: Duke University Press.

Chen Jingkuan 陳靜寬. "Bowuguan de Taiwan shi yanjiu" 博物館的臺灣史研究 (Research on Taiwan history in museums). *Wenjianhua dianzi bao* (March 22, 2011). URL (no longer available): http://www.moc.gov.tw/epaper/20110322/page01.html

Chen, Jo-shui. 1992. *Liu Tsung-yuan and Intellectual Change in Tang China, 773–819*. New York: Cambridge University Press.

Chen, Ming-May Jessie, and Mazharul Haque. 2007. *Representation of the Cultural Revolution in Chinese Films by the Fifth Generation Filmmakers: Zhang Yimou, Chen Kaige, and Tian Zhuangzhuang*. Lewiston, NY: The Edwin Mellen Press.

Chen Ran 陳然. 2005. *Wu chu gaobie* 無處告別 (No Way to Say Goodbye). Nanjing: Jiangsu wenyi.

Cheng Huizhe 程惠哲. 2010. *Dianyin dui xiaoshuo de kuayue—Zhang Yimou yingpian yanjiu* 电影对小说的跨越—张艺谋影片研究 (Film does more than fiction—a study of Zhang Yimou's Films). Beijing: Zhongguo dianying.

Cheng Weijun 成伟均, et al. 1991. *Xiuci tongjian* 修辞通鉴 (Comprehensive dictionary of rhetoric). Beijing: Beijing qingnian.

Cheung, King-kok. 1993. *Articulate Silences: Hisaye Yamanoto, Maxine Hong Kingston, Joy Kogawa*. Ithaca: Cornell University Press.

Chi Li 池莉. 1993. "Ni shi yitiao he" 你是一條河 (You are a river). In Chi, *Yumou sharen* 預謀殺人 (Premeditated murder). Beijing: Zhongguo shehui kexue, 57–129.

Chin Wan 陳雲. 2011. *Xianggang chengbang lun* 香港城邦論 (On Hong Kong as a city state). Hong Kong: Enrich Publishing.

Chinese Literature: Essays, Articles, Reviews. 1985. "Chih-Tsing Hsia (C. T. Hsia) Publications." 7: 217–223.

Chiu, Suet Ying Chiu. 2007. *Cultural Hybridity in Manchu Bannermen Tales (Zidishu)*. Ph.D. diss. Los Angeles: University of California.

Chow, Rey. 1995. *Primitive Passions: Visuality, Sexuality, Ethnography, and Contemporary Chinese Cinema.* New York: Columbia University Press.

——. 1997. "Can One Say No to China?" *New Literary History* 28, no. 1: 147–151.

——. 1998. "Between Colonizers: Hong Kong's Postcolonial Self-writing in the 1990s." In Chow, *Ethics after Idealism: Theory, Culture, Ethnicity, Reading.* Bloomington: Indiana University Press, 149–167.

Chu, Yingchi. 2003. *Hong Kong Cinema: Coloniser, Motherland and Self.* London: Routledge.

Corcuff, Stephane, ed. 2002. *Memories of the Future: National Identity Issues and the Search for a New Taiwan.* Armonk, NY: M. E. Sharpe.

Cornelius, Sheila. 2002. *New Chinese Cinema: Challenging Representations.* London: Wallflower.

Crystal, David, ed. 1997. *The Cambridge Encyclopedia of Language.* 2nd ed. Cambridge: Cambridge University Press.

Cua, Antonio S., ed. 2003. *Encyclopedia of Chinese Philosophy.* London: Routledge.

Cui, Shuqin. 1997. "Gendered Perspective: The Construction and Representation of Subjectivity and Sexuality in *Ju Dou.*" In Sheldon Hsiao-peng Lu, ed., *Transnational Chinese Cinemas: Identity, Nationhood, Gender.* Honolulu: University of Hawaii Press, 303–329.

Cui Yunhua 崔蘊華. 2005. *Shuzhai yu shufang zhijian: Qingdai zidishu yanjiu* 書齋與書坊之間: 清代子弟書研究 (Between study and bookshop: the study of the Manchu Bannermen tales). Beijing: Beijing daxue.

Curtin, Jeremiah. 1908. *The Mongols: A History.* Boston: Little, Brown and Co.

Davis, Rocío G. 2002. "Everyone's Story: Narrative *You* in Chitra Bannerjee Divakaruni's 'The Word Love'." In Rocío G. Davis and Sämi Ludwig, eds., *Asian American Literature in the International Context: Readings on Fiction, Poetry, and Performance.* Hamburg: Lit Verlag, 173–183.

deBold, Elizabeth, Marie Wilson, and Idelisse Malave. 1993. *Mother Daughter Revolution: From Good Girls to Great Women.* New York: Addison-Wesley.

DeGolyer, Michael E. 2007. "Identity in the Politics of Transition: The Case of Hong Kong, 'Asia's World City'." In Kwok-bun Chan, Jan W. Walls, and David Hayward, eds., *East-West Identities: Globalization, Localization, and Hybridization.* Leiden: Brill, 21–54.

Denton, Kirk A. *Exhibiting the Past: Historical Memory and the Politics of Museums in Postsocialist China.* Honolulu: University of Hawaii Press, 2014.

Ding Yi 丁易. 1957. *Zhongguo xiandai wenxue shilüe* 中國現代文學史略 (An outline of modern Chinese literary history). Beijing: Zuojia.

Doležel, Lubomír. 1973. *Narrative Modes in Czech Literature.* Toronto: University of Toronto Press.

——. 1994. "Prague School Structuralism." In Michael Groden and Martin Kreiswirth, eds., *The Johns Hopkins Guide to Literary Theory and Criticism.* Baltimore: Johns Hopkins University Press, 592–595.

Doleželová-Velingerová, Milena, ed. 2006. *Jaroslav Průšek, 1906–2006: Remembered by Friends.* Prague: DharmaGaia.

Doleželová-Velingerová, Milena and Lubomír Doležel. 1972. "An Early Chinese Confessional Prose: Shen Fu's *Six Chapters of a Floating Life.*" *T'oung Pao* (Second Series) 58, no. 1/5 (1972): 137–160.

Drysburgh, Marjorie, and Sarah Dauncey, eds. 2013. *Writing Lives in China, 1600–2010: Histories of the Elusive Self.* Basingstoke: Palgrave Macmillan.

Du Fu 杜甫. "Bing che xing" 兵車行 (Ballad of the army carts). Tr. Dave Bonta. URL (last accessed 4/29/13): http://www.vianegativa.us/2007/06/ballad-of-the-army-carts/.

Elliot, Kamilla. 2003. *Rethinking the Novel/Film Debate.* New York and Cambridge: Cambridge University Press.

Emerson, Ken. 1997. *Doo-dah!: Stephen Foster and the Rise of American Popular Culture.* New York: Simon and Schuster.

Fang Fang 方方. 1996. *Fengjing* 風景 (Landscape). Nanjing: Jiangsu wenyi.

Feng Qiyong 馮其庸, et al. 2000. eds., *Bajia pingpi Honglou meng* 八家評批《紅樓夢》 (Eight commentaries on *Honglou meng*). Nanchang: Jiangxi jiaoyu.

Fanon, Frantz. 1963. "On National Culture." In Fanon, *The Wretched of the Earth.* London: Paladin.

Fong, Gilbert C. F. 方梓勳. 1998. "Gangdu yu ma ji qita—yiming yu yishixingtai" 港督與馬及其他——譯名與意識形態 (Governors, horses, and others—translated names and ideology). In Serena Jin, ed., *Fanyi Xueshu Huiyi: Waiwen zhongyi yanjiu yu tantao* 翻譯學術會議: 外文中譯研究與探討 (Conference on Translation: Studies in Translating into Chinese]. Hong Kong: Department of Translation, The Chinese University of Hong Kong, 420-444.

Fong, Grace S. 2009. "Reclaiming Subjectivity in a Time of Loss: Ye Shaoyuan (1589-1648) and Autobiographical Writing in the Ming-Qing Transition." *Ming Studies* 59 (May): 21-41.

Furth, Charlotte. 2007. "Producing Medical Knowledge through Cases: History, Evidence, and Action." In Furth et al. eds. 2007, 125-151.

Furth, Charlotte, Judith T. Zeitlin, and Ping-chen Hsiung, eds. 2007. *Thinking with Cases: Specialist Knowledge in Chinese Cultural History*. Honolulu: University of Hawai'i Press.

[GLTWLSBWG] Guoli Taiwan lishi bowuguan 國立台灣歷史博物館, ed. 2011. *Guoli Taiwan lishi bowuguan zai Tainan* 國立台灣歷史博物館在台南 (The National Museum of Taiwan History in Tainan). Tainan: Guoli Taiwan lishi bowuguan.

———. 2012. *Situ simin: Taiwan de gushi—Guoli Taiwan lishi boguan daolan shouce* 斯土斯民: 台灣的故事——國立台灣歷史博物館導覽手冊 (Our land, our people: the story of Taiwan—a guidebook for the Nation Taiwan Museum of History). Tainan: Guoli Taiwan lishi bowugan.

Galan, Frantisek William. 1985. *Historic Structures: The Prague School Project, 1928-1946*. Austin: University of Texas.

Gálik, Marián. 1990. "Jaroslav Průšek: A Myth and Reality as Seen by His Pupil." *Asian and African Studies* 7: 151-156.

Gao Mingge 高明閣. 1986. *Sanguo yanyi lungao* 三國演義論稿 (On *Three Kingdoms*). Shenyang: Liaoning daxue.

Gao, Minglu. 2003. "Post-Utopian Avant-Garde Art in China." In Aleš Erjavec, ed., *Postmodernism and the Postsocialist Condition: Politicized Art under Late Socialism*. Berkeley: University of California Press, 247-283.

Ge, Liangyan. 2001. *Out of the Margins: The Rise of Chinese Vernacular Fiction*. Honolulu: University of Hawai'i Press.

Geng, Song. 2004. *The Fragile Scholar: Power and Masculinity in Chinese Culture*. Hong Kong: Hong Kong University Press.

Geng Ying 耿瑛. 1983. "Xu" 序. In Hu Wenbin, ed. *Honglou meng zidishu* 《紅樓夢》子弟書 (The adaptations of *Honglou meng* in the Manchu Bannermen tales). Shenyang: Chunfeng wenyi, 1-10.

Ghymn, Esther Mikyung. 1995. *Images of Asian American Women by Asian American Women Writers*. New York: Peter Lang.

Grantham, Alexander. 1965. *Via Ports*. Hong Kong: Hong Kong University Press.

The Great Ming Code: Da Ming Lü. 2005. Tr. Jiang Yonglin. Seattle: University of Washington Press.

Gunn, Edward. 1980. *Unwelcome Muse: Chinese Literature in Shanghai and Peking, 1937-1945*. New York: Columbia University Press.

———. 1984. "The Process of Wang Wen-hsing's Art." *Modern Chinese Literature* 1, no. 1: 29-41.

———. 1991. *Rewriting Chinese: Style and Innovation in Twentieth-Century Chinese Prose*. Stanford: Stanford University Press.

Guo Ruilin 郭瑞林. 2006. *Sanguo yanyi de wenhua jiedu* 三國演義的文化解讀 (A cultural reading of *Three Kingdoms*). Shanghai: Shanghai guji.

Guo Xiaoting 郭曉婷. 2013. *Zidishu yu qingdai qiren shehui yanjiu* 子弟書與清代社會旗人研究 (The study of the Manchu Bannermen tales and the Bannermen society in Qing dynasty). Beijing: Zhongguo shehui kexue.

Hall, Stuart. 1988. *Black Film, British Cinema*. London: Institute of Contemporary Arts.

———. 1992. "The Question of Cultural Identity." In Stuart Hall, David Held, and Tony McGrew, eds., *Modernity and Its Futures*. Cambridge: Polity Press, 273-326.

———. 2003a. "Cultural Identity and Diaspora." In Ngai Pun and Lai-man Yee, eds., *Narrating Hong Kong Culture and Identity*. New York: Oxford University Press, 7-23.

———. 2003b. "Cultural Identity and Diaspora." In Jana Evans Braziel and Anita Mannur, eds., *Theorizing Diaspora: A Reader*. Malden: Blackwell Publishing, 233–246.

Han Shiqi 韓士奇. 2007. "Xiandai wenren de zichuangzi" 現代文人的自創字 (Modern intellectuals' neologisms). *Shu wu* (March): 79–80.

Hang Ying 航鷹. 1985. *Dongfang nüxing* 東方女性 (Oriental females). Beijing: Renmin wenxue.

Hargett, James M. 2001. "Travel Literature." In Victor Mair, ed., *The Columbia History of Chinese Literature*. New York. Columbia University Press, 555–559.

He Peixiong 何沛雄. 1990. *Yongzhou baji daodu* 永州八記導讀 (Reading on eight records on Yongzhou). Hong Kong: Zhonghua shuju.

He Qinhua 何勤華. 2000 *Zhongguo faxue shi* 中國法學史 (History of Chinese legal studies). 2 vols. Beijing: Falü.

He Shujing 何淑貞. 2011. *Liu Zongyuan ji qishi yanjiu* 柳宗元及其詩研究 (A study on Liu Zongyuan and his poetry). In Gong Mengchang, ed., *Gudian shige yanjiu huikan*. Xinbei: Huamulan wenhua, vol. 12.

Henry, Eric. 1992. "Chu-ko Liang in the Eyes of his Contemporaries." *Harvard Journal of Asiatic Studies* 52, no. 2: 589–612.

"HKU POP releases latest survey on Hong Kong people's ethnic identity." *HKU POP SITE* (6/23/15). URL (accessed 6/26/15): http://hkupop.hku.hk/english/release/release1267.html.

Holman, C. Hugh. 1980. *A Handbook to Literature*. Indianapolis, IN: The Bobbs-Merrill Company.

Hong Zhigang 洪治纲. 2004. *Yu Hua ping zhuan* 余华评传 (A critical biography of Yu Hua). Zhengzhou: Zhengzhou daxue.

Horne, Philip. 2004. "F. R. Leavis and *The Great Tradition*." *Essays in Criticism* 54, no. 2: 165–180.

Hsia, Chih-tsing. 1963. "On the 'Scientific' Study of Modern Chinese Literature: A Reply to Professor Průšek." *T'oung Pao* 50: 428–474.

———. 1968. *The Classic Chinese Novel: A Critical Introduction*. New York: Columbia University Press.

———. 1979a. *Zhongguo xiandai xiaoshuo shi* 中國現代小說史 (A history of modern Chinese novels). Tr. Liu Shao Ming et al. Hong Kong: Union Press.

———. 1979b. *Xinwenxue de chuantong* 新文學的傳統 (The tradition of new literature). Taipei: China Times Publishing Company.

———. 1987. "Dong Xia dao Xi Liu – jian huai Xu Jieyu" 東夏悼西劉——兼懷許芥昱 (Dong Xia mourning over Xi Liu and in memory of Xu Jieyu). *Xianggang wenxue* 30, no. 6: 26.

———. 1999. *A History of Modern Chinese Fiction*, 3rd ed. Bloomington and Indianapolis: Indiana University Press.

———. 2002a. "Zhongguo gudian xiaoshuo zhongyi ben xu" 《中國古典小說》中譯本序 (Forward to *The Chinese Classic Novel*, Chinese version). *Lianhe wenxue* 133, no. 7: 135.

———. 2002b. "Yelu sannian ban" 耶魯三年半 (Three Years and a half in Yale). *Lianhe wenxue* 212, no. 6: 94–115.

———. 2004. *C. T. Hsia on Chinese Literature*. New York: Columbia University Press.

Hu Wenbin 胡文彬, ed. 1983. *Honglou meng zidishu* 《紅樓夢》子弟書 (The adaptations of *Honglou meng* in the Manchu Bannermen tales). Shenyang: Chunfeng wenyi.

———. 1985. "*Honglou meng* zidishu chutan" 《紅樓夢》子弟書初探 (The primary study on the adaptations of *Honglou meng* in the Manchu Bannermen tales). *Shehui kexue jikan* 37, no. 2: 141–149.

Huang, Betsy. 2010. *Contesting Genres in Contemporary Asian American Fiction*. New York: Palgrave MacMillan.

Huang Lizhen 黃麗貞. 1999. *Shiyong xiucixue* 實用修辭學 (Practical rhetoric). Taipei: Guojia.

Huang, Liu-hung. 1984. *A Complete Book Concerning Happiness and Benevolence: Fu-hui ch'üan-shu, A Manual for Local Magistrates in Seventeenth- century China*. Tr. Djang Chu. Tucson: The University of Arizona Press.

Huang, Martin W. 1995. *Literati and Self-Re/Presentation: Autobiographical Sensibility in the Eighteenth-Century Chinese Novel*. Stanford: Stanford University Press.

———. 2001. *Desire and Fictional Narrative in Late Imperial China*. Cambridge, MA: Harvard University Asia Center.

———, ed. 2004. *Legs: Sequels, Continuations, Rewritings and Chinese Fiction*. Honolulu: University of Hawai'i Press.

Huang Shuning 黃恕寧 (aka Shu-ning Sciban). 2013. "Xiandai jiaoxiangyue—Wang Wenxing fantan" 現代交響樂—王文興訪談錄 (Contemporary symphony: an interview with Wang Wenxing). In Huang Shuning 黃恕寧, ed., *Ou kai tianyan qu hongchen—Wang Wenxing zhuanji fangtan ji* 偶開天眼覷紅塵—王文興傳記訪談集 (Glimpses of the world through the inner eye: collected biographies and interviews of Wang Wenxing). Taipei: National Taiwan University Press, 278-305. Rpt. from *Lianhe bao* 聯合報 (United daily), April 28-May 1, 2000.

Hummel, Arthur W. 1943. *Eminent Chinese of the Ch'ing Period (1644-1912)*. 2 vols. Washington: United States Government Printing Office.

Huot, Marie-Claire. 1993. "Liu Heng's *Fuxi Fuxi*: What about Nuwa?" In Lu Tonglin, ed., *Gender and Sexuality in Twentieth-Century Chinese Literature and Society*. Albany: State University of New York Press, 85-106.

Hutcheon, Linda. 2006. *A Theory of Adaptation*. New York: Routledge.

Huters, Theodore. 1990a. "Introduction." In Theodore Huters, ed., *Reading in Modern Chinese Short Story*. Armonk: Sharpe, 3-21.

———. 1990b. "The Telling of Shi Tuo's 'Kiss': Few Words and Several Voices." In Theodore Huters, ed., *Reading in Modern Chinese Short Story*. Armonk: Sharpe, 74-91.

Hutton, Patrick H. 1993. *History as an Art of Memory*. Hanover: University Press of New England.

Idema, Wilt L. 2011. "The Biographical and the Autobiographical in Bo Shaojun's *One Hundred Poems Lamenting My Husband*," In Joan Judge and Hu Ying, eds., *Beyond Exemplar Tales: Women's Biography in Chinese History*. Berkeley: University of California Press, 230-245.

Ingram, Forrest L. 1971. *Representative Short Story Cycles of the Twentieth Century: Studies in a Literary Genre*. The Hague, Paris: Mouton.

Jeremiah, Emily. 2004. "Murderous Mothers: Adrienne Rich's *Of Woman Born* and Toni Morrison's *Beloved*." In O'Reilly ed. 2004: 59-71.

Jiang Tian 江天 , ed. 1988. *Mao Zonggang pingdian: Sanguo yanyi* 毛宗崗評點: 三國演義 (Mao Zonggang commentary: Three Kingdoms). Beijing: Zhongguo wenlian.

Kang, Xiaofei. 2006. *The Cult of the Fox: Power, Gender, and Popular Religion in Late Imperial and Modern China*. New York: Columbia University Press.

Khoo, Tseen, and Kam Louie, eds. 2005. *Culture, Identity, Commodity: Diasporic Chinese Literature in English*. Montreal: McGill-Queen's University Press.

King, Gail Oman. 1987. "A Few textual Notes Regarding Guan Suo and the *Sanguo yanyi*." *Chinese Literature: Essays, Articles and Reviews* 9: 89-92.

Kochis, Bruce. 1978. "List of Lectures Given in the Prague Linguistic Circle (1926-1948)." In Ladislav Matejka ed. *Sound, Sign and Meaning: Quinquagenary of the Prague Linguistic Circle*. Ann Arbor: University of Michigan, 607-622.

Kong Shuyu 孔书玉. 2012. "Jinshan xiangxiang yu shijie wenxue bantu zhong de Hanyu zuyi xiezuo: yi Yan Geling de *Fusang* he Zhang Ling de *Jinshan* weili" 金山想象与世界文学版图中的汉语族裔写作: 以严歌苓的《扶桑》和张翎的《金山》为例 (Imaging gold mountain and Chinese-language ethnic writing as world literature: taking Yan Geling's *The lost daughter of happiness* and Zhang Ling's *Gold mountain* as examples). *Huawen wenxue* no. 5: 5-16.

Kuoshu, Harry H. 2002. *Celluloid China: Cinematic Encounters with Culture & Society*. Carbondale: Southern Illinois University Press.

Lau, Jenny Kwok Wah. 1991. "*Judou*—A Hermeneutical Reading of Cross-cultural Cinema." *Film Quarterly* 45, no. 2: 2-10.

Lau, Joseph S. M. 1970. *Ts'ao Yu: The Reluctant Disciple of Chekhov and O'Neill*. Hong Kong: Hong Kong University Press.

Lawrence, D. H. 1995. "The Rocking-Horse Winner." In Dieter Mehl and Christa Jansohn, eds., *The Woman who Rode Away and Other Stories*. Cambridge: Cambridge University Press, 230-243.

Leavis, F. R. 1937. "Literary Criticism and Philosophy: A Reply." *Scrutiny* 6: 59-70.

————. 1948. *The Great Tradition: George Eliot, Henry James, Joseph Conrad*. London: Chatto and Windus.

Lee, Leo Ou-fan. 1980. "Forward." In *The Lyrical and the Epic: Studies of Modern Chinese Literature*, ed. Leo Ou-fan Lee. Bloomington: Indiana University Press.

————. 2008. *City Between Worlds: My Hong Kong*. Cambridge, MA: Harvard University Press.

Lee, Ming Kwan. 1998. "Hong Kong Identity—Past and Present." In Siu-lun Wong and Toyojiro Maruya, eds., *Hong Kong Economy and Society: Challenges in the New Era*. Hong Kong: Centre of Asian Studies, University of Hong Kong, 153–175.

Lee, Robert G. 1999. *Orientals: Asian Americans in Popular Culture*. Philadelphia: Temple University Press.

Lee, SKY. 1990. *Disappearing Moon Café*. Toronto: Douglas & McIntyre.

Lee, Yee 李怡. 2015. "Houyusanshidai de xianggangliusi" 後雨傘時代的香港六四 (Hong Kong's June 4 in the post Umbrella Movement era). *Pingguo ribao* (May 30): A4.

Leenhouts, Mark. 2005. *Leaving the World to Enter the World: Han Shaogong and Chinese Root-Seeking Literature*. Leiden: CNWS.

Leung Sai-wing 梁世榮. 1998. "Xianggangren de shenfen rentong: lilun yu yanjiufangfa de fansi" 香港人的身分認同：理論與研究方法的反思 (Hong Kong identity: second thoughts on theory and research methods). In S. K. Lau, P. S. Wan, M. K. Lee, and S. L. Wong, eds., *Huarenshehui de bianmao: shehui zhibiao de fenxi* 華人社會的變貌: 社會指標的分析 (Changing Chinese societies: social indicators analysis). Hong Kong: Hong Kong Institute of Asia-Pacific Studies, The Chinese University Press, 189–205.

Li Changzhi 李長之. 2006. *Li Changzhi wen ji* 李長之文集 (An anthology of Li Changzhi's writings). 10 vols. Shijiazhuang: Hebei jiaoyu.

Li Chunyu 李純瑀. 2012. *Liu Zongyuan yu Su Shi shanshui youji yanjiu* 柳宗元與蘇軾山水遊記研究 (A study on landscape essay by Liu Zongyuan and Su Shi). In Zeng Yongyi, ed., *Gudian wenxue yanjiu jikan*. Xinbei: Huamulan wenhua, vol. 14: 1–135.

Li, Hua. 2011. *Contemporary Chinese Fiction by Su Tong and Yu Hua: Coming of Age in Troubled Times*. Leiden: Brill.

Li, Wai-yee. 1993. *Enchantment and Disenchantment: Love and Illusion in Chinese Literature*. Princeton, New Jersey: Princeton University Press.

Li Xiaolu 李曉路. 1991. *Sanguo rencai chenggong shu* 三國人才成功術 (The art of success and talent in *Three Kingdoms*). Hong Kong: Zhonghua shuju.

Li Yazhou 李亞舟 and Li Dingkun 李定坤, eds. 2005. *Hanying cige duibi yanjiu jianbian* 漢英辭格對比研究簡編 (A concise comparison of Chinese and English figures of speech). Wuhan: Huazhong shifan daxue.

Li Yu 李漁. 1992. *Li Yu Quanji* 李漁全集 (Anthology of Li Yu), vol. 3. Hangzhou: Zhejiang guji.

Lianhe wenxue 聯合文學. 2002. "Hsia Chih-tsing zhuzuo mulu" 夏志清著作目錄 (Catalogue of C. T. Hsia's works) 213, no. 7: 164–172.

Liang Jianjiang 梁鑒江. 1999. *Liu Zongyuan zhuan* 柳宗元傳 (Biography of Liu Zongyuan). Guangzhou: Guangdong gaodeng jiaoyu.

Liao Qiongyuan 廖瓊媛. 2000. *Sanguo yanyi de meixue shijie* 三國演義的美學世界 (The aesthetic world of *Three Kingdoms*). Taibei: Liren shuju.

Lim, Sek Pei. 2000. "The Question of Diaspora in International Relations: A Case Study of Chinese Diaspora in Malaysia and South-East Asia." MA thesis. University of Sussex.

Lin Chen 林辰. 1985. "*Honglou meng* xushu zhi wojian" 《紅樓夢》續書之我見 (My view on the sequels to *Honglou meng*). *Guangming ribao* (Feb. 26).

Lin Danya 林丹婭. 2003. *Dangdai Zhongguo nüxing wenxue shilun* 当代中国女性文学史论 (A history of contemporary Chinese women's literature). Xiamen: Xiamen daxue.

Lin Jingjie 林靖傑. 2011. "Xunzhao *Bei hai de ren*" 尋找背海的人 (Seeking the man with his back against the sea). *Yanfen didai wenxue* 33: 25–30.

Lin Junjia 林均珈. 2012. *Honglou meng zidishu yanjiu* 《紅樓夢》子弟書研究 (The study of the adaptations of *Honglou meng* in the Manchu Bannermen tales). Taibei: Wanjuanlou tushu gufen youxian gongsi.

———, ed. 2012. *Honglou meng zidishu shangdu* 《紅樓夢》子弟書賞讀 (Analyzing and reading of the adaptations of *Honglou meng* in the Manchu Bannermen tales). Taibei: Wanjuanlou tushu gufen youxian gongsi.

Lin Yong 林勇. 2005. *Wenge houshidai Zhongguo dianying yu quanqiu wenhua* 文革后时代中国电影与全球文化 (Chinese film and global culture in the era after the Cultural Revolution). Beijing: Wenhua yishu.

Ling Ying 凌影. 1976. *Sanguo yanyi zongheng tan* 三國演藝縱橫談 (A comprehensive discussion of *Three Kingdoms*). Hong Kong: Zhonghua shuju.

Link, Perry. 1993. "Ideology and Theory in the Study of Modern Chinese Literature: An Introduction." *Modern China* 19, no. 1: 4-12.

Liu, Heng [刘恒]. 1991. *The Obsessed.* Tr. David Kwan. Beijing: Panda Books.

———. 2006. *Fuxi Fuxi* 伏羲伏羲. In Liu, *Liu Heng jingxuanji* 刘恒精选集 (Selected works of Liu Heng). Beijing: Beijing Yanshan, 10-71.

Liu, Kang. 2002. "The Short-Lived Avant-Garde: Transformation of Yu Hua." *Modern Language Quarterly* 63, no.1 (March): 89-117.

Liu Shousong 劉綬松. 1956. *Zhongguo xinwenxue shi chugao* 中國新文學史初稿 (A preliminary manuscript of new Chinese literary history). Beijing: Zuojia.

Liu Xiangjun 劉向軍. 2001. *Sanguo yanyi de zhexue yishu* 三國演義的哲學藝術 (The philosophical art of *Three Kingdoms*). Shenyang: Liaoning renmin.

Liu Zengjie 劉增杰, ed. 1982. *Shi Tuo yanjiu ziliao* 師陀研究資料 (Research material on Shi Tuo). Beijing: Beijing.

Louie, Kam. 1999. "Sexuality, Masculinity and Politics in Chinese Culture: The Case of the 'Sanguo' hero Guan Yu." *Modern Asian Studies* 33, no. 4: 835-859.

———. 2002. *Theorizing Chinese Masculinity: Society and Gender in China.* Cambridge: Cambridge University Press.

Lowenthal, David. 1985. *The Past Is A Foreign Country.* Cambridge: Cambridge University Press.

Lu, Sheldon Hsiao-peng. 1997. "National Cinema, Cultural Critique, Transnational Capital: The Films of Zhang Yimou." In Sheldon Hsiao-peng Lu, ed., *Transnational Chinese Cinemas: Identity, Nationhood, Gender.* Honolulu: University of Hawaii Press, 105-138.

Lupke, Christopher. 2003. "The Taiwan Modernists." In Joshua S. Mostow, ed., *Columbia Companion to Modern East Asian Literature.* New York: Columbia University Press, 481-487.

Ma, Eric Kit-wai. 1999. *Culture, Politics, and Television in Hong Kong.* London: Routledge.

Ma, Sen. 1988. "Shi Tuo." In Zbigniew Slupski, ed., *A Selective Guide to Chinese Literature 1900-1949: The Short Story.* Leiden: Brill, 178-181.

Magill, Frank N. 1980. *The Novel into Film.* Pasadena, CA: Salem.

Malcolm, David. 2012. *The British and Irish Short Story Handbook.* Hoboken, NJ: John Wiley & Sons.

Matejka, Ladislav ed. 1993. *Sound, Sign and Meaning: Quinquagenary of the Prague Linguistic Circle.* Ann Arbor: University of Michigan Press.

Mathews, Gordon, Eric Kit-wai Ma and Tai-lok Lui. 2008. *Hong Kong, China: Learning to Belong to a Nation.* London: Routledge.

McDougall, Bonnie, and Kam Louie. 1997. *The Literature of China in the Twentieth Century.* New York: Columbia University Press.

McLaren, Anne Elizabeth. 1985. "Chantefables and the Textual Evolution of the San-kuo-chih Yen-i." *T'oung Pao* 71: 159-227.

———. 1995. "Ming Audiences and Vernacular Hermeneutics: The Uses of the Romance of the Three Kingdoms." *T'oung Pao* 81: 51-80.

McMahon, Keith. 2004. "Eliminating Traumatic Antinomies: Sequels to *Honglou meng.*" In Huang, Martin, ed., *Snakes' Legs: Sequels, Continuations, Rewritings and Chinese Fiction.* Honolulu: University of Hawai'i Press, 98-112.

Mei Jialing 梅家玲. 2006. "Xia Ji'an, *Wenxue zazhi* yu Taiwan daxue" 夏濟安, 《文學雜誌》與台灣大學 (Xia Ji'an, *Literary Magazine* and Taiwan University). *Taiwan wenxue yanjiu jikan* 1: 1-33.

Mencius. 1970. Tr. D. C. Lau. Harmondsworth: Penguin Books.

Meng Shi 孟實. 1937. "'Gu' he 'Luori guang'" 《谷》和《落日光》('Gu' and 'Luori guang'). In Liu Zengjie ed., 1982: 233-236.

Merhaut, Boris. 1966. "Bibliography of Academician Jaroslav Průšek: 1956-1965." *Archiv Orientální* 34: 575-586.

———. 1956. "Jaroslav Průšek: Bibliography 1931-1956." *Archiv Orientální* 24: 347-355.

Morrison, Toni. 1987. *Beloved*. New York: Plume.

Mukařovský, Jan. 1977a. *The Word and Verbal Art*. New Haven: Yale University Press.

———. 1977b. *Sound, Sign and Meaning*. New Haven: Yale University Press.

Murck, Alfreda and Wen C. Fong, eds. 1991. *Words and Images: Chinese Poetry, Calligraphy, and Painting*. New York: The Metropolitan Museum of Art.

Nienhauser, W. H. 1986a. "Prose." In Nienhauser, ed., The Indiana Companion to Traditional Chinese Literature. Bloomington: Indiana University Press, 93-120.

Nienhauser, W. H. 1986b. "Liu Tsung-yuan." In Nienhauser, ed., *The Indiana Companion to Traditional Chinese Literature*. Bloomington: Indiana University Press, 589-592.

Nienhauser, William H., ed. 1986/1998. *The Indiana Companion to Traditional Chinese Literature*. 2 vols. Bloomington: Indiana University Press.

Nienhauser, W. H. et al. 1973. *Liu Tsung-yuan*. NY. Twayne Publishers.

Olney, James. 1980. "Some Versions of Memory/ Some Versions of Bios: The Ontology of Autobiography." In James Olney, ed., *Autobiography: Essays Theoretical and Critical*. Princeton, NJ: Princeton University Press, 236-267.

O'Neill, Eugene. 1988. *Complete Plays 1920-1931*. New York: The Library of America.

Ong, Aihwa. 1999. *Flexible Citizenship: The Cultural Logics of Transnationality*. Durham: Duke University Press.

O'Reilly, Andrea. 2004a. *Toni Morrison and Motherhood: A Politics of the Heart*. Albany: State University of New York Press.

———, ed. 2004b. *From Motherhood to Mothering: The Legacy of Adrienne Rich's Of Women Born*. Albany: State University of New York Press.

———, ed. 2010. *Encyclopedia of Motherhood*. Los Angeles: Sage Publications.

O'Reilly, Andrea, Marie Porter, and Patricia Short, eds. 2004. *Motherhood Power & Oppression*. Toronto: Women's Press.

Ouyang Zi 歐陽子. 1973. "Lun *Jia bian* zhi jiegou xingshi yu wenzi jufa" 論《家變》之結構形式與文字句法 (A discussion of the form and sentence structure of *Family Catastrophe*). *Zhongwai wenxue* 1, no. 12: 50-67.

Palát, Augustin. 1966. "Jaroslav Průšek Sexagenarian." *Archiv Orientální* no. 34: 481-493.

Palumbo-Liu, David. 1999. *Asian/American: Historical Crossings of a Racial Frontier*. Stanford: Stanford University Press.

Pan Wen 潘雯. 2012. "Wenxue yu zhengzhi: Meiguo Yayi wenxue zhong de dongfang zhuyi piping jiqi 'Huaren huayu' jiangou" 文学与政治: 美国亚裔文学中的东方主义批评及其"华人话语"建构 (Literature and politics: the orientalist criticism in Asian American literature studies and its construction of "Chinese discourse"). *Huawen wenxue* no. 5: 19-33.

Papastergiadis, Nikos. 1997. "Tracing Hybridity in Theory." In Pnina Werbner and Tariq Modod, eds., *Debating Cultural Hybridity*. London: Zed Books, 257-281.

"People's Ethnic Identity." *HKU POP SITE*. URL (accessed 7/6/15): http://hkupop.hku.hk/chinese/popexpress/ethnic/.

Plaks, Andrew H. 1976. *Archetype and Allegory in the Dream of the Red Chamber*. Princeton: Princeton University Press.

———. 1987. *The Four Masterworks of the Ming Novel*. Princeton: Princeton University Press.

Pound, Ezra. 1972. *The Cantos of Ezra Pound*. New York: New Directions.

Průšek, Jaroslav. 1962. "Basic Problems of the History of Modern Chinese Literature and C. T. Hsia, *A History of Modern Chinese Fiction*." *T'oung Pao* 49, nos. 4/5: 357-404.

———. 1970. *Chinese History and Literature: Collection of Studies*. Dordrecht, Holland: Reidel.

———. 1980. *The Lyrical and the Epic: Studies of Modern Chinese Literature*, ed. Leo Ou-fan Lee. Bloomington: Indiana University Press.

———. 1987. *Pushike Zhongguo xiandai wenxue lunji* 普實克中國現代文學論集 (A collection of Průšek's essays on modern Chinese literature). Tr. Li Yanqiao 李燕喬 et. al. Changsha: Hunan wenyi.

———. 2002. *China: My Sister*. Tr. Ivan Vomáčka. Prague: The Karolinum Press.

———. 2005. *Zhongguo, wo de jie mei* 中國, 我的姐妹 (China, my sister). Trs. Cong Lin 叢林, Chen Pingling 陳平陵, and Li Mei 李梅. Beijing: Waiyu jiaoxue yu yanjiu.

Qian Zhongshu 錢鍾書. 1985. *Qi zhui ji* 七綴集 (Seven supplemental essays). Rev. ed. Shanghai: Shanghai guji, 63-78.

Qiu Pengsheng 邱澎生. 2008. *Dang falü yushang jingji: Ming Qing Zhongguo de shangye falü* 當法律遇上經濟: 明清中國的商業法律 (When the law encounters economics: Chinese commercial law of the Ming and Qing). Taibei: Wunan tushu.

Qu Jinliang 曲金良.1989. "Lüetan *Honglou meng* zidishu 'Lulei yuan'" 略談《紅樓夢》子弟書《露淚緣》brief discussion on "the Destiny of Dew and Tears"). *Honglou meng xuekan* no. 3: 257-260.

Rich, Adrienne. 1976. *Of Woman Born: Motherhood as Experience and Institution*. New York: W. W. Norton.

Roberts, Moss, tr. 1991. *Three Kingdoms: A Historical Novel*. Berkeley: University California Press.

Rolston, David L. ed. 1990. *How to Read the Chinese Novel*. Princeton: Princeton University Press.

Ruddick, Sara. 1989. *Maternal Thinking: Toward a Politics of Peace*. New York: Ballantine.

Ruhlmann, Robert. 1960. "Traditional Heroes in Chinese Popular Fiction." In Arthur Wright, ed. *The Confucian Persuasion*. Stanford: Stanford University Press, 141-176.

Samson, Anne. 1992. *F. R. Leavis*. Toronto: Toronto University Press.

Sanders, Graham. 2011. "Introduction." In Shen, *Six Records of a Life Adrift*. Cambridge, MA: Hackett, viii-xv.

Sciban, Shu-ning. 1995. *Wang Wenxing's Poetic Language*. Ph. D. diss. Toronto: University of Toronto.

Shan Dexing (aka Shan Te-hsing) 單德興. 1984. "Wang Wen-hsing on Wang Wen-hsing." *Modern Chinese Literature* 1, no. 1 (Sept.): 57-65. Rpt. in Shu-ning Sciban and Ihor Pidhainy, eds., *Reading Wang Wenxing: Critical Essays*. Ithaca: Cornell East Asia Program, forthcoming.

———. 1987. "Wang Wenxing tan Wang Wenxing" 王文興談王文興 (Wang Wenxing on Wang Wexing). *Lianhe wenxue* 聯合文學 (Unitas) 3.8 (1987.06): 166-195. Rpt. "Chuilian wenzi de ren—Wang Wenxing fangtan lu" 錘煉文字的人—王文興訪談錄 (The man who constantly refines his language—Wang Wenxing interview). In Huang Shuning 黃恕寧, ed., *Ou kai tianyan qu hongchen—Wang Wenxing zhuanji fangtan ji* 偶開天眼覷紅塵—王文興傳記訪談集 (Glimpses of the world through the inner eye: collected biographies and interviews of Wang Wenxing). Taipei: National Taiwan University Press, 212-272.

Shangwu yinshuguan bianjibu, ed. 1979. *Ci yuan* 辭源. 4 vols. Revised ed. Beijing: Shangwu yinshuguan.

Shen, Fu. 2011. *Six Records of a Life Adrift*. Tr. Graham Sanders. Cambridge, MA: Hackett, 2011.

Sheng Ying 盛英. 1999. "Manyi muqin shenhua de daota" 漫議母親神話的倒塌 (On the Collapse of the Mother Myth). In Sheng, *Zhongguo nüxing wenxue xintan* 中国女性文学新探 (A new examination of Chinese women's literature) Beijing: Zhongguo wenlian, 102-106.

Shi Shouqian 石守謙, ed. 2004. *Fu'ermosha: Shiqi shiji de Taiwan-Helan yu Dongya* 福尔摩沙: 十七世紀的臺灣荷蘭與東亞 (Ilha Formosa: The emergence of Taiwan on the world scene in the 17th century). Taipei: Palace Museum.

Shi Tuo 師陀. 1952. *Guoyuancheng ji* 果園城記 (Records from Orchard Town), 3rd reprint. Shanghai: Shanghai chuban gongsi.

———. 1958. "*Guoyuancheng ji* xinban houji" 《果園城記》新版後記 (Postscript to the new edition of *Records from Orchard Town*). In Liu Zengjie, ed. 1982: 98-101.

———. 1980. "*Lu Fen duanpian xiaoshuo xuanji* xuyan" 《蘆焚短篇小說選集》序言 (Preface to the *Selection of Short Stories by Lu Fen*). In Liu Zengjie, ed. 1982: 161-167.

Shu, James C. T. 1980. "Iconoclasm in Wang Wen-hsing's *Chia-pien*." In Jeannette L. Faurot, ed., *Chinese Fiction from Taiwan*. Bloomington: Indiana University Press, 179-193.

Šíma, Jiří. 1994. *Jaroslav Průšek: Bibliography 1931–1991*. Prague: Oriental Institute.

Skeldon, Ronald. 1995. "Emigration from Hong Kong, 1945–1994." In Ronald Skeldon, ed., *Emigration from Hong Kong: Tendencies and Impacts*. Hong Kong: The Chinese University Press, 51–78.

Słupski, Zbigniew. 1964. "Some Remarks on the First History of Modern Chinese Fiction." *Archiv Orientálni* 32: 139–152.

——. 1973. "The World of Shih T'o." *Asian and African Studies* 9: 11–28.

Steiner, Peter. 1978. "The Conceptual Basis of Prague Structuralism." In Ladislav Matejka ed. *Sound, Sign and Meaning: Quinquagenary of the Prague Linguistic Circle* (Ann Arbor: University of Michigan), 356–359.

Stevenson, Angus, ed. 2012. *Oxford Dictionary of English*. 3rd ed., online version. Oxford: Oxford University Press.

Storer, Richard. 2009. *F. R. Leavis*. New York: Routledge.

Strassberg, Richard, trans. 1994. *Inscribed Landscapes: Travel Writing from Imperial China*. Berkeley: University of California Press.

Striedter, Jurij. 1989. *Literary Structure, Evolution, and Value: Russian Formalism and Czech Structuralism Reconsidered*. Cambridge, MA: Harvard University Press.

Struve, Lynn A. 2004. "Confucian PTSD: Reading Trauma in a Chinese Youngster's Memoir of 1653." *History and Memory* 16, no. 2 (Fall/Winter): 14–31.

——. 2009. "Self-struggles of a Martyr: Memories, Dreams, and Obsessions in the Extant Diary of Huang Chunyao." *Harvard Journal of Asiatic Studies* 69, no. 2 (Dec.): 343–394.

Sui Sin Far. 1995. "The Wisdom of the New." In Amy Ling and Annette White-Parks, eds., *Mrs. Spring Fragrance and Other Writings*. Urbana: University of Illinois Press, 42–61.

Sung, Tz'u. 1981. *The Washing Away of Wrongs*. Tr. Brian E. McKnight. Ann Arbor: Center for Chinese Studies, University of Michigan.

"Suspend." *Cambridge Advanced Learner's Dictionary*. URL (accessed 7/6/15): http://dictionary .cambridge.org/dictionary/british/suspend.

"Suspend." *Collins Cobuild Advanced Learner's Dictionary*. URL (accessed 7/6/15): http://www .collinsdictionary.com/dictionary/english-cobuild-learners/suspend.

Tan, Amy. 2003. "Confession." *The Opposite of Fate: Memories of a Writing Life*. Penguin Group, 212–214.

Tang Chengfeng [Tang Shingfung] 鄧城鋒. 2012. "Xiaojie jiqiu qingjie de butong changshi: Liu Zongyuan Yongzhou youji de chongxin jiedu" 消解羈囚情結的不同嘗試: 柳宗元永州遊記的重新解讀. (Different trials to release "prisoner's sentiment": a re-reading on Liu Zongyuan's landscape essay on Yongzhou). *Pingdong xiaoyu daxue xuebao* 39: 1–30.

Tawa, Nicholas E. 1980. *Sweet Songs for Gentle Americans: The Parlor Song in America, 1790–1860*. Bowling Green, OH: Bowling Green University Popular Press.

Taylor, Jeremy. 2005. "Reading History Through the Built Environment in Taiwan." In John Makeham and A-chin Hsiau, eds., *Cultural, Ethnic, and Political Nationalism in Contemporary Taiwan: Bentuhua*. New York: Palgrave Macmillan, 159–183.

——. 2006. "The Production of the Chiang Kai-shek Personality Cult, 1929–1975." *The China Quarterly* 185: 96–110.

——. 2009. "Discovering a Nationalist Heritage in Present-day Taiwan." *China Heritage Quarterly* 17 (March). URL: http://www.chinaheritagequarterly.org/articles.php?searchterm=017 _taiwan.inc&issue=017.

——. 2010. "*QuJianghua*: Disposing of and Re-appraising the Remnants of Chiang Kai-shek's Reign on Taiwan." *Journal of Contemporary History* 45, no. 1: 181–196.

Tie Ning 鐵凝. 1992. *Maijie duo* 麥秸垛 (Haystacks). Beijing: Zuojia.

Tihanov, Galin. 2004. "Why did Modern Literary Theory Originate in Central and Eastern Europe?" *Common Knowledge* 10, no. 1: 61–81.

Tosaki Tetsuhiko 戶崎哲彥. 1996. *Liu Zongyuan Yongzhou baji youji kao* 柳宗元永州八記游記考. (Study on landscape essays of eight records by Liu Zongyuan). Tokyo: Chubun.

Tsang, Steve. 2004. *A Modern History of Hong Kong*. Hong Kong: Hong Kong University Press.

Tu, Wei-ming. 1994. "Cultural China: The Periphery as the Center." In Tu, *The Living Tree: The Changing Meaning of Being Chinese Today*. Stanford: Stanford University Press, 1–34.

Varutti, Marzia. 2012. "Towards Social Inclusion in Taiwan: Museums, Equality and Indigenous Groups." In Richard Sandell and Eithne Nightingale, eds., *Museums, Equality and Social Justice*. London: Routledge.

Vickers, Edward. 2009. "Re-writing Museums in Taiwan." In Fang-long Shih, Stuart Thompson, and Paul-Francois Tremlett, eds., *Re-Writing Culture in Taiwan*. London, New York: Routledge, 69–101.

———. 2010. "History, Identity, and the Politics of Taiwan's Museums: Reflections on the DPP-KMT Transition." *China Perspectives* 3: 92–108.

———. 2013. "Transcending Victimhood: Japan in the Public Historical Museums of Taiwan and the People's Republic of China." *China Perspectives* no. 4: 17–28.

Wakeman, Frederic Jr. 1985. *The Great Enterprise: The Manchu Reconstruction of Imperial Order in Seventeenth-century China*. 2 vols. Berkeley: University of California Press.

Walter, Roland. 2003. *Narrative Identities: (Inter) Cultural In-Betweenness in the Americas*. Berm: Peter Lang.

Wang Anyi 王安忆. 1986. "Xiaocheng zhi lian" 小城之戀 (Love in a small town). *Shanghai wenxue* (Aug.): 1–28.

Wang Bomin 王伯敏 and Tong Zhongtao 童中燾, eds. 1981. *Zhongguo shanshuihua de toushi* 中國山水畫的透視 (Perspectives on Chinese landscape painting). Tianjin: Tianjin renmin meishu.

Wang Damin 王达敏. 2006. *Lun Yu Hua* 论余华 (On Yu Hua). Shanghai: Shanghai renmin.

Wang, David Der-wei. 2005. "A Report on Modern Chinese Literary Studies in the English-Speaking World." *Harvard Asia Quarterly* 9, nos. 1/2: 51–56.

Wang Gengsheng 王更生, ed. 1994. *Liu Zongyuan sanwen yandu* 柳宗元散文研讀 (A study on Liu Zongyuan's essay). Taibei: Wenshizhe.

Wang, Li-jung. 2004. "Taiwan Multiculturalism." *International Journal of Cultural Policy* 10, no. 3 (Nov.): 301–318.

Wang Liqun 王立群. 2008. *Zhongguo gudai shanshui youji yanjiu* 中國古代山水游記研究 (A study of the landscape essay in ancient China). Beijing: Zhongguo shehui kexue.

Wang Lieyao 王列耀. 2009. "Beimei xinyimin wenxue zhong de 'linglei qinqing'" 北美新移民文學中的"另类亲情" (A "different kind of love relation" in North American new immigrant literature). *Wenxue pinglun* no. 6: 194–198.

Wang Lieyao 王列耀, and Li Peipei 李培培. 2011. "'Yizu hunlian' yu 'hou liuxue' jieduan de Bei-mei xinyimin wenxue: yi Zeng Xiaowen weiyi" "异族婚恋"与"后留学"阶段的北美新移民文学: 以曾晓文为例 ("Inter-racial romance" and North American new immigrant literature of "the post-international students" period: reading Zeng Xiaowen's stories]. *Zeng Xiaowen's Blog*. URL: http://blog.sina.com.cn/s/blog_49ead53701oorgza.html.

Wang Mingde 王明德. 2001 [circa 1674]. *Dulü peixi* 讀律佩觿 (A bodkin to unravel the Code). Eds. He Qinhua 何勤華, Cheng Weirong 程維榮, Zhang Boyuan 張伯元, and Hong Pimo 洪丕謨. Beijing: Falü.

Wang, Q. Edward. 2002. "Taiwan's Search for National History: A Trend in Historiography." *East Asian History* 24 (Dec.): 93–116.

Wang Weiping 王卫平. 2005. "Cao Yu san da ming ju de jieshou licheng yu dangdai jiazhi" 曹禺三大名剧的接受历程与当代价值 (The reception evolution and contemporary value of Cao Yu's three major plays). *Wenxue pinglun* no. 6: 86–91.

Wang Wenxing 王文興 (aka Wang Wen-hsing). 1973. *Jia bian* 家變 (Family catastrophe). 1973. Taipei: Huanyu. Rpt. by Hongfan in 1978, 2000.

———. 1981/1999. *Bei hai de ren* 背海的人 (Backed against the sea). Taipei: Hongfan.

———. 1995. *Family Catastrophe*. Tr. Susan Wan Dolling. Honolulu: University of Hawai'i Press.

———. 2009. *Jia bian liu jiang* 《家變》六講 (Six lectures on *Family Catastrophe*). Taipei: Maitian.

———. 2010. *Wang Wenxing shougao ji* 王文興手稿集 (The collection of Wang Wenxing's manuscripts). Compiled by Yi Peng 易鵬. Taipei: Xingren wenhua shiyanshi.

Wang, Xiaoying. 2000. "Hong Kong, China, and the Question of Postcoloniality." In Arif Dirlik and Xudong Zhang, eds., *Postmodernism & China*. Durham, NC: Duke University Press, 89–120.

Wang Xuchuan 王旭川. 2004. *Zhongguo xiaoshuo xushu yanjiu* 中國小說續書研究 (The study of Chinese fictional sequels). Shanghai: Xuelin.

Wang Yao 王瑤. 1951–53. *Zhongguo xinwenxue shigao* 中國新文學史稿 (Manuscript of new Chinese literary history). Shanghai: Kaiming shudian; Xinwenyi.

Wang Yichuan 王一川. 1998. *Zhang Yimou shenhua de zhongjie* 张艺谋神话的终结 (The end of the Zhang Yimou myth). Zhengzhou: Henan renmin.

Warner, Nicholas O. 1982. "In Search of Literary Science: The Russian Formalist Tradition." *Pacific Coast Philology* 17, nos. 1/2: 69–81.

Wellek, René. 1936. "The Theory of Literary History." *Travaux du Cercle Linguistique de Prague* 6: 173–191.

———. 1937. "Literary Criticism and Philosophy." *Scrutiny* 5: 375–383.

———. 1960. "Literary Theory, Criticism and History." *The Sewanee Review* 68, no. 1: 1–19.

———. 1963. *Concepts of Criticism*. New Haven: Yale University Press.

———. 1986. *A History of Modern Criticism 1750–1950 Vol. 5*. New Haven: Yale University Press.

———. 1988. "Review on Valuation in Criticism and Other Essays." *The Modern Language Review* 83, no. 3: 707–709.

Will, Pierre-Etienne. 2007. "Developing Forensic Knowledge through Cases in the Qing Dynasty." In Furth et al. eds. 2007: 62–100.

Wong Kar-ying 王家英 and Wan Po-shan 尹寶珊. 2001. "Xianggang de zuqun rentong zhuangkuang: yige tantaoxing de yanjiu" 香港的族群認同狀況: 一個探討性的研究 (Identity among the Hong Kong community: An exploratory research). In S. K. Lau, P. S. Wan, M. K. Lee, and S. L. Wong, eds., *Social Transformation and Cultural Change in Chinese Societies*. Hong Kong: Hong Kong Institute of Asia-Pacific Studies, The Chinese University Press, 431–457.

Wong, Siu Kit, tran. 2007. *An Anthology of Ancient Chinese Prose*. Hong Kong: Asia Education Times.

Wu, Chu-Jen. 2009. *Contestation of National Memory and History: The Case of Chiang Kai-Shek Memorial Hall*. MA thesis. Honolulu: University of Hawai'i.

Wu Hua 吳华. 2010. "Yong 'tamen' de yanjing kan 'women': du Zeng Xiaowen de 'Qiansong'" 用"他们"的眼睛看"我们": 读曾晓文的《遣送》 (Seeing "us" through "their" eyes: a study of Zeng Xiaowen's "Deportation"). *Huawen wenxue* no. 5: 92–96.

Wu, Mi-cha. 2009. "Jianli yizuo guojia lishi bowuguan" 建立一座國家歷史博物館 (Constructing a museum of national history). In *Wenwu, wenhua yichan, yu wenhua renting* 文物, 文化, 遺產與文化認同 (Objects, heritage, and cultural identity). Nantou: Taiwan wenxianguan, 285–292.

Wu, Pei-yi, 1990. *The Confucian's Progress: Autobiographical Writings in Traditional China*. Princeton, NJ: Princeton University Press.

Xi Xi 西西. 2008. *Shoujuan* 手卷 (Hand scroll). Taipei: Hongfan.

Xiao, Hui Faye. 2014. *Family Revolution: Marital Strife in Contemporary Chinese Literature and Visual Culture*. Seattle: University of Washington Press.

Xu Kun 徐坤. 1999. "Nü Wa" (女娲). *Hanqing maimai* 含情脈脈 (Exuding love and tenderness). Tianjin: Baihua wenyi, 23–137.

———. 2003. "Xiandaixing he nüxing shenmei yishi de zhuanxing" 现代性和女性審美意識的轉變 (Modernity and the transformation of female aesthetic consciousness). In Chen Xiaoming 陳曉明, ed. *Xiandaixingxing yu Zhongguo dangdai wenxue de zhuanxing* 现代性與中國當代文學的轉型 (Modernity and the transformation of contemporary Chinese literature) Kunming: Yunnan renmin, 67–96.

Xu Xueqing 徐学清. 2010. "Ping 'Sugelan duanqun he sanyecao'" 评《苏格兰短裙和三叶草》 (Reading "The kilt and clover"). *Zeng Xiaowen's blog*. URL: http://blog.sina.com.cn/s/blog_49ead5370100h417.html.

Yan Yuanshu 顏元叔. 1973. "Ku du xi pin tan *Jia bian*" 苦讀細品談《家變》 (A meticulous discussion of *Family Catastrophe*). *Zhongwai wenxue* 1, no. 11: 60–85.

Yang, Winston L. Y. 1980. "The Literary Transformation of Historical Figures in the San-kuo chih yen-I: A Study of the Use of the San-guo chih as a Source of San-kuo chih yen-i." In Winston Yang and Curtis Adkins, ed., *Critical Essays on Chinese Fiction*. Hong Kong: The Chinese University Press, 47–84.

———. 1981 "From History to Fiction—the Popular Image of Kuan Yu." *Renditions* 15: 67–79.

Yang, Xiaojing 楊曉菁. 1999. "Tan Wang Wenxing xiaoshuo zhong de yuyan wenzi" 談王文興小說中的語言文字 (The language of Wang Wenxing's fiction). In Wu Dayun 吳達芸, ed., *Taiwan Dangdai xiaoshuo lunping* 臺灣當代小説論評 (Critiques of contemporary Taiwanese fiction). Gaoxiong: Chunhui, 31–54.

Yao Ying 姚穎. 2007. *Qingdai zhong wan qi Beijing shuochang wenxue yu jiyi yanjiu: yi zidishu chaqu wei zhongxin* 清代中晚期北京說唱文學與伎藝研究: 以子弟書, 岔曲為中心 (The study of the mid and late Qing performing arts in Beijing by focusing on *zidishu* and *chaqu*). Beijing: Yanshan.

Ye Shufa 葉樹發. 1998. *Liu Zongyuan zhuan* 柳宗元傳 (Biography of Liu Zongyuan). Changchun: Jilin wenshi.

Yeh, Catherine Vance. 2001. "Root Literature of the 1980s: May Fourth as a Double Burden." In Milena Dolezelova and Oldrich Kral, eds., *The Appropriation of Cultural Capital: China's May Fourth Project*. Cambridge, MA: Harvard University Asia Center, 229–256.

Yi Zhongtian 易中天. 2006. *Pin Sanguo* 品三國 (Evaluating Three Kingdoms). Shanghai: Shanghai wenyi.

Yisu 一粟. 1981. *Honglou meng shulu* 紅樓夢書錄 (Bibliography on *Honglou meng*). Shanghai: Shanghai guji.

Yu Hua [余华]. 2003. *To Live, a Novel*. Tr. Michael Berry. New York: Anchor Books.

———. 2004. *Huozhe* 活着 (To live). Shanghai: Shanghai wenyi.

Yu Jianhua 俞劍華 et al., eds. 2000. *Zhongguo gudai hualun leibian* 中國古代畫論類編 (On classical Chinese painting). Beijing: Renmin meishu.

Yuanzhi 原志. 2003. *Bu yiyang de tiankong: peidu shinian jishi* 不一样的天空: 陪读十年纪事 (Of different skies: an account of the ten-year experiences of a Chinese international student's wife). Beijing: Qunzhong.

———. 2008. "Sheng ge Jianada" 生个加拿大 (Jia Na Da/Canada). In Rongrong 融融 and Chen Ruilin 陈瑞琳, eds., *Yidai feihong: Beimei Zhongguo xinyimin zuojia duanpian xiaoshuo jingxuan shuping* 一代飞鸿: 北美中国大陆新移民作家短篇小说精选述评 (Selected stories of North American Chinese writers). Beijing: Zhongguo wenlian, 752–760.

———. 2013. "From *Of Different Skies* to 'Jia Na Na/Canada': Reflections on Women, Marriage, and Family." Guest lecture at Huron University College, London, Ontario, Canada.

Zeitlin, Judith T. "The Literary Fashioning of Medical Authority: A Study of Sun Yikui's Case Histories." In Furth et al. eds. 2007: 169–202.

Zeng Xiaowen 曾晓文. 2012a. "Sugelan duanqun he sanyecao" 苏格兰短裙和三叶草 (The kilt and clover). In *Sugelan duanqun he sanyecao: Zeng Xiaowen zhongduanpian xiaoshuo jingxuanji* 苏格兰短裙和三叶草: 曾晓文中短篇小说精选集 (The kilt and clover: selected stories by Zeng Xiaowen). Beijing: Jiuzhou, 146–166.

———. 2012b. "Qiansong" 遣送 (Deportation). In *Sugelan duanqun he sanyecao: Zeng Xiaowen zhongduanpian xiaoshuo jingxuanji* (The kilt and clover: selected stories by Zeng Xiaowen). Beijing: Jiuzhou, 176–207.

———. n.d. "'Qiansong' chuangzuo tan: bei qiansong de he bei liqi de" 《遣送》创作谈: 被遣送的和被离弃的 (The deported and the neglected: on writing "Deportation"). http://blog.sina.com.cn/s/blog_534c13120100ia7g.html.

Zhang Bilai 張畢來. 1955. *Xinwenxue shigang* 新文學史綱 (An outline of new literary history) Vol. 1. Beijing: Zuojia.

Zhang Huijun 张会军, ed. 2008. *Xingshi zhuisuo yu shijue chuangzao—Zhang Yimou dianyingchuangzuo yanjiu* 形式追索与视觉创造—张艺谋电影创作研究 (Formal exploration and visual creation—studies of Zhang Yimou's filmic works). Beijing: Zhongguo dianying.

Zhang Jie 張潔. 2013. *Zumu lü* 祖母绿 (Emerald). Beijing: Renmin wenxue.

Zhang Ling 張翎. 2007. "Yu zhen" 餘震 (Aftershock). *Renmin wenxue* (Jan.): 29–60.

Zhang, Xudong. 1997. *Chinese Modernism in the Era of Reforms: Cultural Fever, Avant-garde Fiction, and the New Chinese Cinema*. Durham: Duke University Press.

Zhang Yimou 張艺谋, dir. 1990. *Judou* 菊豆 (Judou). Zhongguo Dianying Jituangongsi, Xi'an Dianying zhipianchang, Tokuma Shoten. 2005. *Judou*. DVD. Cineplex Odeon Films.

———, dir. 1994. *Huozhe* 活着 (To live). Metro-Goldwyn-Mayer. 2007. *To Live*. DVD. Twentieth Century Fox Home Entertainment.

———, dir. 2006. *Mancheng yindai huangjinjia* 满城尽带黄金甲 (The entire city be clothed in golden armour). Edko Films. 2007. *Curse of the Golden Flower*. DVDs. Sony Pictures Home Entertainment.

———. 2007. "Extras: Los Angeles Premiere." In *Curse of the Golden Flower*. DVDs. Sony Pictures Home Entertainment.

Zhang, Yingjin. 1996. *The City in Modern Chinese Literature and Film: Configurations of Space, Time, and Gender*. Stanford, CA: Stanford University Press.

Zhang Zhimin 張志民 and Tan Yibing 譚逸冰. 2001. *Zhongguo shanshuihua gouhua yanjiu* 中國山水畫構畫研究 (A study on structural patterns of Chinese landscape painting). Jinan: Shandong meishu.

Zhang Zhonghui 張仲慧. 2002. "Shi Tuo *Guoyuancheng ji* jianping" 師陀《果園城記》簡評 (A concise evaluation of Shi Tuo's *Records from Orchard Town*). *Kaifeng jiaoyu xueyuan xuebao* 22: 21–22.

Zhao, Henry Y. H. 1995. *The Uneasy Narrator: Chinese Fiction from the Traditional to the Modern*. Oxford: Oxford University Press.

Zhao Jianzhong 趙建忠. 1997. *Honglou meng xushu yanjiu* 《紅樓夢》續書研究 (The study of sequels to *Honglou meng*). Tianjin: Tianjin guji.

Zheng Hengxiong 鄭恆雄 (also known as Jeng Hengsyung). 2013. "*Bei hai de ren* shangxia ce zhong de hesheng, duiwei he bianzou" 《背海的人》上下冊中的和聲、對位和變奏 (Harmony, counterpoint and variation in *Backed against the Sea*)." In Kang Laihsin and Huang Shuning 康來新、黃恕寧 (also known as Shu-ning Sciban), eds., *Xuanxiao yu fennu: Bei hai de ren zhuanlun* 喧囂與憤怒—《背海的人》專論 (Sound and fury: critical essays on *Backed against the Sea*). Taipei: National Taiwan University Press, 302–350.

Zhong, Xueping. 2000. *Masculinity Besieged? Issues of Modernity and Male Subjectivity in Chinese Literature of the Late Twentieth Century*. Durham: Duke University Press.

Zhonghua shuju bianjibu, ed. 1964. *Liu Zongyuan ziliao huibian* 柳宗元資料彙編 (Compiled data on Liu Zongyuan). 2 vols. Beijing: Zhonghua shuju.

———. 1979. *Liu Zongyuan ji* 柳宗元集 (Collected works of Liu Zongyuan). 4 vols. Beijing: Zhonghua shuju.

Zhongwen da cidian bianzuan weiyuanhui 中文大辭典編纂委員會, ed. 1962. *Zhongwen da cidian* 中文大辭典 (The encyclopedic dictionary of the Chinese language). 40 vols. Taipei: Chinese Culture University Press.

Zhou Guozheng 周國正. 1994. "Ziyou yu zhiyue: weirao Wang Wenxing *Jia bian* zhong wenzi xinbiande taolun" 自由與制約：圍繞王文興《家變》中文字新變的討論 (Freedom and constraint: a discussion of the linguistic innovations in Wang Wenxing's *Family Catastrophe*). *Xiandai zhongwen wenxue pinglun* 1: 53–78.

Zhou Yizheng 周易正 et al., eds. 2012. *Zuojia xiaozhuan: Wang Wenxing* 作家小傳: 王文興 (Writer's biography: Wang Wenxing). Taipei: Xingren wenhua shiyanshi.

Zhou Zhaoxin 周兆新. 1990. *Sanguo yanyi kaoping* 三國演義考評 (An evaluative analysis of *Three Kingdoms*). Beijing: Beijing daxue.

CONTRIBUTORS

Dušan Andrš is assistant professor at the Institute of East Asian Studies, Charles University. He has published articles on late Qing and Republican-era intellectuals and writers and he has done translations, with accompanying studies, of the work of Feng Zikai (*Nahé srdce*, Brody, 1998), Shen Congwen (*Poslední vítání jara*, Verzone, 2013), and Lo Ch'ing (*Báseň je kočka*, Mi-Lu, 2015).

C. D. Alison Bailey teaches Chinese literature, film, and art history at the University of British Columbia. Her recent publications include, "The Severed Head Speaks: Death, Revenge, Moral Heroism, and Martyrdom in 16th- and 17th-century China," in Carolyn Strange et al., eds, *Honour, Violence, and Emotions in History* (London: Bloomsbury Press, 2014), 23-44.

K. K. Leonard Chan is Chair Professor of Chinese Literature, The Education University of Hong Kong. His recent publications include *Hong Kong in Its History of Lyricism* (2016), *Compendium of Hong Kong Literature 1919-1949*, 12 volumes (chief editor, 2014-2016), and *Discourses on Lyrical China* (2013).

Shelby Kar-yan Chan is associate professor of translation at Hang Seng Management College in Hong Kong. She is author of *Identity and Theatre Translation in Hong Kong* (Springer, 2015).

Chen Pingyuan is professor of Chinese literature at Peking University. He is the author of numerous books on modern Chinese literature.

Kirk A. Denton is professor of Chinese literature at The Ohio State University. He is author of *Exhibiting the Past: Historical Memory and the Politics of Museums in Postsocialist China* (Hawaii, 2014) and editor of *The Columbia Companion to Modern Chinese Literature* (Columbia, 2016).

Gilbert C. F. Fong is Provost and Dean of the School of Translation of Hang Seng Management College in Hong Kong. He is the translator of many of the plays of Gao Xingjian, winner of the Nobel Prize in Literature in 2000. He is also the author and editor of books on Hong Kong theatre.

Anthony Wan-hoi PAK is associate professor of Chinese literature at the Education University of Hong Kong. He is author of *Appreciation of Modern Poetry* (詩賞) (Xuesheng shuju, 2008).

Ihor Pidhainy is an assistant professor of history at the University of West Georgia and editor of the journal *Ming History*. His publications include (as co-editor with Shu-ning Sciban) *Reading Wang Wenxing: Critical Essays* (Cornell East Asia Series) and *History of Chinese Literature* (forthcoming in AAS Key Issues in Asian Studies series). He is currently working on a biography of Yang Shen (1488–1559), as well as a study of the Qing dynasty *Ming History*.

Graham Sanders is associate professor of Classical Chinese Literature in the Department of East Asian Studies at the University of Toronto. His books include *Words Well Put: Visions of Poetic Competence in the Chinese Tradition* (2006), and a translation of Shen Fu's (b. 1763) *Six Records of a Life Adrift* (2011). He is currently translating two collections of Tang poetry anecdotes for De Gruyter's Library of Chinese Humanities.

Shu-ning Sciban is a professor of Chinese at the University of Calgary. She has co-edited the following volumes: *Endless War: Fiction and Essays by Wang Wen-hsing* (Cornell East Asia Program, 2011); *Slow Reading Wang Wen-hsing* (慢讀王文興) (7 volumes) (National Taiwan UP, 2013); and *Reading Wang Wenxing: Critical Essays* (Cornell East Asia Program, 2015).

Ying Wang is professor of Asian Studies at Mount Holyoke College. She has published numerous research articles and book chapters on Ming and Qing vernacular fiction. Her recent scholarship includes the nineteenth-century imitation and adaptation of *The Story of the Stone* in fiction and the performing arts (such as ballad and theater art) and Li Yu's seventeenth-century *chuanqi* plays.

Hua Laura Wu is associate professor of Chinese language and literature at Huron University College, The University of Western Ontario, Canada. She is co-editor of one anthology of studies on diasporic literature (Jinan UP, 2015) and two anthologies of stories by Chinese Canadian writers (Shuiniu, 2004).

Xueqing Xu is associate professor at York University, Canada. She is author of *Life of Confucius* (孔子的故事) (Zhongguo heping, 1990) and editor of *Essays on Chinese Canadian Literature* (枫彩文彰: 加拿大华裔/华文文学研究论文集) (Jinan daxue. 2015).

Li Zeng is associate professor of Chinese Studies at the University of Louisville. He is author of *Tradition and Creation: Essays in Comparative Literature* (Guizhou renmin, 2005) and editor of *Studies of Asian and Asian American Literature*, a special issue of *Language and Literature* vol. 28 (2004).